TOCK TOCK BIRDS

TOCK TOCK BIRDS

A Spider in the Web of
International Terrorism

Tim Hatton OBE

The Book Guild Ltd
Sussex, England

First published in Great Britain in 2004 by
The Book Guild Ltd
25 High Street
Lewes, East Sussex
BN7 2LU

Typesetting in Times by
SetSystems Ltd, Saffron Walden, Essex

Printed in Great Britain by
Antony Rowe Ltd, Chippenham, Wiltshire

A catalogue record for this book is
available from The British Library

ISBN 1 85776 851 5

CONTENTS

MAPS AND DIAGRAMS

PHOTOGRAPHS (BETWEEN PAGES 304 AND 305)

FOREWORD

Tim Hatton's childhood was not untypical of some of his contemporaries although at the challenging end of the spectrum. He gives us an important piece of social history which, in turn, helps us to understand how he was so well equipped for the very exciting first half of his working life. His army training, his immediate rapport with his professional colleagues of every race and creed, his desire to learn their languages and customs enabled him to earn their trust, respect and affection. He clearly loves people and this shines throughout in this book.

Before his twenty third birthday he had seen service in India, Indonesia, Thailand and Malaya. He witnessed with sadness the Partition of India. Given huge responsibility for one so young and junior he made big decisions fearlessly, showing great initiative. Young British officers at that time were expected to cope and those who did were quickly promoted to face further challenges. Life for Tim was clearly exhilarating, exciting, rewarding and fun.

It was no surprise to learn that he returned to Malaya and joined the Colonial Police Service. His military experience and knowledge of languages equipped him for Intelligence work which was to take over his life for the next twenty years. He threw himself into this career with tremendous enthusiasm and, wherever he was posted, he also sought opportunities for new initiatives against terrorism, carrying with him his subordinates and superiors.

The Malayan Emergency, the gradual formation of Malaysia and Confrontation with Indonesia ensured that there was always much to do and that flexibility, initiative and radical change were the order of the day. Tim Hatton not only shone as an operational commander in the fight against communist terrorists, but while still young, found himself acting in a higher rank and involved in mainstream policy making.

Wherever he went he made friends. He made and got to know a large number of interesting and influential people, many occupying high office. Understanding of the needs and aspirations of the Malaysian leaders in particular assisted him when called upon to develop Special Branch policy for the nation. His solutions to different problems were sometimes unorthodox, but always pragmatic and sensible. He reached the top of his profession at the age of forty two, returning to Britain to ensure the education of his young family. His work in Malaysia was widely recognised and acclaimed. It is easy to see why.

Tim threw himself into the second half of his career with the same enthusiasm as the first. He tried the Civil Service, but he is not a bureaucrat. His frustration with some parts of the Establishment reflects mine and crops up from time to time. After a dabble in construction, it was education that hooked him. He clearly felt strongly that young people should have the best possible opportunities. While working professionally in a number of appointments he involved himself in voluntary work, and it was through his connection with Box Hill School as Chairman of Governors that I first met Tim Hatton, taking over as Chairman from him in 1994 after serving a short apprenticeship on the board. Kurt Hahn's work clearly inspired him and he worked tirelessly for Box Hill, the Round Square International Group of Schools and other Hahnian institutions. As a Gordonstoun boy myself, and Chairman of Governors of both Box Hill and Gordonstoun, I can only say that Tim's contribution was greatly valued.

I was also present in Malaysia from 1962 to 1964 and saw quite a lot of that country while touring the peninsula in the days of rafts and unmade roads. Based in Singapore and on active service at sea during Confrontation in Sarawak, sometimes one hundred and forty miles from the sea up the Rajang river, I was able to share in the wonderfully colourful descriptions contained in this enthralling book. It is written with love and compassion, is a fascinating read with a little bit of mischief thrown in.

Vice Admiral Sir James Weatherall KCVO, KBE

ACKNOWLEDGEMENTS

I thank those who have encouraged me to prepare this book especially Lloyd Slater, Adrian Arnold, Dr Rodney Atwood and my beloved wife Sarah, who has also typed endless drafts with patience and growing expertise as she mastered the intricacies of our computer.

I also wish to acknowledge my reliance on the 9th Gurkha Rifles regimental history and newsletters, and the many valuable explanations of Islamic faith and practice from my Muslim friends.

I am indebted to the late Maj General R. L. T. Burges CBE DSO RA for allowing me to quote from his War Diary which describes graphically the horrific situation in Sourabaia, Java, during late 1945 and early 1946.

I am so very grateful for the fellowship, courage and cheerfulness of my Gurkha comrades.

I shall never forget the steadfast bravery of my Malay, Indian, Chinese and European companions in Malaysia during more than twelve long and dangerous years of international terrorism.

I acknowledge the help and professional competence of my colleagues in the state and independent sectors of education in the United Kingdom.

The quotations below each chapter heading are mostly 'other men's flowers'. I hope the reader will find them interesting and amusing.

I acknowledge the sustained help, patience and friendly advice of my publishers.

INTRODUCTION

Some dictionaries state that birds are descended from dinosaurs; the word comes from the Old English 'brid', and describes any feathered, warm-blooded animal, characterised by modification of the forelimbs as wings for flight. Place a word or two in front, and one has game birds, odd birds, wily birds, tough old birds and early birds which do so much better than their tardy competitors. Some birds, such as swallows, are regarded as lucky; others, owls, ravens and crows are said to bring bad luck or bad news. Several birds are protected by superstition; the stork is held sacred in Sweden, the swan in Ireland and the ibis and falcon in Egypt. To be bird-brained is to be stupid; doing bird is to spend time in jail; and to get the bird is to be booed off the stage. I am fond of W. T. Goodge's curious Oozlum bird which is reputed to fly backwards, does not know where it is going, knows where it has been, and keeps the dust out of its eyes.

Young Gurkha soldiers, going abroad for the first time, told me that the one thing which reminded them of their homeland was the ubiquitous kingfisher, seen throughout the Far and Middle East. Field Marshal Sir Gerald Templer told me that the bird which he really liked in Malaya was the racquet-tailed drongo with its elongated two outer tail feathers, bare except for the racquets at the end. He liked to hear its melodic calls and its mimicry of other birds. He enjoyed watching these drongos from his own eyrie on top of the highest part of the Kuala Lumpur Lake Gardens, and admiring their aerial evolutions when catching insects on the wing in the evenings. There was also the large hornbill which provided its owner in Borneo not only with aerial companionship as he cycled to work; but also acted as an umbrella over his head during inclement weather. However, it was the tock tock bird which caught my fancy throughout my time in Malaya.

The tock tock bird is a longtailed nightjar (Caprimulgidae family) and is common throughout the Malay Peninsula. It is mainly grey in colour and has bars of dark brown wavy lines on top; its underparts are lighter, being more of a pale buff. There are noticeable patches of white on its wings, throat and tip of tail. It is nocturnal, becoming active at sunset, hawking for insects and resting in trees; whence it infuriates lightly-sleeping humans with its noisy tympani of tocks, sounding like a series of popping champagne corks. In the late evenings, tock tock birds are attracted to roads on which they are wont to sit in groups, enjoying the warmth of the setting sun, and remaining calm in front of approaching cars. Unsuspecting drivers are alarmed to see in their headlights the birds' unblinking orange eyes staring boldly at them, right up to the last moment, when they take off with an insolent flutter of their white-striped wings.

Their tock tocks have consoled me, entertained me, forewarned me of trouble and cheered me up, depending on the situation and my own feelings. Even today, I continue to hear them in my imagination, long after their actual tocks have become a memory – simplified to slow tocks if I am pleased; and fast tocks if I am annoyed or fearful.

SOUTH-EAST ASIA

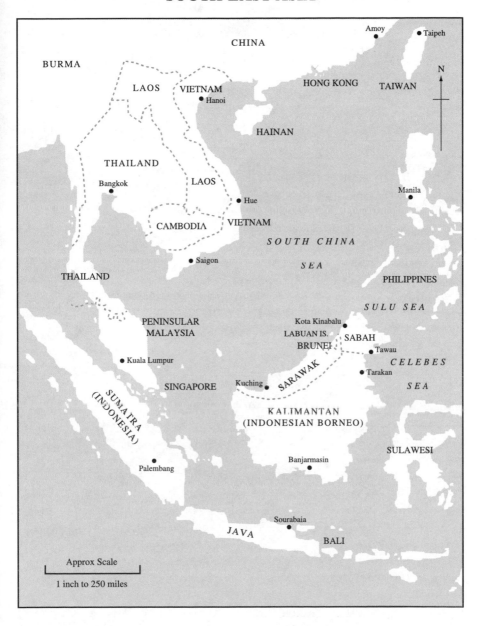

THE MALAY PENINSULA (WEST MALAYSIA)

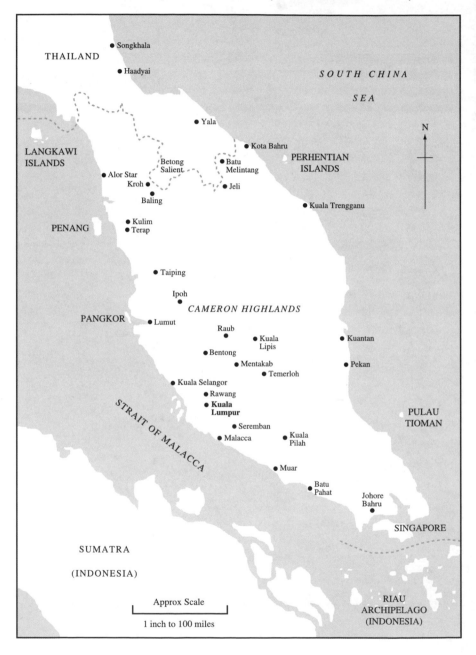

1

Little boy – pair of skates – broken ice – Golden Gates
Little girl – box of paints – licked the brush – joined the Saints

VICTORIAN MAXIM FOR YOUNG PEOPLE

An ear-spitting roar from deep under the ground shattered the stillness of the night. The roof of the little Japanese inn collapsed, the walls bent inward and it began to rain. Ma and Pa rolled sideways out of their futon; all thought of conceiving me evaporated and they scampered out of the bedroom into a mêlée of frightened people in the hall. A little later, they were approached by a small Japanese postman impeccably dressed in his official kimono and a badge of office. With many bows, sharp intakes of breath and a remarkable sense of timing, he handed them a yellow envelope addressed in large black Japanese characters above a magnificent Imperial seal. Pa opened the letter with trepidation and a trembling hand. 'All foreigners are respectfully invited to leave the country immediately,' it said, according to the innkeeper.

Apparently the earthquake of 1923 was so severe that the Japanese government was not prepared to guarantee the physical safety of foreign visitors; so Ma and Pa left the wrecked suburbs of Tokyo for Yokohama and boarded a Dutch freighter bound for Shanghai. This unforeseen interruption of their itinerary compelled Ma to change her plans for my conception from Japan to China, and my prospective nickname from Ito to Wong, which a previous Chinese cook had assured her was the Cantonese word for king.

Much of China had recently been opened to foreigners, and Ma and Pa travelled the length and breadth of the country for a whole

1

year waiting for some sign of my arrival. Sadly this was not forthcoming, despite the helpful intervention of a famous Chinese herbalist at Wuhan whose ministrations proved manifestly uneventful and made Ma sick. Then money ran out. They boarded a steamer at Tientsin and disembarked at Vancouver. A lengthy journey across Canada on the Canadian Pacific Railway took them via Niagara Falls to New York. Here they sailed on a Royal Mail steamer to England, and they motored on to Scotland where Ma was certain the Highlands air and the autumn heather of 1924 would ensure my arrival. Unfortunately, nature continued to be unco-operative and I was not be christened Ian, as newly planned. I arrived safe and sound a year later and was christened Thomas, but nicknamed Tim after Ma and Pa's cat, with no indication at all of where my conception actually took place.

I was born in the summer of 1925 in Denford Mill, one mile across the common from Hungerford in Berkshire, and I was christened in what was to become the Norland Nurses' chapel nearby. The mill was several hundred years old and was built across a swiftly flowing stream, diverted from the River Kennet, which flowed directly under our large sitting room with a never-ceasing swishing noise. I can still recall this room with its thick Turkey carpet and picture windows either side. I remember watching bits of flotsam floating downstream faster and faster towards me, only to disappear with a rush below my feet, then, after dashing to the other side of the room, seeing them reappear bobbing along into the distance. We had a huge water garden, bisected by the road which meandered from the common and over a cattle grid to the Bath Road half a mile away.

One of the great attractions for my parents of living beside the River Kennet was the unlimited supply of trout for which to angle and to eat at table. Of course, fishing the Kennet and Denford millpool produced the usual triumphs, disasters, disappointments and exasperations which make angling such an absorbing occupation. As John Evelyn wrote in his diary for the year 1654, 'Hungerford is a Town famous for its Troutes.'

I was a very active child, and no nanny, Norland or otherwise, could look after me with confidence. I was netted into my bed for rests and at night, but I could easily escape whenever I wanted. I was taken out for walks firmly attached to leather reins. My mother's fears for my safety grew as I learned to walk and run about and explore. 'He really is the pink limit!' she would say to my father. We moved out of the mill into Hungerford town as soon as my younger brother began to show unmistakable signs of appearing on the scene.

Our new house was of Queen Anne vintage. It had dark mysterious cellars full of cobwebs, two floors, an extensive attic area, a two-storeyed block of outhouses and a huge medlar tree in the garden. My brother John was born at home shortly after our move and the procession of my nannies continued unabated. One of these had a boyfriend called Fergie who had dark sallow skin and enormous thick black eyebrows, which he would waggle independently to make me laugh. I was frequently parked outside his ground floor room in nearby Eddington village, and tied by my reins to the handle of the door whilst nanny dispensed her favours inside, such delights being punctuated by hurried peeps from behind the window curtain to see if I was still around. In due course the lady had to leave us because she could no longer disguise her pregnancy. I proudly announced to my surprised parents that I supposed the father must be Fergie – I was right, and only four.

My brother John turned out to be a lovely baby with golden curls, not cut off until he was three years old. He was passive, obedient and much admired. My nannies were replaced by governesses who discovered I liked to read and write. In due course, John and I, aged four and six respectively, were packed off to the Misses Bradnack, who ran a dame school on the south coast at Leas Court, Canford Cliffs, near Bournemouth in Dorset.

The Bradnack sisters took in ten boys whose ages ranged from six to eight. John, though under age, was admitted as a special favour. The Bradnack parents used to run a preparatory school in Folkestone and, when they died, the school was sold and the sisters started their dame school for something to do. Their brother Oswald visited the school once a term to lecture on discipline. The school prospectus stated: The school receives a limited number of the sons of gentlemen – combining for them a thorough education, with a happy home life by the sea ... the school has its own bathing hut ... Sergeant Major Eltham attends regularly for Drill ... inclusive fees are Thirty-Five Guineas a term.

A long list of referees included two Bishops, three Rectors, a Peer of the Realm, an Engineer Commander of the Indian Marine living in Rangoon, two Colonels, a Captain and several Esquires. The List of Requirements attached included an Eton Suit, a Covert Coat, a dark Chesterfield Coat, Combinations and a pair of Navy Blue Knickers for winter wear.

The school building was on the edge of a cliff with wonderful views over a chine across the sea to the Needles. My mother must have had second thoughts when she parted with us, for she took rooms in Canford Cliffs so that she could watch John and me walk by in crocodile formation on the way to play in the woods leading off the high street. She kept this up at great expense for two terms, unknown to the sisters or to us and to the irritation of my father, whose time was fully occupied as captain of the Hungerford cricket team and running his own advertising business in Reading.

Life at Leas Court was great fun in its own somewhat peculiar way. The sisters had never really recovered from the effects of the Great War, in which all but one of their elder brothers, and so many males of their generation, had been slaughtered on the western front. We were brought up to hate the Kaiser, then exiled to Holland, and our hero was King Albert of the Belgians. We had to study selected parts of the Old Testament, which they had laboriously copied out by hand into exercise books, and learn long extracts by heart; even when we went to play in the woods it was always to re-enact Joshua's Battle of Ai. Dressed immaculately in our Eton suits and with our hair neatly brushed, we motored to the nearby church on Sunday in two ancient Rolls Royce taxis with uniformed drivers, but we had to walk back whatever the weather. Three or four times a term we went by the same taxis to the Pavilion in Bournemouth to listen to travelogues given by famous explorers, such as Captain Ladd's on 'Beautiful Belgium, illustrated by 100 coloured slides' and Norman V. Sowden's 'Tyrol – where the Mountains Blush, illustrated by 170 slides of Great Beauty'. Admission charges were two shillings, one and threepence or ninepence. As befitted Fellows of the Royal Geographical Society their talks were well presented and we much enjoyed them. They were followed by delicious *coupe jacques* (ice creams with fruit in long glasses) in the nearby Regent.

The Bradnacks wore long colourful Edwardian-style dresses throughout the year and suffered severely from an excess of air within. Playing in the woods, we always knew where they were by the muffled explosions escaping from their lower regions – rather

4

like steam engines struggling up a hill. Some of us were convinced that they could talk to each other using a sort of secret code of dots and dashes – careful reference to Oliver Byrte's copy of the Morse code did not resolve the matter one way or another.

Perched on top of the cliff meant frightening storms and gales in the winter. When these became really loud and the lightning flashed into our bedrooms, we would be summoned downstairs at dead of night in our pyjamas, dressing gowns and slippers to pray for the safety of sailors on the sea. Miss Bradnack led the prayers and Miss Bea sat at her small harmonium and played the hymn 'Eternal Father, strong to save,' with its refrain, 'Oh hear us when we cry to Thee, For those in peril on the sea'. I well remember crawling under the dining-room table on these occasions to glean the dried-up apple pips which I had flicked underneath for harvesting later at a convenient time. Split open and eaten, they were delicious. Over the next few days, as soon as we heard the newspaperman deliver *The Morning Post*, we would rush downstairs to examine it carefully to discover how many wrecked sailors we had saved.

The language used in our letters home was full of old-fashioned and quaint phrases such as 'fine games of footer', 'ripping teas on the sands', 'flying the Union Jack on Empire Day', 'playing the man' or 'playing the game' and 'being plucky'. I completed reading Robert Louis Stevenson's *Treasure Island* and *Kidnapped* and I won the school chess tournament, all before my seventh birthday. My favourite indoor games were 'Dover Patrol' and 'L'Attaque'.

At home, my parents decided to keep angora rabbits. The first of these were bought from a breeder; in no time more and more little rabbits appeared and the original hutches became inadequate. A rabbitry was built in the outhouses, the gardener was promoted to Rabbit Master and his daughters were employed as Assistant Rabbit Masters. It took off, and we supplied angora wool for the robes worn at the Royal Silver Jubilee celebrations in 1935. I much enjoyed shearing the wool and being careful not to nick the skin. I held a family record for the greatest number clipped in one hour. Alas, a French buck called Napoleon, acquired to introduce a new strain, carried a form of rabbit 'flu and we had to put down the whole lot. Moreover, the bottom fell out of the market and there was no point in starting again. I am sorry to say we got very tired of rabbit stew.

My parents soon discovered that the townspeople of Hungerford held on tenaciously to the ancient traditions of Hocktide, dating back to the fourteenth century and the times of John O'Gaunt. The original celebrations took place over Easter week when, in medieval times, village women would seize their menfolk, tie them up and demand a small payment for their release. Similarly, on the next day the men would ensnare the ladies. Ransoms paid were given to the poor. The American word 'hock' still means to pawn something and comes from the old English custom of Hocktide. In Hungerford a Court was chosen by lot on the Tuesday of Easter week and its task was to elect officials for the following year. The most important of these was the Constable (with limited magisterial powers). The remainder included the Overseers, the Hayward, two Ale-Tasters and the Tutti-men. It was the latter who fascinated me and I followed them closely round the town.

Two of the Tutti-men were given ancient Tutti-poles (long staves) which still retained part of their original gilding and were decorated with pale blue streamers and flowers (hence the word 'tutti', meaning nosegay, posy or bunch of flowers). Each Tutti-man was accompanied by a person carrying a basket of oranges. They visited the schools and demanded a half-holiday for the children, who were each presented with an orange. Old people in the workhouse received a similar gift. The Tutti-men also sold oranges to householders, to journeymen (travelling salesmen) and indeed to any male over the age of twelve. The payment required was 'any coin of the realm'. I noticed that the Tutti-men's poles had a long spike on the end which impaled an orange and a purse. They pointed their poles upwards towards young ladies leaning out of upstairs windows. I was told that the generosity of these ladies was rewarded with a Tutti-man's kiss.

In the evening, the newly-elected Constable presided over a banquet, seated on an antique chair with his horn of office suspended between two Tutti-poles. At the stroke of midnight, the immortal memory of John O' Gaunt was drunk in silence followed by the singing of 'Auld Lang Syne' and 'God Save the King'. All of a sudden the horn was blown. The Constable was escorted to a chair outside and carried home. The horn was blown before him.

In the 1930s, Hungerford was a very busy market town with a large Victorian Corn Exchange where John and I went roller skating in its great hall. We were taken there on Wednesday afternoons and had special small-size skates. We soon learnt to stop with a flourish and to turn corners with reckless abandon. My parents never joined in the fun; but they were good ice skaters and, in the middle of winter, off they went to the canal, strapped on their skates and travelled for miles along the frozen waterway under and over the bridges, interrupted only by the locks. I remember my mother gliding along effortlessly with the wind blowing her scarf behind her, accompanied by my father, resplendent in his cap and plus fours, zipping under Hungerford Bridge with a careless wave, to the delight of passers-by.

There were two doctors in Hungerford; one lived by the crossroads near the Bear Hotel and the other lived in the manor house next to the high street railway bridge. The manor house doctor was Starkey Smith, whose main preoccupation was the resuscitation and repair of erstwhile members of the 'Bloomsbury set', who had taken a large house on the edge of the common. Their excesses and scandalous behaviour would be of little remark today, but then they shocked the public and provided wonderful material for the gossips. The other doctor was bald, smelt of tobacco smoke, had twinkling eyes and always prescribed 'a strong whisky in his smoking room' whenever my father had a cold.

One day my mother and I were walking up the high street when we heard the noise of approaching trumpets and drums – it was the annual circus marching through the town on its way to the great tent erected in a field at the top of the street. Along came the jugglers, acrobats, stilt walkers, clowns, small animals on leads, large animals in wheeled cages drawn by sweating horses, the Fat Lady and a host of mothers, sisters, cousins, uncles and aunts of the performers. A raggle-taggle of boys, girls and stragglers followed behind. After a long gap came a single very large African elephant with magnificent white tusks which, noticing the attractive steps leading up to Dr Starkey's manor house, promptly relieved itself on the topmost and then deposited a large steaming mound. The elephant strode off under the bridge in a cloud of white smoke from a passing steam train and disappeared from view. Just then, dressed in a smart pin-striped suit and wearing spats and a raffish hat, out through the great door came Dr Starkey. He stopped in

7

his tracks, examined the still warm pile, looked left and right and scratched his patriarchal head in disbelief. My mother and I thought it the funniest sight ever.

My father, who was always keen on exercise, took us for long walks in the countryside during winter. We visited the remote place where a policeman was killed by a highwayman more than a hundred years before; we examined the weirs and enclosures on the River Kennet (supposedly declared illegal in the provisions of Magna Carta in 1215) and explored large houses and extensive gardens abandoned by their owners in the Depression. While walking along the Bath Road, I much enjoyed placing my ear on the creosoted telegraph poles, savouring the tar-like smell and listening excitedly to the burring-singing noise made by the wind in the telephone wires. There were perhaps fifty or sixty separate wires which passed through little blobs on the cross-spars; the noise varied slightly with the strength of the wind. I supposed it was the sound of thousands of people talking to each other and I wondered who they were and what they were saying. Were they cross, sad, excited, or what? Often birds would perch on the spars and make a terrible noise in the evenings. When we first acquired a black telephone on a stalk, I answered the phone for the first time. The caller was my father who said he would be a little late for supper. I asked him if he was hungry and he said. 'Yes'. 'Wait a mo,' I said, and ran to the kitchen and found a pan of soup on the range. I ladled out some into a bowl and poured it down the telephone – it seemed a logical thing to do.

During the summers I accompanied my father to cricket matches all over Berkshire and Wiltshire. One day, while watching a match at Littlecote, I was approached by an elderly man in an old tweed suit, who said. 'Would you like to see my house?' in a very pleasant voice. He seemed friendly and nice so I agreed and away we went together. 'I have three hundred and sixty-five windows, or rooms, I forget which; see if you can count them,' he suggested. I lost count because he told interesting stories of ghosts, pregnant servants (I wondered if he was responsible), the Civil War and the Roman occupation. He was Sir Ernest Wills, head of the tobacco company W.D. and H.O. Wills. He always befriended me whenever my father played cricket at Littlecote.

My mother was a practical person. She told us that as a child she had been the middle one of five siblings – too young for the

8

schoolroom and too old for the nursery. She was independent from the beginning, made friends with everyone and was always popular. She played a very good game of tennis, her backhand uninhibited and often unreturnable, until her late seventies. She had two useful tips, delivered on walking expeditions. The first was a cure for tiredness. 'When climbing a hill, ask your companion to place a forefinger firmly in the middle of your back and to keep it there as you walk; you will revive at once.' Her second recommended useful remedial action. 'When walking down a slippery slope, clench your toes and you won't slip.' Ma claimed to be the first person to describe the Zeppelin bomb which fell near London's Victoria Station in the Great war as causing 'damn bombage' instead of 'bomb damage'. Her elder brother became a brigadier general in the Royal Horse Artillery, winning a Military Cross in 1914, and was created Commander of the Most Excellent Order of the British Empire on his retirement; her younger brother became a naval officer serving with distinction in two world wars and became an Officer of the same Most Excellent Order.

My paternal grandfather married at the age of forty and proceeded to have ten children all of whom married and, together with my maternal siblings, produced for me a quiverful of thirty-six cousins. My father's elder brother served in the Territorial Army and was mentioned in dispatches while fighting on the western front where he was severely wounded; he was later transferred to the French Army and was decorated on the field for his bravery, accompanied, he said, by the soggy kisses of a French general. He became one of His Majesty's deputy lieutenants in Staffordshire between the wars and was present in Westminster Abbey for the coronation of King George VI. My father's younger brother won the Military Cross on the north-west frontier of India while serving as a regular officer in the North Staffordshire Regiment.

My father was slightly short-sighted and failed his eyesight test for entry into the Royal Navy; but was accepted as a cadet on the training ship HMS *Worcester*. He served his apprenticeship in sail in the *Romanov* and rounded Cape Horn four times. He joined the Royal Navy in 1914 having cheated the opticians in his medical examination and retired for the first time in 1924. He was called up again in 1941. His last sea appointment was captain of HMS *Tay*, a submarine 'mother' ship.

9

In 1915 Pa was in command of a prize crew on board the recently captured ship, the SS *Nordic* registered with the Swedish South African Line. He was the surprised recipient of the following character reference.

I hereby certify that Captain Hatton was in command of the miserable prize crew that took my ship from lovely Kirkwall to dirty Manchester, all against my wish. It is my duty to warn other unfortunate devils, that said gentleman finished all my good American beer, and damned near all my whisky and cigars. He ate well and slept well and had the whole run of my w.c. I hereby recommend him to anyone who wants a cheerful shipmate, a good talker and a splendid liar. *Gott strafe him and England.*

Admiral in the Germany Navy.
SS *Nordic*, Manchester, May 18th 1915

The signature of the German admiral is indistinct.

The Hatton family of earlier days were very proud of their roots in Shropshire, Staffordshire and Northamptonshire. The family history states of Sir Christopher Hatton KG (1540–1591) that he was born at Holdenby, Northamptonshire, in the rank of gentleman. He was the third son of William Hatton and Alice the daughter of Lawrence Saunders of Harrington. The pedigree of Hatton is 'traced beyond records and consequently to an apocryphal source', states the Victorian historian Sir Harris Nicholas. He goes on to say that Ivor, a nobleman of Normandy, the supposed ancestor of the Fitz-Nigells, Barons of Hatton, and of other families in Cheshire, had a sixth son Wolfaith, Lord of Hatton, from whom descended a long line of knights and esquires of local but little general fame.

Christopher succeeded to the Holdenby estates some time after his father died in 1546. His attractive personality, and his ability as a comely dancer, came to the notice of Queen Elizabeth who took him into her band of fifty gentlemen pensioners in 1564. In 1568 he acquired the abbey and demesne lands of Sulby. Thereafter the royal bounty flowed on him in a copious stream.

10

One day the Earl of Leicester became jealous and, in order to spite Christopher Hatton, drew the Queen's attention to a professional dancer who greatly excelled young Christopher. But, contrary to Leicester's expectations, Elizabeth drew a proper distinction between the merit of an artist and the skill of an amateur. 'Pish,' she said, 'I will not see your man – it is his trade.'

A favoured courtier and trusted friend of the Queen, he appears to have had an intimate relationship with his monarch. Christopher and Queen Elizabeth wrote to each other the sixteenth-century equivalent of love letters, many of which have survived and make fascinating reading. She had given him the nickname 'Lids' (eyelids) and it is with this cipher that he signed his personal letters to her. His letters usually concluded with the phrase 'Your slave and EvcR your own, most dear sweet lady'.

Another anecdote relates that in 1574 Christopher Hatton, with the Queen's approbation, asked the Bishop of Ely to honour his undertaking to grant him the lease of the episcopal house in Ely Place, Holborn. However, the bishop delayed and it was the Queen who wrote to the bishop thus: 'Proud Prelate, I understand that you are backward in complying with your agreement but I would have you know that I who made you what you are can unmake you; and, if you do not forthwith fulfil your engagement, by God, I will immediately unfrock you.'

I spent two wonderfully happy years in Leas Court, leaving in 1934 at the age of eight and a half to enter The Grange in Eastbourne. The Grange was built as a preparatory school in 1878 and provided accommodation for about sixty boys from the ages of 8 to 13. It was cool and airy in the summer but perishing cold in the winter. The school prospectus said, 'The Sanitary arrangements were originally made according to the advice of an eminent London Physician and special care is taken to ensure perfect dryness and drainage. The drains are inspected and tested from time to time by a competent Sanitary Authority.'

I recollect no central heating in the loos and the most fearful lingering smells, especially after school runs. The headmaster was Captain W. L. Herries 'late of the Kings Own, Royal Lancashire Regiment'; his wife Violet was responsible for school welfare. Her mother, Mrs Hollins, was the ancient relict of the previous head and was an all-pervasive '*eminence noire*' as she shuttled around the dormitories dispensing mints. ('She is frightfully mean,' I was told with schoolboy logic. 'She gives you one in case you take two.')

Life at The Grange could not have been more different from Leas Court and I hated my first year. Miss Bea had always encouraged me in my academic work and had requested me to continue to write weekly letters to my parents. Leas Court had become an extension of home, my parents visited us occasionally and I looked after John; the rooms were warm and we were well wrapped up when we went for walks in rain or snow. At The Grange, however, I was entirely on my own; no one from Leas Court ever went to The Grange, and I was cold, lonely, frightened and constipated. I managed to survive, though my letters home in 1934 hint at being homesick; they carried terrible tales of compulsory, but mostly unproductive, dosages of syrup of figs, real barley water, castor oil, senna pods and Parish's Chemical Food.

My first term was really quite traumatic. Twice a day the whole school met for prayers sitting on lockers built on three sides of the big school room. The head boy and prefects sat at one end and, as the latest and most insignificant example of the human race, I sat at the other end. Shortly before Mr Herries came in, the head boy would push against the senior prefect, he would push against his neighbour and so on through the school, round the corners, gathering momentum until, like a forerunner of the Mexican wave, it reached me, perched nervously at the end of the row of lockers. I was shoved firmly into a large waste paper basket placed there for the purpose. Subsequent shouts of laughter, jeers and the clapping of one hundred and twenty-eight hands faded away as Mr Herries strode in, looking very stern with Bible in hand. He did not always have a Bible in his hand; on one occasion he came with a bamboo cane and, to the astonishment of the whole school and without any warning, singled out a small boy only slightly older than me. The boy was accused of deliberately wetting his bed and was made to bend over a table in the middle of the room and was given six strokes of the cane. The whole school was shocked to the core because the boy was very popular – for some reason I escaped my dunking in the waste paper basket for a whole fortnight. But then it started again. Next term I moved up one place and someone else became the unlucky one.

Mr Herries was known to the boys as 'Toad' and it was pronounced with exaggerated distaste. We were told that he had fought bravely on the western front in the 1914–18 war and had been captured by the Germans only to escape back to the Allied lines. This escape was re-enacted every year on the Eastbourne Downs by the whole school. Two boys were selected as the escapees and then taken by car to a remote area of the downs; meanwhile the rest of the school and all the staff were deployed to prevent the escapees returning undiscovered the six or seven miles on foot back to school. It was quite good fun though very tiring for me.

All this time I suffered intermittently from boils, chilblains, earache and toothache. One day, after many complaints, I was sent to the dentist who decided to take out one offending tooth. In my letter home of 31st October 1935 I wrote, 'It was decided to take my tooth out by gas and after several tries they could not get me to sleep. I heard the doctor say to the dentist, "There is nothing like children for holding their breaths, we will give him full pressure and see what happens." Anyway it came out and I am back at school feeling a bit better.'

As time went by I began to settle in and make good friends. With my parents' help I formed a cricket team in the summer holidays and we had some splendid games with other schoolboy teams. I found these games enlarged my circle of young friends at home and, as captain of our team, I began to accept and like responsibility. Freezing winters at school, however, played havoc on my exposed parts: I continued to suffer from chilblains on my fingers, which swelled to twice their size, developing cracks, which had to be poulticed and bandaged throughout most of the winter and spring terms. This enabled me to escape outdoor winter games and to read a great deal. My brother John, who was more robust than me, joined us and we slept in the same dormitory so I was able to keep an eye on him and help him settle in – but not for long.

The school attracted a severe form of ringworm on the scalp and several of the younger boys caught it, including John. My mother came up post-haste and demanded to know how it had been allowed to happen. She would not listen to the Herries's anodyne explanations and decided that nothing short of an inspection of the school by her would reveal the cause. She soon discovered that in the changing room the school kept about twenty communal hairbrushes, which anyone could use prior to marching in to meals. One boy with ringworm could be explained but a series of boys all with infected scalps must have caught it from these hairbrushes. Most of the infected boys were taken home, but John was put into an isolation room in the school, by himself, with only a small window high up on the wall. He had no exercise and his only contact with the outside world was obtained by dragging his bed below the window, and placing a chair on the bed, and climbing up to look out. I saw his sad little face peering from the window and wrote to my mother. She came to the school and arranged for John to be boarded out with 'Chief's' family ('Chief' was the retired Royal Navy chief petty officer responsible for PT and Drill). They had just lost their own son in the Quetta earthquake in India and were only too pleased to have a distraction. My parents took both of us away at the end of term. Paradoxically, I was sad to leave. I was eleven years old and beginning to enjoy myself.

Our next school had a rather strange name which neither John nor I liked to tell our friends: it was Bigshotte, Wokingham, Berks. We had a big black B sewn on our light blue caps. 'Do look,' said our friends at home. 'They've got bees in their bonnets.' I joined when I was eleven and John not yet nine. It was all right for him; but very difficult for me coming in among boys who had already formed their own friendships and had chosen shared desks. I felt rather an interloper; but my morale rose for quite a different reason. I discovered that not only were the loos properly heated; but the matron, school staff, and the headmaster were friendly people who stopped and talked to me. A senior boy was detailed to be my friend for the first fortnight and this helped enormously.

Bigshotte was run by the Master, C.G. Gordon Brierley; his brother, nicknamed Mr B; and the school secretary who was a very efficient Scottish lady. It was essentially a warm school. It had a kindly smell, and even the lack of doors in the loos did not prevent me from putting a wholly honest tick on the specially designated notice board to confirm that daily visits to the 'across court place' had been crowned with success – a very important point from my view. John Stacpoole Haycraft shared my desk for the next two years (in later years he became managing director of the International Schools of English) and we became very close friends. My brother John was the same age as Colin Haycraft (who, later, would control the well-known publisher Duckworths). The four of us all got on famously.

Sometime in 1935, my parents decided to buy a house in St Mawes, opposite Falmouth in Cornwall. We had spent our holidays the previous year in a caravan in a field there overlooking the sea and, although it rained every day and John and I were fractious, my mother decided that St Mawes would be a great improvement on Hungerford. My father, however, had a difficult decision to make. He had been captain of the Hungerford cricket team for many years and was loath to give it up. For him it was as much a social service as playing a game. His captaincy lasted throughout the worst of the Depression and he had kept in close touch with members of the Hungerford cricket team, many of whom had lost their jobs and were living from hand to mouth on a woefully inadequate dole. We adopted privately three families, passing on all our spare clothing and sending them gifts for birthdays and Christmas. My mother had our cook make pies and tarts which were taken round to them from time to time. My father bought most of the cricket gear for the eleven – whites, bats, balls, pads, etc. and the club became very much his hobby. Times in Hungerford were very bad in those days and the Bath Road was travelled by a large number of tramps, who used to gather on the corner where the high street met the Bath Road. They used to walk up to the milestone opposite the Denford turning where they spent their nights in the hedge or in long grass round about. We used to take out all sorts of food and give it to these tramps who, our parents told us, were decent people down on their luck. They never caused trouble and were very grateful for what we did.

My father's advertising firm had just been taken over by one of the larger partnerships and, although not gainfully employed, he had enough money to live quietly, employ a cook, educate John and me, smoke his pipe endlessly and enjoy his many self-imposed responsibilities as captain of the Hungerford cricket team.

My mother won the day and we acquired a four-bedroom house on the hill directly overlooking St Mawes, facing south. The garden was on three levels, about an acre in size and contained a shallow pool and over forty dracaena palm trees. There was a small path from the bottom of the garden which led steeply down the hill directly to the shops and harbour front. The house had an uninter-

15

rupted view of the harbour across the Carrick Roads to Pendennis Castle on the right and to St Anthony Point on the left. Every sort of ship, especially oil tankers, anchored in this splendid natural harbour. My father joined the St Mawes sailing club and our life began to change. We bought a Dolly Varden-rigged clinker-built boat, 18 feet long, called the *Glimmer*. My father taught John and me to sail and then to race. We had marvellous picnics in remote coves along the coast away from the trippers' charabancs on non-racing days.

I learnt to sail and race single-handed; inshore at first; up the Percuil creek for beginners until I was twelve; and then out to sea. We soon sold the *Glimmer* and bought the *Slug* which was 22 feet long, faster to sail and had a cockpit, galley and bowsprit. Its sails were rusty brown so my mother could easily spot us from the verandah. I raced a lot on my own and collected many small silver cups. I also went alongside the three-masted sailing ships which were waiting in the Roads before unloading their cargo in Falmouth docks. I brought newspapers with me and was always made welcome. The *Lawhill* and the *Keloran* were my favourite sailing ships. I succeeded in boarding three Spanish Republican destroyers which sought sanctuary in England during the Spanish Civil War; and in the early summer of 1939 I boarded both HMS *Ramillies* and the German training battleship *Schleswig Holstein*.

We were living in St Mawes when war was declared and my mother stayed on there until mid-1940. My father obtained a job as captain of HMS *Worcester*, an ancient Royal Navy sailing ship-of-the-line, which had become a training ship moored off Greenhithe in Kent for cadets entering the Royal and Merchant Navies. It had been evacuated by the cadets early in the war and became a second home for units of 'The Lower Thames Defence'. My father had been a cadet on board for several years at the beginning of the century and he was tickled pink to return and climb the rigging all over again. The famous wool clipper *Cutty Sark* lay alongside, providing an interesting juxtaposition of two quite different sailing ships, rather like a shire-horse and a thoroughbred. My father stayed there as captain of both ships for a year until he was recalled to the Royal Navy in 1941 at the age of fifty-five. At about this time, my mother examined a map of England and decided that, if Hitler invaded, he would cut off Devon and Cornwall; so she decided to sell the house in St Mawes for whatever she could get, and parked our car at a local farm for the duration. (After the war the farmer confiscated the car in lieu of unpaid rent.)

Meanwhile the house in Hungerford had been let to the Argentine Embassy and the Argentinians were persuaded to buy the freehold for £800 which, even in those days, was a paltry sum. We moved to HMS *Worcester* in the summer of 1940 and watched with bated breath the Battle of Britain being fought above our heads. Because the Germans used the two ships as navigational aids, we were not bombed directly; though one day we all saw a German bomber fly very low over and along the Thames and drop a single bomb down the funnel of an empty tanker. It exploded and the ship sank. My father and four others jumped into motorboats tied up alongside us and managed to rescue all the crew, except two lascars who had been killed by the bomb, both of whom went down with their ship. The greatest danger – but fun for John and me – were the pieces of shrapnel from anti-aircraft shells exploding overhead. They became embedded in the wooden decks and were quickly retrieved by us. A more destructive form of warfare in those days were the parachute bombs. We were really afraid of them and kept a good lookout because they used to drift down from the sky very quietly. That summer, we saw four parachute bombs drift by quite close, to explode dramatically but harmlessly on the nearby mudflats.

All sorts of people came aboard the *Worcester* and looked over the *Cutty Sark*. We lived in the Captain's magnificent quarters in the stern of the *Worcester* with lovely sloping windows leading to a walk-round gallery over the sea. The furniture had been made for the room and was in its original gilded state – all very grand indeed – a lovely place for my mother to entertain the great and the good, scrounging extra food and drink from a variety of mysterious sources. Clement Attlee, the Deputy Prime Minister, was a regular visitor and treated with great respect by Pa; Ma, however, did not take to him and always referred to him somewhat icily as Major Attlee. Nevertheless, John and I liked him because he always stopped to talk to us and had a wry sense of humour. When we asked him what he did he replied, 'I do all the work Mr Churchill does not like to do.' A.P. Herbert called in frequently and became quite a family friend. John and I thought him a delightful person and very funny indeed. He told us that he did not want to apply for a commission in the Royal Navy because he would then lose command of his little motorboat, which was his pride and joy. If he was commissioned, he would probably be posted to a dull shore job pushing a pen and the war would be over before he commanded a ship again. 'I am the Lower Thames defence against the German Navy,' he boasted proudly. Thereafter John and I read his contributions to magazines and newspapers avidly and we all looked forward to his visits.

A host of elderly admirals recently recalled to the colours came on board for a pink gin. The Earl of Winchelsea, said to be a remote family connection, was a regular visitor too; my father felt it was his naval duty to tell him to grow a full beard to offset his magnificent moustache. Our sailing days were over because of the swift tide and John and I spent our time exploring the grounds of nearby Ingress Abbey, playing tennis and collecting bits of parachute and other war material. We drove our mother to distraction by watching the dogfights in the blue skies of 1940. Our cousin Monty Riddell, who had been to RAF Cranwell before the war, was in the thick of things and became our hero. He did not survive the war.

Back in mid-1938 I experienced a severe shock. My father decided that I should go into the Royal Navy and after checking my academic ability with the Master I was entered for Dartmouth. I passed the interview; but I failed the medical because I was found to be short-sighted in my right eye. A string of expensive visits to Martin Sherwood of Park Lane, who operated a system of electrical shock treatment of the eye muscles, did not improve matters and, although my father taught me how to cheat the examiners, I was unsuccessful on appeal. I hoped very much that they would send me to Wellington College for which Bigshotte was a feeder school, but no such luck, I was put down for the Nautical College Pangbourne which imposed no entry restriction on those who were short-sighted in one eye. Pangbourne had its own entry examination and the Master, with my parents' ready assent, put me in for a major scholarship. Unfortunately the exams coincided with an unusual visit to the sick room with a heavy cold, earache in one ear, deafness in the other ear and a very sore throat. I took the exam in bed using a pencil. I was not awarded the scholarship – it went to a farmer's son who had five brothers – but I received a modest exhibition as a consolation prize.

The Nautical College Pangbourne was as much a cultural shock to me as The Grange had been five years earlier. I was very fond of life at Bigshotte and I knew on my first day at Pangbourne that my constipation and other physical ills would return – and they did. My father had already taken me to Gieves, the naval outfitter in Bond Street, and I had been issued with the uniform of a cadet in the Royal Naval Reserve by Mr Kingston, which I wore very self-consciously on my arrival at the college with thirteen others in April 1939. I returned to my spartan life, reporting to my parents, 'I get up at 6.40 a.m., do PT (oddly called activity exercises or "ackers"), cold showers are the order of the day, one is beaten if caught having a warm one ... I can't reach the raised trough to pee in so I have to enter a doorless cubicle sit down and then pretend to do what I don't do. We spend ages making and remaking our bunks without a wrinkle and we march and counter-march for hours on end. Everyone shouts at us as if we are deaf. All the new boys are in the bottom form and we are learning nothing new. I have been put in the Main Top for cricket where those who are not good enough are placed. We have had one game so far: I did not bat and the game was stopped because the ball went down a rabbit hole and no one bothered to retrieve it.'

Six weeks later I crashed my bicycle (called a 'grid'), broke my arm and spent a week in the sick bay before I emerged with it in plaster, only to return the following week with German measles. Next term I was placed in the lowest possible form where most of my companions never read books and were not academically interested in anything. I had no particular friends and went for long walks on my own exploring the beautiful countryside, trying to come to terms physically and mentally with my lot. The junior house was called Croft House and was run by two housemasters who let the Chief Cadet Captain, Cadet Captains, and Cadet Leaders, all seconded from the senior houses, run the place. Our welfare was in the shaking hands of an elderly matron who had been trained at St Thomas's in the nineteenth century. She still retained the distinctive cap which she never removed and in which we assumed she always slept. She had a mangy parrot called 'Cocky' and every evening she came round the dormitories with a squirt which she directed down our throats. Of course we called it 'cocky juice'.

Our Christmas 1939 was supposed to be spent in a large hotel in Torquay, where an aunt of mine lived nearby. Unfortunately, the

Royal Air Force commandeered it as we arrived and we had to go into digs, which could only give us bed and no breakfast. We were rescued by Olive, John and Colin Haycraft's mother, who kindly offered to feed my brother and me while Ma went over to her sister-in-law for meals. This arrangement suited me well and I played chess with John Haycraft all day long. We used to visit the cinemas almost every day; but, for some films children under a certain age had to be accompanied by an adult. Olive Haycraft came to our rescue again and, after a lot of fun dressing up, Colin was disguised as our elderly granny carefully wrapped in a black Indian shawl with his hair whitened by talcum powder. Thus dressed up he chaperoned us to the cinema and we got away with it. All four of us had bicycles and we cycled round the Torquay area picnicking in the winter sunshine – halcyon days.

Amongst the strange new subjects we were taught at Pangbourne was engineering. The person in charge was Engineer Commander Windibank who was said in a ribald school song to have been blown through a bulkhead during the Great War, making him both impotent and deaf. For our practical work we had to make things like hammers and setsquares, and for our academic work we had to reproduce a series of line drawings using soft lead pencils, which needed frequent sharpening by sandpaper. One day I caused amusement when, holding my pencil in my hand, I raised my arm and asked if I might go to the lavatory. 'Windy', seeing my pencil, replied, 'Yes, of course, here is a piece of sandpaper, do it over the wastepaper basket and don't make a mess'!

One day in October 1940 my mother visited the college in order to determine how efficient were the air-raid precautions. On her return, unknown to me, she wrote a letter to Sir Philip Devitt (then chairman of the governors and acting as the hands-on Captain Superintendent) saying. 'From our experiences, living these last few weeks in Kent, we do not think the precautions at Bowden Green are adequate. The risks of colds, coughs, 'flu and pneumonia being caught by going out at night into cold unheated damp shelters seem as great as sudden death from bombs. Could not an efficiently heated and lighted shelter be provided with proper sleeping accommodation? I know that parents would not mind paying extra to ensure adequate protection against illness as well as bombs. Our experience here is that there is very little time to wake up sleeping boys before bombs are dropping all around; often before the sirens and guns have started off.' The original of this letter was returned to me by the archivist in 1996. I do not recollect any bombs falling on the college during my time though a few incendiaries were dropped on the village and quickly put out.

I came top of form 3B (the so-called duffers) at the end of my second term and was promoted to form 3A. I still found work very easy, going over things I had done two years before at Bigshotte. I stayed two terms in 3A and came second, let down in the end by low marks in geometry, which I hated. My parents asked for an interview with Mr Woodall, the Director of Studies, and next term I was given a double move into form 5C. This meant doing School Certificate a year earlier than otherwise. I began to enjoy my work at last having wasted four terms in the third forms learning almost nothing.

George Kitching, an Australian who came up with me from 3A, sat in the desk to my right: he was made Chief Cadet Captain of the college the term after I left Pangbourne. Immediately behind me sat Robin Gillett; he later became Commander Sir Robin Gillett, succeeding his father as Lord Mayor of London, and then became chairman of the Pangbourne governors. Beside him sat Thomas Augustus Courtney Clack later to become the distinguished captain of a Royal Navy atomic submarine.

I gained my athletic colours at this stage and sat my School Certificate examination at the end of the academic year; my results were good enough to allow me to go into 6A, the top form. Other forms at this level were the Royal Navy entry and the Merchant Navy entry. Form 6A concentrated on the Civil Service Commission examinations for the paymaster and engineering branches of the Royal Navy, the Royal Marine entry and the Higher School Certificate syllabus. We were actively discouraged from going on to university and Commander MacIlwaine told me it was an unpatriotic distraction from the war effort. I went for the HSC though, for the experience; I also went in for the CSC exams. Things were not easy for us academically and private study outside school hours was often made impossible. We had to play compulsory games in the afternoons or we were required to plant or lift potatoes. The library was closed every afternoon because it was said to attract shirkers. Anyway it was not well stocked – even naval history, which was a favourite subject of mine, was shamefully inadequate. Nevertheless I very much enjoyed the company of other boys in 6A who, in my opinion, had a much more civilised and relaxed attitude, compared with the frenetic quasi-nautical activity of the aspiring seafarers for whose subsequent careers, of course, Pangbourne had been deliberately designed.

In 1941, after my father had returned to the Royal Navy, my mother bought from her younger sister a seventeenth-century cottage at Chipperfield near Kings Langley in Hertfordshire. It was originally a farmhouse. It had a two-acre garden and an adjoining orchard; there were two spectacular yew trees in front and a rickety barn, formerly used by the village coffin-maker, on one side. My aunt had created a pretty walled rose garden and had replaced some of the cherry trees with apple trees. Our furniture which had been stored at Bideford in Devon was unpacked and room found for the family piano. My mother played it well and had a light touch. However it was really John's delight as he was a born musician and could pick up any tune and arrange it delightfully. He taught himself to play five or six instruments well, but was himself an impossible person to teach. He had a strong baritone voice and was the life and soul of village concerts and the local church. He had little opportunity to develop his musical talents at Pangbourne and, after an unfortunate affair with the second flautist of a national orchestra, he gave up any thought he may have had of playing professionally.

I fell foul of Commander MacIlwaine, the Executive Officer at Pangbourne, whose sarcastic remarks were for years a glowing feature of my termly reports; a sad reflection on my ability to please the naval staff. He was enormously popular with the cadets, a very good navigation instructor (his excellent teaching enabled me to obtain a credit in my School Certificate navigation) and a happy family man whose advice was much sought after by the mothers. He succeeded Jackie Hamilton Blair, a retired submariner who lost his voice escaping from a sunken submarine during the First World War, and had been obliged to learn to speak all over again. JHB was at Pangbourne when I arrived, very small indeed with short fat legs; but sturdily built. He bounced all over the place and was very much on the 'qui vive'. The trouble was I could not understand a word he said to me and he hated repeating himself. He was soon called up and I heard that his stentorian voice had become a navigational hazard off the South Wales coast, especially at night: Old Pangbournians had to be found and dragooned into acting as clandestine interpreters to prevent minor accidents at sea, caused by misunderstandings of his oral instructions.

No male member of the staff bothered to talk to me in my first term except Woodall, the Director of Studies (DOS – an acronym which was invariable reversed), known as the 'The Pink Man' probably because his visits to the Elephant Hotel aggravated a sensitive skin. I think he recognised in me a fellow lonely human being. He often had a cheery word and liked to call me 'Sun has got his', singing the song, 'The sun has got his hat on', loudly, when no one else was around. Our padre was the Reverend Robin Shields, a gentle kindly man who taught chemistry as well as divinity – a dichotomy which prompted him to explain, 'I am a scientific Christian, not a Christian Scientist'. I think I puzzled him because when I came up for confirmation classes I asked about the position of the Holy Ghost within the Blessed Trinity and also why, in the Apostles' Creed, did Jesus descend into Hell for three days. Surely, I thought, Purgatory would have been more appropriate for such a short stay. I felt unable to accept his explanations. He told me that I was the first boy ever to become so 'argumentative' and, to my parents' consternation, I was withdrawn from confirmation by the Bishop of Oxford on the morning of the service. Subsequently Robin Shields lent me various books written by Bishop Gore to study. Next year he decided I was ready for confirmation by Bishop Michael of St Albans. The latter spoke to me at length, holding up the proceedings quite a bit, then confirmed us all and gave me a leather-bound book entitled *The Imitation of Christ*.

Other characters on the wartime staff at Pangbourne included a former colonial district officer, who nearly 'krissed' (knifed) a boy with a ruler while demonstrating painless executions practised by the native inhabitants of North Borneo. Although well over sixty years of age, he was immensely strong and, one day, picked up a boy at his desk and threw desk and boy still firmly together clean through the plywood blackout screen by the door, leaving a recognisable Walt Disney-style silhouette of both on the remainder of the screen. Major R.R. Willis, VC, taught me history and told me how he had won his VC whilst serving with the Lancashire Fusiliers in Gallipoli. When he heard that I had applied to join the Indian Army as a schoolboy cadet, he said he was delighted and set about teaching me Urdu, map-reading and how to use a compass – all as unpaid extra subjects. I was to become extremely grateful for his basic teaching when, only a short while later, I found myself in remote areas of South-East Asia. We kept in contact for many years after I left school, and I was able to write and tell him how his teaching had helped me to survive during troubled times. I owe him a great deal.

After nearly two years my housemaster, whose subject was English language, took an interest in me and encouraged me to found the college Literary Society. I became its first secretary, which enabled me to organise live sessions of interested people to read the plays, and study the books, which were part of my Higher School Certificate English literature syllabus. I also became editor of *The Log*, the official school magazine, for five terms. I acquired an ancient typewriter from a retired couple in Chipperfield whose only granddaughter I was to marry years later.

I confess that I was a total failure by nautical college standards and never got beyond half a term as a Cadet Leader. Nevertheless, I learned to survive and develop wide interests in the unpopular academic side of the school. Beating was a common form of punishment for quite mild offences; but I managed to escape undetected. At that time corporal punishment was administered not only by the Masters-at-Arms; but also by boys, for example the Chief Cadet Captains of the college, often without adult supervision. It seemed to me to be a totally useless form of punishment. The wrong people were caught and the really bad offenders inevitably escaped detection. Bullying was rife throughout my time – some of us fought back, or supported one another, and survived unscathed, being streetwise, others were quite badly affected by the experience. No one in authority made any attempt to restrain excess and much of the bullying became traditional.

A kindred spirit and great friend of mine was Archibald Kennedy. He had an independent nature and disliked routine life at Pangbourne even more than I. We made a list of what we regarded as silly oppressive rules and decided to ignore or break them whenever safely possible. Our minor infringements of the law included illegal sunbathing on the roof, alteration of classroom clocks to provide extended breaks and clandestine replacement of overplayed classical records – deemed appropriate background music for Sunday parades – with much more enjoyable jazz. This certainly quickened the pace of the march past. We also made several long journeys into the world outside, without prior permission, on Saturdays and Sundays. We descended on my mother in Hertfordshire, my aunt near Newbury and his aunt, Lady Kilmaine, who lived on a large estate north of Midgham on the Bath Road.

On one memorable occasion we thumbed down a large black car driven by a uniformed chauffeur with a lady passenger sitting in the shadows on the back seat. A long white face appeared through a lowered window and quizzed us for a moment. Observing our naval cadet uniforms she asked us where we were going. Kennedy said we were on our way to the Nautical College Pangbourne. She hesitated, and then asked us to enter, indicating that one of us should sit next to her on her right and the other should sit next to her on the left. Having entered this very large car we sat down most comfortably as directed. I noticed she was wearing a long, thick light-brown dress and was tucked up warmly under a magnificent blue blanket. Her white hair was full and piled up high, there was quite a lot of it. Her face was chalky white and rather lined, with thinnish red lips and slightly rouged cheeks below lovely bright eyes. Unfortunately I could not determine their colour.

There was a large unopened box of American chocolates (I noticed it came from New York) on the small table in front of her. There was a strong smell of expensive new leather; but there were occasional whiffs and wafts of lavender. The engine was absolutely silent. I was delighted to recognise, almost at once, Queen Mary (the chauffeur called her Ma'am). Sadly I had known no elderly grandmothers with whom to compare her. But she reminded me very much of the elder Miss Bradnack of my dame school days. Her voice was authoritative, modulated and quite distinctive. Neither of us noticed any obvious trace of a foreign accent. We used the royal title 'Your Majesty' when we first replied to her questions and followed it up with Ma'am later. It was all relaxed and friendly and I never felt awed or awkward. She put us at ease effortlessly and effectively. When she asked us which ship we were in, Kennedy said that we were still naval cadets. She then said that the King was a sailor and, afterwards, Kennedy and I thought her voice had a tinge of sadness and that she was referring to King George V (her husband who died in 1936) and probably not to the present King (her son George VI) who had been a sailor too. She asked us lots of questions and became quite animated when she

25

discovered Kennedy's family connections (he later became the Earl of Cassillis and succeeded his father as Marquis of Ailsa). I discovered she knew Sir John and Lady Ward, who lived near Hungerford, whom I had met on occasion and whom my parents knew slightly. She was amusing, relaxed and evidently much enjoyed young company – quite unlike the stern character portrayed in newspaper articles and photographs. She asked her chauffeur to take us back to the college; but we persuaded her to drop us off in Pangbourne village so as not to attract attention and to enable us to slip in quietly. The chauffeur was familiar with the geography and Queen Mary went on her way. Our loyal friends at school asked only one question: 'Was she wearing a crown?'

Unfortunately, Kennedy did not get on with Sir Philip Devitt, the extremely kind and interested chairman of the governors. Kennedy accused him publicly, by way of an unsigned handwritten message on one of the communal noticeboards, of breaking his word following the famous handshake which he gave new cadets on joining the college. He was discovered and very nearly expelled. On learning of his predicament, I knocked on Sir Philip's door and boldly entered his warm drawing room. He was very welcoming and knew my name. I told him what a fine chap Kennedy was and that he was a great credit to his uniform and to the college. Sir Philip listened intently and in silence. I ended my speech saying that, if he was expelled, I thought all the ghillies in Scotland would rise up ... before I could finish Sir Philip laughed loudly and poured out two glasses of sherry saying, 'I hear your message loud and clear, I'll keep him here if he apologises and shakes my hand again,' (which, of course, Kennedy did with good grace). Thus Kennedy survived and managed to complete his time, ending up as a Cadet Captain. I kept in touch with him for years and he was an usher at my first wedding. Another kindred spirit throughout my academic life at Pangbourne and on long-distance runs, was David Kent whose father was the popular marine artist Leslie Kent. We used to cycle to each other's homes and play tennis in the holidays. He, too, didn't make the sea his career; but became a civil engineer and was 'best man' at my first wedding.

While being shown around a local air defence unit Kennedy and I discovered to our delight the following notice, entitled 'Winch drill for Barrage Balloons':

1. Take purity (unless purity is below 50% the operation is unlikely to be successful).
2. Untie petticoat lacing and of slips.
3. Bed down.
4. Inspect all apertures for wear etc.
5. Start up winch and close-haul to point of attachment (N.B. With new winches point of attachment should be well greased.)
6. When winch is thoroughly warmed up, top up using one-way filter (cane stiffeners may be used if required, but should not be necessary).
7. Repeat until storage cylinders are exhausted.
8. On bags.
9. Pay off winch.

The alteration of one letter, of course, provided us with an entirely different meaning.

In 1942 I won the Open English and the Open History prizes, and I became the Vice-Captain of Running, so I suppose I achieved something after all. I also entered a nationwide essay competition organised by the Seafarers' Education Service and, to my great astonishment, was awarded first prize together with a substantial cheque.

The subject I chose was 'Why I Decided to Go to Sea'. Despite my decision to write this essay, I was already beginning to think that the likelihood of a seafaring life for me was becoming remote. It was obvious to all who were trying to educate me, that I did not have the makings of a 'sea dog'. Moreover, I was short-sighted and I began to worry seriously about my future.

I first heard of Indian Army cadetships early in 1943. It seemed a wonderful way of escaping from what I perceived to be the dead hand of nautical officialdom. Changing course would certainly please my mother; but I knew it would bitterly disappoint my father. My great-grandfather on my mother's side, William Master-man Williams, went out to India as an eighteen-year-old ensign in 1846, and eventually became a captain in the Madras Native Infantry. After the Indian Mutiny, he was promoted to the Madras

Staff Corps, but he died soon after as a much-mourned brigade major and the Vice-President of the Trichinopoly Municipality, leaving his grieving wife, my great-grandmother, to bring up their surviving children. Their other children were left behind in the cemeteries of Calcutta, Moulmein and Rangoon – we still have their sad little birth and death certificates. I wrote to my mother's elder brother, who was commanding the anti-aircraft defences of Liverpool, and asked for his advice. He replied at once, saying that he knew very little about the Indian Army, and he put me on to Major General Sir William Twiss, known to us as Oliver, who years ago had been my proxy godfather, in the absence abroad of a full-time one. He replied immediately to my letter and suggested a meeting in Winchester, where he greeted me on the railway station and took me to lunch at a small restaurant which only admitted customers who had given a secret code on the knocker.

Oliver Twiss had joined the 9th Gurkha Rifles in the late nineteenth century. He had served on the Peking Expedition, in the Great War, in peacetime India and had retired as General Officer Commanding in Burma. He was now Commandant of the Observer Corps and Colonel-in-Chief of the 9th Gurkha Rifles. We talked throughout the afternoon and I left carrying home a cake specially baked for him by the restaurant owner. Over tea at his home he said it was up to me to join up, go out to India and obtain my commission. He could not help me with any of this, but, when I was commissioned, he would recommend my application to join his own regiment, the 9th Gurkha Rifles. We exchanged letters regularly for many years and I always made time to visit him and Peggy Twiss at Chilland Barn, near Winchester, on my leaves.

I left Pangbourne at the end of the spring term, 1943, at my own request, and immediately joined Davies, Laing and Dick, the tutors in Holland Park. I found a totally different attitude there towards work. The place was almost entirely run by Jewish mathematicians and philosophers who had escaped from Germany or Austria before the war. Their teaching was the best I had received at any school and I just scraped through my examinations. I had already taken the King's shilling earlier in the year and I was asked to report to the London District Assembly Centre in August a few days before my eighteenth birthday.

I travelled by train to Euston accompanied by my father's ancient narrow naval-uniform black tin trunk and battered suitcase. I hailed a taxi and asked the driver to take me to the assembly centre. He promptly did a U-turn and stopped outside a large building opposite. As I got out, wearing my green trilby hat, a sentry shouted that the main entrance was for officers and I had to enter by the tradesman's door at the back. 'God help England,' said my taxi driver by way of unrewarded farewell.

I soon discovered that I had been appointed to the Queen's Royal Regiment (Second of the Line), and given the number 6100751 and three plastic tags to wear around my person. 'When they find your dead body, they will know who you are, and tell your next of kin,' said the jolly quartermaster sergeant, by way of welcome.

My rank was confirmed as schoolboy cadet and I wore a white flash on my forage cap; my pay was the same as a sergeant – providing me with a pound a week in my pocket. I was issued with an old .303 Lee and Enfield rifle, complete with one of those long bayonets which one used to see in paintings of the South African War. Then, to my astonishment, I was given a very old-fashioned solar topee with fore and aft peaks, usually associated with field marshals, though with less frills – a prize museum piece, it seemed to me. On further examination of this army-issue uniform, a sense of pride in my appearance was shaken somewhat by the length of my khaki shorts – they reached well below my knees. We could not stop laughing at one another as we donned the rest of our tropical fancy dress, surmising it must have been discovered in a remote army warehouse and dumped on us as a convenient way of creating space.

We had frequent inspections of our rifles. This involved opening the bolt and placing a thumbnail at the home end of the barrel, so that the portly sergeant major in charge of us could squint down the other end to see if the barrel was bright, clean and slightly oiled. Unfortunately, my four years at Pangbourne had not prepared me for this. I had to ask my neighbour hurriedly to show me how to open the bolt, and where to find the little black bottle, pull-through and four-by-two cloth which everyone else was using. All my companions seemed to have served in the Officers' Training Corps at school and were *au fait* with this sort of thing. In the end, I accepted with gratitude a cockney soldier's offer to clean my shoes, brasses and rifle and to make my bed with my clothes piled neatly on it ready for daily inspections. He was a permanent officers' batman at the centre and claimed he needed the extra money to play the endless games of housey-housey (bingo), which were such a feature of the other ranks' messes. I gave him sixpence a day to do this and he was very pleased. More importantly, he was a dab hand at obtaining cut-price tickets for the London shows which he sold on to me at a fair profit for himself.

We spent ten days at the centre then joined a large batch of British troops bound for India and on to Burma. Our draft comprised fifty-nine schoolboy cadets, all eighteen years old, and our serial code was RZKOK. We marched across to Euston Station where the elderly porters cheered and wished us luck; then we steamed off on the long slow train journey to Greenock in Scotland. On arrival there we boarded the SS *Multan*, an ancient P&O passenger liner which had been converted into a troopship. Here we were directed down to a temporary deck at the bottom of the ship. My letters home from the *Multan* were heavily censored and arrived looking like Christmas cut-out decorations. Our mess deck, which we shared with three hundred and fifty British other ranks, had first been altered to accommodate one hundred and fifty troops; but it now held over four hundred. We slept in hammocks head to toe by night and sat cheek to jowl by day. I wrote home, 'The heat is unbearable, especially by day when we are kept below hatches for security reasons. Fortunately, I managed to sling my hammock under a ventilator down which I occasionally thrust my nose; apart from a bacon-fat smell, the cool air is quite refreshing. Food every day is stew and caked rice. The tannoy loudspeakers play "Hearts of Oak" endlessly at meals. Everyone has been severely seasick, except me, which means I am an orderly every day and washer-up as well as sick nurse.'

As soon as we were allowed on deck, I hid every night, alone and comfortable in a lifeboat. During long hours of spare time we learnt Urdu from various Indian Army officers on board. A passing interest until we reached Port Said was to meet and talk with a Yugoslav partisan group, led by Mihailovitch, who were hitching a lift from us. As we steamed through the Suez Canal, British Tommies, brown as berries and almost naked on the shore, shouted, 'You're going the wrong way!' On arrival in Bombay we were the last to leave the ship and very fed up with waiting. My tin

30

trunk and suitcase were unloaded separately and sent on to Bangalore. However, I still had with me all my army gear and various bits and pieces in two heavy kitbags, plus my rifle, and myself looking like a Christmas tree. I was physically incapable of carrying the kitbags down the steep gangplank so, as there was nothing breakable in them, I threw both over the side of the ship on to the quay. Unfortunately the OC Troops saw me, jumped up and down and started to shout at me. Good friends on the quayside retrieved the kitbags and, beckoned by them, I dashed to a waiting truck and off we went to Bombay's central railway station.

Just before our arrival in Bombay we had a final kit inspection and, to my horror, I discovered that the sea air had caused my bayonet to rust in its leather scabbard and it could not be withdrawn. I did the obvious thing and exchanged it secretly with someone else's. Our platoon commander went ashore later with my rusty antique swinging proudly on his webbing belt. Minutes before I had innocently displayed my gleaming prize for his inspection.

We were allocated two dirty, smelly, third-class railway carriages for our two-day journey across India to Bangalore. We had no Indian money and of course no one would take our English money. We starved, until we were rescued by our draft conducting officer, who used his own cash to buy us a little fruit and water. That evening a third of us developed severe diarrhoea. We changed trains at a railway junction called Guntakal in Central India. Here there was a long queue of the worst affected for the European-type lavatories, and the rest of us loaded the new train. While doing this, I suddenly saw the train begin to leave in a cloud of steam. By dint of a mad sprint, I just managed to catch up and cling to the last carriage, returning to my third-class carriage at the next station. Some twelve of our draft missed the train and turned up at Bangalore four days later.

Bangalore city was three thousand feet above sea level and inhabited by a million people. The cantonment was outside the city and beyond it was the Officers' Training School (OTS) on the edge of Agram Plain. The weather was cool by night and pretty hot by day. The OTS was heaven compared with the SS *Multan* and the Indian railways. Nevertheless the place swarmed with mosquitoes by night, their whining noise in one's ears competing with the croaking of the frogs outside. We were quartered three British cadets to a small room. My luggage had arrived safely and I was overjoyed to wear clean clothes again. Food in our mess was excellent and we were served by uniformed bearers. However we had to clean our rooms, fetch water, wash our clothes, press our uniforms and clean our shoes, brasses and leather equipment. A block containing a similar number of Indian cadets was next door to us and we discovered they were on the same preliminary course. Our room managed to recruit a small Tamil boy to do some of the hard work, and life became quite tolerable. We were rationed to one airmail letter card a week and one airgraph (a large form which was photographed, sent through the post and delivered in miniature form); I used to draw pictures on the latter and send them home as Christmas and birthday cards.

Major A.R.H. Dee, sometime housemaster at Marlborough College, was the Preliminary Company Commander and I found him helpful and friendly. His sergeant major was said to have the loudest voice in India Command and had the face and moustache of a lead toy soldier. Soon after arrival, I exchanged my field marshal's topee for a pigsticker pith helmet with a white band around the sides, it went well with the highly polished ancient leather equipment which we had to wear. I also had my long shorts or short longs smartly tailored.

I think the permanent staff were taken aback by our tender age and innocent fresh looks because, much to our consternation, we had to attend a two day War Office Selection Board (WOSB). In my letter home I explained, 'The modern army recruits its officers from the ranks and you may think that as schoolboy cadets we were privileged to escape this procedure. Quite the reverse, we attended an unexpected and compulsory WOSB and our mental and physical faculties were endlessly tested by building theoretical bridges over non-existing streams, crossing imaginary barbed-wire fences, writing short stories and giving unrehearsed five-minute lectures. It lasted two full days. They are now making schoolboy cadets do three months in England before coming out here, so that the less able may be weeded out and have somewhere to go. Major Dee told me to grow a moustache and smoke a pipe, both of which I shall attempt! Eleven of us failed and were sent away either as privates to the British Army, or as sergeants to the Indian Army Corps of Clerks. I am one of the lucky ones and have been earmarked for a commission in a Gurkha Regiment.'

Those of us who had been selected for eventual commissions stayed two months in the Preliminary Company and then passed out into the Pre-OTS Company. This meant we could sleep two to a room, share a school bearer, have the communal use of a drunken dhobi (laundryman) and the private use of bicycles at weekends. The latter saved us considerable sums of money previously spent on taxis. Major Dee had his own ideas concerning the implementation of these privileges; after drill one day, he made us form two long lines, one of British cadets and the other of Indian cadets. Each line was told to turn inwards and, behold, our new roommates were facing us. I wrote home, 'My new companion is an elderly Tamil *subedar* (warrant officer) from Southern India. He is a devout Christian, reads the Bible for half an hour every day and is wise in the ways of the world. He has an aggravating habit of asking his friends and relations into our room all day long, thus depriving me of my chair, my half-share of the table and even my bed. I have had to limit the number coming in at any one time and we have agreed no visits before 8.30 a.m.'

As the weeks passed we went from Pre-OTS into D Company of the Junior School. My Indian partner decided to learn English songs and began to sing 'Silent Night' and 'My Bonny lies over the Ocean' endlessly, accompanied by home-made coffee with lashings of locally made rum. In order to escape him at weekends, I joined the Bangalore Sailing Club with a friend whom I taught to sail, and we had many good times. He told me that his grandmother was an author and had written the popular children's book *Little Black Sambo*, a great favourite of mine once upon a time.

D Company won the Wavell Banner for Sports. I contributed by coming equal first in the cross-country race: my co-winner was a Bengali Indian and, on the way, we decided not to race each other into the ground, but to hold hands and come in first equal and save our breath. At this time my platoon consisted of the following nationalities: German-Burmese, Anglo-Burmese, Italian-Burmese, Burmese, Jat, Dogra, Gurkha, English, Punjabi Muslim, American and Madrasee. I passed my preliminary Urdu exam in December 1943 and my main Urdu exam in March 1944, receiving a cash award of 100 chips (rupees). I had plenty of spare time so I decided to go in for the Army Interpreter's exam.

Entertainment at Bangalore consisted of films in the modern and up-to-date OTS cinema and in the city fleapits; excellent ENSA concerts (where I saw Gert and Daisy, Stainless Stephen and Noel Coward) and in local theatres, where I saw a wonderful production of Handel's *Messiah* by the choir of Bangalore's Bishop Cotton School. For reading matter my mother sent me *Punch* magazine every week, which enabled me to keep my sense of humour when times were difficult, and many paperback books.

On 9 July 1944, while planning ten days' local leave in Mysore as a paying guest of the Maharajah, I felt horribly ill and was admitted into a British Military Hospital with infective hepatitis (jaundice). My skin had gone quite yellow and my eyes were like a gorilla's. Luckily, the hospital was entirely Italian-run, having been captured intact during the North African campaign and subsequently transferred lock, stock and barrel to India. The devoted doctors, nursing staff and orderlies were all Italian and quite the kindest, caring people one could possibly hope to find. I was well looked after and I was visited by hosts of friends every evening. My recovery was delayed because I was violently sick every time I stood up. I began to develop growing suspicions that I was missing too much of the course and that I would fail my final exams. Eventually, I left hospital on 26 July and found that I was a 'stateless' person. My depression at this news was compensated a little by the grant of two weeks' sick leave in Wellington, high up in the Nilgiri Hills near Ootacamund in South India.

I left the OTS by victoria for the crowded railway station where I caught a night train to Mettuppalaiyam. Next day I changed trains and boarded the Nilgiri mountain express. I told my parents, 'There were six small dinky carriages each holding about forty people, pushed uphill by a tiny little engine at the back. I travelled first class and the views were magnificent. The hills rise steeply from the plains and on the way, as the little train wound round and round the mountainside, I was able to see for hundreds of miles across the dull-orange, sun-baked plains. The mountain summits were hidden in the clouds and the hillsides were densely covered with trees and other vegetation. At times, the mountain was very close to us on one side and, on the other, there was a vertical drop going down hundreds of feet. I could just make out the tops of trees gently swaying together a long way down below. We passed straight through many waterfalls which were spectacular and sprayed the windows. The train steamed at an average speed of four miles per hour and we arrived at Wellington three and a half hours later.'

Wellington was quite a small place but was said to have the largest parade ground in India. I stayed in Delegation Villa run by a Scottish couple who spoiled me for the next two weeks. Ooty was eleven miles away and I went there by bus to see if I could locate the grave of my great-grandfather; but I was unsuccessful. I was equally unsuccessful in trying to sail efficiently on the lake, because the boats were badly maintained and the sails torn. I soon began to feel very much better and went on long walks, ending up by climbing Mount Dodegetta, whence I got a superb view of the Nilgiri range of mountains through gaps in the clouds.

On returning to Bangalore I found that I did not have to go through the Junior School again and had been posted to the Senior School, though in a different company from my original draft who were soon to receive their commissions. Other news greeted my arrival. My room-mate had been arrested by the military police for drunken behaviour in Bangalore cantonment and had been returned to his unit. His place had been taken by Gian Singh Gurung, an English-educated Gurkha of my own age. As soon as we saw each other, we knew that we would be *sarthis* (friends), and so it turned out. We did everything together, including cross-country running, and thoroughly enjoyed our last two months in the senior company at Bangalore. I helped him with his written reports and I taught him map-reading. He taught me to speak colloquial Khas Kura (the official language of the Gurkhas in Nepal) and to read and write its Devanagari script. This basic knowledge was enormously helpful to me when I joined the 9th Gurkha Rifles Regimental Centre in Dehra Dun as an emergency commissioned second lieutenant (number 15159).

I think that it is of great interest to note the effect of introducing hundreds of British emergency commissioned officers (ECOs), mainly from the Officer's Training Schools in Bangalore, Mhow, Belgaum and elsewhere, into the Indian Army during the Second World War. A cousin of mine had this to say when he joined his Indian Regiment as an ECO: 'Before the Second World War the officer cadre of the old Indian Army (excluding the Gurkha Brigade which did not recruit Indian officers) was divided into two quite separate groups – the British officers and the Indian officers.

The British officers required their opposite numbers to live in "Indianised units" thus consigning them to little ghettoes on their own. There was hardly any socialising between the two groups in these units, and neither had much respect for the other.' He went on to say, 'We were emergency commissioned officers, not regulars, and on our arrival we were shocked to discover the great divide between British and Indian officers. We soon began to make friends with our Indian counterparts and to develop friendly relations after work; becoming close friends and respecting each other's culture, feelings, religion and faith. Later on, when we were called upon to share hardships and danger, the friendships made never failed. I am hugely indebted to my wonderful Indian friends, to some of whom I owe my life.'

Things changed for the Gurkha Brigade after India gained independence on 15th August 1947. Six of the ten Gurkha Regiments were transferred by the British Government to the Indian Government. Every British officer in those six regiments had to be replaced, almost overnight, by an Indian officer. One of these incoming Indian officers, whom I know and greatly respect, eventually reached the rank of major general after a most distinguished military career. He has commented on the situation within the Indian Army, into which he was commissioned before the Second World War, as follows.

'My own recollection on joining the Indian Army, after a few years at school and college in England, was of being aghast at the near-total apartness in the lives of British and Indian officers. That came as a cultural shock after my experiences in the United Kingdom. As I have written previously, there were no friendships between British and Indian officers until the ECOs began to arrive – then the situation changed radically. Very few of the pre-war British officers had a close Indian friend. We Indians lived in our little ghettoes officially called "Indianised units", and we had few contacts with British "colleagues", either at work or at play, even in the same station. This state of officer-duality often had the effect of preventing us from regarding Britain's war as "our" war – until the ECOs began to arrive. We admired the pre-war British officer: but we did not like him (any more than he liked us).'

2

Going into the jungle, my mouth faces homeward.
Going homeward, my mouth faces the jungle.

GURKHA RIDDLE

(Who or what am I? answer on page 354)

Robert Clive's decisive victory at the Battle of Plessey in 1757 established British supremacy in India and opened the door for the expansion of the Honourable East India Company. The Company's influence crept slowly northwards and westwards until it clashed with the interests of the rulers of what is now Nepal. The Nepalese lived high up in the Himalayan mountain valleys and were called Gurkhas, after a feudal village in the city state of Gorkha in Western Nepal. Boundary disputes ensued and the Governor General declared war on Nepal in 1814. After a series of extremely hard-fought battles a peace treaty was signed in 1816; a provision of which allowed the Company to recruit Gurkhas into their armies. The Gurkha soldiers proved brave, fearless and distinguished themselves in local wars and also by their loyalty to the Company during the Indian Mutiny of 1857–58. After the Mutiny ten regiments of Gurkha soldiers were recruited into the Indian Army and fought with distinction in many theatres of both world wars.

It is not well known that the government and the royal court of Nepal gave large sums of money for the purchase of weapons and equipment for the British forces in the Second World War; notably the provision of several fighter aircraft during the Battle of Britain. Considerable sums of money were also donated by the Nepalese to the Lord Mayor of London during the 1941–42 Blitz for the relief of victims in the East End. All this money came from a country which was, and still is by western standards, desperately poor.

37

After the fall of France in 1940, when the British stood alone, the Prime Minister of Nepal sanctioned the recruitment of twenty new battalions for the Gurkha Brigade to serve anywhere in the world remarking, 'Does a friend desert a friend in time of need? If you win, we win with you. If you lose, we lose with you.' He also sent eight Nepalese regiments to India for internal security duties and operations on the north-west frontier. To top it all, a crack Nepalese Brigade was sent to Burma and fought with great courage at the Battle of Imphal.

This was the background I had studied when I was commissioned into the 9th Gurkha Rifles as a second lieutenant. Gian Singh was commissioned into the Jaipur State forces and we parted with sad hearts.

I decided to go back to Wellington for my fortnight's end-of-course leave and once again I walked among the tall eucalyptus trees, smelling the strongly scented air, wandering about the mountains and playing chess with people staying at the villa.

For curiosity, I worked out my expenses over the previous year. My annual pay at about ten guineas a month was £121, plus my first Urdu award at £7, and a clothing allowance of £58, totalled £186. My expenses were £103. Thus I had £83 in the bank after one year in India. My parents had sent me £75; but I had spent this on sending food parcels home, averaging two a month. Of the fifty-nine schoolboy cadets in my draft from the UK, one had died from enteric fever (typhoid), another had been repatriated to the UK with infantile paralysis, eleven had failed the course and forty-six had been commissioned.

I left Wellington on 3rd November 1944 for Bangalore, collected my baggage and returned to the railway station in the late afternoon to catch the train for Dehra Dun, travelling via Madras and changing at New Delhi. The train from Delhi did not leave for seven hours, so I visited the Red Fort, obtaining the services of an excellent guide to take me round. We were the only people there. On arrival at Dehra Dun, I met up with a captain whose *tonga* (small one-horse carriage) I followed in mine five miles along the road to the regimental centre at Birpur. He kindly took me to the officers' mess and introduced me to my brother officers.

Birpur village was situated between the 3rd Gurkha and 9th Gurkha Regimental Centres 2,000 feet up at the foot of the Himalayas. The 9th Gurkha Rifles officers' mess was said, by common consent, to be the most spectacularly situated mess in the whole of India. It had been built at the end of a long ridge with splendid views of the Himalayas, and I simply could not believe my eyes at the sheer beauty of the place. The surrounding garden was delightful – bright green lawns and plenty of colour in the borders. Inside was a very large dining room with ante-rooms and a well-stocked bar. There was a great deal of highly polished wood and plenty of comfortable chairs. A few pieces of regimental silver were set off by a stunning collection of animal heads and antlers on the walls, and various trophies acquired in the Sikh Wars, the Peking Expedition and a large Japanese regimental flag recently captured in Burma. The mess orderlies in their smart Nepali uniforms completed the picture. The extraordinary view by day changed dramatically in the evening as the sun began to set. I could see sheet lightning up in the mountains and this was followed by a strange, eerie atmosphere before the lights of Mussoorie town high up in the mountains came into view – a sort of heavenly settlement twinkling in the night sky. For a moment I was seduced by its natural beauty and I began to envy the permanent staff who were living in this wondrous place.

I was posted immediately to a regimental young officers' course and placed in one of the training companies. My spare time was taken up learning Gurkhali (Khas Kura) which I found quite close to Urdu, both in words and construction, but written in Devanagari script. I also spent my afternoons re-learning to ride properly and to play polo: my instructor was a Sikh *dafedar* (lance sergeant) on loan from the cavalry. Captain Kennedy, said to have been the most senior captain in the Indian Army, helped me with my polo, though he showed little sympathy when I complained at always being given a pony which was blind in one eye – all he said was. 'Get there earlier and pick another,' which I did, despite being so junior. I wrote home, 'One of the ways I have to learn to speak Gurkhali and get to know the men, is to live as a Gurkha recruit by day but returning to sleep in my bungalow at night, and eat in the mess for breakfast and mess nights. It is a very good experience and interesting to see at first-hand how quickly Gurkha recruits from the high hillsides learn to live down below. When they first arrive, they are thirsty because they have never seen a tap and cannot turn it on; they just hit it with a stone. Similarly, they cannot run properly because they live on steep hillsides and have to learn it all when they first come here. This they quickly do and in a few weeks we go "*khud* racing" (rough cross-country) together.'

Immediately after Christmas Day I was posted to the 29th Gurkha Rifles, a jungle-training battalion formed from the 9th and 2nd Gurkha Rifles in the middle of the Siwalik Hills south of Dehra Dun. I shared a tent with another officer who was much older than me and, before the war, had been a borough engineer somewhere in East Anglia. I found I had to sleep on a homemade *charpoi* (bed). There was no furniture of any kind though we had two ancient *lal tins* (oil lamps) to lighten the cold dark evenings. I was pleased to have with me a good thin mattress for my valise (bedding-roll) which I had bought before I left Dehra Dun. The officers' mess, which consisted of three *bashas* (huts) put together, did not have enough crockery or glass or chairs for all of us to sit down together. There was a fire in the ante-room; but chairs for only five people to sit around it; naturally the senior officers had preference for these. There were no windows and no proper doors. Food, however, was excellent. Funnily enough, I found this a much more appropriate place in which to live and work, bearing in mind my projected future in wartime Burma.

I began to settle in well and, when selecting my Gurkha orderly, I chose someone who could build furniture from bamboo, wood and leaves. He was called Palman, and with his *kukri* he built us a small roomful of dinky furniture, including a separate little cubicle with a comfortable thunderbox (loo) and drainage. Army life once again was based on learning Gurkhali and also obtaining experience of living in the jungle and fighting a jungle-based enemy. In retrospect, the training here was very good and I think we became quite proficient. I took part in three detailed inspections. General Sir George Giffard praised us for our realistic training, Lieutenant-General Sir G.A.P. Scoones said we were the best troops in the division, General Lentaign, late of the Chindits in Burma, thought our training area totally unlike conditions in Burma, and General Sir Claude Auchinleck, the Commander-in-Chief, thought we were first class.

Two experiences stand out. Firstly, Lieutenant Colonel C.G. Rogers, MC, the elderly British officer who taught us the culture, language and customs of the Gurkhas, held us spellbound as he explained the meaning of Gurkha riddles, popular Gurkha songs and how to *nautch* (dance) correctly; especially when the worse for drinking rum! At the end of his course, we were taken one by one down the track leading to the Gurkha lines late on a dark Saturday evening and told to make conversation with the Gurkhas as they staggered home from their canteen or as they came off the bus from Dehra Dun. 'Did you meet any girls?' we had to ask. 'Did you make love to them?' we asked again. If they sussed who you were, you failed. If they gave the standard rude and basic answers complete with exaggerated descriptions, you passed. Secondly, Colonel Williams, known as 'Elephant Bill', taught us how to read the jungle, and other war veterans explained how to find and assess tell-tale signs of Japanese troops in the nearby jungle. It was exceptionally well put over and I completed my training by attending a jungle survival course in Shimoga in South India; and an Indian Army engineers' course at Roorkee. On the latter course, while building roads and bridges in the jungle, I supplemented our meagre rations by shooting *cheetal* (deer), wild peafowl and pigeon.

I quote from a letter to my brother in England: 'I have just returned from a tiring expedition in which my training company, in competition with three non-Gurkha Indian Army companies, was supposed to locate and attack a so-called enemy fifty miles away. We were given four days to travel through the jungle, make a recce then launch an attack. We had to travel on foot with mules carrying our rations and tents. I decided that if we ditched our heavy gear and halved our rations, we could take a short cut over the mountains along a little track which I had discovered earlier when fighting forest fires, and make the approach in only two days. My trek proved heavy going. We crossed fast-flowing shallow rivers, skirted fields of hay and sugar cane and climbed higher and higher up the stony banks of rivers. At last we came to the difficult pass and we pushed and pulled our reluctant mules over seemingly impossible obstacles, and then down the other side, where I had to try and find our target. Reaching the bottom tired and exhausted, we pushed along on a night compass march. Luck was on my side. I discovered the "enemy" and the directing staff by the noise they made. They were not expecting us, so we encamped, waited till dawn on the third day, launched our attack and took everyone completely by surprise. My Gurkhas thought it hilarious. The other three companies did not arrive till the next day and I am a bit unpopular; but I don't mind.'

Unfortunately there were no calls for reinforcements from our active battalions and in order to keep me gainfully employed, and to use up my surplus energy, I was given command of the demonstration company (two platoons). I set about putting into practice all I had learnt at the regimental centre and in the 29th Gurkha Rifles.

When at last my posting to the 3/9th Gurkha Rifles came through it was just before the launch of Operations Zipper and Button against the Japanese in Malaya and Singapore. No one in India seemed to know the precise whereabouts of the battalion and I was sent to Comilla in Burma, then on to Rangoon, where I took part in rounding up Japanese soldiers unwilling to believe that their emperor had ordered them to surrender. I was then flown to South India and then to Singapore.

On arrival at Singapore Racecourse camp, I was told that the next available plane to Java, where 3/9th Gurkhas were believed to be located, would be routed a long way round via Shanghai. Our plane carried four Japanese-American officers, whose task was to collect twenty alleged Japanese war criminals, and escort them to a waiting ship bound elsewhere for trial. On arrival in Shanghai I accompanied them as there was nothing else to do. At first we were unable to find the Allied headquarters responsible for handing over the prisoners; but eventually a group of gung-ho Kuo Min Tang Nationalists said they would be delighted to assist. They took us to the local morgue and showed us twenty coffins – they had carried out summary executions not having seen the necessity for a trial. Greatly relieved, the Americans flew to Manila and I flew on the same RAF plane to Batavia (now called Jakarta) in Java. Here I collected a total of 182 reinforcements bound for 3/9th Gurkhas with no accompanying officers. We sailed on to Sourabaia, courtesy of the Royal Navy. Whilst travelling I reflected on the history of this part of South-East Asia.

The Indonesian archipelago is situated in a highly volcanic area where there are at least 150 active volcanoes. It encompasses over 13,000 islands; the exact number varying day by day, being dependent on the activity of volcanoes under the sea. Of these islands 600 are inhabited. The archipelago is 3,000 miles long, by 1,200 miles wide. It is a huge country and has a rapidly-growing population of 220 million people – one hundred ethnic groups and speaking more than 300 languages. Some 90 per cent profess to be Sunni Muslims; the remainder are Chinese, Hindus (mainly on the island of Bali) and Christians.

The identities of the indigenous inhabitants of Indonesia are uncertain; but the early arrival by sea of Chinese from the north and Arabs from the Middle East is well-documented. One of the first empires to arise from within the archipelago was the Sri Vijaya, based in Sumatra, with its strength lying in its control of the Straits of Malacca and Sunda; it had strong Hindu connections and flourished from the seventh to the thirteenth century AD. For a time, the Mataram Empire, based in Java from the eighth to the tenth centuries, coexisted with Sri Vijaya. Today, the Mataram Empire is renowned for its monumental achievement, the magnificent Buddhist temple at Borobudur in Central Java. The Hindu-Buddhist Mejapahit Empire, based in East Java, succeeded Sri Vijaya; it expanded rapidly into Sumatra, the Celebes and the Moluccas; also northwards into the coastal areas of Malaya, Thailand and Indo-China. It flourished throughout the fourteenth and fifteenth centuries. There was also the Menang Kerbau Empire based in Sumatra which, for a time, dominated parts of the Malay Peninsula.

Islam was the religion of the first Arab sea traders, who established themselves in North-West Sumatra; but it was several hundred years later that nearly all Indonesia was converted to Islam.

South-East Asia attracted the attention of European colonial powers – mainly Portugal and Holland – during the sixteenth century; and in 1641 the Dutch captured the strategic port of Malacca from the Portuguese. Thereafter the Netherlands East India Company controlled the economy, trade and politics of the region until the British 'annexed' Java in 1810 during the Napoleonic wars. With the final defeat of Napoleon the British returned Java to the Dutch in 1816, in exchange for establishing British influence in mainland Malaya and Singapore. Thus the Dutch were able to dominate the Indonesian archipelago for a further 125 years. On the whole, Dutch colonial rule may be considered paternal; it is a matter of speculation how so few Dutchmen, and a small number of autocratic Indonesian businessmen and feudal chiefs, were able to rule a mixed population scattered over many islands far from the centre of government in Java.

Suddenly, European colonial domination of South-East Asia

came to an abrupt halt on 9th December 1941 when a new empire – the Japanese – marched across the region. The British administration in Hong Kong, Malaya and Singapore collapsed almost overnight; and a vast army of British and Australian troops surrendered to the Japanese. Weakened by total defeat in their own countries at the hands of the German Army in 1940, the French were chased out of Indo-China and the Dutch fled from the Netherlands East Indies. In their places, the Japanese Empire established a harsh, cruel and unpopular regime: until, equally suddenly, it collapsed in 1945, following the dropping of the atom bombs on Hiroshima and Nagasaki. Educated, ambitious Indonesian politicians were not slow to take up the challenge and demand independence from the Dutch. They received wide popular support from ordinary people. They had been shocked out of their previous docility by the fragility of Dutch colonial rule; and the brutality and arrogance of the Japanese who had shown no respect for Islam, and had deported large numbers of civilians to forced labour camps all around South-East Asia. A typhoon of change began to blow with unstoppable force through the towns and *kampongs* (villages) of the Indonesian archipelago.

On 17th August 1945, Indonesian Nationalist politicians in Java declared unilaterally their country's independence from Dutch rule. They prepared a white flag, covered half of it with their own blood, raised it high in the air and announced the formation of a Republic of Indonesia (which received worldwide recognition in 1949). Attempts were made by these politicians to co-operate with the Allied forces; but they were unable to control all their regular troops or the guerrilla armies – not all of whom were in sympathy with each other. Initially the Japanese Army, carrying out their country's policy of creating a so-called 'Greater East-Asian co-prosperity sphere', continued to arm and train the Indonesian Nationalists' Army. However, the Japanese soon began to lose interest and, in common with their former enemies in the Allied armies, they wished to return to their homeland. Republican leaders (all former political prisoners of the pre-war colonial Dutch authorities) such as Sukarno. a former schoolmaster; Sutan Shahrir, soon to become the first prime minister of Indonesia; and Mohamed Hatta, later to become president of the republic, emerged as popular leaders of the Nationalists. They were greatly encouraged not only by political support from Russia and America; but also by the military inability of the Allied leaders to reinstate the former Netherlands East Indies Empire. They represented the only influential Indonesian politicians with whom the Allied military could negotiate.

The political aims of the new 'Republik Indonesia' were based firmly on Sukarno's five principles (or *pancasilas* – note here the Hindu word used!) first promulgated in July 1945, at a time when the Japanese Prime Minister had just given a degree of independence to Indonesian Nationalists. These five were nationalism, internationalism, democracy, social prosperity and belief in one God. They became the established political aims of all political parties, though, of course, the definitions varied according to circumstances; and the Muslim clerics were not slow to insist that the last of the *pancasilas* should be given the first priority.

Forty-five days after Indonesia's Declaration of *Merdeka* (independence), an Allied military mission was sent to Batavia (now called Jakarta). Its members had been instructed not to interfere in local politics. They were to carry out their objectives through Indonesian 'government' channels. These objectives were to locate and rescue Allied prisoners of war and internees, and to disarm and repatriate the Japanese military. The first large British formation to arrive in Java was 23 Indian Division. Two brigades landed at Batavia, totalling about five thousand men, at the end of September 1945. On 29 October, 49 Indian Infantry Brigade (about 2,500 men), under Brigadier A.W. Mallaby, landed in Sourabaia, a large port in East Java. Brigadier Mallaby's representative immediately attended a conference with Dr Moestopo, the Indonesian Governor of East Java, at which a *modus vivendi* was agreed. The British would concentrate solely on rescuing the Allied prisoners of war and civilian internees, and disarming and repatriating the Japanese. This was accepted by the Indonesian politicians. A signal was sent by 49 Brigade to the Allies' force headquarters in Batavia requesting that on no account should leaflets be dropped from the air on Sourabaia. (Leaflets had already been dropped all over West Java announcing the supersession of local civil government and ordering the disarming of extremists.) Having given this undertaking, it seemed to those who took part, that the Indonesian Government and Regular Army would allow the British to carry out their intentions in East Java. A 'contact committee' of British and Indonesian officials was formed. The atmosphere remained tense.

Contrary to what had been urgently requested, a British aircraft flew over Sourabaia city on 27 October dropping leaflets which made it only too clear to the Indonesians that the British were not only interfering in local political matters; but also intended to disarm all but a small civilian police force. Apart from being completely impractical, these terms nullified the previous agreement between 49 Brigade and Dr Moestopo. It placed the latter in an unfortunate position of appearing to have been double-crossed. The situation deteriorated at once. All that night, Radio Sourabaia broadcast abuse and announced that the British had come to hand the country over to the Dutch. Representatives of the local Indonesian Government in East Java lost control of their army and the extremists. Machine-gun barricades appeared in the streets and Indonesian regular forces regrouped secretly. The result was that each small detachment of 49 Brigade troops in the city was menaced by the guns of far superior forces.

The Indonesian Regular Army in Sourabaia comprised 12,000 ex-colonial soldiers of the former Dutch forces; they had been fully armed and trained by the Japanese. The well-organised armed mobs in the city and in the surrounding villages, controlled by Indonesian extremists, were estimated to number a further 75,000.

The following day a serious clash occurred. The mob, incited by Radio Sourabaia to violence, and also by the 'Black Buffalo' secret society (an extremist organisation), poured out of the villages. British lorries which were going about their work in the city were trapped without warning. Eleven officers and fifty other ranks were captured and shot out of hand. A convoy of Dutch women and children being driven into the Dharmo internment camp was attacked. Nearly all the lorries were set on fire. Despite a prolonged and gallant defence by the small escort of Mahratta Regiment (Indian Army) soldiers and by the drivers, only three out of the twenty lorries escaped. Many of the European and Eurasian women and children together with their military escorts were massacred with the utmost brutality. Very few escaped with their lives.

After desperate efforts, Brigadier Mallaby arranged a truce until the arrival of the divisional commander, Major General Hawthorne, next day. However, the Indonesians ignored the truce and continued to attack. The situation was now extremely grave. The Allies' troops, dispersed around the city in penny packets, had no ammunition except that actually carried on the men, and all reserves were still some distance away in the docks.

The Allies' radio station was set on fire, ammunition ran out and as the surviving (Indian Army) Mahratta defenders fought their way out of the flames, they were killed by overwhelming numbers of Indonesian swordsmen. One company of the Rajputana Rifles (also Indian Army) was overpowered, and the survivors butchered in the jail they were guarding. The Brigade Headquarters officers' mess was overrun and the mess servants and orderlies all killed. During this time Radio Sourabaia continued to broadcast appeals for a national rising. Threats were issued to poison water, burn down the city and torture prisoners and internees.

The situation in the city was now very serious. It was clear that the moderate leaders of the Republic had lost control. The extremists had the bit between their teeth and nothing but force would stop them. Another truce was demanded, but the Indonesians paid no attention. Brigadier Mallaby, seeking a new approach in a desperate situation, proposed sending out British officers, together with Indonesian Regular Army officers, to tour the city and attempt by personal efforts to contact local Indonesian leaders in the streets and to bring about a ceasefire. He himself was untiring in this cause, exposing himself to the mob by whom he was murdered on 30th October. At about the same time two platoons of the Rajputana Rifles, stationed south of the Dharmo internment camp, were overwhelmed and killed to a man. Many units of the brigade were cut off in the city and reduced to less than ten rounds of ammunition per man. Brigade Headquarters had sustained twenty-five per cent casualties. The Indonesians themselves announced later that they had suffered six thousand casualties.

The new commander of 49 Brigade issued immediate instructions that no withdrawal should take place without his orders. Troops by the harbour were ordered to hold the airfield and docks. Administrative units such as the Dock Operating Company of Hull stevedores, the Indian Pioneer Corps, Field Bakery, Supply and Issue Sections, Workshop Units etc. were to contact the Royal Navy and obtain arms; so that they too could defend the port. Indonesian demands for surrender were rejected out of hand. Plans were set afoot to regroup the brigade into two main areas – Dharmo and the internment camp: and Tanjoengperak and the docks. Negotiations were then reopened with the former city authorities to abate the fighting and enable the main forces to withdraw from the centre of the city.

The brigade regrouped successfully after protracted local negotiations, ammunition supplies were reassured and the immediate danger passed. During this period of fighting 18 officers and 374 men had been killed, wounded or were missing. Much equipment had been lost and the brigade had little more than it stood up in. Arrangements were now made to supply the isolated garrison in Dharmo by air and to bring out the internees.

On 2nd November Major General E.C. Mansergh, CBE, MC, commanding 5 Indian Division, arrived in Sourabaia by air. Although 49 Brigade was somewhat depleted in strength, they were firmly established on the ground and were still in contact with the Indonesian politicians. The dock area was safe, which enabled 9 Indian Infantry Brigade (about 2,500 men) to land safely. They were soon followed by 123 Indian Infantry Brigade (also about 2,500 men). With the co-operation of regular Indonesian troops, some 6,100 women and children internees were safely extricated from the internment camp at Dharmo. Meanwhile the mobs were still armed in strength and based on the surrounding villages.

A moving incident occurred as two landing craft came from Sourabaia out of the sunny haze, passing close by the convoy of reinforcing troops on its way into the docks. These two craft were seen to be carrying the Dutch women and children rescued from Dharmo, and were so packed with people that their superstructures were hardly visible for people. The women and children. many in rags, waved and cheered. Thus the Indian Army soldiers could see at first-hand the main reason why they were coming to Java.

Thousands of Indonesians were still massed outside 49 Brigade's perimeter, and an uneasy peace reigned while the two new brigades landed. General Mansergh attended a meeting with the Indonesian leaders on 7th November; the Indonesians were led by the erstwhile Governor of East Java. It became clear that the Indonesian Army was now doing its best to take control from the mobs. However they would not agree to release any more internees or prevent extremist activities. The general told them once again that it was his intention to free all those held in captivity and to disarm the Japanese prior to their repatriation. He gave the Indonesians two days to reconsider their position after which he would then enter the city, by force if necessary. No reply came from the Indonesians.

A start was made at 6.00 a.m. on 10th November; 123 Indian Infantry Brigade, including the 3/9th Gurkha Rifles, moved forward and found the Indonesians in strength and armed with tanks, guns and mortars. The brigade suffered a number of casualties from these heavy weapons and also from small arms. One of the first casualties suffered by 5 Indian Division was the brigadier of the Royal Artillery, who had accepted an offer from the RAF to make an aerial recce in a Mosquito aeroplane. Unfortunately the plane disintegrated in the air soon after take-off and crashed, killing its occupants. There were suggestions, afterwards, that the glue sticking the wooden plane together may have softened in the tropical heat. General Mansergh decided that no progress could be made without heavy loss and ordered pre-arranged targets to be engaged for five minutes by the RAF, artillery and naval ships. After a short pause the troops continued their advance. By evening, the Kali Sosok jail had been reached by the 3/9th Gurkhas. Inside were 3,000 Dutch and Allied internees crammed into a space normally occupied by 1,200 prisoners. Unfortunately, entry into the jail was blocked by a huge, locked, iron gate covered by Indonesian snipers. An armoured car was driven at the gate but it only dented it and it jammed. The Gurkha company commander decided to blow a hole in a nearby wall with a 'Bangalore torpedo' (explosives at the end of a long pole). This produced an entry and the Gurkhas dashed through. As the men, women and children escaped there were extraordinary scenes. The sexes had been segregated throughout the war; no one knew if his or her spouse or family were still alive. The sight of their reunions made the Gurkha soldiers weep with joy. In fact, their freedom came in the nick of time. The Gurkhas were able to prevent the Indonesians from setting the place alight and burning alive the prisoners inside. Petrol had already been poured over the roofs.

During succeeding days there was close-quarter fighting. The division was forbidden to use aircraft and no aerial bombs could be dropped. Dutch camp areas and certain specified buildings had to be preserved for peacetime occupation. The supporting squadron of Sherman tanks was only allowed to fire its 75mm guns on direct orders from a brigadier. The Indonesians counter-attacked again and again regardless of life, suffering proportionate losses from machine-gun fire. The Chinese and other small communities refused to evacuate their corners of the city centre, fearing that their houses would be looted. House-to-house battles took place in this region for thirty-six hours. Indonesian resistance began to stiffen as they brought up more guns and tanks. Like the Japanese who had trained them, they would often fight to the last man in their strong points. By the time the residential areas of Dharmo and Goebeng were reached, the Indonesian military began to withdraw from the centre of the city. Companies of the 32nd Punjab Regiment were greeted with kisses and flowers by the blockaded Armenian, Arab and Chinese womenfolk.

The military occupation of Sourabaia was completed on 28th November 1945 after nineteen days of heavy fighting. The determination of the Indonesians to continue the struggle was unimpaired and much time was spent in searching for armed men in the city, now in mufti, and for caches of arms. The Indonesians reacted by organising a number of fighting patrols from bases outside the perimeter. These were usually twenty to thirty strong, armed with light machine-guns, grenade dischargers and rifles. They ambushed our patrols and attempted to attack our perimeter bases. Their own bases were protected by armoured cars (some of them were originally British, captured in 1941 by the Japanese in Malaya), 75mm guns and anti-aircraft guns. Patrols from both sides clashed frequently. Each of 123 Brigade's patrol bases on the perimeter was supported by a troop of the Berkshire Yeomanry's 25-pounder guns. A gunner officer was posted to each infantry company making it possible to bring down artillery fire accurately on a specific target at very short notice. However, there were never enough troops to man the perimeter effectively since the third brigade of 5 Indian Division had been diverted to West and Central Java where serious battles were also in progress.

On 11th January 1946, Lieutenant Colonel Saljit Singh Kalha, DSO and bar, the commanding officer of the 2/1 Punjab Regiment; Major Hugh Whitcombe, the commander of 396 Battery of the Berkshire Yeomanry, and an infantry platoon from the Punjabis were ambushed near one of the perimeter bases. Saljit Singh, Whitcombe and eight Punjabis were killed and two Punjabis wounded. The remaining soldiers under a Punjabi *subedar* (warrant officer) beat back four sustained attacks by the Indonesians. The subedar was awarded a Military Cross and a gunner signaller, who had been wounded, was awarded a Military Medal.

It is strange that this campaign in Indonesia, especially in Java, should have been played down in the British press. Nothing much appeared in the papers or on the radio of what was really going on. The impression given by occasional 'communiques' in *The Times* was that our troops were merely involved in a series of isolated terrorist incidents.

The 3/9th Gurkha Rifles had been sent to the Netherlands East Indies, as part of 123 Brigade of 5 Indian Division, to help the Allied forces disarm the Japanese and arrange for their repatriation; and, more importantly, to recover and evacuate Allied prisoners of war and some 1,200 civilian internees. Earlier Allied action had been prevented by the Indonesian nationalists who had decided on a coup d'état aimed at freeing their country once and for all from colonial Dutch rule. Our troops thus became involved in a bitter war not of their making and against people with whom they had no quarrel. The legal government was still in the hands of the Dutch, but they had utterly lost the confidence and friendship of their colonial people and, moreover, had insufficient administrators and too few troops to re-establish their authority. Thus the 3/9th Gurkhas, together with their British and Indian comrades, found themselves in a serious war situation, at a time when ordinary soldiers of the British and Indian Armies were expecting to go home on long-delayed leave or to be demobilised.

I already knew that Sourabaia, at the east end of Java, had been an important Dutch naval base before the war and about half a million Indonesians were living in or around the city. The Dutch had encouraged and recognised inter-racial marriages and the result was a flourishing middle class who were accustomed to living very comfortably in modern Dutch-built suburbs. The city appeared largely undamaged after the war, and the destruction I saw when I landed had taken place over the previous few weeks. Slogans were everywhere especially on the sides of the huge warehouses along the docks. Some were freezingly polite, such as, 'Gentlemen, what is the meaning of the Atlantic Charter?' and, a little more explicitly, 'We're Fighting for Freedom'. Some urged us 'Don't believe the Dutch', or asked 'Mook, or what are you doing here?' (Van Mook was the Dutch Foreign Minister), or demanded with an air of finality, 'Van Mook, Get Out', and *'Merdeka!'* (freedom). Another common slogan was 'Respect our Constitution'. Perhaps, some of us thought, the sloganeers had been given something nasty to eat.

I reported to Lieutenant Colonel Alec Harper DSO, the commanding officer of the 3/9th Gurkha Rifles, and handed over the Gurkhas I had collected from the transit camps. I reflected on the history of this extremely experienced battalion. It had been raised on 1st October 1940 and fought in the Arakan. It was then selected for service in Special Force, created for long-range penetration behind the Japanese lines in Burma, under General Orde Wingate. The general was not a typical staff-trained soldier; but an independent spirit who had his own ideas about fighting the Japanese. 'There are no lines of communication on the jungle floor,' he said. 'Bring in the goods, like Father Christmas, down the chimney.' And so the idea of air transport to ferry troops and supplies into the deep jungle was born. The 3/9th and the 4/9th Gurkha Rifles glided into Burma as part of the Chindits. The regimental history has this to say of the Chindit campaign in 1944. 'The regiment has every reason to take pride in its role in Special Force, to which it had contributed two battalions – more than any other regiment in the Gurkha Brigade. The Chindits were a *corps d'élite* ... their mission demanded the utmost in endurance and in courage. On no battlefield did fighting men face greater hardship ...' One posthumous VC, several MCs and many high Indian Army decorations for bravery were awarded to the 3/9th Gurkha Rifles.

This, then, was the battalion I had joined. The British officers and the Gurkha officers were all very experienced soldiers and, together with the Gurkha other ranks had won a hard and difficult war suffering enormous privations. I was barely twenty years old and, of course, my colonel became my ideal and I hero-worshiped the company commanders with whom I was to serve and learn to soldier. Mike Drinkall DSO, Scott Leathart, Bill Towill, Geoffrey Jackson, Reggie Twelvetrees MC, 'Butch' Passmore MC and Mike Bates (later to act on television in *Last of the Summer Wine*, *It Ain't 'Arf 'Ot Mum* and in several shows in the West End), were for me names to conjure with and they were all very good company. I consider myself fortunate indeed to have had the privilege of knowing all these lively, brave and friendly men.

On arrival at our mess in Sourabaia I discovered that my friend R.C. Edgar, who had been transferred to the 3/9th Jats (Indian Army), had just been killed and Vicary, who had come out from England with me, had been severely wounded outside the Kali Sosok jail, while engaged in freeing the civilian internees. The battalion had suffered many casualties in the short time it had been in Java. I was posted as a company officer to Geoffrey Jackson's company on the city perimeter in a village called Warogoenong, on the main road to Driaredga by the west bank of the Kali Mas river. Alec Harper gave us strict instructions to defend our perimeter; but not to start a war. However, he allowed us to patrol outside the perimeter to ensure our safety.

Two days later the neighbouring company reported that they were expecting an imminent attack from the Indonesians opposite them, and they requested urgent reinforcements. Jacko did not think there was any likelihood of a major attack; but, as he had been asked for help, he took a platoon and off he went. Soon after he left, we heard several plops ahead of our positions and mortar shells exploded harmlessly close in front of us. We stood to and took cover in our slit trenches. There were more plops, but this time the bombs exploded on the bank of the river opposite which was held by 9 Brigade troops. A cross and tired Jacko returned the next day; he had been called out on a wild-goose chase. The following night more mortar bombs were fired and exploded opposite us across the river. We had expected this would happen, and, at the time, I was on patrol a mile or so up the road sheltering among a group of abandoned bullock carts. I remembered Major Willis's instructions on how to use a compass, and took a couple of bearings on the area from where the mortars were firing. Jacko contacted our 3-inch mortar officer and, with the agreement of 9 Brigade, we lobbed twelve mortar bombs on the Indonesians. Troops from 9 Brigade followed up and recovered four Japanese mortars, a great deal of ammunition and a Japanese anti-aircraft gun, which had just been prepared in a horizontal firing position. They also found the bodies of two uniformed Indonesians. Our sleep was not disturbed by mortar fire for the next two weeks.

Other troops in our area were 145 Field Regiment (Berkshire Yeomanry) with their 25-pounder field guns, a troop of Stuart tanks and 1/17th Dogras armed with medium machine-guns (Vickers MMGs). The guns were used to break up Indonesian concentrations and to provide defensive fire, the tanks escorted us up and down the exposed road alongside the Kali Mas river; and the machine-gunners covered small combined operations with 9 Brigade on the opposite bank, as well as being able to provide defensive covering fire on selected target areas. I was engaged in various patrols over the next ten days during which we clashed with armed Indonesians on most occasions, our combined firepower was used to great effect and we broke up what we thought could possibly develop into raids on our positions. I do not recall anyone wearing tin hats but I do remember Subedar Kehar Singh's Gurkha hat was singed by a bullet and he always wore it nonchalantly thereafter. Following a small night raid on our position we found a dead Japanese non-commissioned officer, caught on the barbed wire (he was probably leading an Indonesian patrol) – he had his sword strapped around his waist and my application to keep it for myself was approved by Alec Harper.

We were relieved eventually and went back to quarters in the city. Here Alec Harper told me that as I was the last officer to arrive I would have to be the first to go to Brigade and relieve Bertie Lane as brigade orderly officer. Brigadier E.J. Denholm Young, DSO, became my commanding officer, the brigade major was Major Weston GM; but I was under someone else called a DQ, who seemed to spend his time either concocting weird schemes to prevent our soldiers from catching VD (which was rife and seriously reduced the efficiency of all our troops), or trying desperately to recover army issue watches from people going on leave. I stayed in Brigade for about a fortnight. My spare time was spent learning to ride a motorbike and being taught to speak a little Dutch. Then I talked Alec Harper into allowing me to return to the battalion.

General Sir Miles Dempsey visited us and said that we would all be out of the Netherlands East Indies by the end of February 1946 and home by September. General Stopford was taken by our colonel to the top of a water tower on the perimeter used by us for observing the enemy, and shown the area which we patrolled. 'How many enemy are there?' the general asked. 'Armed groups of between twenty and a hundred and fifty,' was the reply from our colonel. 'Armed with shotguns and spears?' he supposed. 'No, rifles, machine guns, tanks and 75mm guns', came the reply. 'I had 'no idea,' the general said. climbing down hastily as a sniper's bullet whistled overhead. Another visitor was the elderly diplomat Sir Archibald Clarke Kerr, who was acting as mediator between the Indonesian Nationalists and the Dutch. Of his address to a large crowd of British troops, I wrote home. 'He started by talking about his time in Russia and his personal experiences of Stalin and Molotov. The British other ranks thought this outrageously irrelevant and interrupted him again and again demanding to know when they were going home. When he did not answer them, they barracked him so much that he had to stop.'

We left Sourabaia on 14 March 1946 having handed over to a Dutch Marine outfit which had been armed and trained in the USA. We had suffered 18 killed and 62 wounded in 131 days of active service there in Java. We embarked on HM Tank Landing Ship *Sansovino* for Singapore and entrained for Kota Bahru in Kelantan on the north-east coast of Malaya. On arrival five days later I was promoted, though still a lieutenant, to acting company commander and posted to South Thailand with platoons in Songkhla (Singgora), Yala and Haadyai. The name Siam had recently been replaced by Thailand, or Land of the Free.

When I arrived in Yala to establish my company headquarters, I found a large abandoned school, the best building in the place, occupied by a company of unarmed and unemployed Japanese Army engineers awaiting repatriation. As we had won the war against Japan, I turfed them out and loaned the Japanese the ancient pre-war tentage we were supposed to inhabit. I also talked the Japanese company commander into making the entire school waterproof, and then building garages with a driveway from the school to the main road. In return he taught me Japanese chequers. I also went on long visits to my platoons in Haadyai, the local district capital with a thriving shopping area, and to Singgora which had a beautiful clean beach and boats with which to play around. The Gurkhas thought this was great and I switched the platoons around weekly so that everyone had a fair share.

It has been my experience in the Far East that railwaymen have a special empathy for the British and almost every stationmaster I met in Thailand, and later in Japan, seemed to have been trained in England. Invariably they gave me special favours which, in Thailand in 1946, produced for me two jeeps fitted with special wheels to travel on the railway lines; and a small carriage, formally used by the Japanese Inspector of Railways, as my personal transport in South Thailand.

Our military task was to identify war criminals, round up armed terrorists, arrest looters and not to annoy the Thai civil authority. Part of the region was dominated by the Communist Party of Malaya (CPM), which had retained most of its weapons and organisation intact after the end of the war. They had embarked on a thorough overhaul in preparation for civil war later. I came into contact with them frequently as they were supposed to be friendly and on our side. The Thai authorities at that time were scared stiff that the British would take over South Thailand as part of a peace treaty with Britain (they had sided with the Japanese during the war) and subsequent war reparations. This part of Thailand had an irredentist population of Malays clamouring to join the Federated Malay States as an independent state within the Malay Federation, and the Thais dearly wished to keep their frontiers unchanged. Therefore, the Thai population was officially anti-British and no public signs, advertisements, or notices could be in English. Similarly, no one was supposed to speak English. But this was really a façade and I made many Thai friends behind closed doors.

At about that time, I acquired a Siamese cat – or rather a ginger and white cat born in Siam – which I named 'Billy' after the Gurkhali word *bilalo*, meaning cat. It was a beautiful moggy and became the company mascot throughout our peregrinations over the next eighteen months.

Not long afterwards, military decisions were taken elsewhere and we had to return to Kota Bahru, Kelantan, in North-East Malaya, without replacement. Before we left, the three local Thai district officials. who were very pleased with the reconstruction work at their school, gave my company of Gurkhas a series of parties accompanied by Ramwong dancing, Thai kick-boxing and some quite innocuous bullfights. In return we entertained them to a farewell *nautch* (Gurkha celebrations including dancing, singing, eating and drinking).

Having had what I considered to be the best possible company posting, we were immediately given what became for us the worst possible posting. We returned to the frontier between Malaya and Thailand, but this time it was on the unmapped, sparsely-populated

56

Malayan side. We went by three-ton lorries to Tanah Merah, on by jeep to Nibong, then twenty-five miles on foot through the jungle, accompanied by a series of very heavy thunderstorms, to Jeli, on the upper reaches of the Pergau river. (Some decades later the Pergau River area became the site of an enormous, controversial and very expensive reservoir.) Here I relieved Dave Sheaves and his company; they had nothing favourable to say about the place and were delighted to leave. The next day I established one of my platoons several miles up river to the north-west at Batu Melintang.

My only contact with the outside world was through a temperamental 22 wireless set, driven by a chugging engine which broke down frequently. I considered it important to secure our extended line of communication with Kota Bahru so I took out a lease on two elephant and the service of their two *mahouts* (minders) with my own money. They did the two-day trip from Jeli to Nibong and brought back our food (the boring Pacific and K rations), and our mail which included my *Punch* magazines and the overseas *Daily Mail*. Elephant in this part of the world worked in pairs, male and female; no other combination would work; they lived off the land becoming very attached to each other and quite inseparable. I named the male elephant *Gurung da Guroong* (onomatopoeic Gurkhali word for thunder) and the female *Pirudli-Pirudli* (Gurkhali word for lightning). After a month, I promoted both elephant to the rank of lance *naik* (lance corporal). Our adjutant in Kota Bahru was somewhat puzzled when I put both elephant on the company's nominal role, and claimed payment for little treats to be included in their rations. To supplement our meagre food, we caught fish (the Kelantan Malays showed us how to organise 'fish drives' using a jungle poison which knocked out the fish, but was harmless to eat), shot wild pig and captured mouse deer and jungle fowl, at all of which the Gurkhas became supremely adept, much to the surprise of the Malays.

My headquarters was on a bluff overlooking the Pergau river next door to the Kelantan Malay *pengawa* (headman). He had a substantial wooden house and a large family. I was the subject of great curiosity and my every move was closely watched. Soon we began to talk, and I was given lessons on the ways in which the Kelantan Malays' way of life differed from the customs and language of west coast Malaya. In return, I gained an unwarranted

57

reputation as a witch-doctor. I wrote home 'The locals come from afar, usually with splinters in their septic feet, which I pull out with my tweezers and they get better. Dave Sheaves had already introduced sick children to the curative aspects of Smarties (each colour being prescribed for a different medical condition) and I continued the good work with miraculous success. One old fellow produced a magazine about King George VI's 1937 coronation; and another asked me to sign a book with signatures from passing travellers and messages dating back half a century, including two from Force 136 officers in 1944 who had been parachuted behind the Japanese lines. I am fascinated by the houses here and I am sketching all the different ones.' In my spare time at Jeli I made a butterfly net out of a piece of old mosquito netting and started a collection of butterflies and moths.

The greatest drawback of this remote place was the leeches. I described them to my mother thus 'Leeches here are prolific. If you look carefully on the ground, you can see them inching their way along, stopping every so often to lift one end and sniff around for blood. They are about one inch long; when they climb on to you they dig in and hold on. You don't notice anything at first, it is only when you feel warm blood running down your leg or arm that you discover, to your horror, a bloated ugly slimy slug with one end deeply embedded in you. The only way to dislodge them is to burn them out with a lighted cigarette. When you take off your clothes, you find at least ten of them sticking all over your body – it really is most repulsive. Wherever we go, I make the Gurkhas operate in pairs and flick them off each other's uniform. Thank goodness we are not fighting a jungle war in this part of Malaya.'

In addition to the leeches, there was an infection in the river which resulted in the men coming out in dreadful skin rashes; all cuts became septic and almost everyone nursed some sort of annoying skin condition. To counter this we dammed a small stream coming down the hill behind us, channelled the water along split bamboo pipes and created a jungle bathroom, complete with four efficient showers. These proved very popular so I banned washing in the river and our health improved a little.

Our task was supposed to be the rounding up of local bandits and keeping an eye on the Communist Party units in the jungle. Our only success was to capture, by chance, three of the former bathing under a waterfall, with their arms and equipment piled up on the bank. We sent them under guard to the police station two days down river at Kuala Krai, but they escaped from the civil jail a week later. We discovered two Communist training camps in the jungle well inside Thailand. Not knowing what to do with them, and also not wishing to cause an international incident, we accepted cups of tea in male bamboo mugs, and passed on our way, noting everything we could and envying their modern carbines.

Batu Melintang, a small Malay village along the upper reaches of the Pergau river, was dominated by an ancient, tall Punjabi Muslim, who told me that he had fled there in the late 1920s, having discovered another man *in flagrante delicto* with his wife. He killed them both and ran away. He eventually set up home in Batu Melintang, adopted another name and, as a devout Muslim, he was accepted into the community. Accepted was clearly the correct descriptive word. Not only was he much taller than any of the villagers – even in his old age – but he had a very large, long nose. I couldn't help observing that the physiognomies of many young men and women round about, including some in Jeli, were distinguished by a similar large proboscis; clearly a sign of the attraction and, indeed, affection with which their father had been held by his many wives. When I met him he claimed to be one hundred and twenty years old, but looked about seventy. He was regarded by the villagers as their influential leader and his word was law.

We kept ourselves busy by living off the jungle. A visit from Anker Rentse, a local Danish character from Kota Bahru, inspired me again to use my compass, as taught by Major Willis VC at Pangbourne, and draw a map of the area. As I had found the official map lacking in detail and not at all helpful, I was really quite pleased with my efforts! My journeys took me upriver west of Batu Melintang to Belum, over the State border into Perak State and on to the outskirts of Grik where I liaised with the outposts of another Gurkha battalion. We decided to travel the last leg of our return journey by river; so I paid the Malay *kampong* people to build us three rafts. This they did in no time, using bamboos tied together by jungle creeper with a little shelter in the middle for our packs. When we got on board, the Malays nearly split their sides laughing at us and said we would drown in the rapids. Swallowing our pride, we took a pilot on board each raft. It was lucky that we did, because we had no idea how fast the river flowed through the narrow parts into quite scary white-water rapids. We proceeded very fast and by evening we were floating serenely down towards our base in Jeli. As the skies darkened we noticed the animals on the mudflats, where the tributaries joined the river, especially wild elephant which we took by surprise as we floated quietly by into the sunset. Another splendid treat was the sight of two well-marked healthy young tigers rolling in the shadows showing off their soft white tummies. On our return we were greeted by my subedar who had just returned from *shikari* (hunting) with four wild pig, three jungle fowl and two small deer.

The next day, a senior officer of the British Military Administration came up unannounced by outboard motorboat from Kuala Krai for what I can only describe as 'a swan'. He and his bodyguard consumed all my gin, all my tinned fruit and they pinched my cutlery, my orderly's knife, my spare belt and 350 cigarettes from the men's tobacco ration. As I said in my letter home, 'Not a bad haul!' Manbahadur, my orderly and the oldest rifleman in the company, said with a hesitant look on his face, 'I think they will drown because I replaced the cork in the bottom of their boat with leaves.' I heard later that the boat duly sank and the personage and companion had to walk the last twenty miles along the bank of the river back to Kuala Krai.

Eventually we returned to Kota Bahru for a much-needed rest. Virtually all of us were suffering physically and my leech sores began to play up. I thought people might accuse me of 'self-inflicted wounds' so I tried to carry on; but our Indian doctor intervened. He gave some of us a week's light duties and masses of penicillin which worked wonders. I brought back with me from Jeli two mouse deer – a boy and a girl – which we hoped might breed. Unfortunately the male died six weeks later, but my Siamese cat took on the female mouse deer and they remained inseparable companions for the next eighteen months.

Kota Bahru, the capital of Kelantan State, was a pretty little town near the coast with large cast-iron cannons dug into the riverbank as mooring posts for fishing boats. Our quarters were in unoccupied government officers' houses and our mess was delightful and civilised. HH the Sultan of Kelantan proved a kind and generous host and entertained us at all sorts of parties, making us feel wanted and at home. A relative of his, Prince Mahiyuddin, had invested in a modest tourist development on the east coast facing the China Sea. Here the beach was clean and sandy and the sea was warm and clear. Little *pondoks* (shelters) among the casuarina trees could be hired for one day, or weekends, and the whole place was called *Pantai Chinta Berahi* which, translated, meant 'Beach of Passionate Love'.

The prince was a large jovial man, who spoke English, and was usually dressed in a faded grey tee shirt and a green Kelantan Malay sarong; he always had a number of smiling ladies in his entourage. With one exception, I never discovered who were wives and who were girlfriends; they were all very attractive and I understood some were Thais. The exception was a White Russian lady whom I called Mummy; she was a little older than the others and ran the place efficiently. She always gave us preference for booking, and insisted on providing us with ice-cold gin and tonics and the best of Kelantan Malay cooking, occasionally spiced with herbs from Thailand. Mummy told me that her family originally came from Moscow where her father was a civil servant working in the household of the Tsar. The family survived the Revolution of 1917; but life under the Bolsheviks became impossible and they were forced to flee across Russia to China and settle in Shanghai, where she was born and educated. As soon as she reached her eighteenth birthday, she ran away to French Indo-China with a young White Russian student, and they lived together in Hanoi. When the Japanese invaded that country in 1942 the student was arrested and was never seen again. In order to survive, she pretended to be a Vietnamese, dressed accordingly, worked in a coffee-shop and lived in a small room above. When the war came to an end she met a French officer who took her to Singapore. Apparently they did not get on, and she was extremely unhappy until she met her handsome prince by chance when he was sheltering in the rain just off Orchard Road. He took her out to supper. She stayed the night with him in his hotel, he proposed to her next morning and she returned with him to Kota Bahru three days later. She said they had fallen in love with each other at first sight and had no trouble at all in fitting in to his Islamic *ménage à cinq*.

Several years later, I was taken by the Director of Singapore Special Branch to a restaurant called 'Old Russia', in the Tanglin area of Singapore, and who should I see welcoming her guests and wearing a beautiful Russian dress but Mummy – I stared hard, not believing my eyes. She recognised me at once. 'Teem,' she said, 'lovely to see you,' and drew me to her substantial bosom where I was overcome by what I recognised to be Himalayan Bouquet scent. We talked and talked in her boudoir, behind a life-sized recumbent image of a babouska. high up in an alcove above a most realistic imitation fireplace. She had not changed a bit; though I had not known her that well, despite her presence on the 'Beach of Passionate Love'. I discovered that her prince had died, and she had become of little importance in the family as a junior wife in a Muslim household. So she packed up, obtained a 'quickie' divorce and travelled down to Singapore. Here she met a mysterious, sunburned, saturnine Frenchman who had spent much of the last few years going to and fro between Singapore and North Vietnam, doing unexplained business involving what he called 'import and export', stating this with an enigmatical smile at me. They had invested her savings in 'Old Russia'. It had taken off dramatically and was patronised by all the great and good in Singapore society.

I tried to arrange a visit to 'Old Russia' whenever I visited Singapore until one day I found it had closed. Mummy, her mysterious Frenchman and the lofty babouska were no longer there; no one could tell me where they had gone. It was not until the mid-seventies, when I was walking down Horseferry Road behind Westminster Abbey in London that I saw the familiar sign 'Old Russia' outside a small roadside boite. I went inside and there was the Frenchman cleaning glasses behind the bar. There was no sign of Mummy. 'I'll call her', he said, in answer to my unspoken question. A bell rang in the depths of beyond; but nothing happened. We conversed and it appeared they had grown tired of Singapore and left to start a new life in Australia and then again in New Zealand. I supposed he had no one and nothing to spy upon or be mysterious about ... then in swept Mummy in a large diaphanous flowery dress. 'Oh, Teem,' she said, and, once again, I found myself engulfed and struggling for light and air in her even more voluminous bosom. I was disconcerted again by clouds of newly-donned scent which, this time, I identified as Chanel No 5. 'Where is the babouska?' I asked, as soon as I was free. 'I am the babouska,' she said, and I changed the subject. She looked a little larger, a little older and seemed a little slower; but her manner was the same and her eyes were bright and never still. I called in several times during the next two years then, as I knew it would be, I found the place deserted. No one knew their whereabouts. I have not seen them again and I miss them – just a little.

I borrowed boxes, setting boards, relaxing fluid and pins from the Sultan of Kelantan and arranged my lepidoptera in as professional a way as possible according to a book my mother sent out via Foyles in London. On leaving Kota Bahru, I gave the Sultan my collection which complemented his own and, indeed, which added quite a number of new specimens to his cabinets and replaced some badly set ones of his.

We departed from Kota Bahru on 8th July 1946 by train and after a thirty-six hour journey through South Thailand and North Malaya we arrived at Sungei Pattani in Central Kedah. As we had no idea when or where we were going, I spent the next ten days in the surrounding countryside practising with our newly-arrived wireless sets. They were better than our old 48s – less noisy and sent out a stronger signal. We left Sungei Pattani on 19th July by train to Prai opposite Georgetown, Penang, whence we embarked on the troopship *Dunera*. In my letter home I said, 'This is the best ship I have ever been in. Extremely comfortable for the Gurkhas and ourselves. It took us three days to arrive off the mouth of the Palembang river in Sumatra, the large island at the north-west extremity of the Indonesian Archipelago. Here we were loaded on to naval barges, commanded by very young Royal Navy officers who had no navigational charts of the river or nearby swamps. We went aground several times and the only way of freeing ourselves was to line up on the port side of the barge and, with great difficulty, run across together to the starboard side, and back again. After one or two hilarious confusions, we improved our performance and managed to float off successfully. Eventually we completed the sixty-mile journey through the mango swamps and arrived at Palembang town itself. The sailors were in constant fear of an ambush and took cover at every bend in the river, our men had nowhere to go and were spread all over the hatches and decks.'

Palembang turned out to be an oil refinery town of 100,000 people. We were to be responsible for the defence of a section of the perimeter round the old Dutch quarter of the town including the Governor's palace, which became our mess, and a pretty lake

63

surrounded by gardens. The military situation was entirely unlike Sourabaia. Here there was an uneasy truce between the Dutch and the Indonesians; this allowed the latter, armed to the teeth, to wander at will round the city and the surrounding countryside. I wrote home, 'This is a ghastly place. Our perimeter is undermanned and we have no mobile reserves. We are not allowed outside to patrol our fronts therefore the enemy can do exactly what he pleases – bring up artillery, tanks, men. We have no artillery, no planes and no tanks. Our supplies come up sixty miles of vulnerable river and the airfield is seven miles away through enemy territory. It is military planning gone wild and a frightful gamble. The colonial Dutch army, who share the defence with us, are entirely unreliable and their section of the perimeter is easily distinguishable by the sounds of gunfire as their patrols shoot at one another.'

My company took over from the 1st Burma Rifles which, somewhat to my surprise, was made up half by Sikhs and half by Punjabi Muslims. They left the place in a frightful state which annoyed my men and made me realise how lucky I was to be serving with Gurkhas. I found the Sumatrans more like the Malays than the Javanese – less fiery than the latter and of a more genial disposition. My bungalow was next door to the unmanned city perimeter and close to an amusement park; the harmonious bells of an Indonesian gamelan orchestra kept me awake every evening till the early hours. It was rather like the music of the Thai Ramvong which also went on into the small hours when I was stationed in Thailand. Highlights of my stay in Palembang were visits to the Indonesian Cultural Association and the wonderful *wayang kulit* (leather puppet) shadow plays which depicted various colourful Hindu myths. The Gurkhas, as Hindus, were fascinated by these performances, not having realised that there had been a Hindu empire in this area several hundred years ago, before the locals were converted to Islam.

Militarily, there was a company of 3/4th Gurkhas on our left flank and a company of Japanese soldiers under my direct command to the right. Immediately after the surrender in August 1945, the Japanese commander in Palembang decided, off his own bat, to prevent the Indonesians destroying their valuable industrial sites. Our arrival late on the scene was to enable the Japanese to go home having handed over their responsibilities safely to us. The 1st Battalion the Lincolnshire Regiment, the 1st Burma Rifles and the 3/4th Gurkha Rifles were already there. The Japanese had been allowed to keep their infantry side arms and, indeed, they were given special permission by the Allied Command to take these weapons with them when eventually they were repatriated to Japan. Once again, I found my Japanese opposite number to be an educated man who kept his men under very strict control. They never caused us the slightest worry and they always honoured their undertakings. Nevertheless my company subedar, Yembahadur Khattri MC, never trusted the Japanese and thought me mad when I went to talk to them.

Poor Yembahadur, who had fought gallantly in the 3/9th Gurkhas' Chindit campaign, was to suffer grievously in Palembang. One night a runner hammered on my door shouting that Yembahadur had been killed and was calling for me. Ignoring the lack of logic, I dressed quickly and ran round the lake to our perimeter base. There was Yembahadur, with blood streaming out of a hole in his head, blind drunk and in a fearful temper. Apparently he had been struck with a bottle by a *naik* (corporal) who was equally drunk; and all hell had been let loose. On seeing me he collapsed and passed out. My orderly found a jeep and a driver; but I could not find our doctor so I decided that, to save his life, I would have to take him to the Charitas Hospital, run by a nursing order of nuns, in a supposedly enemy area some miles outside the city perimeter. We drove through at speed, taking various Indonesian sentries by surprise, and up to the Mother Superior's door. She turned out to be a practical Irish lady and took control of the situation. A surgeon was found and I watched him gently remove several large pieces of broken glass from Yemmie's brain. I stayed with him until his operation had been completed. On returning the next day – after bribing the Indonesian roadblocks with gifts of cigarettes – I found him sitting up in bed, complaining of having nothing to do and squashing a pat of butter in a vain attempt to rewax his little moustachios. He appeared none the worse and claimed he had made a complete recovery.

After discussions with my Gurkha officers, I decided that we should bend the rules and carefully recce the area in front of our positions, so that we would be better prepared if a surprise attack was launched on us from outside. After a good look round, I decided to light a small fire to burn down the scrub which blocked the view directly in front of our positions; this nearly got out of hand and, in the subsequent stand-to necessary to put out the fire, I made sure as many people as possible got an idea of the lie of the land. The perimeter itself meandered across a large hill used by the Chinese as a burial ground. Their families used to come to the graves with lighted candles and food for the gods which, as I had to explain later to Terence Philips our over-anxious acting colonel, obviously caused the fire. The Chinese cemetery became the cause of considerable concern for me. Several of the men would wake up at night shouting their heads off in a wild dream; it was only after dire threats of disciplinary action that I discovered the cause – each man affected admitted to peeing on graves in the cemetery while going on, or returning from, sentry duty. This had clearly offended the departed spirits who had returned to haunt the culprit in his dreams. Peeing in the cemetery was made a disciplinary offence and the shouting at night abated.

At about this time my permanent company commander returned from leave in the UK and, once again, I had some spare time. I started teaching six of our men to use the Japanese medium machine-guns stationed on our flank in case we needed them. This meant seeing quite a lot of the Japanese soldiers and we were greatly surprised to find how well equipped they were. Each man had his own mattress, all the officers and NCOs had magnificent highly polished calf-high leather boots and everyone seemed to have an endless supply of good quality uniform. This was in stark contrast to our two suits of faded jungle green, poor quality Indian-made boots and ancient blankets.

We left Palembang on 20th October 1946. The Royal Navy landing craft took us downstream to the mouth of the river where my boat, which was in the vanguard, got hopelessly lost. The RN lieutenant navigator was using a pre-war Shell map and he mistakenly put us alongside the Dutch trooper *Plancius*. We were made most welcome on board and enjoyed a splendid meal and a singsong, half in Dutch and half in Gurkhali! Having consulted the Dutch navigators, our lieutenant located His Majesty's Troopship *Dunera*, our old friend, just over the horizon. The battalion was still boarding the ship. The OC Troops, who was unknown to us, was keeping a suspicious eye on our men as they climbed wearily aboard. Suddenly he espied an 'illegal animal'.

'What's that piglet doing?' he cried.

'What piglet?' enquired our acting colonel.

'I definitely saw a piglet in that man's arms,' thundered the OC Troops.

'I can't see one,' replied our acting colonel, adding hopefully, 'are you quite sure? Perhaps it was the movement of the ship?'

'It's not just a piglet,' said a friendly member of the crew *sotto voce*. 'The place is alive with animals.'

'And so it was – for a moment or two – then in a twinkling of a Gurkha eye they disappeared as if by magic into packs, kitbags and upturned saucepans. Thus escaped my Siamese cat and her pal the little female mouse deer, both tucked safely inside the pack of dear old Balbahadur, the battalion ammunition *naik* (corporal).

Boarding having been successfully completed, the OC Troops decided to hold an inspection, aimed at locating the illegal livestock. Obviously he could not do this entirely on his own; so he asked an advance guard of 1st Lincolns to search our men. As is well known, the British Army gets along well with Gurkha soldiers; not a single animal was found and honour was restored. There was soon to be a *quid pro quo* for us. Someone, I think it was the Dutch commander who took over from us in Palembang, accused 1st Lincolns of looting, and who should be detailed to search 1 Lincolns when they arrived later in Malaya, but us. Strangely enough, nothing incriminating was found, leaving the Dutch to mutter harmlessly up their wretched river.

We landed at Port Swettenham and went to Perak State in Central Malaya. The battalion headquarters was in a former convent at Lumut, a pretty little Chinese fishing village on the west coast (Lumut is now a large brash tourist resort.) I became a temporary company commander again with my headquarters in Parit Buntar, halfway between Taiping and Penang, some one hundred miles away from my battalion headquarters. Once again, we began to enjoy life to the full, supposedly in aid of the civil power. Our duties were not strenuous; though I had quite a job keeping the company reasonably intact without too many guard duties on rice mills, etc. We managed to get in some wonderfully productive wild pig shooting east of Selama. The Gurkhas excelled themselves in cooking the pork. They built a huge fire, burned off the hair, shaved the skin, roasted the carcass on a home-made spit and cut it into one inch cubes. The trick was to avoid proffered entrails, and other so-called delicacies, and to eschew the occasional square bits which, on close inspection, still had one side lined with skin and singed hair. Although I hesitate to admit it, I slipped some of the pork to a freelance Chinese cook (in a nearby coffee shop) who would prepare for me a delightful dish to the European taste but with delicious Chinese flavours.

Before leaving Sumatra, I had put in for two months' leave in the UK prior to eventual release from military service and suddenly it came through. I handed over my company and flew to Singapore and then to Heathrow. While on leave I saw as many London shows as I could fit in, taking my parents and as many girlfriends as I could manage. I stayed with my parents in Chipperfield and occasionally helped my father deal with the stateless Latvians who, at that time, were under enormous pressure from the British government to return home. The Latvians themselves had no wish to start life again under Communist rule and many, with justification, feared for their lives in that country if they were discovered by the Communist authorities. It was a question of getting official approval for them to remain in England or, if not, to help them emigrate to the USA. My father studied the Latvian language and made their welfare his postwar personal cause devoting a great deal of his time trying to help them.

As I was about to leave Malaya, my colonel asked me to buy 12-bore and 16-bore shotgun ammunition for the mess and also to collect green berets from Lock & Co. of St James in London. I bought as much of the former as I could carry away in two visits, and I collected a large box of the latter. I also visited Brigadier Ponting, who had recruited me in 1943 as a schoolboy cadet. I called upon Lieutenant Colonel Noel George in the War Office, a former gallant commander of 3/9th Gurkhas in Burma, and I was invited to Winchester for long talks with Major-General Sir William Twiss. I think I conveyed to them both the thoughts and feelings of my two recent commanding officers regarding the future of our regiment in the British Army.

I went to Southampton docks on 17th April 1947 and boarded the *Arundel Castle*, an old passenger liner converted into a very comfortable troopship, bound for Bombay via the Suez Canal. A large number of officers were on board and three of us shared a four-berth cabin. As we left Southampton the mist lifted and we passed close to the *Queen Mary* which was in dry dock. Soon we saw the *Queen Elizabeth* lying at anchor looking superb with its paint glowing in the morning sun; then along came the *America*, steaming slowly towards the dockside with hundreds of gum-chewing ladies excitedly awaiting its arrival. The fourth officer on board the *Arundel Castle* was an Old Pangbournian whom I knew and liked; we passed the time pacing the deck from eight to ten every evening.

The ship docked at Bombay and I caught a train to Madras. Here I had to wait ten days and then travelled across to Cochin to board the *Nevasa*, a troopship owned by the British India Line, bound for Singapore. I was made the ship's adjutant which gave me plenty to do. On arrival at Singapore I took the train to Kuala Lumpur where I spent a day with my parents' friend C.R. Howitt. a senior Malayan civil servant. I reported for duty in Taiping on Whit Monday and handed over the berets and the ammunition.

While in Taiping I became a temporary company commander again and I was also the mess secretary, something I really loathed, which, *inter alia*, involved finding and supplying the right sort of chocolate bar for certain greedy people and persuading the perennially broke to pay their mess bills in full and on time. A more interesting task turned up when our subedar major asked me to run the battalion's bingo evenings. The Gurkhas were all familiar with some of the numbered descriptions – legs 11, pair of ducks 22, etc. – both in English and Gurkhali; so I invented some of my own and, for all the rest, quoted the last two digits of the army numbers of popular characters. It was all good fun and helped pass the time. I also received my War Gratuity (the British Government's thank-you for my war service) amounting to the princely sum of £48.

The only active patrolling we did, as a complete company, was when we were sent down to Sitiawan in West Perak to search a jungle area in support of our company based in Lumut. Our aim was to find and arrest an armed kidnap gang from Penang but, by chance, we discovered another Malayan Communist Party training camp, this time in the middle of Malaya. It was rather more sophisticated than the camps we had come across on the Thai border. It had well-used parade grounds, weapon-training schedules, school buildings complete with desks and blackboards, two flagpoles, bathrooms and a well-stocked kitchen. It contained at least 200 men and women, some with children. It was like a small village. The Communist leaders were furious when we walked in, and went into a grand sulk. Once again I noted down all I could find or secretly take away. When no one was looking, I pocketed a long list of names and duties and passed them on to the British District Officer who could hardly believe what we had seen. A year later, the Malayan Communist Party, in conjunction with similar parties elsewhere in South-East Asia, launched its armed struggle, taking the British Colonial Office if not by surprise, certainly unprepared, ill-equipped and mentally unwilling to accept the gravity of the situation.

However, the worsening situation in Malaya was not our main concern. The Independence of India in August 1947, the rioting between Hindus and Muslims in the Punjab and Bengal, the future role of the Indian Army – especially the ten Gurkha Regiments – the location of our regimental centre, the welfare of our men and their families all were matters of increasing importance and worry as the days passed by.

Before we left Malaya for India we celebrated *Dashera* (or *Durga Puja*, the worship of Durga Devi, the goddess of victory). It is the greatest of all Hindu festivals, and takes place over ten days between the end of September and the middle of October, depending on the phases of the moon. Although Gurkha soldiers are Hindus, their celebrations are often constrained on active service by local commitments. The origin of the word Dashera and the many legends surrounding the fabulous Durga, go back to the time when, as Hindu mythology relates, quarrelsome gods ruled the world.

One of the legends concerns King Dasrath whose son Rama-chandra decided to rid the world of an evil giant called Rawan. He prayed for nine days asking the goddess Durga for strength, this was granted and he slew Rawan on the tenth day. Subsequent celebrations commemorate the killing of Rawan and were named Dashera after the king.

Another legend introduces Durga Devi, who seems to have been a most remarkable lady. It all started when King Rambha was granted a boon by the god Brahma, pledging that no female would resist him and that his son Mahisashura should rule the kingdom of Tribhuwan. One day, a beautiful milk-white cow, feeling much attracted to Rambha, left the herd with which she was grazing and

70

followed him home. Angry at this, the shepherds, and buffaloes in the herd, killed Rambha, and placed his body on a funeral pyre, then set it alight. When the flames were at their height, the milk-white cow jumped into them and from the ashes of the pyre was born a huge buffalo-headed demon, Mahisashura who, in turn, was granted by Brahma a boon pledging he would not be killed by a male. The evil Mahisashura then attacked the gods, overpowering the great Indra, god of rain. While the gods were appealing for help from the Hindu holy trinity (Brahma, Shiva and Vishnu) a beautiful maiden called Durga appeared. She set about organising the gods' resistance to Mahisashura. Durga was extremely well-endowed for the battle – she had three eyes and eighteen arms. The gods gave her their own weapons. Vishnu gave her his wheel, Shiva his trident, Indra some thunder and lightning, Agni a bow and arrows and Biswakarna gave her his sword, an axe and a *kukri* (large knife). Other gods gave her additional weapons for her remaining hands.

After saying a prayer, Durga mounted a lion and galloped towards Mahisashura and his accompanying band of demons. At the end of six days fighting one of the leading demons was killed and, on the next day, the gods made offerings of flowers. (This seventh day of Dashera is called *Phulpatti* and, nowadays, is celebrated by the picking of local flowers which are placed at the scene of an approaching sacrifice.) On the ninth day, Mahisashura climbed on to a large bull and attacked Durga furiously. She responded with her kukri and cut off Mahisashura's head. She celebrated her great victory by quaffing a small cup of his blood.

Our own celebrations of Dashera concentrated on the last most important night. Merrymaking, drinking *rukshi* (rum) and age-old tribal dancing by men dressed as *pursengis* (male dancers) and *marunis* (female dancers impersonated by men) took place, after the blessing of weapons by the battalion *bhawan* (priest). A carved and painted post decorated with flowers was placed in the middle of the parade ground and a young male buffalo was tied firmly to it. A specially selected soldier was chosen to sacrifice the buffalo, using a kukri to sever its head in the presence of the whole battalion of excited and expectant men. It is of the utmost importance that the animal's head is severed in one stroke; if the execution fails it is a sign that Durga has rejected the prayers and sacrifice. In our case, the head was not severed in one blow. Instead

71

of cheers, loud shouting and the blowing of bugles, the failure was greeted in shocked silence – except for the nightjars tock-tocking away in the distance trees. I noticed, with a feeling of awful dread, that the surrounding midnight bonfires revealed expressions of utter dismay, disbelief, fear and foreboding on the faces of six hundred men. The omens were very bad and we all knew the battalion would be in for a bad year.

3

In a turquoise twilight, crisp and chill,
A cafilla camped at the foot of a hill.
Then blue-smoke haze of the cooking rose,
And tent-peg answered to hammer nose;
And the picketed ponies, shag and wild,
Strained at their ropes as the feed was piled;
And the bubbling camels beside the load
Sprawled for a furlong down the road.

RUDYARD KIPLING

In my opinion, which was also widely held by those who served with him, Field Marshal Lord Wavell was a first-class viceroy and we all trusted him to find a workable solution to the handover of power in India. We understood that his plan was likely to involve partition of India and that he required sufficient time to organise the safe transfer of all the people involved. He had a timetable and proposed to stick to it. Unfortunately the politicians in London wished to settle matters as fast as possible. They requested Lord Wavell to bring back his intended date in 1948 for the handover by one year to 15th August 1947. When he objected, Lord Wavell was sacked. His successor, the charismatic Admiral Lord Louis Mountbatten, became Viceroy of India in March 1947.

For some time, Lord Mountbatten had been our commander-in-chief and he was very popular, especially with the British troops. Although we much regretted Wavell's abrupt departure, we thought we had acquired a winner in his place. However, our confidence in Mountbatten's ability was quickly shattered when he confirmed that the date for the partition of India into two independent countries with dominion status would be 15th August 1947.

We knew this would not give time for the politicians and the mapmakers to draw up and agree the boundaries between the two states of India and Pakistan, or for their armies, police forces and civil services to redeploy their multiracial constituents. Moreover, it seemed to us that it was most unwise to divide Pakistan itself into East and West regions, both with creaky infrastructures, separated from each other by a distance of over 1,000 miles across the unfriendly Indian continent.

It also became obvious to us that, although Mountbatten and his family developed friendly and close relations with Pandit Nehru, the equally charismatic Hindu leader, he simply did not get on with the ascetic Jinnah, the acknowledged leader and negotiator representing the Muslim populations. Jinnah was dedicated to the division of the subcontinent into India, West Pakistan and East Pakistan. Although he got his way, it left the Indians with the lion's share of industry and commerce.

The 15th August 1947 became Independence Day and the separate Dominions of India and Pakistan became independent countries within the Commonwealth. India became a republic in 1950; Pakistan became a republic in 1956. East and West Pakistan fought a civil war in 1971, after which East Pakistan became Bangladesh, an independent people's republic.

The Indian national flag is a horizontal tricolour with bands of deep saffron, white and dark green in equal proportions. There is a navy blue wheel in the centre of the white bar; this is a symbol of Asoka, the Indian emperor who converted to Buddhism c.250 BC. In Sanskrit Asoka means 'without flame' or 'causing no hurt'. It was hoisted proudly on the *maidan* (square) at Dehra Dun on Independence Day. It rained that night and the colours ran. Many Indian observers thought the gods were crying – not at the demise of the British Raj – but at the troubled times soon to come. India and Pakistan, both of which claim to have the atom bomb in their arsenals, have fought three major wars since August 1947 and many savage low-level battles have taken place for control of the remote Siachen glacier in Kashmir.

The seeds of war in Kashmir were sown in 1947, when the 500-plus rulers of the princely states were compelled to make up their minds to join either India or Pakistan. For most of them it was a *fait accompli*, and the great majority joined either one or the other country. But the Hindu Maharajah of Kashmir could not make up his mind. On the one hand Pandit Nehru, himself of Kashmiri origin, was pressing him to opt for India; on the other hand, the large majority of his Muslim subjects, urged on by Pakistani politicians, were agitating for Kashmir to become part of Pakistan. Eventually he decided that his state should join India. The local Muslim population took great umbrage and an unwinnable war broke out which continues to flare up dangerously, as India and Pakistan strive to dominate this mountainous region.

In mid-October 1947 we sailed by troopship from Malaya bound for India. On arrival we entrained for Delhi and three days later, on October 21st, we found ourselves in Khyber Barracks. My company was first stationed at Humayoun's Tomb on the outskirts of Delhi, and then New Delhi airport, where our tasks were to defend specific perimeters. While at the airport I witnessed part of the exodus of Muslims by air from Delhi to Pakistan. Several thousand Muslims wished to leave but few had valid tickets. They camped in the ticket halls and round about, causing extreme confusion, compounded by a thorough blockage of all the lavatories. This situation was exploited by a host of touts attempting to re-sell tickets at over £1,000 each. Large numbers of forged tickets were also changing hands at similar prices. When the owner of a forged ticket discovered that he had been deceived, off he went to a hopeful newcomer and sold his forgery for an even larger sum. The police were unable to control this; we even caught one policeman trying to sell forged tickets.

We did not stay long in Delhi and soon moved 15 miles south west to Gurgaon, a town near the borders of Alwar State. As a temporary company commander I was stationed just outside the town. This time, my designation as temporary was for two reasons; firstly, the permanent company commander was on leave in Delhi prior to returning to the UK; and, secondly, an Indian officer was due to relieve me, following the British Government's decision to transfer four Gurkha regiments to the British Army and allow the other six regiments, including the 9th Gurkha Rifles, to serve in the Indian Army. If my immediate future was uncertain at this time; so were the futures of my men and especially their Gurkha officers. None of the Gurkha rank and file within the regiments to be retained in India were given the chance to opt into either the Indian Army or the British Army; but those going to the British Army had to say whether or not they wished to go. This caused a great deal of anger and sadness in the regiment. Moreover, Indian officers who, previously, had not been permitted to serve in Gurkha regiments were themselves coming into unknown situations, both in regard to their relations with the departing British officers and their relations with the Gurkha officers and the men.

Scott Leathart, who served many years with the battalion and was wounded in Burma in the Chindit campaign, had this to say in his splendid book *With the Gurkhas*, of his own feelings at the time: 'I felt that I was abandoning to the unknown, men who had served me loyally through thick and thin. They were my friends of dangerous moments and happy times, some of them had saved my life, all of them had trusted me without question. What was I to say to them?'

It was this worrying uncertainty which was to form the background to my service in the Punjab in this later stage of the partition of India. Our Indian officer replacements were said to be on the way, but had yet to arrive.

The situation in Gurgaon during early October 1947 had been fairly quiet. My commanding officer told me that it would be my task to escort and protect a foot-and-cart convoy of up to 40,000 Muslims along the grand trunk road to the Pakistan border. The other rifle companies would be similarly employed, or would escort groups of 1,000 Muslims at a time, who were about to travel to Pakistan on the local railway line. Our battalion headquarters would be responsible for supplying us with basic needs and we were to have wireless communication. Details of the foot-and-cart convoy (known to my Gurkhas as the *cafilla* party) would be arranged by the local Indian District Officers and the local Indian police commanders. He reiterated that my involvement must be limited to escort and protection. I was not to give advice to the Muslim population. The pages which follow are based on a daily diary which I kept over the next two months. I had celebrated my twenty-second birthday a few weeks earlier.

It was just before Id, the great Muslim festival, that I visited the Muslim village of Mehrauli. There was much heavy fighting elsewhere in the Punjab. Railway trains were being attacked, roving bands had put whole villages to the sword; but the fighting had more or less bypassed this area between Delhi and Alwar State. In both Delhi itself, and elsewhere in Alwar State, there had been vicious rioting earlier in the year. Very large numbers of Muslims had been killed, compelled to leave their homes, or had been forced to become Hindus. It was feared that trouble would soon start locally. The rural population here was almost entirely Muslim; although there were a few Hindu-Jat villages scattered about. Just before our arrival reports began to come in of isolated incidents, small in themselves, but all pointing to trouble brewing for the future. There had been important changes in the local government and in the police. Many of the *tehsildars* (Muslim police officers) had been transferred or had retired, their places had been taken by inexperienced younger men. Almost everyone of these was a Sikh. The Muslim civilians were very worried by their presence, for this was not a Sikh district and there were no rural Sikh communities in the region.

Most of the rich families and educated Muslims had already left for Pakistan. Those who could afford it, and could procure the petrol, went by car, lorry or hired bus and, as I had seen recently, others went by air. The great trek had started, the unhappy events of the next few weeks in this part of India would soon unfold. That the mass exodus of the Muslims in this particular area was planned in advance, and actively encouraged, by a few well-placed extremists in the local Hindu authorities became plain to see.

The total number of Muslims involved in this area was estimated by the civil authorities to be around half a million, of whom a large number were either old, sick, infirm or very young. These particular Muslims, whose correct designation is Meo, were originally Hindus, but had been converted to Islam by the invading Moguls three centuries before. To an inexperienced eye like mine their looks were indistinguishable from their Hindu neighbours. The Meos were stubborn, clannish farmers living in a region known as 'The Mewat', at subsistence level and heavily indebted to *banias* (Hindu moneylenders). For three hundred years, it was said, they had fought regularly with their Hindu-Jat neighbours, much as English villagers played cricket with their neighbours on the village green; but with swords, guns and knives in place of pads, bat and ball. The Meo were demonstrably unpopular with most of their Islamic brothers, who seemed to regard them with the greatest disdain. The Hindus too had very little use for them, and viewed their about-to-be-abandoned land and property with envy and greed; while the local government officials regarded the prospect of vacated land as an ideal solution to impending problems following the arrival of incoming Hindu and Sikh refugees from Pakistan. Altogether, it seemed to me that the Meos were a most unfortunate race; few had reached any position of eminence and a large majority whom I met were completely illiterate. Before the Second World War, hardly any had left their villages and they were not regarded by the government as a 'military caste'. During the war, however, some individuals had volunteered for service in the armed forces, and now they were returning to their villages having experienced the world outside. I was soon to discover, to my dismay, that not only were these people almost leaderless; but also nearly all their females were in strict purdah.

As we began to understand the situation, fresh disturbing factors emerged to complicate matters. Interested people were campaigning to win the confidence of the Meos. There were four main groups involved. The Indian police, who were mainly Hindu, wanted the Meos to go to Pakistan; representatives from the Pakistan government wanted them to go to Pakistan for political reasons; the Indian Muslim community, based in Delhi, wanted them to stay in India; a few extremist Sikhs were exploiting the situation, as part of a long-term plan for the creation of an independent Sikh State, separate from the Punjab. All were working hard to achieve their ends.

The misuse of force became a dominating factor once again. Various bands, their task of loot and murder at an end in other districts, were taking full advantage of the new developments. In Alwar State a general massacre was taking place. Men, women and children were coming across the border, telling appalling tales of slaughter, mutilation and horror. On a visit to the border I talked to a number of these people as they streamed across. Their stories certainly proved to me that either the Alwar State government had no control over its own State forces, or that it deliberately supported them. I saw a large number of gunshot wounds, sword slashes, severed limbs and deep festering wounds on men, women and children. At no time did I see any arms of any description in possession of the Meos who began to camp out in the open fields, and had brought little food with them. Winter was approaching.

My commanding officer had to reckon carefully. The Meos were most likely to leave their land and go to Pakistan as soon as possible. It was obvious that local politicians were preparing to evacuate half a million people from this and neighbouring areas, with considerable impedimenta and only animal transport, before winter set in. A very limited number of troops were at his disposal. British troops were required to remain in their barracks after the proclamation of Indian Independence on 15th August and could not be used. His task would be the military protection of the 'evacuees'; the civilian authorities would be responsible for the rest of the administration. In practice, however, we were all engaged acting as catalysts by helping, suggesting and urging the civil authorities to do their jobs fairly, efficiently and speedily. Many of the Indian officials I met worked really hard and often courageously; but their determination and confidence were continually undermined by a few active extremists who, from time to time, were able to orchestrate complete breakdowns of the civil power.

Mehrauli was the largest village in my company area. On 27th October 1947 I went there to announce that a foot-and-cart convoy was to leave in ten days' time. Those who wished to travel with it were to rendezvous at a certain milestone on the grand trunk road by noon on the ninth day. This convoy would go to Pakistan on foot by stages. I assured them that the army would provide adequate military protection, and that the district officer had accepted responsibility for making arrangements for the supply of food and fodder and various other matters. I met the local *lambedar*, or village headman. He turned out to be an elderly former *subedar major* of a famous Indian Army regiment, who had married a Meo lady, and had retired on pension some time before the war. He was now an honorary captain and a *Khan Sahib*, the father of a large family and the village patriarch. He was held in the greatest respect by everyone. As soon as my jeep was seen, word was sent to him and he came hurrying up to greet me; followed at a discreet distance by a few white-bearded, hollow-eyed cronies with whom he had just been talking. He turned out to be a great character with a deep husky voice, a thick white beard and a pair of eyes twinkling behind two bushy white eyebrows. These eyes were the first thing I noticed about him. If any man could talk with his eyes, it was the Khan Sahib. Although we spoke in Urdu throughout, I discovered that he could speak quite good English; but never did unless he chose to do so. In earlier days he must have heard and understood the unguarded conversations of unsuspecting British officers – maybe that accounted for his dry sense of humour.

Today he was in uniform. Evidently something was astir for he was wearing his full complement of medals which included the Order of British India (OBI, 1st class), the Indian Order of Merit (IOM) and the Military Cross. The latter would have been an award for bravery in the field, a visible reminder of some almost forgotten prewar campaign recorded, perhaps, by a few faded lines in the regimental history, or among rambling reminiscences during a regimental dinner in a famous London club. Anyway, he shook hands with me and invited me over to his house. This turned out to be a two-storeyed building, built more or less in the European style, of which both he and the entire village were clearly proud. Its ground-floor windows were of glass and the roof was tiled. There was not another such house for miles around, except the *dak* bungalow (rest house), and even that had only iron bars and metal anti-mosquito netting in its windows.

Having given instruction for my Gurkha orderly and driver to be given a chair and a glass of fresh milk, he began to apologise for bringing me to his poor abode and for what he described as his miserable surroundings; all this, it seemed to me, in a voice not completely devoid of pride. After a few pleasantries we got down to business. He told me he was about to hold a much enlarged *panchayat* (council of village elders) in an hour's time. Its main objective was to discuss monthly pensions payable by the civil and military authorities. These had not been received for three months and much hardship was the result. The District Office, and the District Soldiers' Board, had been informed many times and they had at last told him to say that steps were being taken to pay all pensions as soon as possible. Unfortunately, the army pension office had been at Lahore, the scene of violent fighting recently, and had been completely wrecked. It would take some time to get things back to normal. He had called all the local leaders together to tell them to be patient and that they had not been forgotten. I then explained my mission. He received the news in silence and pondered over it for several minutes, before asking me if we might inform the panchayat, to which I readily agreed.

By this time, the village elders had gathered outside the house and were waiting expectantly for us. We went outside. There, in a semicircle, about fifty silver-bearded white-clothed ancients were waiting for us; they salaamed respectfully and then stood in silence. One or two at the back turned round angrily to quieten some eager youths, who were braving the staves of their elders and betters to catch a glimpse of me. There were a few empty chairs reserved for us in front; but we did not need them. The Khan Sahib, having introduced me, gave out our news. To my surprise it was well received and they broke into small discussion groups. They appeared greatly relieved that something was being done and, it seemed to me, that they had already decided in their own minds that they should abandon their homes and go to Pakistan with their families, their household goods and their animals. Every day they had seen an increasing number of distressed refugees from Alwar State camping in their fields; many were related to them, having gone to Alwar State to work or to marry.

As I went among them, a few showed me their discharge certificates from the armed services: for these people their only form of regular income was their pensions. Although this was not nearly enough to live on, it provided extra cash which enabled an older man to be independent and make ends meet. I wondered who would pay their pensions when they arrived in Pakistan. Worse still, I discovered they were all in great financial trouble. The banias, or moneylenders, suddenly realising that their erstwhile clients were on the brink of imminent departure into the unknown, began to look after their own interests. They had already ceased to lend cash when the troubles started and they were aggressively calling in their debts. Old men gathered round with tears in their eyes, literally throwing themselves at my feet and begging for help; some had served the British Raj in one capacity or another during the war years. The British had let them down and were leaving them to starve, to have their homes stolen from them and even to be murdered. Why were the British going so abruptly? Until quite recently everyone had been content; now everything was in turmoil and the bottom had fallen out of their world. Their familiar British Sahib had not come round to visit the pensioners and their families this year; the new Indian Sahib was only a *batcha* (boy) who had not been to see them, because he was a family man and never had the time. Why had not the British said goodbye to their faithful servants, having made proper arrangements for their welfare and their safety?

Life, they explained, had become impossible. No one cared for them any more. No one came to give advice, they had no one to listen to their troubles. Would I, as a British officer, whom they were indeed very glad to see, help them and give them advice as to whether or not they should pack up, leave their villages and take their families to Pakistan? I was a man of the outside world and would understand how difficult it was to move their families by road into Pakistan, with all the privations and embarrassments for women travelling in purdah. Should they stay at home or should they move to Pakistan? If they stayed, who would protect them from the roving bands of cut-throats? Would I, as a British officer who knew everything they wanted to know, tell them what they ought to do? They added that they would do anything I ordered – no matter what it was. The Khan Sahib remained quiet and gloomy. They were disappointed when I said that I had orders from the Indian government in Delhi not to influence their decisions in any way. Even the Khan Sahib looked at me straight between the eyes for a few moments, making me feel as if I had been weighed and found wanting in his great hour of need. He questioned me closely as to the state of the roads, the amount of baggage that could be taken, etc. Fortunately, I had already worked out most of the answers for which I would be responsible and which I had thought likely to arise. I left an hour later with a heavy heart, knowing full well they were thinking that I, too, had let them down. Before going, I agreed to return in two days' time to collect the estimated numbers of those who wished to travel in the foot-and-cart convoy.

I returned to the dak bungalow which I was using as my company headquarters. Patrols had been going out and coming in all day long. Their task was to spread the news of the cafilla party over as large an area as possible, in the shortest space of time. To help in this tiring and dusty task I had acquired a civilian publicity van and a number of young policemen. The van turned out to be an ancient Ford chassis, on which had been constructed an enormous loud-speaker, fixed to a swivel and looking rather like a mobile search-light. This loudspeaker, together with two large and brightly polished brass headlamps and an enormous squeeze-bag horn, gave the contraption a distinctly Martian appearance; indeed this effect was emphasised by the facial characteristics of the Mitra twins who jointly owned the van. Each had a magnificent full Rajput warrior moustache. They were quite tall, pleasantly rotund, pop-eyed, very good company, ready to work all hours of the day and only too willing to go anywhere or do anything. Both had a ready sense of humour and were to prove their worth many times over in the weeks to come. Apparently their previous occupation had been the playing of recorded music for Hindu weddings. They set about their new task with enthusiasm and visited all the villages which were accessible by road or track; I never discussed with them who paid their salaries or where they obtained seemingly unlimited supplies of petrol.

Just before lunch, three large black Buick saloons drove up outside the dak bungalow. A dapper man, complete with a spotless white pith helmet, was handed out of the second car: he was surrounded by about twelve police constables. As I approached I heard him order the cars to go to the police station and to await him there. He then introduced himself as the new police superintendent and declared his intention to go on tour: I asked him to join me for lunch at the dak bungalow and during the meal, with a punkah gently swishing overhead, he told me that it was his intention to visit all local police stations, and give 'each and everyone of his idle policemen one big pep talk.'

After my guest had departed my Gurkha subedar came in and reported that there was a delegation waiting outside, near the well, and they had an *urzi*, or plea. Should he tell them to go away? Clearly this was what he wanted to do; but I saw some smart-looking soldiers among them. I asked him to call the soldiers over. When they arrived, after much salaaming and many polite words, they informed me that they were serving soldiers of the Pakistani army, whose homes and families were living in the area. Would I give them transport to take them and their families to their regimental centres in Pakistan? As it was our agreed policy to give our Pakistani colleagues all the help we could – and I had been warned that such requests might arise – I had already earmarked a temporary transit camp for these people. When the camp was full, our battalion headquarters informed the Pakistani Army authorities that arrangements would be made for a lorry convoy to take them to New Delhi for onward despatch to Pakistan.

I had the pleasure of telling these men the good news; but I warned them that, while they were here, they would have to provide their own food and tentage. I asked them for a nominal roll-call of families, and was agreeably surprised when a number of these were handed to me straight away. They had evidently been prepared carefully beforehand, and were very neatly written in

English. However, I was concerned to see that the first five men's families comprised 167 souls; an average of no less than 33 per family. I had intended to suggest that each man should be limited to taking a smaller number of dependants. In fact, I had given the matter insufficient thought and it soon dawned on me that they intended to take everyone with them and to leave none of their families behind. I agreed and handed the whole show over to these Pakistani soldiers for them to look after themselves. One of the senior men among them was a Royal Indian Army Service Corps *jemadar*, who asked to stay on in the little transit camp as general factotum, until the camp closed a few weeks later. Having moved into an area under some trees which had three wells, they scrounged some tents from brigade headquarters and the place soon became a hive of activity, causing me no problems.

As the days passed by, it became only too obvious that the Meos were definitely going to move to Pakistan. More tales were coming in about how the police were physically forcing people to leave their homes. These were hard to believe until, one day, I decided to go and investigate myself. A Meo youth had arrived that morning in a breathless state crying out that his younger brother and two sisters had been kidnapped by the police. On being asked the reason for this, he said that police, armed with *lathis* (long wooden staves), had entered the village that morning and ordered the Meos to leave on the foot-and-cart convoy. Only the day before a well-dressed Muslim gentleman from Delhi had arrived and distributed pamphlets advising the villagers to stay in India; promising them special privileges, including a new school should they decide to stay. Following these honeyed words, they had all undertaken to remain at home and enjoy these good things and the gentleman had proceeded on his way. When the police came along the next day and ordered them to go they plucked up courage and refused, whereupon the police had kidnapped a number of children, among whom were the three youngsters who had been playing outside his house.

I went around to the police station with the man who was now trembling with apprehension, and found the police inspector inside; he was a young Sikh who was entirely new to the district in general and to police work in particular. He still wore the uniform of a lieutenant in the Indian Army. He agreed to come with me and we set out for the village with my escort. Here we found about ten policemen in khaki uniform each armed with a large wooden lathi having an argument with the villagers. There was quite a tumult with women and children crying, angry men shouting and dogs barking. We asked the constables what it was all about, and they said that they had been unfairly accused of kidnapping children. At these words, several villagers protested vigorously saying that the police were lying. The inspector asked his men if they had arrested or taken the children away; whereupon they denied vehemently all knowledge of any abduction. We confronted them with the man whose siblings they were supposed to have taken; but the police said that the man was deliberately inventing the story. At this point, several villagers stepped forward and claimed that they had seen the police drag the children away; furthermore, they said, the police had declared subsequently they would return the children if the whole village gave its word to pack up and leave with the cafilla party. More prolonged wailing from the women greeted this; and one of the policemen expectorated noisily, as the rest looked towards the Sikh inspector. The latter turned to me and said, in English, that the villagers were born liars and that it was their intention to get the police into trouble. It was the word of the villagers against the word of the police, and I departed. The children were returned later in the afternoon. This was typical of the many complaints against the police and, I thought, an increase in this bullying of the Meos was probably the direct result of the police superintendent's earlier pep talk.

Over the next few days more and more people arrived to join the cafilla party. Preparations were made to keep the people in a defined area, according to the villages from which they came. Even then, crops round about were trampled down and there was some looting and a few minor thefts.

The day before the cafilla party was due to start I persuaded the District Officer to call a conference. This was necessary because it was very doubtful if the civilian 'heads of department' knew their responsibilities or had initiated any action. The manifesto issued by the government to the Meos clearly stated that medical supplies, food, farrier and cart-repair facilities would be made available. However, the estimated numbers had now reached the hundred thousand mark and to supply all these people and their cattle would be a task of Herculean proportions.

The conference was called for 9 a.m. on 5th November. I arrived punctually and we were joined a short time later by the others. When the District Officer arrived well after 10 a.m., he was deep in conversation with a man wearing a spotless white dhoti and the ubiquitous Congress Party cap. We all filed into the conference room and sat down at a large table. The District Officer took the chair. He was rather large, and was dressed in badly fitting European-style clothes; doubtless he was feeling the heat for he kept tugging at his outsize collar, pulling his tie well over to one side, and thrusting his chin forward in an effort to encourage the perspiration to run down inside his collar. On his left sat an equally fat bull-necked Indian *babu* (clerk) who breathed heavily as he began to sharpen a pencil. He wore European-style clothing and, perhaps, had long since forgone the pent-up inward effort required to enable his youngest relation to button up his waistcoat. Another concession to the heat was to let his shirt-tails hang out fore and aft in the current fashion; to complete this splendid example of oriental scholarship his unlaced shoes were upon unsocked feet.

The Congress man sat on the right of the District Officer, looking very smart in the national clothes of India and having a most disdainful air about him. He was obviously annoyed with the District Officer, and the latter was acutely aware of it, for he kept glancing nervously in his direction as he addressed us. Having looked at us closely the Congress man proceeded to examine his fingernails intensely for some time. The police superintendent, now in uniform, looked bored and restless. The local stationmaster, despite the heat, wore a thick army pullover dyed black. The Khan Sahib was there with two other Meo leaders. The civilian doctor wore tiny spectacles in a battered metal frame and was asleep. The schoolmaster sat on the extreme edge of his chair continually scratching himself with the end of a well-worn pen holder. On the other side of the table, adding a final touch to the incongruous, was a thin horse-faced man chewing betel-nut with every sign of enjoyment; I thought he was either uninterested in the whole proceedings, or did not understand what was going on. I later learned that he was the farrier who was to play a most courageous part in the survival of the cafilla party. Significantly, there was no representation from those responsible for supplying food and fodder. The conference soon developed into a classroom squabble with each man voicing his own entirely different point of view. I said that, although time was short and the foot-and-cart convoy could not be cancelled, it might with advantage be postponed for a day or two. At this there was much wild gesticulation. The effect on the Congress man was extraordinary. He looked up and asked lots of questions; eventually, he and the District Officer agreed to a delay of two days. A detailed plan was hammered out; and I left much relieved that the Congress man had proved so helpful and that he would remain in the District Office for the next few days, and deal with the food supply situation.

It took me four hours to travel the fourteen miles from the district office to the dak bungalow: I had with me the Meo leaders for whom there was no other way of returning. The roads around for miles and miles were almost impassable to motor traffic. Thousands of men women and children, with all manner of animals, were converging on the starting point. Already the camp boundaries had been enlarged several times and still the people drifted in.

That afternoon I contacted brigade headquarters some thirty miles away, and asked for an Auster aeroplane to fly over the area and let us know how things looked from above. A reply came through straight away, saying that the brigadier himself was just about to take off. When his report came in by radio, it gave us some idea of the tremendous scale of our undertaking. The roads for ten miles around in every direction were packed solid; and vast concourses of people were making their way across country. The whole land over some hundred square miles seemed to be closing in. As evening fell, his view from above had become obscured by the dust which hung like a mist over all, and he had experienced considerable difficulty flying safely home.

Fortunately, at this point there was little danger of a serious attack from the outside on the Meos. The main danger was the ever-present possibility of losing control and becoming engulfed in the mass of moving humanity. Very gradually things began sorting themselves out; my Gurkhas were doing a magnificent job. For three consecutive days and nights a company of ninety men, with only token support from the police, had managed everything. This demanded endless patience, an iron constitution and, above all, a sense of humour – all qualities which Gurkhas have in abundance. I doubt whether other troops could have stood it so well in these conditions; and then to travel for four weeks through dust and heat by day and the bitter cold by night The Gurkhas remained completely impartial throughout. They treated Hindus, Sikh and Muslims alike and with unfailing courtesy and kindness. In addition to the normal discomfort of bodily dirt, our dark olive-green uniforms had been bleached almost white by the extremes of temperature. Everyone had developed coughs and colds and we had nasty sore throats.

The evening before the cafilla party was due to start, several other military units joined us. Two platoons arrived from a Punjabi battalion which had been transferred to the Pakistani Army: the remaining platoon had got lost *en route* and did not join us till much later. These Punjabi troops (all Muslims) had just come from across the border and were to act with us as part of the escort; they had their own rations and motor transport but were under my command till the cafilla party reached the frontier with Pakistan. At first, we were rather alarmed, for their presence might cause friction when we passed through Hindu-Jat, or Sikh-populated districts; and I wondered how they would be received by the Meos. We were not left in doubt for very long. They proved tough, reliable and well-disciplined soldiers. Their commander, who joined us later, had a forceful character and spoke upper-class English and down-to-earth Urdu. He had the knack of getting on well with everyone he met and was a most ingenious man for compromise, saving the situation several times when the Meos were about to get excited.

I made a special point of keeping my Gurkha officers and the Indian Army officers and VCOs (Viceroy Commissioned Officers) attached to me as fully briefed as possible throughout our journeys towards Pakistan. They all proved utterly loyal and I valued greatly their support, ideas and suggestions.

With the Punjabis came a troop of mounted cavalry and three tanks. The civil authorities sent two motorised forges and three farrier units. Later came six modern ambulances and four motor buses which, together, formed a mobile hospital and was serviced by a posse of tough, friendly, efficient, mainly Parsee nurses. The doctor was the same man who had slept soundly at the conference the day before. There would be no sleep for him during the next month.

That evening the Khan Sahib came round to my tent with ten men whom he introduced as additional leaders of the people. They were all elderly and had held various posts in the armed services or in their old villages. I was extremely glad to hear that, between them, they expected to be successful in dividing the cafilla into geographical groups with their own original village leaders in command. This would facilitate control at the end of a day's march, and at the journey's end over the border in Pakistan, where they expected to be resettled by their villages. The first man to whom I was introduced was a retired subedar who still wore the faded badges of the Indian Pioneer Corps; later, I was to learn that he was a Pathan and had once been the *jemadar* adjutant of a battalion of the Frontier Force Regiment. His brother had been hanged for murder, and he had been obliged to transfer from his regiment to the Pioneer Corps. The most striking things about him were his blue eyes. The second man was a Royal Indian Navy petty officer, an intelligent man of about forty who spoke good English. He was small, very thin and suffered from TB, which had been the reason for his discharge from the service. When he spoke he emphasised the points he was making by prodding the ground with a hockey stick which he always carried with him wherever he went. Next was an ancient *Risaldar*, heavily bemedalled and bearded. He wore a skintight pair of cavalry breeches which, he said, were part of his mess kit twenty years ago. The rest of these leaders were in the same mould – tall and thin, with leathery faces, and wearing some sort of army uniform.

Having tried to memorise their names, I gave out the orders for the next day's march. Broadly speaking, the cafilla was to consist of an estimated 100,000 people with their camel carts and bullock wagons, and men, women and children on foot, together with herds of cattle, sheep and goats. An advance party consisting of five Meo leaders would accompany a platoon of my Gurkhas and a platoon of Punjabis at 5.30 a.m. the next morning travelling in one of the buses. Their combined task would be to organise the reception of the cafilla as it came into the new camp area. The time for the main party to get started was 6.00 a.m. sharp. The carts and wagons were to travel head to tail on the road, close together, four abreast. Those on foot, and the free-ranging animals, would keep to the left of the carts, but must not extend more than fifty yards from the road. This would leave the right side of the road for the free movement of my troops. There were to be no halts on the road. The day's march would end near a specified milestone on the grand trunk road where they would camp within a defended perimeter for the night. On arrival there, the head of the cafilla would be directed to the far end of the reception area and would be guided in by members of the advance party.

As for our own troops, my chief concern was to avoid foot marching as much as possible, and yet provide sufficient protection for both sides of the cafilla party. We had to have an advance guard and a rearguard; the one to prepare the night camp, and the other to help the leaders organise the cafilla party as it streamed out of the camp. After consulting the Punjabi captain, my Gurkha officers and the attached VCOs, I decided to picquet the road with sections every mile or so, sending them out by lorry in the morning and picking them up in the evening. This would save them a certain amount of fatigue and would not require extra petrol. The tanks were to head the cafilla party and the mounted cavalry would bring up the rear. The tank commander insisted on conducting a tour of the whole perimeter at different times in the evening, so that he might get some idea of the lie of the land and deter any organised attack from outside.

The duties of the advance guard were important and, after several mistakes, we found that certain conditions were essential before establishing a camp. The camps had to be near wells and our own base had to be windward of the cafilla and of the road. The cafilla's camp could not be sited on soft ground in case cartwheels became bogged down. I usually selected the campsites myself; but, in case I was elsewhere at the time, my Gurkha second-in-command always went with the advance party. At the very end of the cafilla were to go, by short bounds, the civilian authority's buses. These included the 'hospital' and the Mitra twins with their precious loudspeaker. All through the night late arrivals came streaming in. The shouting of the men, and the answering grunts of their animals, adding to the cacophony which never abated for a single moment. The last thing to happen that night was the breakdown of our wireless communication. This was not a complete disaster for it enabled our tired signallers to get a rest. My colonel expected me to get on with things, which suited me well, and my headquarters kept us regularly supplied with food and water via a number of small side roads and tracks. Suddenly, brigade headquarters bombarded us with signals from New Delhi, asking us to receive and entertain important visitors. A Mountbatten daughter was insisting on flying in by Auster to inspect the cafilla's latrines. The latter were nonexistent; but I did not object to this request, trusting that the enormous dust cloud would protect us and prevent her landing from the air. This assumption proved correct and no one, not even the Mountbatten daughter, bothered us after all.

On 8th November at 5.30 a.m. we were ready. The advance guard set off successfully. The section picquets had left in the lorries to be dropped off at selected points along the route. Just then the Khan Sahib arrived with the Sikh police inspector in the latter's newly acquired British Army jeep; something was clearly wrong for they were in vociferous disagreement. The Khan was red in the face and spluttering. I enquired what the trouble was, and was told that the Khan had been arrested for arson. Apparently, on the previous evening, a police patrol had entered Mehrauli and found the Meos setting the village alight. They had reported this to the police inspector, and he had just arrested the Khan as being the person responsible. The Khan's story was quite different. The police had come around the evening before, and had threatened to kill anyone who remained the next day, and who was not going on the cafilla. There had been a great deal of argument and more threats; but eventually the police departed. He himself, with the whole village, left a little after midnight; but had not destroyed or set anything alight. The police contradicted all he said. They declared that the Meos had burned their homes. As far as I could make out, the police had not arrested anyone on the spot and they had no witnesses. I persuaded the inspector that in view of the Khan's importance to me he should be released, and the inspector did so with bad grace.

My Gurkhas told me that the villagers bought themselves out of trouble with the police by the gift of a goat, or some other equally acceptable present. They said that the police station, which was next door to their tents on the outskirts of Gurgaon, was teeming with a great many bleating animals. In the end, I concluded that the village of Mehrauli had been burned by persons unknown.

After the police inspector left, the cafilla began to start. I took my stand on the right side of the road with the Khan still muttering and the doctor wide awake. The wind was behind us. First of all came the Stuart tanks, the crews seemed happy enough and the commander of each tank stood black-bereted in his turret waving to us as he passed. I could hear the Mitra twins going hard at it in

91

the distance on their loudspeaker. The early morning mist slowly dissipated as the minutes passed. Presently, came the first of a long line of camel wagons creaking along at a fast walking pace. They gave the impression of being really roadworthy. Each camel was slung between two enormous shafts of wood; the wagon itself was square in shape with small wheels at each corner. Inside were the women, rigidly in purdah, about to undergo great privation from the heat and lack of water. In some wagons there were as many as twenty women and young children. On the top, sides and at the back were stowed, hooked or slung all the household goods imaginable; varying from large steel trunks to the ubiquitous sack of fodder tied between the axles of the wheels. The camels looked very proud as they stalked solemnly along without the least apparent effort. Beside the wagons came great families of old people, women and older children intermingling with the goats and herds of cattle. Occasionally there came by what looked like a double-domed mosque on wheels; it was just like an ordinary wagon but two large domes had been build upon the body. These were on a wooden framework covered with dark red silk and looked beautiful if incongruous. Both domes were crowded with women and babies.

The Meo womenfolk might well have been fair to look upon, but the great majority were travelling in purdah and, as they were forbidden to let a man see their faces, it was impossible to tell. However a few women had either given up purdah or were of too low a class to be in purdah. These ladies tramped along barefoot behind the carts, wearing men's rough faded shirts outside dark brown cotton breeches. Many carried heavy boxes on their heads; others had babies at their breasts. On seeing these unfortunate women, I turned to the doctor and asked him if he thought they could survive the 250 mile walk to their new homes in Pakistan. He replied, with a shrug, that they had far better constitutions than the men. As we were talking, the doctor pointed out a woman carrying a box on her head. He told me that she had given birth to a child the evening before and, having killed it herself, she had buried it and was quite prepared to walk fourteen miles. His matter-of-fact tone of voice left me speechless; much later I was overcome with feelings of pity, anger, frustration and sadness – all of which I discovered was felt by everyone of the escort party. It grew worse every day.

The cafilla party's trek had begun, tens of thousands of people uprooted from their homes were starting on their journey into the unknown. They were not doing so without good cause; but few, if any, considered or understood the tremendous difficulties which lay ahead. To reach the Pakistan border they had to travel an average of ten miles a day, often through hostile country. Winter was approaching fast, the rainy season was about to start; extensive flooding of the rivers was an ever-increasing danger. Those on foot would suffer severely, many of the elderly, the infirm and the very young would certainly perish. When the Meos reached Pakistan their troubles would not be over, for they had to settle down in a strange land with no established homes, schools, shops, crops or cash. Those who were prepared to talk seemed to view all this philosophically; and did not worry about the future, preferring to place their trust in Allah and to take comfort in the safety of numbers.

I was thinking of these things as the cafilla creaked by. Then I saw that, if I did not start soon, I should never be able to overtake them: so I gave my last-minute instructions to the rearguard commander and set off in my jeep and trailer to the next day's camping place. It took us some time to overtake the head of the cafilla; but by dint of much hooting, shouting and cajoling we eventually heard the sound of the tanks and caught them up. My Gurkha driver was swearing away, his one adjective being applied to all objects, animate or inanimate, but he drove safely and well. Several times we had to stop and order people to keep over to the left of the road, and to take their cattle with them.

When we reached the spot near the designated milestone we found our advance party. My subedar had chosen the sites well and areas had been allocated for the mobile hospital, the forge and the publicity van. At about 11.00 a.m. the noise of the approaching tanks could be heard and soon they came into view. One stayed at the side of the road opposite the entrance to the main camp, and the other two went into harbour.

Then along came the camel wagons and, with babies wailing, women shouting and buckets clanging to and fro, they bumped across the uneven ground towards the far corner of the camp. Here they unhitched their animals, brought water from a well and gave them as much fodder as they could spare. The older children lit fires and parties of young men went out to collect firewood; they proved extraordinarily agile and climbed the most difficult of trees

93

like monkeys. Others less inclined to shinning up trees, tied together two poles at the extremity of which were bound long curved knives. With these instruments they cut down quite large branches and, by occasional use of not too gentle prods, kept away the human monkeys who were encroaching on their territory. The place soon filled up; we were hard pressed persuading them to keep together. It had been agreed that this work was the responsibility of the police, but there was no sign of them. We did our best and kept things more or less under control. We could do nothing to save the roadside crops and the next day, after the cafilla party had passed by, both sides of the road, for miles back into the distance, looked as if a swarm of locusts had eaten everything in sight. The beautiful roadside trees had gone, the wells were dry and the crops had completely disappeared. All that was left, was a mile wide swathe of dust, excrement and rubbish beyond description. The number of sad little graves left behind increased daily. Vultures circled overhead and had the time of their lives.

We soon regained limited wireless communication by using the tanks' radio sets, and we resumed contact with the rearguard. The latter reported that the cafilla was still coming out of the original camp, and that it was not nearly finished. This meant that, apart from the fourteen miles of road packed tight with moving people, there was still a considerable number yet to come. A police section of ten men, whose sole job it was to stand on the road, counting the evacuees as they passed, reported approximately 60,000 people on the road. This was beginning to look as if the revised estimate of a 100,000 would prove correct. Meanwhile the poorer people, who had not brought sufficient supplies, or could not afford to buy them, were sending deputations asking for food. Fortunately, the Viceroy's Commissioned Officer (VCO) in charge of the tanks, who was a Muslim serving in India's army, happened to be going via the district office to his headquarters. I asked him to take a written message requesting urgently the promised food and supplies.

By the later afternoon, the incoming column had broken down into groups of stragglers. Some of the wagons had collapsed en route; these were arriving, painfully and slowly, to join the queue at the farriers' and the makeshift repair stations. Back came the 3-ton lorry which, in the late morning, had made its way down the road distributing tea to the picquets. Having completed the trip it had turned round and collected the first section picquets after the last of the column passed by.

Eventually, as the sun was going down, along came a sleek civilian limousine and three large vans. These turned out to contain the District Officer and the police. I asked him when the food was coming. He shrugged his shoulders, threw out his hands, waved them in the air and said that they should have been here already. This was his last visit. We would soon enter another district and a new man would take his place.

We were joined by the doctor who had a sad tale to tell. His nurses had attended 89 deliveries; he surmised there were at least ten times that number at which they had not been present. He also said that he had seen 47 old people and 9 small children die, in addition to the many babies killed at birth. His medical supplies were running out. He was fearful of the future. I told him that I would get what I could from military resources; the District Officer, clearly guilt-stricken, said he would endeavour to get some too. The doctor looked very tired indeed. I was horrified to hear he had no relief, no assistant and, until one of the Meos volunteered, he had been driving his vehicle himself. The pay of this very gallant individual was less than £3 a week. He had a wife and six children living on the India/Pakistan border, from whom he had no news since severe rioting there some weeks ago. He was the only doctor for 100,000 people – and this was the first day of a journey which might last over a month.

We said goodbye to the District Officer, and soon more deputations from the Meos came up with their *urzies*; a word that we seemed to be hearing so often. Unfortunately, we could not help them. Just before it got dark I had a stand-to for the whole escort. This was necessary in case there were raids during the night. It entailed two thirds of my company being in section posts on the perimeter, and the remainder with me for any emergency. The tanks did their *chukka* round the perimeter and, when they returned from this circumnavigation, we stood down. Four separate patrol posts were established, because we expected some of the more enterprising local youth would make raids on the ill-controlled herds of cattle. We had less than 200 men of whom only one third were on duty at any one time. Hence we could not hope to stop every act of pilfering – only something in the nature of a large raid. In fact, it transpired that, at this time, most of the petty thieving which took place was carried out by the Meos among themselves. One thing which struck me as a little strange, was the way the thousands of animals stuck close to the cafilla and obeyed their owners. There was almost no straying away. I assume this was the result of a close affinity with their owners and a wish to remain as close as possible to their source of food and water.

It was a noisy night. The awesome croaking of the camels kept me awake. I found this to be a most disturbing sound, seeming to come from the depths of the animal, combining great physical discomfort with an apparent desire to end its life with the least possible delay. Indeed, I shall never forget the sound of a very large number of camels chiming like hounds in English kennels. The troops slept under the inner fly of 180lb tents, sixteen to a fly. Although this was very crowded, a third of them were always on duty. Sleeping close together kept the remainder warm, for it was getting very cold at night. I usually slept in the back of an army truck and got up early every morning, very stiff. The sentries said they were cold, despite wearing the greatcoats which I had cadged some time before from our regimental centre in Dehra Dun. Next morning the procedure for leaving the camp was the same as used on the first day. This time the escorts changed over duties; except the men of the two Punjabi Muslim platoons, who had especially asked to continue to march with the cafilla party. They did not wish to go with the advance or rear parties; but wanted to be on foot all day in contact with the Meos.

I decided that the next halt would be for nearly 48 hours because I had just been told by a motorcycle messenger that arrangements were being made for some of the Meos to travel to the frontier by train. The railway station was near a town; and two refugee trains a day were being run up to the border. According to the message we would be allocated one train a day, for three or four days, and that the escorts would be supplied by another company from our battalion. I set off with the advance guard; a rather larger one than usual. Having selected the various camping sites, I told them that their special duty would be to prevent anyone leaving the perimeter of the camp. It was quite possible that large numbers of Meos might flock to the station causing chaos. Strictly speaking, this was not my task but I felt quite certain that the police would let us down. I then went along to the railway station to find the stationmaster.

Despite the hour, he was in his office and pleased to see me. I had heard that he had the reputation not only of being efficient and reliable; but also cheerful and helpful – attributes rare in my recent experience of officialdom. He was expecting me and passed on another message from our headquarters. A train would leave the next morning taking a maximum of a thousand people to the border. This was what I wanted to know. I agreed to ensure that about that number would be on the platform by 4.00 p.m. next afternoon. He warned me that there was fighting up the line between trainloads of evacuees and refugees as they passed each other. Although the passenger carriages on this line had still not been cleaned, the train would be empty of people and the escort carriages were usable.

On returning to the camp I saw the head of the cafilla party visible along the road a mile or so away. Neither the police nor the civil authorities had turned up. Once again it was left to us to receive them. At about 3.00 p.m., just as we were all very busy indeed, three large lorries and a huge bus arrived, without warning, laden with food. The lorries drove right up to the edge of the camp and stopped there. Immediately, groups of men women and children started running from all directions converging on the lorries; within a minute a dense crowd had formed with everyone pushing, stumbling and shouting for all they were worth. Soon a great groan rent the air; the food had come to an end and there was nothing left. The man in charge seemed quite content and drove away. All this took place before our unbelieving eyes in under ten minutes.

Half an hour after this episode, the new District Officer arrived and with him came the same Congress man. I told them the story of the food and asked them to use whatever influence they had to persuade the police to do their duty. The Congress man seemed surprised and very angry at the absence of the police. While we were talking, the police vehicles drove up to us and came to a standstill in a scurry of dust. Their arrival heralded a torrent of abuse from the District Officer but the police inspector, not to be outdone, retorted with equal vehemence. Meanwhile, the police constables, newly armed with rifles, gathered around adding their oral share to the proceedings. They leaned on their rifles as if they were walking-sticks, the sight of which made the Gurkhas present burst out laughing. I went off to lunch, having being called away by my Gurkha orderly, freshly employed as 'cook'. When I returned there was no sign of the official, the Congress man, the police or their transport.

During the next few days the cafilla party continued its journey up the grand trunk road to Pakistan without any major incident. As the Meos' strength became weaker I felt it necessary to arrange shorter marches, to enable the stragglers to catch up and the mobile hospital to deal with an increasing number of the seriously ill. The doctor wished to send the latter to hospitals in Delhi; but many of their families would not let them go, preferring to take them away to die on the march. Fortunately, the new Indian authorities began to send us large quantities of medical supplies and several enthusiastic doctors arrived with ambulances a week after we started. I was also given a platoon of Madras Sappers and Miners. I suspected that their arrival might have been ordered by the highest authorities in Delhi to provide the missing latrines so I discussed the situation with them and with brigade headquarters. It was agreed that, for the time being, the sappers would be attached to the cafilla party's escort. Their cheerful acceptance of the most arduous duties proved invaluable.

We used the little railway four times, commandeering civilian buses to take them to the railway station. To avoid a stampede, I always selected the last thousand or so people in the cafilla party, wherever possible from the same village and in family units. Once we got into the rhythm of the daily march, nightly stops and rests in between, I was able to improve our own *bandobust* (administrative arrangements). We were all in need of a decent bath, physical rest out of the heat and dust, and a change of clothes. This was quite difficult to achieve. However, I was able to arrange informally for an exchange of men temporarily with the battalion head-quarters company in Gurgaon. I asked our quartermaster to send me my 16-bore shotgun, together with another shotgun, and some of the cartridges which I had brought from England. Jemadar Tejbahadur and I took time off to go hunting. Unfortunately, because of the upheaval in the countryside, we did not find many *cheetal* (deer), but in the evenings we had a splendid time shooting pigeon over nearby *jheels* (lakes) and supplemented our boring rations accordingly. We were able to do this with a clear conscience throughout weeks two and three. Later I wrote in the 9th Gurkha Rifles (UK) *Regimental Newsletter*, 'I got to know Jemadar Tejbahadur quite well when he was a platoon commander in my last

98

days with the 3/9th in 1947 ... He was a brave, unflappable, tireless, intelligent, amusing and much respected Gurkha officer; a likeable gentleman and wonderful company in the middle of nowhere.' His service medals are now in the Gurkha Museum in Winchester.

The next two weeks proved to be much more difficult from the guard and escort point of view. So I had to put a stop to our little treats. We were passing through Sikh territory, and there were large numbers of well-armed Sikh bands roaming around attacking anyone who got in their way. We began to experience small but vicious raids at night directed mainly at stealing cattle; occasionally, our patrols intercepted this activity and an exchange of shots preceded a Sikh withdrawal. The police in the new district we passed through were much more efficiently organised; though their attitude towards the Meos was as hostile as ever. Some of their officers and men were Sikhs and I always took a Sikh officer with me when I reconnoitred new sites for the night stops. The great thing was to talk plainly, and apply as much pressure as possible on the local Sikh community leaders to let the cafilla party go by without harm. The trouble was that tempers would rise in the whole community whenever a Sikh refugee train arrived from Pakistan; particularly if the passengers had been killed or wounded on the way. Dreadful revenge attacks often followed and my cafilla party was a sitting target. I kept in constant contact with the Sikh community leaders, and I think the cafilla was fortunate indeed to reach the border of Pakistan more or less intact.

None of my men had been hurt through enemy action though we were all in poor physical condition. The Punjabi Muslim soldiers suffered more than us, because they had insisted on marching alongside the Meos. Shortly before arriving at the border on 10th December, I handed over the cafilla party to my newly-found friend, the Punjabi Regiment captain, said farewell to the Mitra twins whose eyes were as gaunt and hollow as the rest of ours; and had a last word with the doctor whose hair was now as white as our bleached uniforms. There was no sign of my old friend the Khan Sahib or his family in the Mehrauli village group; I was told they were some distance away near a ruined mosque. Here I found him lying quietly on a litter surrounded by his womenfolk. His eyes lit up as I approached and he mumbled something which I could not catch. He seemed to have aged a hundred years in a few weeks and it was clear to me that he was on his deathbed. He told me that he could not eat, go to the lavatory or move to say his prayers. I did not stay long and, as I left, he managed a very weak wave of his hand – originally a cheery gesture which I had come to know so well. I walked away in sadness with my head turned away for I was ashamed they would see my tears. I was told that he died the same evening, and that the Royal Indian Navy petty officer with the hockey stick had also died on the same day.

I visited the same area fifty years later. Gurgaon is now a huge town, and one cannot move for crowds of shouting people, scurrying around everywhere. Mehrauli is part of an unrecognisable suburb – all white concrete walls, bright red tiles and shiny glass windows. The route we took along the grand trunk road has long returned to its former rustic beauty. Great tall spreading trees have reappeared, like captive dowagers, along the roadside and villages have sprung up everywhere. In the early morning dew, I noticed that the fields were full of women, wearing multicoloured saris, gently supervising little children in rows engaged in fertilising the fields There were no signs of the passing of our cafilla party – no sad little graves, no ruined mosques though there were plenty of pigeons striating across the sky from one beautiful jheel to another. What of our cafilla party? How did they fare in Pakistan? Was their escape from India worthwhile and were their hopes fulfilled? Are they still a recognised community in Pakistan with access to schools, shops, pension payments ... or did they perish in the floods which followed shortly after their arrival? I do not know the answer to these questions.

We returned to our first company headquarters near Gurgaon on 12th December. I had no opportunity to make a formal report to anyone, and no one had the time to hear of my adventures. On my arrival at the officers' mess, I was told that our efficient adjutant had fallen foul of the Indian authorities and had been forced to fly for his personal safety immediately to the United Kingdom. His place would be filled by one of the Indian officer replacements who were to arrive in a day or two. Our colonel had left some time ago to go on retirement. His Indian replacement was in New Delhi. I was told to go to the regimental centre in Dehra Dun prior to returning to the UK. My replacement was an Anglo-Indian captain whom I had not met before. That evening all the remaining British officers were asked by the subedar major (the senior Gurkha officer) to a farewell reception in the Gurkha officers' mess. About 15 minutes after I arrived, the A and B Company Gurkha officers asked me to their own combined farewell, and off we went together. They were in a terrible state. On the way they reminded me that some time ago they had carried out an unofficial poll of both companies. Not a single soldier had wished to stay in the Indian Army, half wanted to transfer to the British Army and the other half wished to go back to their homes in Nepal. The men were gathered round an open space between the tents and were trying to be as cheerful as possible. Goats had been killed and cooked; there was plenty of rum to drink; and all ranks including the riflemen launched into reminiscences, mostly about the battalion's exploits in Burma (before I joined) and in Java (some of which I shared). After many tearful farewells we departed, with very sad hearts, at 2 a.m.

A month before, knowing that my time in the 9th Gurkha Rifles was soon to come to an end, I had arranged with a silversmith in Dehra Dun to make me ten half-pint Indian-silver flasks. I presented them to the Gurkha officers, the *havildar* majors and the quartermaster *havildars*, who had served with me during my time with the battalion. I had them inscribed in English: 'From a Friend' which was not very original – but all I could think of at the time. Apparently they had the same feelings because, in return, they gave me a full-size silvered kukri and, much to my great surprise, my orderly gave me his army-issue kukri, which had been his constant companion throughout his army life.

According to my relieving Indian officer, in a cheerful letter addressed to me at home in England, he had been made welcome by the company. He had been pleasantly surprised by the co-operation and help which he received from all ranks. My orderly, who was still the oldest and wisest rifleman in the company, had not volunteered to serve him: but, apparently, he had recommended another person who was pleased to do so. I was delighted to hear this, because I understood that some of the relieving Indian officers had experienced difficulties in this respect.

I quote below two verses from a poem entitled, *A Gurkha*,

101

written by Lieutenant William Ross-Stewart of the Indian Medical Service and the 1/4th Gurkha Rifles at Gallipoli in 1915. They move me to this day.

> Faith there's little small about him
> Save the question of his size
> From the mountains which begat him
> To the laughter in his eyes.
> His sport, his love, his courage
> Preserve the sterling ring
> Of the simple-minded hillman
> With the manners of a king.
>
> I have seen him broken, mangled
> With his life-tide running low,
> And the tears welled deep within me
> As I watched the last thing go.
> But it triumphed ere it left him
> And stifled every moan,
> 'Twas the little chunk of cheerfulness
> Being gathered to its own.

I think these words describe the personal feelings which are deeply held by those who have had the great privilege to serve with Gurkhas, and also by those in other regiments who have fought alongside them.

When I returned to our regimental centre in Dehra Dun I found the record office in a complete shambles, and my own records were incomplete and incorrect. There was no one available to bring them up-to-date. No arrangements had been made to provide me with a place to sleep. I cut my losses and proceeded direct to Bombay, pending embarkation for the UK.

On arrival home in the United Kingdom, I followed up applications for jobs which I had sent off from Malaya. I turned down firm offers to plant tea in Assam; to join Unilever's groundnut scheme in Africa; and to administer a small oil company in the West Indies. I pursued my application to go up to Oxford University. The government approved an annual grant of £203 and I was allocated provisional places in two colleges for the autumn of 1949. My preference, however, was to join the Colonial Service and be posted to Malaya as soon as possible. Unfortunately, I could not obtain a definite reply from the Colonial Office. C.R. Howitt, a senior official in the Malayan Civil Service and an old family friend, then intervened and said he expected to be the Chief Secretary of the Malayan Union and would like me to become an ADC to the Governor, Sir Edward Gent. Shortly after that, Sir Edward was killed in an air collision. Charles Howitt's reaction was to suggest that I should join the Malayan Police Service at once. On my arrival in Malaya, he would arrange for my transfer as permanent ADC to whomever became the next governor. As I was not looking forward to a fifteen-month wait before going up to university, I decided to fall in with his suggestion.

I have never regretted this decision. Of course I would have liked to have broadened my mind by the study of politics, philosophy and economics – with a bit of luck, I might have obtained a decent degree to help me earn a living. However, the experience I gained during the same period in Malaya certainly broadened my mind, although I must admit it did not seem to have been of much practical assistance twenty years later, when I was forced to adopt completely different careers.

During our friendly discussions, Charles Howitt made it very clear that my duties in Malaya would involve helping to create conditions for the independence of that country from colonial rule. He said that I must not regard service there as a permanent career and thought, perhaps, a five-year period was the maximum I could expect. He put this in writing to my parents, and made the point again to me at one of the further interviews I attended at the Colonial Office. Sadly, his estimates of the time required for the transfer of power were shattered by the Communist Party of Malaya's armed bid for power.

4

Follow after – follow after! We have watered the root
and the bud has come to blossom which ripens soon to fruit.

RUDYARD KIPLING

The British Military Administration (BMA) took over temporarily the reins of government in Malaya following the defeat of Japan in 1945; and was responsible to the Commander-in-Chief South-East Asia Command, Admiral Lord Louis Mountbatten. Meanwhile, the British Government in London wished to grant Malaya a new streamlined constitution from which independence, preferably within the Commonwealth, could gently flow. Unfortunately, the bellicose Communist Party of Malaya had already been legally recognised by the British, although its sole aim was to work for a Communist-dominated Republic of Malaya. This created a political situation which infuriated the loyal Straits Chinese who had been born and educated in Malaya and mystified most of the other inhabitants of Malaya.

Sir Harold MacMichael was despatched to Kuala Lumpur with instructions to negotiate a new political set-up to be called the Malayan Union. On his arrival in Malaya, Sir Harold, at the behest of the Colonial Office, was in a hurry to obtain the agreement of the Rulers of the nine Malayan States to come together with Penang and Province Wellesley, and Malacca to form a single union; which would guarantee the political rights of all races living in the country. He put considerable moral pressure on the Rulers, allowing insufficient time for them to consult among themselves, discuss details with the politicians or indeed to ascertain the wishes of their Malay subjects. Although the Rulers thoroughly disliked the 'MacMichael Treaties', they relied on the good faith of the

British, and reluctantly agreed to the formation of the proposed Malayan Union. They naively signed away their sovereign rights and Malaya became a British colony. All was achieved within Sir Harold's tight schedule. Colonial Office officials in London were delighted.

When they realised the implications, the Malay population became greatly worried that they would be swamped by alien cultures in their own country; especially in the fields of religion, politics, commerce and industry. They complained bitterly that the new constitution took no account of previous treaties with the British, which dated back to the 1870s. Their politicians pointed out that the Malay States had never been British territory: they were under British protection, and the position and authority of the Rulers had never been in question. All had been done in an unseemly rush and the Rulers were wrong to have given in without consulting anyone.

The consequence was that when Sir Edward Gent (introduced as a Malayan affairs expert from the Colonial Office) was installed as the Governor, no Malay Ruler or Malay official attended his ceremonial installation. It was widely reported that, having apologised for not knowing the names of the Rulers, he was told, 'Well, at least we know your name, because it is on every railway station platform in the country.'

Malay politicians got together and formed a new political party under Dato (the title of a Malayan knight) Onn bin Jaafar, called the United Malays National Organisation (UMNO). Its main aim was to persuade the British Government to scrap the unpopular Malayan Union; and to restore the *status ante*, prior to negotiations for complete independence from colonial rule. After much recrimination, but with the personal support of Sir Edward Gent, the Malayan Union was replaced in 1948 by the Federation of Malaya – a British Protectorate comprising the nine Malay States, each retaining the sovereignty of its Ruler, together with Penang and Province Wellesley, and Malacca – to which Sir Edward Gent become the High Commissioner.

The Federation of Malaya became an independent state within the Commonwealth on 31st August 1957. The Federation was enlarged by the accession of Singapore, Sarawak and British North Borneo (later renamed Sabah) to become Malaysia on 16th September 1963. Singapore seceded from Malaysia to become an independent republic within the Commonwealth on 9th August 1965.

My journey back to Malaya started four days before my twenty-third birthday. Edmund Ward, then a partner in Melvin Gollins and Ward, the London architects, drove me in his splendid Riley sports car to London airport on Wednesday 25th August 1948. The take-off was delayed several hours by fog; but it cleared eventually and my last sight of England was Brighton Pavilion which I could see glinting in the evening sun as we sped southward. The plane was a converted Skymaster, and there were sixty of us on board en route for Malaya all packed together like sardines. I sat on three pieces of canvas and leaned back on two narrow strips.

We flew over the fairy lights of Marseille; and later saw the coast of Sardinia by moonlight. Suddenly one of our engines coughed, spluttered and failed. We had to make an emergency landing on Malta and stayed in Valetta for twelve hours while the plane was being repaired. I was lucky enough to find among my companions a knowledgeable senior member of the Palestine Police to take me round Valetta and the ruined castles of the Knights of St John. We left Malta late on Thursday evening and arrived in Damascus for breakfast on Friday. We stopped at Basrah for lunch. As we were about to leave, the repaired engine refused to start; and we had to spend two hours in the sun cramped together without air condition-ing or liquid sustenance, until suddenly it came to life. We landed at Karachi for breakfast on Saturday morning, then Calcutta for lunch, followed by Bangkok for dinner. We stayed six hours in Bangkok to give the crew a rest; I managed to board a bus for a splendid meal on my own in the Oriental Hotel, made famous by Somerset Maugham – no one else had the energy or the will to accompany me! We landed in Tengah airport in Singapore, in time for a late breakfast at Nee Soon Camp where I had stayed for a few days in 1945. It was Sunday 29th August – my birthday – and I began to look forward with great expectations to my new life.

We stayed three days in Nee Soon and I was able to buy the necessities of life. We had been allowed to take only hand baggage with us on the plane. (The Colonial Office delayed sending on my heavy luggage and, after many complaints, it arrived at Port Swettenham via the SS *Denbighshire* in mid-1949.) I sent six food

106

parcels to my parents and my brother, and then searched through the quite thin Singapore telephone directory, to see if I knew anybody. I discovered Bertie Lane, a customs officer who had served with me in the 3/9th Gurkha Rifles. He told me he was married and had a baby; he kindly invited a friend and me to supper on Monday and Tuesday evenings. Their civilised household made life tolerable again after our unpleasant journey from England. We had all suffered physically from the lack of pressure in the cabin of the plane, and many of us had developed severe gumboils. Derek Mole, whom I had known well in the OTS Bangalore, lost several fillings from his teeth and some of us experienced severe earache each time the plane took off and landed.

Most of us went up by train to Kuala Lumpur (KL). On arrival there, we were welcomed by two enormously fat police officers wearing wide shorts and khaki stockings. They carried swagger sticks and looked just like Tweedledum and Tweedledee. They were very friendly and had laid on transport to take us to our quarters. It was then that I discovered our various ranks. I was a cadet assistant superintendent of police. Most of the remainder were European Sergeants (E/Sgts) recruited from the Palestine Police, who had dealt with terrorist activity in Palestine; they were posted on to mainly European-managed rubber plantations and tin mines to organise defence against Communist terrorist attacks.

The origins of Communism in Malaya and Singapore are probably to be found in 1919, with the newly-formed Third International in the Soviet Union, whose aims included the establishment of Communism (Marxism-Leninism) throughout the world. The Communist Party of China (CPC) was formed in 1923. A year later it extended its influence among overseas Chinese living round the Pacific rim. In late 1927, official representatives of the CPC arrived in Singapore from Shanghai and began organising the Nanyang (South Seas) Communist Party. In April 1930, the Nanyang Party convened its Third Representatives' Conference and promptly dissolved itself to form the Communist Party of Malaya (CPM). Its object was to establish a Republic of Malaya and operated, for the time being, under the aegis of the Soviet Far Eastern Bureau of the Comintern based in Shanghai.

The following years saw many ups and downs for the CPM. By 1936 it had organised itself sufficiently to promote severe labour troubles throughout Malaya. The worst of these took place at Batu Arang, an opencast coal mine which supplied fuel to Malaya's railways and power stations. Six thousand strikers overran the property; they celebrated their success by setting up a Workers' Committee to deal with criminals and to settle labour disputes. The army and the police reacted quickly, stormed their way through improvised defences, and restored order to what had become a trial of strength between the Communist Party and the government. It is interesting to note that, eleven years later, shortly after the State of Emergency had been declared in Malaya in 1948, the CPM attacked Batu Arang again; overran its defences, killed five people, attacked the police station and sabotaged much valuable equipment and transport before withdrawing unscathed into the surrounding jungle.

When Japan invaded China in 1936, the CPM received considerable support from the Chinese population in Malaya. In 1939 the Soviet Union's non-aggression pact with Germany resulted in a violent anti-British campaign, organised by the CPM throughout Malaya and Singapore. It was not until June 1941, when Germany launched its attack on the Soviet Union, that the CPM changed its tactics and decided to co-operate with the Malayan Government, and to cease its attacks on the capitalist system. Things changed dramatically yet again, when Japan invaded Malaya in December 1941. The CPM promised the Governors of Singapore and Malaya all-out co-operation against the Japanese; the party mobilised its members to resist the Japanese in the towns and the hinterland of Malaya. Thus the Malayan People's Anti-Japanese Army (MPA JA) came into being.

The Sixth Central Extended Conference of the CPM was held in 1939 and Loi Tuk, alias Mr Wright, a much travelled Annamite from French Indo-China and close friend of Ho Chi Minh, was elected as the party's first Secretary-General. He was a good linguist and an efficient organiser. But he was also an opportunist, whose identity was known to few in the party. He absconded with the party's funds in 1947 and was probably murdered in Thailand later by agents of the Communist Party of Siam.

The Central Committee of the Communist Party of Malaya was shocked to the core by Loi Tuk's unexpected disappearance; they

108

carried out a lengthy investigation led by 27-year-old Wong Man Wah, better known by his alias Chan Peng. The result came as an even greater shock to the party. It became clear that Loi Tuk had cooperated with French Intelligence in Indo-China before he came to Singapore. During the Japanese occupation of Singapore, he sold himself to the Japanese authorities there, betraying virtually the entire Communist Party leadership in Singapore to the Japanese; but 'escaped' arrest himself by fleeing to mainland Malaya. Here, too, he had continued to work assiduously for Japanese Intelligence until his greatest betrayal of all took place on 1st September 1942. A meeting of the Communist Party's Central Committee near Batu Caves, just outside Kuala Lumpur, was interrupted by Japanese soldiers. Twenty senior Communist leaders were killed and many more were captured. At a single stroke, the majority of the party's experienced leaders were removed. Communist Party morale was greatly shaken and the effectiveness of the Malayan People's Anti-Japanese Army was very severely reduced. Chan Peng's report concluded that after the war Loi Tuk had worked for the Malayan Police intelligence service. Chan Peng's detailed report, his youth and his unblemished military record resulted in his own appointment as the new Secretary-General of the party. The party announced that 1st September would be regarded as a day of mourning for the 'Nine-One Martyrs'.

During the British Military Administration the CPM became a legal party and Chan Peng, its new Secretary-General, was made an Honorary Officer of the Most Excellent Order of the British Empire (OBE) The award could not be handed to him personally by the British High Commissioner in Malaya because, by then, he had taken to the jungle and was busily directing the armed revolution against the same Empire.

After the Second World War, the CPM continued as a straightforward Communist Party on well-defined Marxist-Leninist-Stalinist lines; with special notice taken of Comrade Zhadanov's encouragement of liberation movements in South-East Asia, expressed by him during the first meeting of the Cominform at Moscow in 1947. Representatives of the CPM attended the International Communist Conference at Prague in 1947, the Conference of British Empire Communist Parties at London in January 1948 and, in February of the same year, they attended the important

Soviet Union-sponsored Youth Conference of Asian and Australian Communist Parties in Calcutta. No less than sixteen Russian observers attended this conference and Lawrence Sharkey, President of the Communist Party of Australia, was one of the delegates. It is clear that, at this conference, Asian Communist Parties in Burma, Indonesia, Malaya, India and the Philippines were given the green light to go ahead with their own armed struggles in their own way and in their own time, but they were told not to expect material, financial or military support from outside their own countries. This may have been one of the factors which compelled the CPM, later on, to amend its monolithic reliance on Marxism, Leninism and Stalinism, by the substitution of the last 'ism' by Maoism; and a switch from urban war plans to the development of secure rural bases in the countryside.

On 19th June 1948, Sir Edward Gent declared a State of Emergency in the Federation and the Singapore Government followed suit four days later. This belated action was taken after it had become clear to all in Malaya, that the Communist Party was mobilising for an armed struggle. A series of Communist-organised raids and murders were already taking place up and down the country. A prominent headline in the English-language newspaper *Straits Times*, told the High Commissioner, 'Govern or Get Out!' It summed up succinctly the strongly felt feelings of the European, Malay, Chinese and Indian communities.

While the decision to declare a State of Emergency was being agonised over by the colonial government, the Malayan Communist Party had sufficient time to mobilise, and arm, thousands of ex-members of the Malayan People's Anti-Japanese Army. The party also persuaded many educated young men, who had joined the party during the period 1945–48, to take to the jungle. Virtually all these people were Chinese. However, there were small groups of Tamils (mainly trade union activists working on the rubber estates), Malays (mainly from Pahang – many of whom were the descendants of those who took up arms against the British during the Pahang Wars of the late nineteenth century), a handful of Japanese (low-grade deserters from the Japanese Army who had taken to farming in remote rural areas) and a few aboriginal people (mainly from Central Malaya). The terrorists were armed with modern rifles, carbines, handgrenades and some light machine-guns, which had been deliberately hidden away after the end of the Japanese occupation in 1945.

The Communist Party's general plan was to look inwards, and create 'liberated areas' deep in the jungle, from which they could establish support organisations in the countryside. Once these were working successfully, the next step would be to look outwards and return to the towns, and organise a programme of subversion in the schools, trade unions and political parties. The eventual aim was to take over the country, and form a republic of Malaya, either directly by military means, or by way of a 'united front' of willing political parties.

This was all very well in theory, especially as the party's Central Committee knew they could not rely on outside military support from Russia, China or elsewhere. Moreover, it soon became manifestly clear that they had grossly overestimated the sympathy and practical support of the Malayan public, which had suffered hugely from both Communist and Japanese atrocities during, and immediately after, the Japanese occupation of Malaya. The common people were not prepared to underwrite an armed struggle against a colonial government, which was already talking about the political rights of all races. There was no political support from Malays, the urban Chinese were not interested and the labour forces remained largely indifferent.

When the Malayan Communist Party took to the jungle, it severed nearly all its communications with the outside world, and abandoned its political work in favour of piecemeal Shangri-Las in the so-called liberation areas. The mental processes of its political leaders soon began to cloud over, as intellectual life in the jungle became lonely, blinkered and out of touch with what was taking place in the world outside. Nevertheless the armed struggle policy continued for three long years.

I was in a somewhat peculiar position, having been recruited originally by C.R. Howitt, the Acting Chief Secretary, as ADC to Sir Edward Gent, the High Commissioner. Unfortunately he had been killed a few months before in an air collision over London airport, and I had drifted into the Malayan Police Service in August 1948 as an alternative to a recently offered place at Oxford

University for October 1949. The idea was that I would still be an ADC; but would be on secondment from the Malayan Police Service. The day after my arrival in Kuala Lumpur, I purchased a decent tropical suit, run up for me in one day by a Chinese tailor; and I presented myself to Sir Henry Newboult, the Acting High Commissioner. We talked for an hour or so, and got on very well; but I was somewhat dismayed at his insistence that I should play tennis every day and escort various females to parties in the evening. This was at a time when I knew that the few friends I had in Malaya would be up to their necks fighting the Communist Emergency. I felt that, with my army experience, I was probably of more value supporting them; rather than socialising among the fleshpots of Kuala Lumpur and Singapore. Honour was saved when it was decided that a knowledge of the Malay language would be a requirement of the appointment and, of course, I could not speak Malay at that time.

The lowest permanent unit in the Malayan Police Service was the Police Station, usually comprising about ten men under a corporal or a sergeant. Then came the District which had between five to ten Stations, followed by the Circle with up to three Districts, then came the State (e.g. Perak or Selangor) with three or four Circles. Superimposed on all these were the CID, the Special Branch, the Special Constabulary, the Auxiliary Police and police units such as jungle squads and, later on, jungle companies.

Next day, 2nd September 1948, I was posted to Kuala Lumpur North (which included a large area of the North Selangor country-side) as assistant officer in charge of the police district. I was delighted to discover that my boss was to be Solly Graham. Solly was a pre-war officer and one of the youngest prisoners of war sent by the Japanese to build the Thai-Burma railway. Unlike so many older officers, who had suffered grievously under the Japanese, he was energetic, enthusiastic, helpful, strongly opinionated and great fun. Above all, he knew the country well, spoke the language and was experienced in all sorts of exotic pursuits. Other ex-Gurkha Brigade officers in Selangor State were Duggie Farnbank, Derek Mole and Ted Rainford. Len Comber, whose army group photograph was displayed for several years in a Chinese photographer's shop in Batu Road, was an ex-Indian Army officer; he was our co-operative next door neighbour in KL South. He later married Han Su Yin, the author of *Love is a Many Splendoured Thing* and many other books. After leaving the service, Len became a distinguished academic and a successful author himself.

I was allocated a room in the Venning Road mess, a wooden colonial building with a large dining room and an adjoining ante-room. There were several roomy bedrooms on both sides flanked by two long corridors. A number of small bungalows on the estate were occupied by senior people, one of whom was my overall boss, H.G. Beverley – 'Bev'. He had also been a prisoner of war of the Japanese and had been very ill, but he had made a complete recovery and was full of energy and wisdom. Before the war, he was at RAF Cranwell and went on to train as a pilot. Unfortunately, he told me, he crashed so many aeroplanes he was asked to leave and, not knowing what else to do, he joined the Colonial Service. His hobby was building model aeroplanes. He had ginger hair, laughing eyes and a huge old-fashioned ginger moustache. When I first met him officially in the office, all he said to me was, 'I want a little more order and a little less law in this place. Solly Graham is my best officer, go and learn from him. I'll see you in the bar at seven.' This was to become the first of many informal and enjoyable chats with him. Bev had recently conducted a most distinguished, brave and successful operation against the armed Green Mountain secret society gang: he treasured a local press photograph showing him, carbine in hand, pointing to a dead terrorist who was still clutching a pistol and saying, 'That one was mine!' Bev had a red MG and usually was accompanied, off duty, by a gorgeous blonde.

My pay in those early days was very meagre. The Colonial Office had omitted to give me any allowance for war service and I was on the second from bottom rung of the incremental scale. Brother officers, with less service and therefore junior to me, had been given larger salaries and I felt put out by this. I was told the reason was that I had been appointed ADC, and I was expected to qualify for all sorts of perks. On Bev's advice, I complained to the Malayan Establishment Officer and eventually I was given the correct salary, although it was not backdated. Things were made worse in a way, because I needed a car in order to carry out my duties; and I did not have a civilian driving licence. Nevertheless, I bought a brand new Austin A40 for £450, funded generously by an interest-free government loan repayable monthly over three years. I passed my driving test at the second attempt, having rammed a bullock cart on my first. I discovered that I could be paid seventy dollars a month to recruit an orderly with the rank of Emergency police constable; so I asked the mess sergeant to find me someone. He produced a group of hopefuls, from whom I chose Abdullah. He was the oldest of the bunch and had himself been a forced worker on the Siamese death railway. He was a Kelantan Malay with a light skin, a happy disposition and was married with two beautiful children. He and his wife were very intelligent, and wanted to learn English, which suited all of us as I needed to practise my Malay. I did not have enough spare money to join any of the four KL clubs so I took my evening meals in the mess, or they were left in my room when I was late.

The mess was situated among tall trees in the boughs of which perched many longtailed nightjars (the Latin name is *caprimulgus macrurus bimaculatus*). The kampong Malays called these birds by a variety of names of which the most common was *burong malas* (lazy bird) because they slept all day. They would glide down to earth in the evenings and sit on the roads where their unblinking eyes would shine orange-red, reflecting the lights of approaching cars, remaining there until the very last moment, then escaping just in time to avoid certain death. They would become particularly vocal on clear moonlight nights, emitting a loud tock tock noise, hence their onomatopoeic name of tock tock bird. My European colleagues found the tocks very irritating; but Abdullah and the other Malay orderlies took much pleasure in gambling on the number of tocks a bird would make without a break. I preferred to play a kind of dab-cricket, scoring imaginary runs in test matches between England and Australia (uninterrupted tocks were the runs: a batsman was out each time there was a pause between the tocks). I would fall asleep long before my imaginary game could be completed. The tock tocks of these birds haunted me throughout my life in Malaya and they have played a significant part in my imagination ever since.

An amusing incident occurred at this time. Bev complained to some of us that a certain officer was entertaining a female in the mess late at night; the noise of her taxi turning in the drive on her arrival and departure kept him awake. He asked us to do something about it, but not to cause a fuss. After several drinks at the bar, we purchased a pair of Chinese slippers, and placed them one night on the verandah outside the culprit's bedroom. Sure enough that evening a taxi drew up, a shadowy figure emerged, climbed the steps of the verandah and clip-clopped towards the bedroom door. Here the clip-clopping stopped. A short silence was broken by an angry sigh followed by the tinkles of broken glass as first one slipper, and then the other, were hurled through her paramour's window. A faster, and very determined, clip-clopping reached our expectant ears as she retraced her steps. The returning taxi was caught just in time and she disappeared into the night, and that was that.

Exams in law and the Malay language had to be passed as early as possible so I engaged a *munshi* (teacher) to teach me Malay and its *jawi* script. I was helped quite considerably with the script, because I had already passed my three Urdu exams in army days and had a good working knowledge of the same script – a form of Arabic. This turned out be a great bonus because, somewhat cheekily, I was able to write my exam papers in jawi script, instead of Romanised Malay: I am sure this gave me a few extra marks with the examiners. Law was mainly a question of reading manuals on the penal code, the criminal procedure code and a long list of relevant enactments. My duties took me into court from time to time, where the judges were very fair to me, as well as to the accused persons.

After a month, Solly Graham was appointed ADC to Sir Henry Gurney, the newly arrived High Commissioner: Sir Alec Newboult reverted to being his deputy, or chief secretary, and I became OCPD KL North. Soon after his arrival, Sir Henry called me up for lunch, and said he would like me to be an honorary extra ADC to serve on duty from time to time, if I was willing and free. Thus I went to King's House, on the King's business, occasionally until October 1951, when Sir Henry was ambushed and murdered by Communist terrorists on his way to Fraser's Hill in Central Malaya.

As soon as Solly became the Governor's ADC, he moved into King's House. I took over his rooms in a large house at the top of Bluff road, in the centre of KL, overlooking the *padang* (a large area of grass between the Secretariat and the 'Dog' club). I shared a Chinese cook with Jack Gladwell, a former London policeman, who was in command of the KL 'flying squad', which had been hurriedly put together to deal with Communist and militant secret society gangs. They considered themselves rather élite, and had been given most of the automatic weapons and modern transport available to the police at that time. They were dressed in smart khaki uniforms and Jack drove himself around KL in a yellow jeep. Jack, aged forty-one, was soon to marry the Chinese lady with whom he was living. They were very approachable and we became good friends. Upstairs was occupied by Christine and Douggie Weir, complete with newly-born baby.

A week or two before I arrived in Kuala Lumpur, Solly Graham was permitted to recruit fifty young men from the regular police service to form his own Kuala Lumpur North anti-bandit squad. It comprised twenty Malays, ten Punjabi Muslims, ten Sikhs, five Chinese detectives and five Tamils – three of the latter were licensed dog-shooters. The creation of an anti-bandit squad, from the ranks of the regular police, was a unique thing to do. Their average age was twenty-two, and only ten were married men. Fortunately, I already spoke Urdu/Punjabi and I was learning Malay fast. All members of the squad could speak Malay and a little English, but not much. Getting to know them and keeping them busy, and out of mischief in quiet periods, was not easy. My day-to-day police work had to continue. I decided to train up junior leaders and delegate to them much of the routine work. I chose Inspector Kartar Singh as my second-in-command, and I appointed a Malay sergeant as platoon commander and four corporals as section leaders – a Malay, a Chinese, a Punjabi Muslim and a Sikh. With the agreement of all concerned, the sections were multiracial and, wherever possible, friends could serve alongside each other. They mixed very well and we had no racial problems of any kind.

Unforeseen problems arose as we trained together and took part in operations. A number of the younger men, who had suffered from malnutrition during the Japanese occupation, had poor eyesight and failed my weapon training requirements, and had to be replaced. One or two others developed allergies and skin complaints which made them itch and move about in ambush positions. They had to go too. Smoking on patrol was banned. Snoring at night was a cardinal sin, not only for members of the squad, but also for any accompanying 'informer', guide, member of the security forces or journalist. All snorers were sent home. There was also a question of being accused by the public of stealing, looting etc. while searching houses in the city, or squatter huts in the countryside. To deal with this, all cash had to be left at home and the men had to search each other at random before and after operations.

The only person not to be searched was me. This searching was not at all popular at first, but it was soon accepted.

When I took them over they too were dressed in khaki and travelled around in ancient soft-skinned ex-military vans. My immediate boss, whose title was the Officer Superintending the Police Circle (OSPC), was H.J. Spink, a traditional Malayan police officer, whose father had also been in the police service in the Federated Malay States. I nicknamed him Daddy Spink. He was a very good policeman, an extremely kind man, a stickler for method and followed the laws of the land to the letter. Moreover, he had a distinguished record as a prisoner of war under the Japanese and was one of Kuala Lumpur's most respected citizens. The trouble was he did not go along with Bev's theory of 'a little more order and a little less law'; and he had no time for Solly Graham's involvement with the Emergency. Daddy was a great paper man and, because I spent so much time out of the office, he was prone to issue polite little notes, which started off, 'I think you should . . .', and 'What have you done about . . .?' As the Emergency situation in and around Kuala Lumpur got worse, so the Spinkers became more prolific and found themselves impaled upon a spike, which I had created for the purpose, on my desk.

On one such occasion, he complained bitterly about my intention to dress the jungle squad in jungle green, and to train them in the use of modern automatic weapons, e.g. Bren guns and Sten guns, using up-to-date ammunition. He took his complaint through Bev to the Deputy Commissioner. All three came to my office, curious to know what was going on. I asked for a day's grace to mount a demonstration in the nearby jungle; on the following day, I placed men in khaki alongside men in jungle green, and asked the Deputy Commissioner which man was easier to distinguish. I also arranged two mock ambushes, at very short range, using rifles for one (about ten rounds fired as single shots which resulted in only one imaginary dead 'bandit'); and using automatic weapons for the other (about a hundred rounds fired and many more dead 'bandits'). These simple demonstrations were effective and that is one reason why operational police, after proper training, were issued with automatic weapons. However, a difficulty arose because the police stores were empty and I was obliged to go hunting. I already knew most of the Gurkha units in Malaya, which had been transferred to the British Army after India had achieved independence. Some of these were based in military camps near Kuala Lumpur, and I knew they were greatly under strength. For some reason, unknown to me at this time, very few serving Gurkhas in the battalions which had been transferred to the British Army had volunteered to serve His Majesty. This meant that these new battalions had to recruit and train on a large scale, and were unlikely to be fully operation for a long time.

I begged for help. They kindly gave me all the jungle green uniform and equipment that I needed. I also discovered an embryo Gurkha Signals unit in a camp in Kuala Lumpur. Its commanding officer had been given a large amount of unissued arms and ammunition for safe keeping. I signed my name away again and returned with two lorry-loads of Bren guns, Sten guns and a goodly supply of modern ammunition (1944 vintage).

All this was very popular with the men and we trained together, whenever the Spinkers were reduced to an acceptable number. I also found a helpful American tin miner, Norman Cleaveland of Pacific Tin, who was prepared to fix light armour plating to protect the drivers' cabs and engines of our trucks. The plating was later extended to spread the weight, and give two feet of protection to the occupants in the back. This armour plating saved many lives in the early days of the Emergency, when we were occasionally shot at while answering calls for help. Most unfortunately for me, one of my vehicles overturned; the driver and passengers, including me, escaped serious injury. I was deemed financially responsible, despite a strong defence mounted by Daddy Spink, Bev and Norman. The mining company's experts said that the added weight on the vehicle had been evenly balanced. I produced written evidence to show that the truck had been passed as previously roadworthy by the Registrar and Inspector of Motor Vehicles, both before and immediately after the incident. Anyway, with Bev's support, I refused to accept financial responsibility. The accounting officer, who was a senior official from the Malayan Civil Service attached to the police, was evidently not confident enough to institute disciplinary proceedings. I am pleased to say that my 'accident file' was destroyed nine years later by the Malay Commissioner of Police when Malaya achieved independence in 1957.

In these early days of the Emergency, we always referred to terrorists as 'bandits' and it was much later that the official term Communist terrorists, or CTs for short, came into general use.

Peter Wright Nooth, a keen young former army officer, who became my Assistant OCPD Kuala Lumpur North, has this to say of his early days during the Emergency in Malaya.

'Tim Hatton, ex-Gurkhas, was the OCPD. He spent most of his time running a ferocious-looking jungle squad and hunting for 'bandits' (or, as they were called later, Communist terrorists) in the jungles north of Kuala Lumpur and left the policing side to me . . . Tim's jungle squad had to be seen to be believed, it consisted of about 30 Malay and Indian policemen dressed in jungle green and armed to the teeth, brandishing rifles, Sten guns and Bren guns with hand grenades hanging from their belts. Every now and then one of the section leaders, a large and imposing Sikh sergeant, would march into the office which Tim and I shared, give a butt salute on his Sten gun, receive instructions from Tim, shout "Sahib" and march out. Then chaos ensued as Tim and the jungle squad piled into their vehicles and went roaring out of the station compound.'

The Emergency took over our lives. I was kept extremely busy, not only reacting to terrorist incidents as they occurred, but also trying positively to prevent trouble by developing tactical intelligence for use by our anti-bandit squad and the military. In the early days, trained army units were few and far between and it was only after several weeks that we were able to call upon the 2nd Battalion the Scots Guards and the 4th Hussars. Before that, the Malayan Police Service had many exciting adventures as the Communists attempted to create what they were pleased to call 'liberation areas' in the remoter parts of Central Malaya. The Communist Party of Malaya organised its armed forces into regiments, companies, platoons and armed work forces based generally on each of the Malay States, Penang and Province Wellesley, and Malacca. These armed units were entirely dependent on the Party's permanent district and branch organisations, situated inside the jungle, who were in direct contact with their outside civilian organisations. The latter were called the *Min Yuen* (or People's Army) which was responsible for supplying food, money, recruits and local intelligence to the Communist armed units inside the jungle. [See Diagram 1 on page 120]

Former members of the Malayan People's Anti-Japanese Army and the recently banned Communist Party, formed the nucleus of the Malayan People's Anti-British Army, later to be called, in a

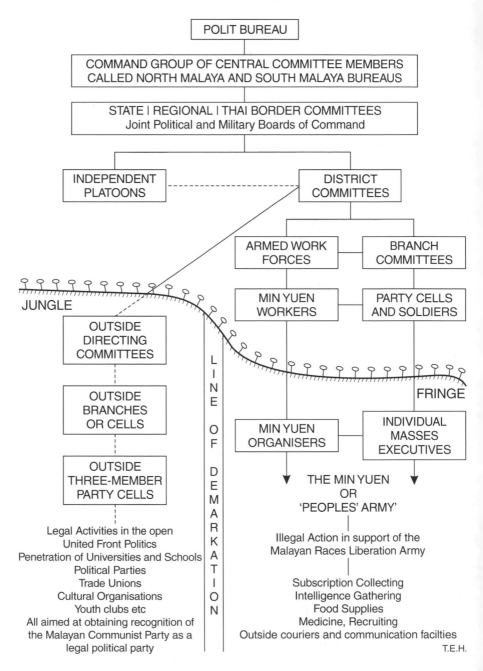

DIAGRAM 1

Simplified structure of the Malayan Communist Party during the Emergency 1948–1960

POLIT BUREAU

COMMAND GROUP OF CENTRAL COMMITTEE MEMBERS
CALLED NORTH MALAYA AND SOUTH MALAYA BUREAUS

STATE | REGIONAL | THAI BORDER COMMITTEES
Joint Political and Military Boards of Command

INDEPENDENT PLATOONS

DISTRICT COMMITTEES

ARMED WORK FORCES

BRANCH COMMITTEES

MIN YUEN WORKERS

PARTY CELLS AND SOLDIERS

JUNGLE

OUTSIDE DIRECTING COMMITTEES

OUTSIDE BRANCHES OR CELLS

OUTSIDE THREE-MEMBER PARTY CELLS

LINE OF DEMARKATION

FRINGE

MIN YUEN ORGANISERS

INDIVIDUAL MASSES EXECUTIVES

THE MIN YUEN
OR
'PEOPLES' ARMY'

Legal Activities in the open
United Front Politics
Penetration of Universities and Schools
Political Parties
Trade Unions
Cultural Organisations
Youth clubs etc
All aimed at obtaining recognition of
the Malayan Communist Party as a
legal political party

Illegal Action in support of the
Malayan Races Liberation Army

Subscription Collecting
Intelligence Gathering
Food Supplies
Medicine, Recruiting
Outside couriers and communication facilties

T.E.H.

120

vain attempt to attract support from the Malay and Indian communities, the Malayan Races Liberation Army. Of course, these forces in the jungle caused the government great concern, in case they should launch a concerted attack on the main towns – especially Kuala Lumpur – where our forces were in penny packets under different commanders. On the other hand, it provided some of us with interesting opportunities to exploit. Our operational intelligence at that time was surprisingly productive, but entirely short-term, aimed at breaking up large groups of terrorists in jungle camps. Often we were able to send informers straight into these camps as recruits to work for us; and sometimes disillusioned recruits (surrendered enemy personnel or SEPs as they were soon to be called) would escape, and come to us with operational information.

A minor example of this occurred on a Saturday night just as I was preparing to go as an invited guest to the Selangor Club. A British Army lieutenant from the Royal Engineers was put through to me by the telephone exchange, and reported that his Chinese *char wallah* (tea person) had information of a bandit meeting place: he wanted to lead the security forces to attack it. I was not very impressed, and thought it might be a trick, but I turned out the stand-by section of my anti-bandit squad and two Chinese detectives. We met up with the lieutenant at a nearby crossroads and we debriefed the char wallah. He turned out to be a member of the MPAJA, who had been called up to rejoin the terrorists in the jungle: his motives were clearly short-term and financial. Although I decided to believe him, I was very conscious that it might prove to be a trap. Unfortunately. the meeting place with his comrades was in a Chinese village in KL South District. I had to waste time on a Saturday evening obtaining clearance from Len Comber to go into his area (luckily, I found him sitting very comfortably in the Venning Road mess).

It was dark. As we entered the village dogs started to bark, and I began to wonder if we were going to find anyone at home. The char wallah was clearly disappointed with our progress and when we arrived at the large *attap* hut, where the meeting was supposed to take place, he went to pieces and lost his voice. We surrounded the house and on breaking down the door we were confronted by a Chinese male, who seemed surprised and anxious, but no one else appeared to be around. I was starting to regret my missed

121

dinner in the club, when one of my detectives shouted in English, 'Look out! There's a man on the roof and he has a grenade on his belt!' For some reason no one moved. I reacted by asking the detective to tell the man to climb down and that, if he made any attempt to grab his grenade, he would be shot immediately. This was accompanied by a nervous clicking of safety catches on the ground. The man climbed down carefully and was shaking all over. I arrested him, together with the person we found when we entered. I arranged to meet the char wallah at a safe place later, thanked the lieutenant, and returned to the fleshpots of KL via High Street Police Station where we handed over our two prisoners for interrogation.

Next morning, Sunday, I received a telephone call from an excited Bev to say that the OC Detectives, who was a notorious storyteller, had arrested an armed Central Committee Member of the Malayan Communist Party. His Chinese detective sub-inspector had identified him as the CPM's State Committee Secretary for Trengganu State on the east coast, who had been lying up in Kuala Lumpur, pending the arrival of a jungle courier to take him back to Trengganu. A young man, arrested with him, was his bodyguard, and the house they were hiding in was a former Anti-Japanese Army office. I was able to say with some glee that, whatever the OC Detectives may have said, he had not been involved. Nevertheless, I felt a little embarrassed to report that the arrests had actually been made by us on the information of the British Army lieutenant and his erstwhile char wallah. Although the prisoners had little tactical information to give, and we were unable to persuade them to continue their journey back to Trengganu and work for us; they proved extremely helpful over several years. I think that they were the first captured terrorists to be reclassified by the legal authorities as having surrendered.

I spent the next three months calling on all the estates and mines in KL North District and bought a pedigree Scots terrier puppy, called George, to keep me company at home and in the office. I rearranged my Malay lessons for 6.00 till 8.00 a.m. and read my law books whenever I had spare time. I attended to my police work, which included a post-mortem (never again!), prosecuted minor offences in court, and danced the night away with taxi dancers (ladies who sat in chairs, around the side of the dance floor, waiting to be hired for a dance) in the Happy World and the

Eastern Hotel. Here the senior hostess was an elderly Chinese dancer, known as the Japanese Flower Lady – an exotic relict of the recent past – who was presented with a bunch of flowers at the beginning of every evening session by an anonymous admirer. Above all, I continued to be heavily involved in the Emergency. Peter Wright Nooth first saw action with us when I left him in charge of an ambush position in the jungle, as part of a complicated series of ambushes around the Sungei Buloh Forest Reserve. My detectives had reported a reorganisation of terrorist forces; and we were able to forecast their possible movements from an old MPAJA-annotated map, which we had found during a previous raid on a house in nearby Ampang village. Ambushes were laid around the Sungei Buloh Leper Settlement and in other areas south of Rawang, eighteen miles to the north. Although Peter's ambush did not achieve anything, it scared the life out of the approaching terrorists. I warned Duggie Farnbank in Rawang, using the Gurkhali language on the telephone, that up to eight terrorists had left Peter, retreating helter-skelter northwards. Duggie joined one of his ambush parties and, next day, killed three armed terrorists, recovering a pistol, two hand grenades, two rifles and some ammunition.

Duggie Farnbank himself was wounded on 11th December 1948 in a terrorist ambush, while driving his red Morgan sports car in the Kanching Pass north of Kuala Lumpur. I took out my whole squad, less one section, and drove straight to the Sungei Buloh Leper Settlement. Here we debussed and started off through the jungle over Dog's Head Mountain (Kow Thau Sun is its Chinese name, which became so familiar to me over the next year) to see if I could cut off the terrorists. We found a recently evacuated camp from which, it seemed, they had laid the ambush. I laid a counter-ambush. In the middle of the night, I saw the flashing of a torchlight snaking up the mountain track. Fortunately, none of us got over-excited. When it arrived a few feet away, we opened fire at short range. I was able to visit Duggie in hospital late next evening to say that we had killed the leader of his ambush, and we had recovered a silver-plated pistol. We found out later that the ambush of Duggie in his red sports car had been deliberately planned and that afterwards the ambush party had scattered. fearing a major follow-up from the security forces.

I also discovered that the lilies I had sent for the funeral of a

European tin miner, killed in nearby Serendah, had been sent to Duggie's room; the flowers I had ordered for Duggie had been sent to the miner's funeral. Duggie had woken up after the operation to remove the bullet from his leg, to find himself surrounded by white lilies and, for a moment, he thought he had died and his nurses were angels and he was in heaven!

On Christmas Day 1948, I was invited to lunch by Mr and Mrs Neville Godwin and had a wonderful relaxing time. We heard the King's speech clearly and I returned home late. Next day, two Chinese informers came to see me and reported that twenty armed Communist terrorists – the Gombak Armed Work Force – had arranged to meet villagers the following evening near a rubber estate managed by Peter Lucy. Peter himself rang up an hour later to say he had received similar information. I took two sections of the anti-bandit squad and set up a temporary camp in the jungle nearby. It rained all night and through the next day. We were close to the Kuala Lumpur-Bentong road, and could hear cars and lorries going over a wooden bridge, creating a resounding bumpty-bump noise and preventing us from sleeping. Later that evening and with complete surprise, we raided the village hall and arrested twenty Chinese males. They were all unarmed. On interrogation, it turned out that they were indeed the complete Armed Work Force on a recruiting mission among Peter Lucy's rubber tappers. Next day, the legal authorities allowed me to do a deal with them and, eventually, we recovered all their arms and uniforms hidden in a small cave nearby. Most of them proved co-operative, and were drafted into *hantu* or 'ghost' groups, dressed as Communist terrorists, to operate most successfully against specific targets in the jungle.

A summary of our efforts with the Kuala Lumpur North anti-bandit squad over a period of four months from September to December 1948, shows that we contacted the terrorists 35 times on our own initiative and without military support. We killed 22 armed men; captured 9 armed men and 6 other terrorists wearing MRLA uniforms, plus the 20 men from the Gombak Armed Work Force and all their weapons. We also recovered a Lewis gun, 22 rifles, 19 pistols, a Tommy gun, a carbine, two Japanese machine-guns and 4,700 rounds of ammunition. I kept the carbine, which had a folding butt, for myself.

Duggie had to be replaced. I was posted to Rawang as OCPD

and Peter Wright Nooth took over from me in KL North District. Peter was wounded by a terrorist bullet a short time later; but he soon recovered and earned for himself the nickname 'Ulu' (jungle), because of his successful work chasing bandits in the jungle. Rawang District was twenty miles north of Kuala Lumpur astride the main north-south road through Malaya. Batu Arang, which had been overrun by Communist terrorists in the early days of the Emergency, was a large opencast coal mine a few miles to the west and was part of my new district. There were also many European-managed rubber estates and tin mines. The Scots Guards, commanded by Lieutenant Colonel Sanderson, were based in Batu Arang with companies out on nearby estates; the 4th Hussars were based near KL under 'Colonel Henry', and the Coldstream Guards under Lieutenant Colonel Fitzgeorge Balfour were soon to take over responsibility for North Selangor and South Perak. As these troops finished their training and joined us in the war against terrorism, we learned to work together and many friendships developed between the young men in my squad, and the British soldiers.

Trouble started again soon after my arrival. On a routine patrol, late one evening and in darkness, we clashed with terrorists intent on burning down Serendah railway station. We killed two of them, both armed with rifles. Two hours later the terrorists came into Rawang town, close to where I lived. A mixed patrol of my jungle squad, and Right Flank company of the Scots Guards under Major Fane Gladwin, killed one of them and wounded and captured another. On the evening of the same day, I received an unwelcome visit from the OC Detectives Kuala Lumpur. He had travelled up in one of three small armoured cars available to the Selangor police. Having announced his intention to go for a drink, he walked down to the town leaving me to clear up some accumulated paperwork.

Suddenly, my ancient telephone made its usual gurgling sound – it was the officer-in-charge of Serendah police station, who reported in Malay that terrorists had burned down the Serendah Boys' Home, run by Mr Blake on behalf of The Save the Children Fund. I commandeered the armoured car and its driver and off we went the five miles to Serendah. There was nothing we could do for poor Blake. He had been murdered in cold blood by a passing group of Communist terrorists just as he was unloading Christmas presents for his charges. All I could do was to rescue the Fund's minibus from a locked garage beside the burning house. It was too dark to organise a follow-up; I arranged for the local police station wives to help look after the children and I returned home to find the uninvited OC Detectives snoring loudly in my bed! When I visited Duggie in hospital, the following weekend, he was very cross to hear the news, because, he said, the Fund had repeatedly refused police protection and Mr Blake had been a personal friend of his.

At about that time, another former army officer joined me as Assistant OCPD. On his very first patrol, he came across an armed party of terrorists confronting him on a jungle track. They threw a hand grenade at him, but it exploded without hurting anyone. His patrol killed one of the terrorists who was armed with a loaded Luger pistol. This officer was later posted to South Perak, where he was said to have arrested and tortured a terrorist suspect. The case was taken to court and he was found guilty and sent to Kuala Lumpur's Pudu Jail for a long term of imprisonment. I had found him to be a gentle, mild and kindly person . . .

Colonel Sanderson of the Scots Guards and his officers were a great help to me and extremely good company. I had never come across the Guards Brigade before. They played hard, worked hard and were devoted to fighting the Emergency. I dare to think they learned a great deal from us about counter-terrorist work in a very short time after their arrival. The battalion's discipline was far stronger than anything I had seen before in the British Army. If an officer made a mistake, he would be sent back to England in disgrace. The men became proficient in jungle warfare and were very fit and enthusiastic. The Colonel himself was a real ball of fire and visited me frequently at home in Rawang and later in Kuala Selangor; in return, I became a temporary member of their officers' mess in Batu Arang and visited the company commanders outstation. Police and army had excellent personal relationships based on their help and support for Balwant Singh, my station inspector in Batu Arang, whom they nicknamed 'Balloon Singh', because of his shape and irrepressible sense of humour. Batu Arang coal mine was managed by Mr Warmington who, quite naturally, insisted on a strong defensive posture and deplored my attempts to carry out planned offensive patrols. 'Don't disturb the hornets,' was his war cry.

Early in January 1949, I was ambushed alone walking from my house down to the police station. I was struck by a tommy-gun bullet, which singed my leg on its way through my trousers. Inspector Kartar Singh, my second-in-command of the anti-bandit squad, was walking up the overgrown road to meet me. We both opened fire and nearly shot one another. We took pot-shots at the sniper as he scooted through the *lallang* (long grass) into the jungle leaving behind his pack and four spent cartridge cases. Inside the pack we found a rolled slip (letter) from a local Communist leader instructing his armed cell of three people to murder me and two of my detectives. One of the latter, a particularly brave man and a practising Roman Catholic with eight children, was murdered six months later on a remote railway station while on leave.

In mid-January 1949, I was contacted by Mr Park, formally of Force 136, who had been dropped behind the Japanese lines during the war. He wished to visit his old camp where he had lived before the Japanese surrendered. We found it near the edge of the Kanching Pass, on a col between the main range and a large rocky limestone outcrop. We retrieved the remains of his Force 136 wireless set. He showed me the cairn which had been built in 1942 over the grave of a British Army sergeant, nicknamed by the Anti-Japanese Army guerrillas 'Markus' after Karl Marx, because he had a fiery red beard.

In order to ensure better communication between those of us on the ground, and others who ran the operations rooms, a number of civilian liaison officers were appointed. One of these was Commander Kerrans RN who asked to be attached to me. One day he accompanied us on patrol in the jungle off the Kanching Pass. Shortly after we left, I received a signal on my 48 wireless set requesting him to go back to KL immediately. I took him to the main road, thumbed down a Chinese lorry and put him on board. That was the last time I saw him. He flew to China, took command of HMS *Amethyst* and sailed down the Yangtse river past the Communist Chinese artillery positions to the safety of the open sea and won a well-deserved DSO. He later became an MP.

On 25th January 1949, the terrorists attacked a group of European tin miners in Serendah, killing Messrs Green and Barbour and a special constable. Another constable was wounded and all their weapons were taken. Curiously enough, one of these bandits surrendered the next evening personally to me in my house at

127

Rawang, carrying a rifle and a primed hand grenade. He offered to take us back to his occupied camp. Unfortunately, one of the European civilian liaison officers who was having supper with me on his way to Kuala Lumpur, leaked this out to the RAF. Bev told me that we had to wait until the camp had been bombed from the air, and he asked me to try and obtain a six-figure map reference of the camp. Time was of the essence; there was no time to mount a photo-reconnaissance and wait for an interpretation of the results, so I decided to see whether or not I could locate the camp on the ground, using the informant and two detectives. This was agreed with Bev, and we discovered the camp quite easily on a bluff east of the main KL-Ipoh road. We could hear domestic noises coming from the camp in the distance; so we knew it was occupied. Because of the terrain, I was able to take only one reliable bearing with my compass and, to obtain an accurate visual sighting on Bev's requested six-figure map reference, I took off my white underpants and hung them on a tree, some five hundred yards away from the camp overlooking tin tailings below, in sight of the road, and visible from the air. On hindsight, I was to wish I had gone straight in with my anti-bandit squad and not listened to the honeyed voices of the RAF. As it happened, at dawn the next day, the RAF decided to fly a dummy run over the camp: the occupants took flight, the bombs were dropped a few minutes later on a large, hurriedly evacuated camp, complete with flagstaff and parade ground. The informant was distraught, I was distraught and members of my squad were distraught. Worse still, my pants were left hanging on the tree, and I was to glare at them every time I motored by over the next five years.

One day, I was told that Sir Henry Gurney, His Excellency the High Commissioner, wished to accompany a police patrol and see for himself how the other half lived. He would be kitted out with a pistol, which I was assured he could handle, and would wear jungle green. It would be my responsibility to lay it on. Bev had approved. His own staff at King's House, with one exception, had not been told. We were to meet in an abandoned smoke-house near Kepong, at an agreed time and date. This was a great surprise; but on hindsight I should have refused to do it. We duly met. The great man was in boyish spirits. He wore an immaculate jungle green uniform and took his place, well protected by members of my patrol. I chose to visit a typical squatter area about five miles away, approaching it via logging tracks through the jungle. My plan was to raid an empty house on the jungle edge which we knew was occasionally used by the terrorists as a postbox. The patrol proceeded normally and we had a pre-planned break for tea. This enabled me to send out a recce party to locate the hut. When we approached it, I sent some of us to the left to enter the house and others to the right to cover the entry. My party with H.E. would join the others, if all was well. Indeed it was, though nothing was found and no one was at home. On our arrival at the house, Kartar Singh asked, 'Where is H.E.?' and I replied, 'I thought he was with you.' No H.E. No one knew where he was. Oh calamity! Suddenly we heard plaintive cries coming from the bowels of the earth; and, on investigation, we discovered His Majesty's crestfallen representative sloshing around in mud at the bottom of a ten-foot-deep pig trap. We rescued him, dusted him down, or rather dried him off, and his high spirits quickly returned. I omitted to tell him that pig traps usually had *panjies*, sharpened bamboo spikes, at the bottom. Having indulged in a picnic lunch, we escorted him back to the main road where he changed into civilian clothes and I drove him back to King's House. His escapade remained a secret.

One of the major lessons I learnt in jungle warfare, was to travel light and travel fast. Many of the army units with whom we worked, in the early part of the Emergency in Malaya, carried far too much on their backs. It made them tired, and slowed down their reactions when most needed. Contacts with the enemy were usually in poor visibility and at short range: few shots could be fired with any degree of accuracy at sighted targets; and it was usually over in a few seconds. Stand-up 'battles' were few. We much preferred carbines to .303 rifles; light Sten guns to heavier Bren guns, best of all, was the Austen gun which we were given to test. It suited us well because it fired silent shots and did not give our positions away. Although we gave it an enthusiastic report, we never saw Austen guns again.

On 19th February, I was transferred to Kuala Selangor, the next-door district from Rawang. It shared the same Emergency problems; however, my house was in a comparatively safe area some miles away from the nearest bandit camps. I stayed the night with ff. Sheppard, the District Officer Klang. His Malay wife was an excellent cook. George, my Scots terrier, accompanied me. I kept him upstairs in case he offended the feelings of my hosts. On the next day, as I was waiting in the sitting room for dinner, I heard a little splash-splash as water dripped through the ceiling on to the polished wooden floor. I rushed upstairs and confirmed my fears that George had been taken short. I realised the situation could easily get out of hand, so I persuaded ff. Sheppard that I had to go to Kuala Selangor sooner than planned and I motored there the next morning.

Kuala Selangor itself was a small town, some forty miles north-west of Kuala Lumpur, at the estuary of the Selangor river; the government officers' bungalows were on a small rocky wooded hill, among the ruins of an ancient Malay fort. David Borrie, the District Officer (DO), and his wife kindly offered to put up Abdullah, his family, George and me, whilst my departing Malay predecessor packed up and left. We had a good handover. His home was originally dedicated for use by the Malay Assistant District Officer and the police bungalow was inhabited by the European Assistant Drainage and Irrigation Department Engineer (DID). The other occupants of the hill were the European DID Engineer and his wife, the European Public Works Department official (PWD) and his wife.

I soon found that Kuala Selangor had a peculiar smell of its own – a sort of wet muddy 'pong' – which became recognisable a good ten miles away. On returning from a jungle patrol or from a long day in the Kuala Lumpur courts, I always felt a strange feeling of welcome directly my nose registered the last stage of the journey home.

When I moved in to my new house, I discovered that it was on the edge of a Chinese cemetery and that it was *cheng-beng* time (grave cleaning). This was achieved by burning the *lallang* (long grass) and *beluka* (bushes) and cleaning the overgrown area round the graves. The wind blew the smoke inside my house for a fortnight and it was a great nuisance. I hired an elderly Chinese cook and bought some china and cutlery from Robinsons, the large European-run departmental store in Java Street, recently renamed Mountbatten Road, in Kuala Lumpur. I acquired an antique ice-box from a local planter, and I arranged for a large block of ice wrapped in sacking to be put on the evening bus from the Singapore cold storage depot, forty miles away, for daily delivery to my door, having shrunk to about a quarter of its original size. Three months later, the assistant DID engineer left and I moved into my official quarters which, although much larger, was forty-nine steps up a steep hill. It had a wonderful view across the Selangor river to the extensive padi fields and oil palm plantations beyond.

Thus I escaped the effects of cheng-beng. But a new peril soon emerged. Kuala Selangor hill was the home of a rare breed of blue monkey which bred orange babies. Every morning about sixty of them decided to tour the treetops. Their smooth passage was interrupted by my house and garden. They were compelled to jump down from the trees, and run across the roof of my house, onto a long corrugated-iron passage leading to the kitchen roof, then back into the trees. Their procession was accompanied by a thundering noise of many little feet, followed by a very loud clattering and another thundering noise as they disappeared into the branches. This cacophony lasted two minutes, and was accompanied by the shrill screams of the monkeys, and George's excited barking. Sometimes, they decided to go out for a run in the middle of the night and, if I wished to scare the wits out of an unwelcome or uninvited visitor, I would omit to warn him in advance and, quite naturally, he thought the end of the world had come.

I had no electricity and so had to rely on Aladdin lamps. My telephone was an old army field contraption which I had to wind up furiously to obtain a ring at the other end. I made do with a zinc bath and a wormy thunderbox (mobile loo).

Whilst in Kuala Selangor, I was able to organise my professional life on better lines. I had 55 rubber estates, several oil palm plantations and a few tin mines, which had to be protected from terrorist attacks; some were very large, such as the Nigel Gardner/ Sungei Tinggi Socfin group, which had a small army of special constables to defend it. I had 150 regular policemen living in 10 police stations, 950 special constables on the estates and mines, and a miscellaneous headquarter group of about 30 clerks, junior court prosecutors, drivers, dog-shooters etc. I even had an official pun-kah-puller to work the Heath Robinson contraption, designed to keep me cool in the office; soon after my arrival I demolished the machinery and transferred him to one of our new jungle squads. The special constables were officered by twelve European Ser-geants (E/Sgts). Once the latter settled in, they became extremely keen to learn the language, understand the requirements of work-ing in a multicultural environment and train their men. I completed previous negotiations for the rent of a large house for six of them, as a safe defended base from which they could supervise their areas. The remainder were housed on the rubber estates in fairly comfortable plantation bungalows.

My eastern border adjoined Rawang District and was full of active terrorists; the area to the north of the Selangor river was a vast government-financed flat rice-growing area, criss-crossed with irrigation canals fed by a system of locks and gates controlling the water supply. Naturally enough, the terrorists based their supply organisation on the jungle edge adjoining the rice-padis but, because it was such a productive region, they limited their activities to the collection of food from the farmers and money from the shopkeepers. The area to my south adjoined Klang District, and its eastern border was also the home of several active terrorist units. The Malacca Straits, to the west, were the scene of constant smuggling and illegal immigration. An occasional island off shore provided wonderful picnic sites and, occasionally, when I was able to make the time, I would hire a fishing boat and enjoy life with invited friends.

I set about visiting every mine and rubber estate in my district and spent at least two nights a week in one of my police outstations. I discovered to my horror that only half my special constables had rifles and that their ammunition was usually of 1938 vintage which often misfired. Many of them had no uniforms. I set about obtaining two uniforms for each man from Kuala Lumpur headquarters, and arranged for the European Sergeants to visit each estate at least once a week. Later on, most estate managers were given the rank of honorary inspector and some, with no experience whatsoever, seemed to think that, with their more senior rank, they could boss my increasingly efficient European Sergeants. I bombarded headquarters with letters deploring the introduction of the rank of European Sergeant. However, it was a long time before this rather silly rank with its unnecessary ethnic connotations, was replaced by the much more appropriate title of Police Lieutenant.

I sat and passed my Malay Standard 1 and my Law Parts 1 and 2. When a visiting football team complained that they could not distinguish our barracks from their murky muddy background, I inveigled the local Public Works Department to give us unlimited white paint and we transformed the place. I trained up two jungle squads, each of twelve men, placing one under a European Sergeant on Nigel Gardner estate; and the other under a European

Sergeant in Sekinchang, a remote Chinese fishing village many miles to the north. Both did very well, and carried out some extremely well-planned ambushes. Routine police work took up a lot of my energy. National Registration identity cards were issued throughout Malaya at this time, and many difficulties arose as hundreds of illegal Chinese and Indonesian immigrants were landing secretly along the west coast.

A worrying problem after my arrival was a nasty smell in the main police station coming from the cells. On investigation, I saw six emaciated Chinese lying in rags on the floor. They were in a distressed state. I asked my predecessor who they were; he said they had been arrested at sea by the Royal Navy because they had plundered an inshore junk and murdered its crew. The arrests had taken place outside Malayan territorial waters; and the Malayan High Court had ordered their detention in local police cells, pending a legal decision regarding a trial. They had been there thirteen months under local police lock-up rules, which prevented proper exercise, restricted bathroom facilities and limited the amount and quality of their food. Moreover, the mainly Malay police families, who lived in government quarters within the perimeter of the police station, had increased in number following the declaration of the Emergency. They objected strongly to sharing washing facilities and lavatories with these people. The prisoners had no money to buy fresh clothes, food or soap, having thrown overboard their belongings and their loot before the Royal Navy boarding party arrested them. I gave them a small amount of cash, improved their living conditions and phoned Bev in Kuala Lumpur. He was shocked and contacted the Attorney General. In the end, he told me to get rid of them. I had them examined by Dr West, our helpful civilian local doctor. On his advice I fed them up for a fortnight, allowed them an increasing amount of exercise and then arranged for them to be taken back by ferry to Sumatra, where they said their families lived. We were all very relieved to see them go – it took ages to get rid of the smell they left behind!

I explained in a letter home, 'Life on the hill has its moments. Mr D.I.D. had an unexplained row with Mr P.W.D. and, in reply, Mr P.W.D. accused Mr D.I.D. of encouraging his dogs to eat Mrs P.W.D.'s chickens; next time he caught them at it he would shoot them dead. (Mr P.W.D. rang me up and asked to borrow my shotgun.) Mr D.I.D. replied that, if Mr P.W.D. shot his dogs; he

133

would shoot Mr P.W.D. (Mr D.I.D. rang me up and asked to borrow my shotgun). Then Mrs D.I.D.'s cookie was thought to have run off with Mrs P.W.D.'s *amah* (children's nanny) and the situation became quite tense. Good sense prevailed when the missing couple returned separately from their grave-cleaning duties. Meanwhile George has grown tired of chasing monkeys, and has turned his attention to small girls attending the Chinese primary school. They loved to tease him and yesterday a poor little girl fell over and George gave her a nip. The District Officer came to hear about it, and started to mutter about rabies and hydrophobia – possibly because he recalled that my predecessor's dog-shooter had shot his dog (said to have been suffering from mange).' I concluded in my letter home, 'If D.O. shoots George; I shoot D.O.'

Solly Graham was married in Kuala Lumpur Anglican church in April 1949 and he invited me, and the KL North anti-bandit squad, to his nuptials. I wrote home: 'It was a grand affair. Sir Henry Gurney made a speech and Sir Alec Newboult played the organ. We had plenty to eat and drink and a good time was had by all and sundry. Among the latter, were members of our old anti-bandit squad who enjoyed shaking Lady Gurney's hand. and slaking their thirst by drinking copious amounts of champagne. The former exercise was limited to one occasion per person; but not so the latter – to their great pleasure. Soon the time came for them to go home quickly if not all that quietly!'

A very nasty incident happened on 20th May 1949 at Bukit Mayong, a hill off the 28th milestone on the Kepong/Kuala Selangor road. A number of ambushes had taken place nearby and I had myself been fired at twice while motoring along the road, receiving yet more bullet holes in my car. I mentioned this on a visit to the Scots Guards at Batu Arang and we decided to search the hill the next day. Our plan was to enter the jungle, prior to crossing a swift-flowing river at the foot of the hill. A Scots Guards officer called Paul would take ten guardsmen and cross the river to the left, where we had seen fresh tracks. Ossie Priaulx, who was the Company Commander, and I, together with my police corporal and a section of Scots Guards, would cross over a short distance downstream, fifteen minutes later, and recce the area opposite. The rest of the Scots Guards platoon and my jungle squad would remain on the home side of the river to await results. We crossed the river safely; but Paul's group came under fire and Paul was killed. I heard the firing just before we came under heavy fire ourselves. Corporal Abdul Samad, who was standing beside me, was shot in the head and his brains and bits of skull came all over me. Sergeant Lea of the Scots Guards was killed on our left and, in the ensuing fire, four more guardsmen were wounded. During the battle the bandits shouted at us in Malay and English from their positions above us. They had sited a Lewis gun enfiladed along the line of the river; fortunately it jammed before it could do serious harm. Our reserve group, somewhat exposed on the other bank, decided to disperse quickly and regroup among the rubber trees about 800 yards away. This left Ossie and me on the wrong side of the river. We survived probably because we were below the terrorists' line of fire; their bullets and grenades went over our heads. I was armed with my carbine and had thirty rounds. I could not see anyone in front of me and I only fired eleven shots at an angle of about forty degrees. Suddenly, a bugle blew and the enemy retreated leaving behind one or two snipers who kept firing pot-shots in our direction from a distance of 50 or 60 yards. Ossie and I thought discretion the better part of valour, and retired slowly to the river where we were faced with the wounded men and three demoralised non-swimmers who were wandering around in a daze. We kept each other covered and we took it in turns to help them all to cross the river. It was getting dark and the tock tock birds started up, but we soon managed to locate the rest of our patrol. With much difficulty, I then dragged poor old Abdul Samad to the other side of the river, and we carried him some distance to the roadside where I stopped a bus and we went home. I saved his rifle and ammunition belt, noticing that he had fired eight rounds before he died.

On arrival I had the awful task of informing his wife. I still had the uneaten remains of the lunch which she insisted on cooking for me whenever I went out on patrol. Adbul Samad was forty-two years old, had twenty-one years' police service and many children. He was captain of our football team. Next day Colonel Sanderson arranged for an air strike, random machine-gunning from the air and, for good measure, bombarded the place with his 3-inch mortars. Ossie and I, accompanied by a platoon of Right Flank, went back across the river to where we had been shot at the day before. To my amazement, I discovered that we had been within 10–15 feet below a well camouflaged dug-in trench position. The place was littered with cartridge cases and I found twelve used hand-grenade rings. About one mile away, on the reverse side of the hill, we discovered a very large camp for from 70 to 100 persons; complete with schoolroom (for Communist indoctrination), two dining halls, blackboards, wash places, three sewing machines and even a well. A number of rude notices were left pinned to trees and I dismantled one obvious grenade booby trap. On the way back, I caused wry amusement by hauling in a short jungle creeper line and retrieving an army Bren gun, which I had deposited in the river the previous evening because I had other priorities and it was too heavy for me to carry.

Meanwhile a rumour started that I had been killed and, according to Cookie, a certain European and his wife visited my bungalow and took away my radiogram. When I returned very late the same night I had not seen anything amiss. I was out all the following day. The couple returned the radiogram surreptitiously, having found that rumours of my demise had been exaggerated.

I continued to arrange police and army ambush parties on two tracks leading to the camp from a nearby squatter area. We were rewarded a fortnight later when a small group of terrorists walked into one of the ambushes in the middle of the night. The army opened fire and next day recovered a one-star Communist cap. On searching the area carefully with my jungle squad I found, by chance, the body of a uniformed male Chinese about half a mile away. Documents he was carrying revealed he was the company commander and district committee member in charge of the Bukit Mayong camp, and was returning with his bodyguards from a meeting several miles north in Perak State. So, in a way, we were able to avenge the death of our comrades. The captured documents were of great value and we made successful operational use of them in three different areas of Selangor. Some time later, a Bukit Mayong Communist terrorist surrendered and told us that they had suffered four wounded in the battle, of whom one had died from his wounds. He went on to claim that they had killed thirty European soldiers!

As has been seen, not all our efforts were crowned with success. We suspected there must be a large Communist terrorist camp, somewhere between Sekinchang on the coast and Nigel Gardner Estate to the east, from which a series of particularly vicious attacks had been made on Socfin personnel and property. Maria Sube, the

French manager, had himself discovered a sunken log path under the swamp leading into the thick jungle; he was certain it was by this track that CTs entered his estate. I contacted the Air Photography Section in KL and they flew over the area. Their experts confirmed that an occupied terrorist camp was flourishing in the middle of the large jungle area to the west of the estate. There were no civilians within miles. Unfortunately for us, they told their RAF liaison officer at Operations Headquarters in Kuala Lumpur, which decided that the RAF should bomb the area on what they assured us was a six-figure map reference. The bombing took place on 15th September 1949 and missed its target by a long way. One Chinese female civilian was killed near Sekinchang itself, two Chinese male civilians were badly wounded and two children slightly wounded. I had recently persuaded the local Chinese *towkays* (heads of families and shopkeepers) to help us build a brand new police station in Sekinchang, and I had just stationed there twenty Malay and Chinese policemen, together with a jungle squad. The RAF's misreading of the map was a disaster and set back our efforts to win the hearts and minds of the people for years. The District Officer and I had to deal with a long list of complaints; intelligence of terrorist activity dried up in that area and never really recovered.

Sometimes, however, we had a bit of luck and one day we arrested a Chinese suspected of drug smuggling. On searching him, we found he had a rolled slip (a letter) written in Chinese characters; he admitted he was a Communist courier. To save time, I sent the slip to H.T. Pagden, the government entomologist, then a civilian liaison officer in Kuala Lumpur. He had a tame Chinese translator and he phoned me the results. It contained an instruction, some time, to murder Browne, the D.I.D. assistant, who was living in an unprotected house on the coast near Tanjong Karang. I phoned Browne at once and told him to come down to Kuala Selangor post-haste. The terrorists burnt his empty house that very night.

Once I was attacked by bees as we were preparing an ambush. I was in real trouble and ended up in Dr West's house receiving painful treatment for twenty-four stings on my face and neck. On another occasion, I was struck by lightning in the rain on top of a hill in the jungle. All I knew about it was a loud bang, a burning smell, a blue flame and my carbine leapt out of my hand. This caused much merriment among my companions when they discovered I was unharmed, if a little shocked! I was luckier than Derek Mole who only just survived a severe bout of scrub typhus, probably picked up from rats in a bamboo clump while he was chasing bandits in the jungle south of Kuala Lumpur.

In December 1948, occurred what was to be called by the press the 'Batang Kali massacre'. Batang Kali was east of Tanjong Malim and some way north of my District. Nevertheless, when Bev heard that about twenty terrorists had been killed on a remote Chinese-owned rubber estate near Batang Kali by the Scots Guards, he wanted to know the details and arrange for the High Commissioner to congratulate the security forces involved. All the local police and army commanders were engaged on the ground and could not be contacted, so he asked me to go up there to see what I could find out. On arrival next day, I photographed the dead people still piled together on the back of a truck. I was disturbed to see how white were the palms of their hands, and I was surprised to see that they all wore singlets and underpants. I did not wish to determine whether they were men or women. They were not at all like the Gombak Armed Work Force, whose hands were dark and rough. Moreover, no weapons had been found and no one had been wounded. They were all stone dead. I returned to Rawang and discovered that one of my Chinese detectives came from that area and he volunteered to visit his aunt's family. On his return, it was clear to me that these people were not terrorists; but civilian rubber tappers on one of the local absentee landlord Chinese-owned rubber estates. I told Bev and Colonel Sanderson of my suspicions. The former went straight to the Attorney General and warned the High Commissioner of impending trouble; both launched their own immediate investigations. I heard later that the patrol was commanded by a sergeant, and that no officer was present. I took no further part in the investigation.

Local information about Communist activity in the towns, and in the inhabited countryside, was normally obtained from registered informers or from people known personally to members of the security forces. Equally important, however, was the flow of fortuitous information from the general public, which often produced good and often unforeseen results. The RAF's ill-fated bombing near Sekinchang and the Scots Guards unfortunate shooting of the rubber tappers, were not only heartbreaking for so many

138

families; but also put a brake on voluntary intelligence from the public over a wide area of North Selangor for a long time afterwards.

As I was leaving my office on 12th July 1949, the telephone rang and it was Ted Rainford to say that a section of my old KL North anti-bandit squad, then based at Rawang, had been engaged in a serious battle with a much greater number of terrorists. My great friend and colleague, Inspector Kartar Singh, had been killed; so had Sergeant Tara Singh, the tallest man in the Malayan Police Service, and a great raconteur; together with five regular police constables. Two other police constables had been wounded. The Scots Guards were following up, but there had been no subsequent contact. This was terrible news. My mind was full of memories of the extraordinary experiences I had gone through with these brave and cheerful men. It took me a long time to get over the shock.

The rest of 1949 was taken up with training, inspecting the defences of police stations and estates, and acting on operational information against the terrorists. Ordinary everyday police work could not be ignored. Apart from the Emergency, which had to be given priority, we were also closely involved with putting up investigation papers requesting decisions to be approved, or disapproved, by the CID and/or by the deputy public prosecutor. Suicides, murders and thefts had to be investigated, thieves and robbers brought to justice. Opium smuggling had to be frustrated and the distributors identified and prosecuted. Illegal *samsu* stills, which produced strong liquor from heated rice stills driven by noisy old motor-car engines, had to be located and destroyed: similarly, 'toddy' factories which produced an alcoholic liquid from the sap of the palm tree had to be broken up. Failure to do these things, it was thought, might encourage public criticism of the administration and the police and, worse still, allegations of bribery and corruption!

Routine police work in the padi fields north of the Selangor river was a nightmare, especially if there was a sudden death reported to us several days after the event (suicide, illness, murder and the unexplained). The law of the land required us to bring the body down to Kuala Selangor for a post-mortem. In the rainy season the journey had to be made on foot for up to twenty miles through storm and mud; crossing flooded canals and deep drains, where motorised vehicles could not go. The only conveyance available was a bicycle. The corpse's feet were strapped to the pedals, the body was tied to the saddle then, depending on the state of *rigor mortis*, the shoulders and arms were attached to the handlebars. The longer we took over this, the smellier the corpse ... No one liked this task; but I was allowed to pay the pall-bearers a small sum from a special fund. Another *ex officio* role I took on was chief of the Kuala Selangor Fire Brigade, for which I had at my disposal a monthly sum of $25 (about £8). I earmarked ten people as firemen and let them share the money between them. Unfortunately, because of distance and the lack of communications, most of the fires we attended had burnt out before our breathless arrival.

Mr W.N. Gray, the Commissioner of Police, visited Kuala Selangor alone on 15th August and I took him on a tour of the vast padi area around Tanjong Karang and Sekinchang. We had lunch in the grounds of my newly-built Sekinchang police station, and I introduced him to the policemen and my local jungle squad. On 28th September I went on leave. I handed over to Phil Murch whom, nine months before, I had discovered in a ditch off Ampang road, having broken his neck in a motor accident, from which he had made a miraculous recovery. I motored up north as free as a bird in the air, calling on mutual friends in charge of police districts on the main trunk road through Malaya. I also called on 2/2nd Gurkha Rifles in Ipoh and 2/6th Gurkha Rifles in Sungei Pattani.

In Taiping I looked up Albert Edward Rowley, our former quartermaster in 3/9th Gurkha Rifles. He told me that he had joined the Malayan Prison Service and was the chief hangman in Taiping jail. He was paid an extra sixty dollars a drop, he said. He had married a Malay and was enjoying his work. I was quite glad to leave him and his tales of horror. When I arrived in Sungei Pattani, I was invited to join the Gurkhas for their Dashera celebrations. After that I visited Alor Star in Kedah and returned home via Penang, much refreshed. It was very interesting to meet the small number of young, mainly former Indian Army officers, engaged in the sort of anti-terrorist work with which I had become so familiar. It seemed to me that in these early days of 1948, and the first few months of 1949, the safety of the country depended so much on so few junior leaders; the hastily put-together police anti-bandit squads; the brave Malay policemen in their lonely countryside police stations; and especially the European Sergeants who soon began to play such a vital role in these early days. Later on, when the Gurkha battalions became operational, and other troops from England and the Commonwealth gained experience, the national danger would recede and it would become a war of attrition. A combined national command headquarters would be established under a director of operations. War by committee would be formed at State- and District-levels; the twelve-man jungle squads would become hundred-man jungle companies as part of a centrally-based police field force. However, all this was in the future.

Deepavali, a Hindu religious festival, was celebrated on 21st October 1949. European Sergeant Barraclough rang up late that night to say he had been shot at by a group of drunken Sikh special constables on Sungei Tinggi Socfin Estate. He thought he had a mutiny on his hands and what was he to do? I told him to meet me at the estate crossroads. On arrival there he briefed me. Apparently the eight Sikh special constables on guard had acquired some illegal samsu and had celebrated Deepavali much too well. They were in a happy mood, firing their rifles and shouting challenges at anyone who approached them. Barraclough was a reliable and courageous man; however, he could not speak Urdu and his Malay was still a bit basic at that time. I went up close to the guardroom and, standing behind a concrete water-butt, started talking to the men in Urdu (Punjabi), recalling much of the Sikh phraseology I had learnt in my journey through the Punjab two years before. Two shots were fired in the air and a drunken cheer went up, followed by a loud argument. When their chattering died down. I said that they would have to lay down their arms and surrender. One of them acted as a leader and we began to parley for about five minutes. I told them that I was a marksman (actually, I am a poor shot!) and I was prepared to shoot them one by one. In the end it was agreed they would do as I asked; on my side, I promised that I would treat them fairly and not have them shot out of hand. They piled their rifles against a wall and came forward, giving me what was meant to be a salute, and then stood around rather sheepishly.

I called in their scared and angry wives and told them to take their drunken husbands back to the lines. Meanwhile, a somewhat relieved Barraclough took charge of the rifles and unloaded them. Then we left the office area of Sungei Tinggi Estate to guard itself for the next twelve hours or so. Next morning, I took the sobered-up and repentant Sikhs in a police van to the Kuala Lumpur Sikh *gudwara* (temple) and I asked the priest in charge, whose services I had used twice before, to deal with the situation. In the end, the eight men apologised to Barraclough and donated a day's pay to the *gudwara*, promising not to get drunk on duty again. My action had nothing to do with police disciplinary regulations and I was lucky to get away with it. The eight Sikhs caused no more trouble and I understand that their behaviour was exemplary for the rest of their service. Socfin reacted by asking me to take over the security of their estates in South-East Asia, at a vastly increased salary, and no end of perks. I had no hesitation in politely turning down this unexpected offer.

When I first arrived in Kuala Selangor, I was welcomed by a Scottish rubber planter who had served in the 3/9th Gurkha Rifles. He had been invalided out of Burma (the Chindits) and I had never met him. He was a remarkable character with a strong Scottish accent and had taken over the management of Kampong Kuantan Estate; his predecessor having developed tropical neurasthenia after four of his special constables had been killed by locally-based terrorists. He was a great man for the taxi girls in Kuala Lumpur, and soon formed an alliance with a certain lady, whose main claim to fame was the possession of a huge grand piano in her little bedroom in an attap house (a simple hut) off Campbell Road. In these early days of our acquaintance, I met in his bungalow what seemed to me an endless stream of taxi girls, not all of whom were prostitutes. Many were on the lookout for a husband – preferably a British serviceman! The majority were single girls with one child and they desperately needed the money. They came in all shapes and sizes including Malay, Philippino, Chinese, Indonesian, Vietnamese, Thai, Australian and two wayward daughters of another Scottish planter. He invited groups home every weekend, entertaining them at his expense on what he described as purely platonic visits. It was a curious situation, quite beyond the borders of my innocence. We would talk for long periods on every subject from the everyday life of a taxi girl, to reasons why they liked their occupation. I much appreciated their views on the male species! We never discussed our work, or the Emergency. He eventually married the lady, and her grand piano came too. For many years afterwards I, and then my wife, and then my family, stayed with them over Christmas. Of course, by then, the taxi girls had become very much a thing of the almost forgotten past.

When his wife went into Bungsar hospital to have her first baby I escorted her inebriated husband to Nanto's bar in KL's Batu Road, and waited for a telephone call as we listened endlessly to Teresa Brewer singing 'Music Music Music' on the bar's nickelodeon. The bell rang eventually and the barman told him that he was the father of a baby daughter. I drove him up to Bungsar Hospital where the nurses on duty in the maternity ward took pity on him, and put him to bed in the public ward.

I remember with pleasure two officers in Right Flank of the Scots Guards. Lord (David) Ogilvie, later to become the 13th Earl of Airlie and Lord Chamberlain of the Queen's Household, was a wonderful companion and told amusing stories of his military adventures on duty at 'Buck House' and in the Tower of London. He was the first person to point out, while we were travelling in an open railway wagon on a jungle logging line, that my hair was going grey. The other officer was Captain Murray de Klee. He was an enthusiastic patrol commander and an outstanding athlete. On his first encounter with the bandits he was wounded; but captured his attacker. It appeared that his wound was caused by the bandit's bullet hitting the foresight of his rifle, which broke off and entered his forehead. For ages afterwards, he was wont to ask me to listen carefully as he shook his head to make the foresight rattle around inside! He was ambushed and wounded again in June 1950, on his way through the Kanching Pass north of Kuala Lumpur; his jeep crashed and he was thrown clear, covered in blood. The terrorists left him for dead, but he survived to complete a long and highly distinguished military career.

I was a great favourite with the mothers whose first and only anxious question was, 'Are you permanent and pensionable?' I always answered 'yes', although I was still only a cadet on probation. They then abandoned their daughters to my wily ways. Actually, things did not pan out as wily as I would have liked. I usually worked seven days a week and often eighteen hours a day. Occasional visits to Kuala Lumpur were limited to conferences and attendance at the High Court, and I returned home as soon as I could. The young ladies expected a good time in the clubs, or to dance the night away at the Griffin Inn (where Colonel Sanderson, who commanded the Scots Guards, might occasionally be seen of a late evening, playing the drums in a most professional and energetic manner). The ladies soon transferred their affections to the lounge lizards of the capital!

At the end of my first year in Malaya my bank statement showed a credit balance of four pounds, so I was not doing all this just for the money!

5

Just a moth-eaten rag on a worm-eaten pole
Hardly a sight to stir a man's soul.
'Tis the deeds that were done 'neath the moth-eaten rag
When the pole was a staff and the rag was a flag.

FROM A MEMORIAL IN SHERBORNE ABBEY

In January 1950, I heard that Mr William Nicol Gray, CMG, DSO, the Commissioner of Police (CP), had arranged for me to go to Kuala Lumpur as his Personal Assistant (PA) with the status of aide-de-camp. Apparently the *Mentri Besar* (Prime Minister of Selangor State), the District Officer and my immediate boss had jointly opposed my transfer – I suspected that they had little interest in me, but resented interference from the Commissioner. Anyway their protests were in vain. My wishes were not consulted and I had mixed feelings: the more positive of these was a realisation that a move to KL would allow me to live a more settled life and that I would meet interesting people.

My successor in Kuala Selangor would be a former officer in the 9th Gurkha Rifles whom I had never met. He duly arrived and we had a very busy handover attending many parties all over the district given by the district office, my policemen, the army, rubber planters and the tin miners. He had come from Pahang State and had much the same experience of fighting terrorism. I thought he would fit in well.

I reported to the Commissioner of Police's office high up the hill on Bluff Road, overlooking the *padang* (open ground), quite close to where I used to live with the Gladwells. My new office had easily the best view of Kuala Lumpur and the mountain range beyond. I met Paddy Giles, the incumbent PA, who had been in

145

post for five weeks only, and he gave me an excellent briefing. I was to move into a large house on Federal Hill next to the official residences of the Chief Justice, the Attorney General and the Solicitor General. This house would be shared with Nicol Gray, Dick Catling (who later became Sir Richard Catling) the Police Secretary, Nicol Gray's dachshunds and me. Abdullah and family had to be left behind in Kuala Selangor with George.

Although the handover went very well on the work side, little else did. Unfortunately my successor had no money to pay for my kerosene fridge, the Aladdin lamps, paraffin iron, the soft furnishings, or any of the other basic necessities which I had acquired to keep me fairly comfortable. Naturally, I needed the cash to pay for similar items using electricity in KL. In the end, I agreed to let him have them.

On moving into 8 Federal Hill, I discovered that Nicol Gray's elderly Malay bearer called Roose had a son, Ahmad, and I was expected to take him on which, of course, I did. I also discovered that I had responsibility for Nicol Gray's dachshunds and, moreover, he was extremely fond of them and would play endless games with them on the lawn. We lived as bachelors employing five servants – the Malay father and son, a Chinese servant for Dick Catling, a Tamil gardener and a Chinese cook who, in addition to cooking our meals, had to feed the multitude who came to breakfast, lunch and dinner, and sometimes stayed the night or even long weekends. We entertained a great number of people from all round the world who happened to be passing through Malaya. They included politicians, diplomats and senior service officers from England, the USA and Australia.

I was responsible for running the household, ordering the food, determining precedent at table, and making sure we had sufficient drinks, cigars and eats available to meet any eventuality. The official part of this entertainment was funded by government, for which Dick Catling kept a special purse, and we shared the rest of our expenses between us. The result was that, once again, I was broke and, in addition, I had to purchase a decent suit and full mess dress, complete with tight trousers, boots and spurs. The wearing of the latter was a tradition dating from the days when the Malayan Police Service was mounted, and known as the Malay States Guides. Unlike me, my colleagues in the little clique of

Kuala Lumpur ADCs were kept by their masters and so could save the cost of their board.

My work proved very interesting indeed. I was involved with all Nicol Gray's day-to-day business. except certain policy matters and 'difficult cases' which Dick Catling tackled with enthusiasm, firmness and a wry sense of humour. The considerable amount of paperwork we produced was efficiently organised by a tireless European Sergeant, later Police Lieutenant, George Wynn. He stayed with us in the office, or at home, during late hours and most weekends, without a grumble or a long face. I developed good relations with the staff in the federal operations room, which was becoming the heart of security force strategy against the Communist terrorist organisation. Its very efficient director for many years was Richard Buxton who was another former 9th Gurkha Rifles officer. I came to know and like Jamie, ADC to the General Officer Commanding (GOC); also H.E.'s ADC (Dennis Drayton, yet another former Gurkha Brigade officer) and I think we became a good team. Much of my time was spent travelling around the country with Nicol Gray, or undertaking special missions on his behalf. We saw quite a bit of South Thailand staying in Songkhla with Captain Dennis RN, the British Consul. He had commanded the battleship from which Nicol Gray led his Royal Marine Commando into France on D-Day 1944. It was good to see Songkhla again, little changed from when I was last there in 1946. I became quite deeply involved with intelligence operations which we were running in conjunction with the Thais. We also visited the States of Perlis, Kedah, Perak, Pahang, Kelantan and Johore, meeting the British Advisers, police chiefs and military commanders. All this gave me a much enlarged overview of the security situation, and the personal difficulties faced by the Commissioner of Police.

On the day of my arrival, Nicol Gray took time off to tell me that he expected my loyalty and support; much of my work would involve secret matters and I was not to gossip. He said that he would often express his off-the-cuff feelings to me, and I was not to regard them as set in tablets of stone; sometimes they could be altered after mature reflection. He invited, and indeed expected, criticism and ideas from me. He ended up by saying he suspected I had not been keen to come to Kuala Lumpur; but he hoped the calibre of people whom I would meet would enlarge my experience. Richard Buxton and I drafted many of his speeches – often at the last minute – which he usually accepted, without any changes. However, it was Dick Catling who provided the guiding light, dynamism, originality and flair at Bluff Road.

I discovered that Nicol Gray had made many loyal personal friends among the armed services, journalists, middle rank civil servants and the commercial community. They proved very helpful and understanding on difficult days. Malcolm MacDonald, the Commissioner General for South-East Asia, who lived on Bukit Serene in a splendid palace beside the Johore Straits opposite Singapore, was a very real friend to Nicol Gray, sending him letters of support and keeping in touch by telephone. I found him a very approachable person and always ready to listen. He was amusing, full of ideas and had a way with the local people unlike many stuffy British politicians who came our way. He mixed well with all nationalities and seemed to know everyone of importance in the Far East. He was a famous host and was a 'wow' in Chinese female circles! Nicol Gray had a number of enemies, too, including some long-established members of the Malayan Civil Service and some senior planters and tin miners, especially those who had been prisoners of war in Japanese hands. These over-powerful voices sometimes exerted what we believed to be baleful influences in local commercial circles. A significant number of civil servants tended to ignore the Emergency altogether, carrying on as if they were living in pre-war days. For example, senior civil servants responsible for supervising precedence at official functions, took pleasure in placing Nicol Gray and the General Officer Commanding well below the salt among junior officials. Sir Henry Gurney himself decided to intervene and more appropriate places were allocated to both.

When touring Malaya, we always combined it with inspections of newly-built police stations. The modernisation and accommodation of a much-enlarged police service in Malaya was one of Nicol Gray's great achievements. We would attend morning prayers (war briefings), lunch with outstation planters or miners, visit European Sergeants' messes, and encourage informal discussions over supper with our hosts. We tried to lodge with people we knew, or needed to get to know. For instance, Tapah in South Perak was a favourite watering place not only because Solly Graham, who had retired from his service with the High Com-

148

missioner, was the senior resident police officer there; but also because he was heavily involved in the Emergency, and had strong views about the way security forces operations were conducted. I had another reason – there was a Chinese-owned delicatessen nearby, which sold exotic food and drink imported from France for consumption by the local French community. I was able to slip away and arrange to top up our reserves at home, thus maintaining Nicol Gray's reputation for civilised food and post-prandial liquid refreshment. Above all, these visits enabled Nicol to keep in touch with people at the sharp end of the Emergency, brief himself regarding the security situation on the ground and to listen to the views of those involved.

It was unofficial government policy to maintain contact with the overseas Chinese Nationalist Kuo Min Tang organisations in Malaya. They had supported Chiang Kai Shek's war against the Communists, by providing the Chinese Nationalists with large amounts of foreign currency. However, following Mao Tse Tung's victory in 1949, they had lost their enthusiasm for supplying overseas aid, and were looking to increase their influence in local affairs in Malaya. Unfortunately, many of these Kuo Min Tang organisations – both secret and overt – were riddled with secret society affiliations and were corrupt and untrustworthy. Nevertheless, they had provided some useful intelligence on local Communist Party members in the early days of the Emergency, and they had a somewhat shady army of inactive guerrillas left over from the Japanese occupation. Moreover, our own small overworked intelligence organisation – the Special Branch – was almost entirely engaged on short-term operational activity; there were few regular Chinese members of the police rank and file. I was involved on the fringes of this interesting development.

My first experience of this was when I was OCPD, KL North in late 1948. Bev wanted us to make Kepong police station, about six miles north of KL, a strong base for patrolling the Sungei Buloh Forest Reserve and he asked Peter Wright Nooth to set it up. In order to involve the Chinese community, 25 Chinese youths in Kepong were persuaded to join the special constabulary. I inspected them later the same day and noticed they were very weedy specimens: I did not envy Peter his conscript army. Later, to his surprise, they all reneged on their commitments; but, to save face, they produced 25 replacements all of whom claimed to be experienced Chinese Nationalist anti-Japanese fighters. They announced their wish to defend the town against militant Communism. We turned down six of them for Triad secret society involvement; the remainder were allowed to join the special constabulary and proved loyal and hardworking.

Nicol Gray asked me to act as his personal contact with the Thai Police. We obtained the agreement of the Thais, and the British Embassy, to post a British-Malayan police officer as the British Vice-Consul in Songkhla. Our aim was to obtain intelligence on Communist influence in South Thailand. We also shared with the Thais a mutual interest in Communist penetration of the irredentist movement among the Muslim population in that area. Sometimes, a senior diplomat from the British Embassy, who was extremely suspicious of our intentions and wanted to avoid a diplomatic 'incident', sat in on our meetings. It was all very interesting and I learnt a great deal about intelligence collection, subsequent assessment and long-term planning.

In the spring of 1950, General Sir Harold Briggs arrived in Kuala Lumpur as the first Director of Operations; responsible for combining the separate efforts of the civilian government, the police and the military into a unified and properly co-ordinated organisation to fight the Emergency. In my view at that time, the police and military co-operated very well; but many members of the civil service still lacked leadership and were deeply divided amongst themselves (such as those who had been 'in the bag', i.e. prisoners of the Japanese; and those who had not). The Communist armed struggle had been contained; yet there was no long-term planning to deal with the Emergency. I and my young friends hugely welcomed his arrival on the scene.

I was asked by Nicol Gray to suggest an ADC for General Briggs. I immediately thought of Duggie Farnbank, who was not only a former Gurkha Brigade officer; but had been severely wounded in the leg and needed a 'rest'. His recent conversion to Islam was not considered to be a drawback. He was interviewed by General Briggs and they got on famously. Duggie was intelligent, literate, had distinguished military experience in Burma and in Malaya and mixed well with people. Another excellent appointment was Richard Buxton's mother as General Briggs's secretary, hostess and general factotum. Her husband, I believe, was a Harley Street doctor; on his recent death she was looking for an exciting job in Malaya, and to be near her son. As expected, her appointment was an immediate success and it was over Harold Briggs's dinner table, liberally supplied with good food and wine, that we hammered out together the draft of what was to become the hugely successful Briggs's Plan for resettlement of Chinese squatters throughout the country. It was at the same table that, with patience and persuasion, many 'doubting Thomases' were won over to the plan. Nicol Gray's idea was to include Robert Thompson, DSO, MC (later Sir Robert) in our little group. It took Sir Henry Gurney's intervention to prise him away from his civil service duties so that he could become staff officer (civil) on Sir Harold's staff. Robert stayed on in Malaya after Independence until 1961, when he was appointed head of the British Advisory Mission in South Vietnam until 1965.

Our UK visitors included James Griffiths and John Strachey, ministers in the British Labour Government, who came to see us on 26 May. Mr Griffiths turned out to be an understanding, helpful person who took an interest in everything and asked lots of questions. He wore a white sun-hat and was very popular with all of us. Mr Strachey, on the other hand, hardly spoke a word. He was clearly bored with the visit, became quite aloof and made no effort to be friendly. In a letter home, I described him as starchy, awkward and remote. The two ministers could not have been further apart in manners, looks or humour. In October, Lord Listowel and a delegation of MPs visited us; we thought they had been properly briefed beforehand and would help us when they returned to the UK.

I collected Sir William Jenkin from the airport in June and took him round Kuala Lumpur to sign the books (even then, this was very much a civil service social requirement). Sir William was a distinguished former member of the Indian Police, and an international expert on intelligence. He had been asked to review the composition and work of the Malayan Police Special Branch and to make recommendations. A month or so before, Nicol Gray had asked me to rent and furnish a house pending his arrival and I had sought the help of a senior colleague's wife. Everything went smoothly and I think Sir William appreciated the results of our efforts. I took to him at once, although I could see that he was not a good mixer and he gave an initial impression of being bad-tempered and rather humourless. On reflection, I think this was because he resented being responsible to Nicol Gray who was a younger man; and he desperately wanted to have an executive function, not limited by the word 'advisory' implied in his contract. Furthermore, he had been imposed upon an overworked Special Branch, whose senior members generally regarded him as an interfering stranger in their midst. He badly needed friends to help him settle in. He did not sleep well and, as we were both early risers, we had many dawn walks round the Lake Gardens and long talks during breakfasts together. I did my best to brief him as fully and as efficiently as possible. I think I was able to help him in his first few weeks though, of course, there were many people, much senior to me, who gave him their advice. Eventually, when Lady Jenkin joined him, and as he got the hang of things, he began to relax and enjoy himself.

His main task was to persuade the Colonial Office to provide the Malayan Government with sufficient funds to build a strong intelligence organisation, based solely on the existing Special Branch. His plans involved the establishment of an intelligence training school; a Chinese language school; and the construction of a 'purpose-built', strictly controlled, interrogation and planning centre as a base for long term intelligence projects. All these new organisations would come under senior police officers chosen for their flair, initiative, reliability and charisma. Dick Catling and I were asked by Nicol Gray and Sir William to suggest names, for by then we had met and talked with nearly all the senior police officers in the country. I am glad to say that all our suggestions were supported by Nicol Gray though, again, many additional recommendations came through from other sources. I believe strongly that Sir William Jenkin's forward planning was responsible for the first vital phase of the extremely effective Special Branch expansion, which came into play over the next two years. I think he was right not to create an entirely independent intelligence organisation – separate from the police service – for which there was strong support among some senior civil servants opposed to what was considered empire-building by Nicol Gray. General Templer's direction later for further major expansion of the Special Branch was a natural development of Sir William's original plan.

Life on Federal Hill, in between our travels, was really great fun. I discovered that the Chinese servants in the Chief Justice's house used to work for à Becket Terrell the pre-war Chief Justice of the

152

Federated Malay States. He was a connection of my family and my parents had known him for a long time. This Chinese family showed me their old photographs which they had kept safely hidden throughout the Japanese occupation. I exploited my newly-found friends by borrowing the Chief Justice's crockery and glass, and sometimes even his cook, for our larger parties. In May, I had to sack our cook because his meals had become boring and uninspired. With a little help from the Chief Justice's cook, I recruited a superb replacement and there were no subsequent criticisms of the kitchen – indeed our table regained its fame and became the envy of our friends and their wives.

Chief Justice Spenser Wilkinson was much too important and busy to be a special friend; but he was good company and had a very loud laugh which, at night and with the wind behind it, could be heard a mile away across the valley through the Lake Gardens as far as Carcosa and King's House (important government residences). Mr Justice Foster Sutton was a closer acquaintance of Nicol Gray and sometimes acted as Chief Justice, or as High Commissioner, in the absence on leave of the incumbents. On one of these occasions, when I was his temporary ADC, we had to attend a large parade. He did not possess a suitable colonial uniform, and he considered his legal outfit inappropriate, so we had to borrow Sir Henry Gurney's. But he was a larger man than Sir Henry, and only just squeezed himself into it after quite a struggle. We entered the car without incident and drove to the setting-down point for the ceremony. When the driver opened the door for him to descend, he did not budge. His face became very red and he spluttered, 'Give us a push', so the driver pulled from outside and I pushed from within till, with a great effort, we managed to decant him successfully. He took a deep breath, his face recovered its normal colour, and he walked slowly and majestically to the dais taking the salute with confident aplomb. When limited national service was introduced by him, his name became well-known throughout Malaya. Those enlisted were called 'Sutton Boys'.

Our great friends on Federal Hill were Attorney General A.G. Brown (and wife) and Solicitor General M.J. Hogan: both staunch supporters of Nicol Gray, and we gave enjoyable parties in our homes. One of the best of these was a tripe and onions dinner given by A.G. Brown when we all dressed up as London Cockneys.

I also found time to organise an Old Pangbournian dinner at the Griffin Inn having located four other OPs – a rubber planter, the chief signals officer in KL, a major in the 6th Gurkha Rifles and an elderly Malayan Police inspector – sadly, not a sailor among them.

Having completed six months as PA to Nicol Gray, I began to hint that it was time for another posting and eventually he agreed to look out for a replacement. I declined to suggest anyone because it was important for him to choose someone he could get on with. Three months later, in November, he chose the Assistant OSPC Kulim in the northern State of Kedah. He was another former Gurkha Brigade officer who, after our arrival together in Malaya, had been posted to Kedah. He was invited down to Kuala Lumpur for interview by Nicol Gray and Dick Catling. It appeared they both liked him and Nicol Gray took him away on a week's tour of Perak, based on Fraser's Hill. Before going, Nicol Gray said I could have three days leave before taking up my appointment as Assistant OSPC Kulim.

I motored down to Singapore and spent two nights with the Scott Leatharts. Scott had left the Gurkha Brigade to recruit, train and command the Gurkha contingent of the Singapore Police. At that time, he had hand-picked 149 Gurkha policemen for employment on internal security duties. It had become his special interest and the contingent had already won praise, as much for their military efficiency and reputation for fair play, as for their bearing and turn-out on parade. They had also taken part in several successful security force operations against Communist terrorists in South Johore, opposite Singapore Island. It was a great experience for me to see such an enthusiastic group of people. Plans for housing their families, education of their children and general welfare were in full swing. The introduction of Gurkhas into the Singapore Police continued to be a huge success. Fifty years later, the Singapore Gurkha contingent comprised over 2,000 men.

On my return from Singapore, I went to various farewell parties and we had a good handover. I was, however, quite glad to leave and surrendered my responsibility for looking after Nicol Gray's dachshunds. I said my own farewells to George Wynn, Ahmad, Roose and his wife, Dick Catling's Chinese servant, our splendid cook and the gardener – a very loyal and willing group with whom it had been a great pleasure to work. I collected Abdullah and his wife from his sister's house in Kampong Bahru – a delightful orchard area in Kuala Lumpur populated by Malays, with mostly wooden houses on stilts with large verandahs – together with George and my belongings. We all set off by car for Kulim, not forgetting to muzzle George when we entered the rabies area north of Tanjong Malim. My heavy baggage was to follow later by road.

Reflecting on the way, I decided I had been most fortunate to have had those nine months in KL. I now had a good understanding of the Emergency. I had talked with, and listened to, the country's leaders and a host of distinguished visitors. I had met a wide cross-section of European planters, tin miners, civil servants and the judiciary: I had looked after all sorts of visitors, and had taken foreign delegations round the country. I had travelled throughout Malaya, spent more time in South Thailand, and I had made some useful contacts all over the place. As an Honorary ADC to Sir Henry Gurney, I had met many more people and, just before I left, the Gurneys kindly invited me to a farewell supper. I was never to meet them again.

Before joining Nicol Gray's staff in Kuala Lumpur, I had no idea of how the country was run and how the army and police liaised to fight the war against Communist terrorism. I soon became aware of the difficulties faced by Nicol Gray in his relations with many senior officers of the Malayan Civil Service and the lack of support from certain officers in a divided police service. On the other hand, I saw at first hand the wonderful encouragement given to Nicol Gray by Malcolm MacDonald, the Commissioner General based in Johore Bahru; the friendliness and understanding of General Urquhart, the General Officer Commanding; and the growing respect of many of the rubber planters and the tin miners. Above all, I had been involved with the arrival of Sir William Jenkin, whose clear and forthright views on the creation of a new and effective intelligence organisation under police control, was a huge step forward. I had witnessed daily the initiative and drive of Sir Harold Briggs and his resettlement programme for the rural Chinese: I now realised that, at last, something practical was happening and there was increasing hope for the future. It had been a most interesting and constructive time for me and I had been extremely fortunate to have had this experience.

*

Whilst I was in Kuala Lumpur I had managed to keep in touch with my friends in Rawang and Kuala Selangor; and I had continued to visit regularly three Gurkha civilian families, who all suffered horribly from leprosy in the Sungei Buloh Leper Settlement. Unfortunately, all but four of these people had died in the previous six months. It was very sad to say goodbye to the survivors. I arranged with the local shop to send them regular supplies of food and cigarettes. In April 1951, the settlement superintendent wrote to say that the remaining four had died the previous week.

I had the shock of my life when Abdullah, his wife and I arrived by car in Kulim. My new boss, the Officer Superintending Kulim Police Circle (OSPC), was formally of the Indian Police; he had kindly invited me to share his house just outside the town. To our surprise, no one was there to greet us, but the place was swarming with Tamil rubber tappers crying their eyes out and asking for money! Apparently, he had been out shooting snipe and had accidentally fired into the tappers' lines, peppering the inhabitants with small lead shot. Some had taken exception to this and were now loudly demanding compensation. There was no sign of him. I had never met him, and we were very tired from our long journey. No one else was around, and I was beginning to wonder what might happen next, when along he came, with a shotgun under his arm, looking every inch a worthy English farmer. He greeted us cheerily, 'Hello, have you settled in?' then without a pause, 'I am off to have a shower. Oh,' on seeing the madding crowd, 'shot some coolies, eh? Tell them to buzz off.' He disappeared and I was left to deal with them. Their leader was a Conductor (supervisor) and spoke good English. I could not find evidence of any bodily damage, so I apologised on my boss's behalf and handed out 25 dollars (about £3) of my own money. Away they went, with every sign of satisfaction, leaving me greatly relieved that they were unhurt and happy with the outcome.

Poor old chap; he had returned from home leave, having just buried his wife who had died of cancer. She was an amateur artist and they had spent their last days together, painting in the south of France. He spoke of her frequently and was rapidly going downhill. His servants had left him, the men were frightened of his unpredictable behaviour, and the morale of the police in his Circle was rock-bottom. I was very cross with my predecessor for not warning me of this extraordinary situation; when I telephoned him, he said his former boss was quite mad and he was glad to get away.

Abdullah and his wife cooked Malay food for all of us until I found a Chinese cook. Unfortunately, the van transporting my possessions from Kuala Lumpur to Kulim went over the edge of a precipice in the Kanching Pass; my fridge was a write-off and the remainder of my impedimenta was now at various police stations up and down the main road. It took weeks to get this sorted out; but luckily, in a rare moment of financial foresight, I had insured my household contents for the princely sum of £100.

On arrival at Circle headquarters next day, I was met by the officers in charge of Kulim and Serdang Districts; the Circle CID and Special Branch officers; the inspectors and the police lieuten-ants (formerly called European Sergeants). I had hoped to speak to each of them individually; but they insisted on speaking to me as a group. They were all very open about the state of affairs in the Circle. Even the non-English-speaking Malay sub-inspector (the most senior member of the rank and file) said that his OSPC was *gila* (mad). I was told that the jungle squads lacked discipline and, on examining the operation room records, I discovered that, although they had notched up a remarkable number of terrorist kills, very few arms had been recovered; whereas it had been my previous experience in Selangor that dead terrorists were almost always armed. I found this extremely worrying.

During the following week, in the absence of my boss elsewhere, my presence was requested at two meetings of the District Planters' Association; one in Kulim Club and one on nearby Dublin estate. The planters claimed, somewhat arrogantly, that they had success-fully removed a previous holder of my appointment (a former shopwalker in Harrods whom they called 'Blockhead') but they reckoned that his successor was much worse. Then one of them started to query my experience, and my professional ability, remarking that as a former Palestine policeman and a crony of Nicol Gray, I was unlikely to be of much use in an area notorious for its Communist terrorism. I made the point that the OSPC was not present to answer questions, so I could only comment on what I knew about myself and my career to date. I put them straight on these. I also said that I would pass on their anxiety to higher authority. Things cooled down in the bar afterwards, though I was the surprised recipient of much strong criticism of the way the Emergency was being handled by the police in South Kedah.

My new boss asked me to accompany him to each police station in the Circle, where it was customary to sign the visitors' book kept in the charge room. However, he not only signed the books; but he also wrote long rambling essays in English and spoke to the Malay constables in Urdu. Then, to my horror, he told me that he intended to 'court-martial' a senior European police officer for cowardice; he had already typed out himself the necessary papers for onward transmission to the Chief Police Officer Kedah State in Alor Star. On our return, I asked to see the papers and I realised at once that the accusation was wholly illegal and factually incorrect; he had made a terrible mistake and he had been extremely unfair to the person concerned, who had no idea what was going on behind his back. This was the last straw. I asked to see the Chief Police Officer immediately about all these disconcerting matters.

He was my old friend Neville Godwin who had been a great help to me in my Rawang and Kuala Selangor days. He had a very nice wife, too, and invitations to lunch with them had always been gratefully received. His office was in Alor Star in North Kedah about thirty-five miles away. Before I could say a word, he said he wanted me to take over as Acting OSPC Kulim until a more senior officer could be appointed. He obviously knew of the peculiar situation in the Circle. Neville Godwin agreed with my proposals to disband the jungle squads and to redistribute their personnel. To my great relief, he said he would examine the court-martial file. I also told him of my intention to reduce road ambush casualties, by requiring passengers in police vans to disembark from their vehicles, and walk around notoriously dangerous sections of the road. I said that I proposed to recruit unpaid volunteer auxiliary police (APs) from among the Malay kampongs (villages), and to attach them to outlying police stations. We talked all day on these and other problems. I came away well satisfied, and in the knowledge that I had plenty of wholly unexpected things to do.

On my return to Kulim, my boss informed me that Neville Godwin had phoned him to say he was to go on promotion to Alor Star and would leave before Christmas. He regarded the intervening period as a handover to me and said he was pleased with his transfer. This gave me *carte blanche* to do what I wanted. We continued our tours of the two districts. I did not spend any nights in police stations, as had been my previous practice, but I accepted invitations to inspect the defences of rubber estates as often as I could get away. Neville Godwin came down the following week and I cleared my detailed plans with him. He spoke privately to the author of the court martial file and made him destroy it.

We were supported militarily by the 2nd Battalion of the King's Own Yorkshire Light Infantry (KOYLI); one of their companies was based nearby. This battalion had an excellent reputation for fighting the terrorists, and for co-operation with us; I considered myself fortunate to be working with them. One day, a very strange thing happened. A platoon was out on night ambush in the Karangan tin-tailing area when, in the middle of the night, a single shot was fired and killed a member of the platoon. It was assumed that a terrorist had spotted him. His body was brought back to Kulim for a routine post-mortem and, to everyone's astonishment, the medical officer's conclusion was that he had been strangled by a cord, almost certainly originating from a Japanese jungle boot; and that he had died before he was shot. This was a civil matter; but the army wished to study the case in detail. The dead man's platoon commander, whom I had met, had been with the platoon since before they left England for Malaya and, without doubt, he was an efficient reliable officer. He knew his men well and was held by them in the greatest regard. Neither he, nor anyone else, could think of an explanation for the death of a man known so well in the platoon. All sorts of explanations went the rounds for this unfortunate death. As far as I know, the mystery was never satisfactorily resolved.

Service in Kedah meant a major change in the way I planned my diary. I explained this in a letter home the day after my arrival. 'Kulim is a very busy place and I am not sure I shall like being here – my main complaint being a goofy boss who lives for weekends when he can go snipe shooting. However, there are compensations for he keeps our table well supplied . . . some of the customs of this State are interesting . . . to suit the Malay padi planters, the day counts from dawn to dawn and not, as we calculate it, from midnight to midnight. Thus, at 6 a.m. the clock strikes one, and so on until 5 p.m. and 5 a.m.; when it strikes twelve times. Our weekends are on Thursday afternoons and Fridays; and our Saturdays and Sundays are working days. In practice here, we work throughout the week, without a break, though occasionally I sneak across to Penang on a Friday. Unkind colleagues elsewhere say we only work a three day week!'

Until now, virtually all my social contacts outside the security forces had been British, and nearly all the government officers whom I had met were also British. But Kedah was a Malay State and I began to meet Malay officials of all grades. The District Officer Kulim was a Malay, and I called on him immediately after my arrival. He proved very friendly and extremely knowledgeable about his work: he had twelve children: enough, he said, to make a cricket team, with a reserve in hand. His assistant was Tunku (Prince) Fariduddin – one of a hundred princely grandsons of the late Sultan of Kedah. We all became close friends and Tunku Farid took in hand my colloquial Malay and Jawi script. His wife was a really good cook and introduced me to traditional Kedah Malay cooking, as well as some exciting Muslim dishes from South Thailand. I managed to slip away from my official duties to explore with him the architecture of the Royal Malay cemetery at Langgar, various beautiful mosques throughout the State, and the green and yellow painted royal palace outside Alor Star. He also laid on for me a special playing of ancient Malay music in the Balai Nobat, a two-storey tower in the centre of Alor Star surmounted by a cupola, from which Muslims were called daily to prayer. He introduced me to His Highness the Sultan and members of his family. We also went on photographic expeditions, and he showed me the royal archives of which he was the unofficial curator. He copied for me a photograph of a mid-nineteenth-century Kedah State Police guard of honour outside the royal palace, which I used as a greetings card in 1951. Tunku Farid later went on a *haj* (Holy Pilgrimage) to Mecca and, on his return, he became known as Tunku Fariduddin Haji.

After some time, Tunku Farid and his wife became very keen for me to learn something about Malay culture and customs. They told me that the words Malay and Malaya were probably derived from a place in East Sumatra called Meleyu. According to anthropologists, I was told, the Malay race could be divided into two different types: Proto and Deutero. The Proto-Malays appeared to be the ancestors of all the people now considered to belong to the Malay-Polynesian group, living in countries from Madagascar to the Pacific Ocean. They were believed to have come from Yunnan in China some 5,000 years ago, bringing with them the neolithic civilisation. Today, these Proto-Malays were called Jakun and their tribes were variously called Orang Bukit, Benua, Udai or Orang Laut (Sea Jakuns). The term 'Abo' (short for aboriginals) was considered an insulting and demeaning word. Proto-Malays appeared to have made their homes also in Sumatra, Kalimantan (Borneo), the Celebes, Tidore and parts of Indo-China.

The descendants of the Proto-Malays were pushed inland by the arrival of new immigrants, the Deutero-Malays. This second wave of immigration was believed to have taken place several hundred years before the present era, and to have its origin in North Indo-China and adjacent areas. They brought with them iron tools and weapons into the island world. Thus, people generally known as Malays had been in mainland Malaysia for over two thousand years. No one has ever told me if South-East Asia was inhabited before the arrival of the Proto-Malays.

My friends quoted from early historical records (the Greek *Periplus of the Erythraeanic Sea*) which indicated that, in the first century AD, the Greeks referred to the Graeco-Egyptian trade in what seems to have been the Malay archipelago; and Ptolemy described the 'Golden Chersoneus' in Book IV of his *Geographia* with its inhabitants (in the Malay peninsula) organised into communities. Chinese annals, e.g. *The History of Liang*, continued the story, identifying civilised inhabitants at various early times in North Malaya. A century or so later, the Buddhist Sri Vijaya Empire, based in Sumatra, extended into West Malaya and this was eventually replaced in the fourteenth century by the Hindu-Buddhist Mejapahit Empire. European colonial powers – Portuguese, Dutch and British – vied for the control of trade, and the important port of Malacca; until the British, by a series of treaties with the Malay Rulers, brought the country under the protection of the British Empire.

The greatest impact on culture in South-East Asia was the arrival of Islam. Marco Polo described in 1292 how Islam had established a foothold in Sumatra; but it was not until the early sixteenth century, following the conversion of the Malay ruler in Malacca, that Malays embraced Islam.

161

Tunku Farid explained to me how rich the Malay language was in words and expressions from other languages. The earliest of these came from Sanskrit during the Buddhist period of the Sri Vijayan Empire (Palembang in Sumatra, he said, was a centre of Buddhist learning, when the Chinese traveller I-tsing spent six months there in 671 AD). Then came the cultural influence of Hinduism during the Mejapahit Empire, and the introduction of many Hindu and Indian words and music into the language and customs of the country. With Islam, came the language of the Koran and the assimilation of Arabic words. The port of Malacca, from the sixteenth century to the early nineteenth century, saw the introduction of Portuguese and Dutch words into the language; and, of course, the British presence added much more to the language. A further influx of Arabic words came as more and more people undertook the haj to Mecca. Universal knowledge acquired from radio, television and the internet are having unforeseen and extraordinary consequences for the Malay language and for the education of Malaysian children.

I much enjoyed delving into all this in my talks with Tunku Farid; and later, too, with Syed Nasir bin Ismail, the Director of the National Language Institute in Kuala Lumpur. Other important social manners I learnt, as I mixed with my Malay friends, were that a person's head is sacred – it is an insult to touch it without permission. Equally, it is an affront to place one's foot on a table or chair, or to touch anyone with one's feet. Pigs and dogs were regarded as unclean. To enter a house with shoes on was very bad manners, as also was the use of the left hand for eating (it has other less hygienic uses throughout the East).

I was often asked to marriages of friends, or their children, and it was most interesting to observe the ceremonial involved. I went to marriages in Kedah, Pahang and Selangor and, although customs varied in detail, as did the wealth of those involved, the overall rituals were similar. These marriages usually went through three stages – the Proposal, leading up to the Engagement; the Religious Ceremony; and the *Bersanding* or Celebrations. It was the Bersanding Ceremony to which I was usually invited as a guest.

Long before the Bersanding Ceremony took place, the girl's family would be busy preparing a new bridal bed and also a *Pelamin* (sometimes a bed; but it was usually two chairs side by side, or arranged as a double throne). Three days before the

Bersanding, the bride's and groom's fingernails would be dyed red with henna. On the Bersanding night, the groom would be dressed in an elaborate traditional wedding dress. The bride, dressed in a specially made sarong and *baju* (top) and very heavy headgear, would be the first to sit on the Pelamin. The groom would come in procession and would be ushered into the house. He would not be permitted to join his bride on the Pelamin until he had paid a small fee to the 'sentry' on guard. Two important items would be placed in front of the couple – the *nasi kunyit* (rice) and the *bunga telor*, (hard-boiled egg).

As soon as the groom took his place beside his bride, the family and guests would try to make the couple smile, by making funny remarks as they ate the rice. After some time, the bride would join her little finger to the groom's and pull him slowly to the bedroom. The guests would depart, each having been given a hard-boiled egg.

Kulim was the headquarters of the survey department and I persuaded the chief surveyor to produce large-scale maps of both districts. I had these made up and put around the walls of a new operations room. The enlarged maps were annotated to provide an accurate historical record of terrorist activity; such as camps, supply lines, ambushes, attacks on estates, rubber tree slashing, lorry burning, armed robberies, identity card destruction, etc. We were then able to carry out better-informed forward planning, and to extract quickly meaningful operational intelligence from surrendered and captured terrorists. It also helped us brief and debrief informers and to analyse captured documents. Air photography, and Auster plane recces, were becoming more widely used at this time, and we were able to ask for coverage of specific jungle areas. The air photography people in Kuala Lumpur soon improved their expertise on interpreting the information revealed.

I gave annotated area maps to every police station; so that the officers-in-charge could plan random foot patrols in their station area, and not just sit on their bottoms all day. My plan for the occupants of police transport to get out and walk around ambush black spots was introduced. and seemed to work, though it was not at all popular. I am sorry to say I always ignored my own instructions on this matter.

The Director of Operations, Sir Harold Briggs, wrote to me informally towards the end of January and said he proposed to see what I was up to in Kulim. Next month, he arrived with a retinue of sixteen. He said he was most impressed with my new operations room. We took him on a lengthy inspection of Kuala Nau resettlement area, one of the largest in the country. Later, I asked him to talk informally to my (now, not so) 'difficult' planters after a lunch hastily laid on at the Kulim club. It proved a huge success from my point of view, and we had nothing but friendly co-operation from the European planters after this.

Meanwhile, terrorist activity continued apace and I kept in regular contact with our local KOYLI company commander. My diary records that a senior British rubber planter was wounded on 10th November, and his clerk killed. Two Chinese-owned lorries were burned on 14th November. My police sergeant at Karangan was killed by terrorists on 23rd November and a constable and a civilian were wounded; the KOYLI killed an armed terrorist and captured another during the follow-up. Mr Bulteel, a senior police officer, and a constable were ambushed and killed over the border in Alor Star on 1st December. Mr Stork, the security officer on Dublin estate, escaped from an ambush on 21st December which, according to a surrendered terrorist, was meant for me.

My boss left on transfer to Alor Star on 23rd December 1950, having completed our lengthy handover. I moved from my temporary office in the operations room into his office and inherited 'the chair'. This was the pilot's seat of a crashed Second World War Japanese Zero fighter. It was very comfortable though rather narrow.

We began recruiting something like 1,200 unpaid volunteer Malay auxiliary policemen, and placed them under the officers-in-charge of police stations and the police lieutenants. Although only about fifty of them, each armed with a shotgun and ten rounds of ammunition, were on duty at any one time, they proved surprisingly useful for 'sitting on', and disrupting, terrorist lines of communication. They assisted security force activity, such as manning roadblocks, carrying out identity card checks and raising morale in isolated police outstations. Later on, these and similar bands of auxiliary police were formally recruited into a national organisation and given the title Home Guards.

There were several Europeans living in Kulim at that time; one of them was Walker Taylor whom I got to know well. One day, he told me in an offhand way that he had watched two suspicious men meet three Chinese squatters on the jungle edge, quite close to his house. Next day I called on him for tea and he took me up to his bedroom. 'There they are again,' he said, and produced a pair of binoculars. I had a look; there they were, large as life, two armed terrorists wearing simple green uniforms collecting something from two Chinese squatters only 500 yards away. I could not believe my eyes. To cut a long story short, after rigorous practice sessions, four of us managed to capture both terrorists cleanly and without a fight, together with a carbine, a pistol, and a primed hand grenade. Quite illegally, but with Neville Godwin's enthusiastic agreement, I classified them as having surrendered to us. They helped us enormously over the next few weeks by leading us to two small, occupied, terrorist camps and by identifying leaders of the Communist organisation *Min Yuen* outside the jungle. Actually, Neville Godwin's enthusiasm was not wholly limited to the reclassification. He drove down to see me straight away. He said he was really quite angry with me for putting the lives of my colleagues at risk, and ordered me not to try on anything like that again. Of course, he was absolutely right.

Before I arrived in Kulim, the State government had decided to disrupt terrorist supplies over a large part of South Kulim district, by regrouping all the absentee Chinese landlord rubber estates into seven resettlement areas, bordering the two main roads. Each area would be defended by fifteen special constables. I came on the scene after the decision had been taken and became involved in setting up defensive positions. As the area was populated entirely by Chinese rubber tappers, we tried hard to help build communication bridges between the Malay policemen and the Chinese population; we were helped greatly with this task by the extremely efficient Chinese Affairs Officer for Kedah/Perlis. Immediate proof that this huge undertaking and expense was worthwhile came from the terrorists themselves, who mounted desperate attacks in an attempt to prevent resettlement taking place. More lorries were burned, more rubber trees were slashed and intimidation became commonplace. On our side, increased contacts with the terrorist organisation resulted in seven armed terrorists being killed. a further two were captured and five surrendered. Not long after that, the Communist Party decided to withdraw its two hundred armed terrorists from this large area of South Kedah. A real victory for the security forces and the Kedah Government. Even more importantly, it brought safety and prosperity to the local population, which had suffered grievously for so long from the attentions of the so-called Liberation Army.

Elsewhere in the Circle the Emergency continued apace. In February 1951, a police van was ambushed and one constable was killed and two were wounded. In our follow-up my patrol killed an armed terrorist on the jungle edge, but the remainder escaped. Detective Sergeant Ismail and a number of civilians were killed on Sungei Dingin estate. Half of Terap village was burned down by terrorists in March and we had to evacuate the inhabitants so that the Chinese Affairs Officer could find them homes. The army killed or captured six armed Communist terrorists during this period.

In March, I went to Penang and met my successor as OSPC Kulim on board the SS *Carthage* and returned to Kulim with his baggage. Next day, I collected him and his wife from the *Carthage* and drove them to Kulim. They retrieved their belongings from South Perak later; I moved into a large two-storeyed house nearby, to share with the inspector of mines for Kedah/Perlis.

My new home was formerly occupied by the *Kempei Tai* (the Japanese secret police) during the Japanese occupation of Malaya, 1941–45. It was known to be haunted and no one of any nationality liked to live there. The concrete floor of the garage had only recently been dug up and twenty decapitated bodies were given a decent funeral in the Chinese cemetery. According to local people, the missing heads had been placed by the Japanese on top of poles, opposite the police station, to serve as a warning to others. The house itself had different auras in the rooms. Lights would go on and off. The wireless would suddenly start playing and change stations automatically; sewing machines would switch themselves on. My companion was in a state, because none of his Chinese girlfriends would stay there. Abdullah said that stones were thrown, his wife had heard screams in the jungle behind the house and George would start to whine and growl for no apparent reason. We reported this to our splendidly black-bearded local Jesuit priest. He summoned two colleagues and, having heard all we had to say, agreed to exorcise the house, garage and garden. During the proceedings, things were held up by what he described as a troubled cloud in a small room next to the garage. We broke up the floor and discovered three more decapitated bodies in the ground below. After that strange diversion, the place was thoroughly exorcised according to Roman Catholic tradition. My sleep was interrupted thereafter only by my companion's noisy returns from Penang in the early hours.

My successor was a former Indian Army officer and had plenty of experience fighting terrorism in Perak. As I had been doing two jobs over the last four months, I was glad to revert to the operational side and he took over the administration, and the chair, though our work overlapped, depending on day-to-day developments.

In late March, I left Kulim for Kuala Lumpur, stopping at various places on the way and spent the night with Roy Henry, the OCPD at Tanjong Malim. Next day, I called in at Rawang to see Ted Rainford and found the place in an uproar. Earlier that morning, an RAF Regiment platoon had fought a battle with terrorists and suffered five killed and five wounded. Apparently the platoon had then surrendered and handed over to the terrorists two Bren guns, two Sten guns, fourteen rifles and no end of ammunition – a black day for us. Whilst in Kuala Lumpur, I was invited to lunch by Mr W.D. Robinson, the acting commissioner of police during Nicol Gray's absence on leave, and I brought him up to date with my adventures in the north. On my way back, I called in at Tanjong Malim again where Right Flank of the Scots Guards had just brought in the dead bodies of ten terrorists. This cheered me up a little.

Shortly after my return to Kulim, I was driving along the road when I heard the sound of firing towards Labu Besar, a few miles north of Kulim, and found Police Lieutenant Wride and two special constables lying dead on the road beside their burning Land Rover. I loaded the bodies on to a passing bus, sent them to Kulim under escort of my driver and telephoned Major Murray of the KOYLI. I collected ten men from two local police stations; but, despite finding tracks, we did not catch up with the terrorists. During my Malay lesson a few days later the telephone bell rang and I was told that Mr Stork, his driver and a Tamil civilian had been ambushed and killed near Dublin estate. While organising the follow-up, a Chinese terrorist surrendered bringing lots of operational information. I handed him over to the army.

167

Friday 13th April was unlucky for me. The local military had just completed training one of my twelve man re-formed jungle squads. I took them on their first operational patrol, with yet another brand new surrendered terrorist to attack his former jungle camp. All went very well. But as we took up our chosen positions, a police constable accidentally shot himself in both legs with his Sten gun. The terrorists upped and ran. We managed to wound and capture one and we also captured another. Eight of them got away. We recovered a pistol, a hand grenade, a great deal of equipment, a lot of .303 ammunition and a valuable haul of documents. I decided to abandon the chase as it was all we could do to carry my poor constable and the wounded terrorist back to hospital and guard the captured terrorist. I had also to preserve the anonymity of the surrendered terrorist.

On a second visit to Kuala Lumpur, I was invited by the Acting Commissioner to lunch, over which he asked me if I would like to learn Chinese. I said that I would, very much. I reported home as follows: 'I think I stand a good chance of being selected as I am sure I have passed the last of my Malay exams ... knowledge of Chinese will be important anywhere out here, and will be an excellent insurance if I am ever out of a job ... I can now speak Urdu, Gurkhali, Malay and, of course, some Indonesian. I can also write in *jawi* and *devanagari* scripts. Perhaps I am too optimistic ... I have to pass a tone test and, as you may recall, I was in the groaners' section of the Bigshotte Preparatory School choir.' Surprisingly, I passed both the Cantonese and Hokkien tone tests and was allocated to the Hokkien Course which, apparently, was the harder and less popular one.

The arrival of my successor gave me an opportunity to take up some of my accumulated local leave. I drove down to KL for two nights, picked up Derek Mole, turned round and drove across the border to South Thailand via Kulim and Penang. We stayed in Songkhla in the Vice-Consul's house for three nights and I renewed my acquaintance with Captain Dennis, the British Consul, and some of my Thai friends. We left by woodburning train to Sungei Golok on the Thai/Kelantan border, where I had spent the night with the stationmaster in 1946, and then trans-trained to Kota Bahru in Kelantan State. Here we hired an ancient Ford and drove to the Beach of Passionate Love. I renewed my acquaintance with Prince Mahiyuddin, a younger brother of the Sultan, and his exotic

White Russian wife, known generally as Mummy. They had modernised their beach homes, one of which Derek Mole and I used as a base to explore the places I had known so well in 1946. A week later, we retraced our steps via Songkhla and returned to Malaya.

The rest of my time in Kulim was as busy as ever, marred greatly by the murder of a KOYLI private soldier by terrorists on 20th May. I left Kulim by car for the Cameron Highlands hill station, to join the Chinese language school, leaving behind some very good friends; including Tunku Farid and the Soon family (Hokkiens) whom I knew quite well in Penang. I was very sad to leave my brave Malay policemen in their lonely outstations. The loyalty and cheerful service of these people during difficult times have left an unforgettable print on my memory, and I often think about them. Tunku Farid's wife gave me a sumptuous farewell dinner; cooking many separate Malay dishes, so that I could sample each one. George was not allowed to leave Kedah, which was still a rabies area; a local rubber planter's wife kindly agreed to look after him for me.

I made a point of saying goodbye to my former boss in Kulim, who had settled down well as an administrative officer in Alor Star, sharing a house with the Deputy Chief Police Officer. He had gradually recovered from the shock of losing his wife. I still find it grossly insensitive of the police headquarters in Kuala Lumpur to have posted him to Kulim where so much terrorist activity was going on. I think his removal by Neville Godwin prevented a serious tragedy. Neville Godwin himself was murdered by Communist terrorists a short while later on a mountain road in Central Kedah. I think he was the most senior British Police Officer to be killed during the Emergency. He and his family had been great friends from early days and, though I missed him terribly, for them it was a really terrible disaster.

Having arrived in the Cameron Highlands, I wrote home saying, 'The Cameron Highlands Hotel, where we are staying, is over 5,000 feet above sea level. The weather is invigorating and quite the right atmosphere for mental work. The food is good. We live in wee cubicles – a simile of monks on a mountain top is too apt to bring a smile! Dr Nicholas Bodman, an American linguist, is our headmaster and he is assisted by Dr Ngo, an old-fashioned professor from Amoy university in China; and by Mr Yap, a former editor of a Chinese mosquito (gossip and scandal) newspaper in Singapore.

Thus we have a mixture of the old and the new. Dr Bodman's family – his wife, boy and girl – are with him, and so are the wives of Dr Ngo and Mr Yap.'

The Hokkien language, said to be one of the earliest literary languages of China, is spoken not only by Chinese living in Fukien Province of South China; but also in the nearby large island of Taiwan (called Formosa when it was occupied by the Japanese). For centuries, Hokkien seafaring merchants from the port of Amoy, its nearby islands and from the surrounding countryside, ventured overseas and settled in South-East Asia. On reaching the Malay Peninsula, they established themselves in Singapore, Malacca, Klang and Penang. They also travelled inland and founded rural Hokkien communities.

They brought with them their ancient customs and traditions such as commercial guilds, clan associations, secret societies, the use of drugs (mainly opium) and maintained strong financial and family links with their home regions in China. A few brought their womenfolk with them; others married Malay girls or lived with concubines (*mui-tsai*). Their businesses flourished and they began to control most of the booming Malayan economy (rubber and tin, mainly). They gained the respect of the pre-Second World War British administrators, who gave them the much-valued designation 'Straits British'. However, the surrender of the British in 1941 and four years' bitter experience of the Japanese occupation, destroyed for ever the *ancien regime* and brought terrible disasters to the Hokkien community. They suffered greatly at the hands of the Japanese *Kempei Tai*; many were murdered, thousands went missing, never to reappear. After the war they strongly supported British proposals for the Malayan Union. When these were withdrawn, they went into local politics proper and joined the Malayan Chinese Association (MCA).

The MCA entered into political partnership with the United Malay National Organisation (UMNO) and the Malayan Indian Congress (MIC); thus uniting the ethnic communities in Malaya to form the Alliance Party. In 1955, a general election was held throughout the country and the Alliance won a landslide victory. After Malaya gained its independence from the British in 1957, the Alliance formed the new government, with the MCA in control of the financial portfolios. The next two decades saw the

MCA lose political and financial power to UMNO, but that is another story.

There were two Malayan civil servants and eight police officers on my Hokkien course, three of whom were married – the wives were allowed to join the class. The hotel was managed by an Indian; the staff were Chinese, whose children had rosy cheeks in the cooler climate. We used to go to the European-owned Smoke House Inn for social entertainment and had many convivial evenings with David Marshall, a frequent visitor, who later became Chief Minister of Singapore. My particular friend on the course was John Lawrence MCS, who worked in the Kuala Lumpur and Singapore Secretariats (centres of government), and I took my daily exercise following him as he hit a ball round the beautifully laid out golf course. I played tennis every weekend. Links with the outside world were maintained by an armed convoy of vehicles which went 35 miles down the hill to Tapah every morning, and returned every afternoon. Although it had been a notorious area in the past, we were ambushed only once and there were no casualties. The greatest dangers were the landslides which occurred after every storm; these had to be cleared by Public Works Department labourers, employed specifically for that purpose.

My concentration on learning Hokkien was rudely interrupted by some dreadful news on 20th August 1953. Ted Rainford, who had won the DSO and MC in Burma, had been ambushed and killed near Rawang. His obituary in *The Times* included this anonymous tribute: 'Mr E. Rainford was the epitome of the British character ... after a most distinguished war record in the Gurkha Rifles, he made himself a legend as a bold and fearless police officer in Malaya ... with his red beard and hearty open countenance ... he represented a strange survival of Elizabethan chivalry, the more especially because of his gallant and courteous manners ... and the fact that derogatory words concerning others never left his lips.'

And I wrote, also anonymously, in our police magazine: 'With his red beard, faded jungle green and clear blue eyes, Ted was a great leader. I shall never forget the vivid impression he made upon me one night in 1948. It was just after he had been ambushed

171

by terrorists on the Kuala Kubu/Rawang road, and his Sikh inspector had been shot in the shoulder. His men were very young and this was their first time in action. Despite being in an unarmoured district van, with its tyres shot to pieces, all had fought well; driving off numerous terrorists who were running alongside the stricken vehicle – from tree to tree – pouring in their fire. These young Malays were in extremely high spirits when I came upon them and in a most pugnacious mood, although half of them were wounded. Ted would be the last to admit that he became their idol from then on, but it was obvious.' We discovered, later, that his youngsters had wounded nine terrorists, three of whom had died subsequently of their wounds in the jungle.

When Dr Bodman was described to us in our joining instructions, he was said be a linguist and, quite naturally, we thought he could speak Hokkien fluently. We soon discovered he could not speak a word and, on occasions when he tried, his tones were distinctly faulty. In *The Shorter Oxford English Dictionary*, which I had specially imported from England to help me do *The Straits Times* weekly prize crossword puzzle, a secondary definition of the word linguist included the word philologist from the Greek love of words, a person versed in the science of language. I supposed he was a philologist. Speaking a language himself did not concern him at all. But the history and construction of languages were his lifelong interests; and teaching willing students became his living. His method was based on a weird and wonderful ancient tape machine using wide transparent plastic tapes, which broke down frequently. Fortunately, Mr Yap, the practical man of our three teachers, could repair the machine and was required to do so several times a week. We spent hours and hours of repetitive work, first on words and then on sentences. He asked us not to make notes but, with some reluctance, he agreed that we could make word lists. I manufactured a series of cards, with the English version on one side and the romanised Hokkien version on the other. I made an average of twenty-five cards a day. and played with them while shaving in the morning and sitting on the loo. I left them in all sorts of places round my room and I took the week's collection with me to church on Sundays. Dr Bodman had not prepared the teaching syllabus in advance. As we progressed, he devised fresh lessons the night before each session, often with the help of one of his students – usually me.

We discovered that every word in Hokkien had its own tone and any mistake in that tone produced an entirely different meaning. For example, the word *kau* (pronounced cow) could mean monkey, dog, hook, to arrive and the figure 9 depending entirely on the tone. Worse still, words in combination changed their tone, so that one had to remember not just the original tone, but its change in combination. Even now, if I discover a Hokkien waiter in a Chinese restaurant, and I order a bowl of soup, I sometimes get it wrong and I am confronted with an unwanted bowl of sugar, accompanied by an innocent smile on the waiter's face.

I managed to escape three times from my incarceration in the Cameron Highlands. While spending a weekend visiting Kuala Lumpur to see friends, I was contacted by General Sir Harold Briggs who asked me to drinks. He talked about the slow development of his Plan, and then told me that he was retiring back to Cyprus in October. He was clearly tired and frustrated and critical of the civil service, its ambivalent attitude to the Emergency, and silly nit-picking limitations on his powers as Director of Operations. I also drove to Ipoh where I attended a Chinese dentist who removed an aching tooth most professionally. My third and last visit was up to Penang for a short holiday at a Chinese-run beach hotel with Dr and Mrs Ngo. Here I discovered that Mrs Ngo had herself been a university professor and, before the Chinese Communist victory in 1949, was a renowned calligraphist. I asked her to write my name on a visiting card – it was a work of art. I have it by me as I write.

Nicol Gray rang me up in August to say that I could go on leave at the end of the course, providing I passed the final exam, and urged me to take up golf. Sir Henry Gurney, the High Commissioner, was murdered by terrorists on his way to Fraser's Hill on 7th October 1951. Subsequent interrogation of those responsible, together with a study of documents captured later, showed that his death was not pre-planned or the result of a breach of security – it was fortuitous. But it was a disaster for the country. M.J. Hogan took over as officer administering the government on 8th October; General Sir Harold Briggs retired to Cyprus in November; General Sir Rob Lockhart late of the Indian Army, and aged nearly sixty, was appointed the new Director of Operations. Mr Oliver Lyttleton, the Secretary of State for the Colonies in the Conservative Government, came out to Malaya on 29th

November to see things for himself. As a result, in February 1952, General Sir Gerald Templer was appointed the new High Commissioner, Commander-in-Chief and Director of Operations with very wide powers.

This was the background to the last half of my Hokkien course and, as my work improved, I began to enjoy the language. Unfortunately for me, Dr Bodman discovered that not only was I a former officer in the Gurkha Brigade, but he also discovered a Gurkha change-of-air station in the nearby village of Brinchang, high up in the hills, where men serving in the Gurkha battalions stationed in Malaya were sent in turn on local leave. He got quite excited over this and decided to record the languages of the East Nepal/Tibet region. I was dragooned into acting as interpreter and we inflicted ourselves on the hapless Gurkhas. Between us, we wrote down and recorded the basic languages of the Gurungs, Magars, Rais, Tamangs, Limbus and three other smaller tribes. Eventually, his colleagues in America were very pleased with our work which, apparently, they rewrote into booklets – perhaps for use during mysterious operations of the CIA in that region! He was delighted when we were invited to the local Gurkhas' Dashera celebrations in October.

Our Chinese language exams started in late December. The first was set by Dr Bodman and his staff; the second by the Chinese Secretariat in Kuala Lumpur. I came first in Dr Bodman's exam, and equal first with a Great Credit in the Secretariat's exam. I completed the course with a working vocabulary of three thousand words and I was capable of talking fairly intelligently with ordinary Hokkien people of all ages. I decided that my weak points were, firstly, that I had a tendency to be lazy about my tones; and, secondly, I was not fluent enough and lacked practical experience of talking to people. Fortunately, if I forgot a word or phrase, it was often acceptable to slip in the corresponding Malay expression, as many overseas Hokkiens were bilingual in Malay. As soon as I knew the results, I took two days off for shopping in Kuala Lumpur, returning to the Cameron Highlands Hotel on Christmas Day.

Who should I see ensconced comfortably in front of the fire before dinner, but Nicol Gray. I described what followed in my letter home. 'He said that he was fed up with Kuala Lumpur and had come up here to spend Christmas with young people for a change. We persuaded him to put on a suit and took him to a cocktail party (our own farewell at the Bodmans' home). Then back to the hotel for Christmas dinner. I was elected as one of two hosts. We did him very well and he stumped up half the cost of the champagne. After dinner, we organised an impromptu dance finding many willing partners from among the young female staff of Miss Griff's (Griffiths) nearby school.'

In fact he was very depressed with the way things were going, especially with the death of Sir Henry Gurney; the departure of Sir Harold Briggs; and the arrival of Sir Rob Lockhart, Sir Harold's somewhat elderly raw replacement. We talked at length the next day and I could see that he was equally frustrated with the continuing lack of support for his ideas on fighting the Emergency among a few influential senior civil servants. He left us the next day and returned to Kuala Lumpur. On 13th January I received this letter from him. 'Just a line to thank you for all you have done for me and to say how grateful I am for your help, support and loyalty. It is a pity I cannot see you to say goodbye; but I think that if I started a tour merely for that purpose it would add to the difficulties of the Force and those in it ... let me know how you get on. Come and see me when you are on leave.' And so he left Malaya for good. I saw him in July 1952 at the 'In and Out' club in Piccadilly and he came with his wife to my wedding in England on 13th October 1956.

During the previous six months, many of my heroes had been murdered, or had died, or had left the country; even George, my much-loved Scottish terrier, had been bitten by a snake in Kedah and had died. Some thirty years later, an article in *The Times* about cicadas recalled him to me, and I contributed the following postscript:

Sir, your Science Report on cicadas reminds me of an evening alone in my bungalow on the jungle edge in Malaysia. A cicada flew into the sitting room, crashed against the ceiling and hit the floor making loud, characteristic noises. George, my Scots terrier, pounced on the cicada and swallowed it whole. The cicada protested loudly from within for a full two minutes. The expression on the dog's face was unforgettable.

*

175

Abdullah and his wife now had two more young children and they decided to stay in Kulim. I came down from the hills into a very different world from the one I had left only six months before.

On arrival in Kuala Lumpur after Christmas, the Deputy Commissioner of Police gave me a letter from an official of the Chinese Secretariat asking me whether or not I would be willing to take over from Nicholas Bodman, whose contract would come to an end after a year. I had no difficulty in turning this down because I did not feel I would make a good headmaster. I was also offered a year's study in Taiwan, with all expenses paid; though sorely tempted, I turned that down as well. However, I agreed to be interviewed on radio by the head of the Chinese section of Radio Malaya about my recent Chinese language course. Following this, I was asked to take part in a series of six five-minute sketches in Hokkien on contemporary subjects. Each episode received two broadcasts and appeared quite popular with the listening public; I received twenty letters from Hokkien Chinese fans! As a follow-up, I received many invitations to attend dinners, over the next few weeks, hosted by the Hokkien communities in Penang, Kuala Lumpur, Klang and Malacca, during some of which I made several useful contacts.

I reported to Mr Thompson, the Chief Police Officer of Negri Sembilan State, on 5th January 1952; he told me that I was to go to Kuala Pilah as Officer Superintending the Police Circle. It was a larger Circle than Kulim and had four Districts. Bearing in mind that I was already overdue for home leave in the UK, I thought it rather a strange posting. Evidently the District Officer thought so too. He became stuffy and difficult and started to agitate; making life so unpleasant for me that I decided to put in for a transfer to the Special Branch where, perhaps, I could use my languages to better effect, before taking up my overdue UK leave.

Mr Thompson proved sympathetic. He managed to find someone else to go to Kuala Pilah and offered to share his home with me. My posting to Special Branch came through immediately; but there was not a vacancy in Negri Sembilan State. With Mr Thompson's agreement, I took off for Singapore on local leave, and joined the household of some Chinese friends of Mr Yap, who ran a death house down by the muddy Singapore river. It was patronised by rich Hokkien families, whose dying relatives were encouraged to gratify their failing senses by over-indulgence in rich food, expensive drink, large Havana cigars and attentive female company. Not exactly, 'one more crust before I bust', but something like it; though on a grander scale. I purchased two pairs of black trousers and two white shirts, consumed masses of Chinese food with lashings of garlic, and did my best to fade into the murky background of an ancient Chinese house, off the 'five-foot-way' (the pavement), along the riverbank.

There were plenty of Hokkiens in Singapore with whom I could chatter all day long and most of the night. Eventually, I decided on a change and went to live, on extended local leave, in a large Chinese temple in Kuala Lumpur. I continued to practise my Hokkien and spoke no English to anyone.

Before my arrival there, I had imagined that the main activity of the temple would be centred round religion, but it soon became apparent that most of the praying was for two desired eventualities: the birth of a son for the younger couples; and a successful win on the racecourse for the older visitors. Whilst people were given every type of food and comfort in my death house, pending the end of their lives in this world, the temple also provided inexpensive, easily obtainable, luxuries of every description for personal use in the next. But they were all made of bamboo and paper. I started off by helping to build houses, limousines, aeroplanes, racehorses, ships, pretty ladies, handsome gentlemen, dogs and fabulous beasts; all of which were made of paper and thin strips of bamboo. But I suspect my clumsy efforts were not fully appreciated, for I was soon taken off this work, and encouraged to spend my evenings tearing up bits of flimsy coloured paper, with circles of silver foil glued in the middle, representing vast sums of money for use in the world to come. All these replicas and the paper money were burnt together at funerals, and joined the souls of the departed on their journeys to another world. My colloquial Hokkien improved enormously, as did my knowledge of Chinese family life with its lack of privacy and its strange mixture of lingering smells.

Mr Thompson proved sympathetic and understanding of my wish to practise the language and, on my return to duty, said that I could take over the interrogation section of the Negri Sembilan Special Branch. I was delighted and, for the next three months or so, I managed the interrogation of surrendered and captured terrorists. I contacted Colonel d'Arcy Mander DSO, who was commanding a battalion of the Green Howards and married to my cousin Eileen. He introduced me to Nigel Bagnall (later to become a Field Marshal) who, he said, was his best company commander. We hit it off and, I think, I helped the company by giving them a regular supply of willing former terrorists to guide them into camps, supply points, courier posts etc.

When it was announced that General Sir Gerald Templer (later Field Marshal) was to replace Sir Henry Gurney as the High Commissioner for Malaya, we looked up his track record, and found he was fifty-four years old and had served with courage and great distinction in the Second World War. We were delighted beyond bounds to hear that not only was he to be the High Commissioner; but also Director of Operations. A combination, which we realised at once, would unite the civilian and military efforts, thus ensuring his undivided direction of the war against militant Communism. It soon became crystal clear that he had a very strong character. demanded the highest standards and was prepared to dismiss, or retire compulsorily, those who failed to obey his orders or conspired against him. Quite a number of senior European officials quietly disappeared off the stage during his first year of office.

I first met him shortly after his arrival in 1952. when I was at odds with the British Adviser Negri Sembilan (my old friend ff. Sheppard) regarding the classification of a recently captured high-ranking Communist terrorist. My request to have him reclassified as having surrendered and made available to the security forces was turned down. At Mr Thompson's suggestion, I made an appointment to see General Templer urgently in King's House Kuala Lumpur. I had already thoroughly approved of all I had heard about him and I was agog to see what he was like. I was ushered through familiar rooms by one of his military staff, and found him looking across the valley with his feet firmly planted in an open drawer of his desk.

'What's that up there?' he said.

'A racquet-tailed drongo,' I replied.

'What do you want?' he demanded.

'I've got a really good captured terrorist on my hands, he's got bags of operational information. No one knows we have captured him. He's come over to our side and I want to hand him over to the army. Unfortunately, ff. Sheppard won't let me reclassify him as a surrendered person. Please help.'

The General replied with a sigh. 'I wish all my problems had such an easy solution. Don't waste any more time, go ahead. I'll telephone Sheppard, what does ff. stand for? A bloody silly name. I won't see you out, you know the way, my back is giving me hell and I am resting it.'

I asked him if he had been wounded in the war.

'Christ, no,' he said. 'A bloody great grand piano fell on top of me.'

I fled.

I went out on operation with the army several times and on one occasion they shot dead one of my informers, by mistake, and I had a lot of trouble persuading them he was on our side and could not be counted as an addition to their tally of kills. On the whole, however, I was mostly deskbound; but the interrogations were very rewarding. They gave me a really good insight into individual Communist thinking and way of life in the jungle. I made friends with a senior Punjabi Muslim police officer called Mobarak Ahmed, who was arguably the best operational agent handler in the Malayan Special Branch; and he invited me to join him on several of his exciting and sometimes dangerous activities.

At the request of Mr Thompson, and with the agreement of the Head of the Negri Sembilan Special Branch, I prepared a paper on how General Templer's order to expand the Special Branch – a major expansion of Sir William Jenkin's plan – might be carried out in practice on the ground. I consulted my friends, who already had similar experience fighting the Communist terrorist organisation, and I talked at length with Mobarak Ahmed and others in Seremban, drawing on my early experiences in North Selangor and recently in Kedah. My conclusions were pretty obvious. Draft into Special Branch all those who pass out of the Chinese Language School; double the number of Special Branch inspectors in Circles and Districts; and provide them with office staff, translators, homes for their families and schools for their children; ensure each Circle and District Special Branch officer had sufficient support to mount medium-term intelligence projects aimed specifically at the penetration of the party at District level, and their jungle courier links elsewhere. The Special Branch School should focus on this at once. Its students should include police uniform branch officers involved directly with the Emergency on the ground; and all Military Intelligence officers should attend the school on appointment. Of course some of us were aware of Sir William Jenkin's advice on this subject, and had been doing just this in our own way, often with success. But, generally speaking, Special Branch and its facilities at this time were still far too small to cope with both tactical operations, and the development of longer term intelligence projects across the country. Above all, it was important to explain to the Military Intelligence officers that short-term results, important for battalion 'scores', would sometimes have to give way to more important and productive long-term projects. Among those to whom my paper, suitably edited by the Director of Special Branch in Kuala Lumpur, was sent, were General Templer (apparently at his request) and the head of Special Military Intelligence Staff (SMIS) who was responsible for administering the Military Intelligence officers.

I left Seremban by train for Singapore and flew to Ceylon, where I stayed ten days with my cousin, who was then the secretary of the Ceylon Planters' Club, and his wife, a former Royal Navy Wren. They gave me a super time. I then flew home, via Rome, where another cousin arranged for me to be entertained by a delightful female companion, who showed me the sights and took me to the opera.

I spent six months in England and had a wonderful leave escorting girlfriends to shows in London. I drove my parents on a tour of Wales in my brand new Austin A40. My enjoyment of leave was dampened, however, by the illness of my father who had developed cancer and a duodenal ulcer. When I said goodbye on leaving England for Malaya, I watched him drive away in his ancient motor car – then, as he waved goodbye, I knew that I would not see him again. He died the following year.

6

If the good people were clever, and all clever people were good,
The world would be nicer than ever we thought it possibly could.
But somehow, 'tis seldom or never the two hit it off as they should;
The good are so harsh to the clever, the clever so rude to the good!

ELIZABETH WORDSWORTH

When I flew out of England on 12th January 1953, I discovered
that Scott Leathart, who was commanding the Gurkha Police
contingent in Singapore, was on the plane together with his sister.
This cheered me up immensely on our long journey. We stayed
twenty-four hours in Beirut; there was another stop in Karachi,
and we landed at Singapore on 14th January. I spent the night at
the Adelphi hotel and handed slices of Christmas cake from the à
Becket Terrell parents to their two daughters, then working in
Singapore. I was invited to supper with the Director of the Singapore Special Branch and his wife and he brought me up to date
with the security situation there. I flew up to Kuala Lumpur the
next day and reported for duty. I had lunch with the Malayan
Director of Special Branch, Harvey Ryves, who told me that I had
been posted as Circle Special Branch Officer Mentakab in Pahang.
He said that my task would be one of the most important on the
ground in the country. This was because South-West Pahang was
the jungle home of the Communist Party's politburo, the Battle
News Press, and from where the party controlled its courier routes
throughout the country, inside and outside the jungle. In addition,
the Temerloh area on the Pahang River was the headquarters of
the Malayan Communist Party's Department of Malay Work and
the 10th Regiment (mostly Malay personnel) of the so-called
Malayan Races Liberation Army. He noted I had useful experience

181

and that I had a good working knowledge of Malay and Hokkien. 'Go to it,' he said, 'Build up intelligence coverage in the Chinese and Malay communities.' I realised at once that it was an important posting in a very remote and dangerous area. I flew by Beaver aeroplane to Temerloh.

I discovered that almost all the gazetted police officers, inspectors and detectives in the Circle were being replaced. I was expected to build up a completely new Special Branch organisation and an old friend, Jock Neil, had just been appointed to take charge of the uniform branch. I took over as the Circle Special Branch Officer on 24th January 1953. My predecessor went southwards to Negri Sembilan as head of the Special Branch there, we continued our friendly liaison on secret projects across our borders for some time.

I shared a large bungalow with Jock Neil. He was a marvellous character who started his army life as a medical orderly at the outbreak of the war. He was in the thick of the fighting in Italy, France and Germany, ending up as a major in the Glider Pilot Regiment. He had been awarded an immediate DSO for outstanding gallantry in the field during the Battle of Arnhem. A canny Scot with a bent nose and a roving eye for the girls, he was a member of the Kuala Lumpur Flying Club and had access to a small aeroplane which we kept hidden in the jungle just off Temerloh airstrip. He used the plane to bring back a Red Cross nurse for recreation; flying in visiting politicians and miscellaneous journalists wishing to see something of the Emergency on the ground; and for me to spy indirectly from the air on camps or jungle cultivation areas occupied by terrorists. He was a very experienced pilot and took much pleasure in scaring the life out of unpopular visitors by gliding sideways to land accompanied by loud and increasingly desperate 'Oh dears', then straightening up at the last moment for a faultless landing. Jock was responsible for the administration of the Circle; I had independent executive responsibility for providing the intelligence on which the security forces could take action. We experienced no problems between us and we worked well together.

Our bungalow was light and airy with a huge garden full of cannas and orchids. It was on a hill, behind the District Hospital, and had a panoramic view over 40 miles of jungle to the range of mountains in Central Malaya. We enjoyed wonderful sunsets lasting fifteen minutes every day, accompanied by an eerie light which made everything seem extremely clear.

My mode of travel whilst living in Mentakab was different; but interesting. Three armoured trains ran between Kuala Kurau to the north of us, and Negri Sembilan to the south and I used them from time to time. The Pahang River flowed fast through the district and I was able to borrow the government houseboat, and sometimes the Sultan's personal houseboat, with their respective crews. If I was in a hurry, I used Jock Neil and his aeroplane (he never needed to be asked twice). I had acquired a secondhand Canadian-built Chevrolet in exchange for my nearly new Austin A40. I had been confirmed in my rank as an assistant superintendent of police, before going on leave, thus ending seven years' cadetships, though they were not consecutive. This did not entail an increase in pay, so I was as short of money as ever; but there was not much to spend it on.

Soon after my arrival, I attended a month's Special Branch course in Kuala Lumpur directed by Claude Fenner (later to become Sir Claude Fenner, the Inspector General of the Royal Malaysian Police Service). Most of my postings in the Indian Army and Malaya so far had given me great independence, away from daily contact with my headquarters (for example, when I was in charge of Rawang Police District I never saw the District Officer or even the Officer Superintending the Circle, both of whom ignored me entirely). I was content with this and I did not mind being left to get on with the job in hand. This first posting to Pahang was no different. Nevertheless, I determined to be as co-operative, friendly, loyal and obedient as distances and time would allow.

Following talks with David Henchman, who was the head of Special Branch in Pahang State, living in Kuala Lipis some 70 miles away by road, it was agreed that my main responsibilities would be to organise the Special Branch contribution towards a major food denial operation which would take place in the Triang/Mentakab area of South Pehang, in conjunction with the 4th battalion of the Malay Regiment. My task was to penetrate the outside Communist organisation (Min Yuen) which supported the Communist Party headquarters (at that time believed to be in the area), and the Communists' Battle News Press in the jungle between Mentakab and Bentong. He also asked me to do something positive about civilian Malay support for Malay terrorist organisations among the riverine kampongs along the Pahang River. I requested him to let me approach His Highness the Sultan of Pahang, Sir Abu Bakar KCMG, for his help in solving the problem. He agreed at once, on condition that I cleared it with the British District Officer in Temerloh.

At that time, the British District Officers in Central and North Pahang were not particularly helpful and, as far as anyone knew, they did not appear to have any special personal relationship with the Sultan. They were not Emergency-minded and rather resented any intrusion into their administrative responsibilities; however, they raised no objections to my plans, so I contacted the Sultan's palace on the east coast in Pekan, the royal capital at the mouth of the Pahang river. The comptroller of the Sultan's household was Norman Bewick, an English gentleman of the old school, an old Malaya hand and a personal friend of the Sultan for many years. He proved a great friend to me, too, and we worked closely together in Pekan and again in Kuala Lipis later on.

Before approaching the Sultan, I did some research in the museum libraries in Singapore and Kuala Lumpur to discover all I could about the history of Pahang, and the Malay uprisings against the British some three generations ago. As a member of the Malayan branch of the Asiatic Society, I was able to research former journals and I came across a volume from June 1936. This was a detailed history of Pahang State and included a lengthy article on the Bahaman Wars of 1890–95. I was able to relate these, both historically and geographically, to the present situation. I also discovered that Dato Abdul Razak, then *Mentri Besar* (or prime minister) of Pahang, was a direct descendant of Bahaman, and he very kindly allowed me to examine his family documents relating to those early days. This was the beginning of a long and friendly relationship with the Dato, who later became a *Tun* (a Malayan peer) and Deputy Prime Minister of Malaysia. I also picked the brains of my locally-born Malay detectives, to discover more about the current background of the Sultan and other local Malay leaders. A loose feudal system still operated amongst the Pahang Rawa Malays (who originally came from Sumatra). The Sultan was not only powerful, but also highly respected among his subjects and was a strong and cheerful character.

To my great surprise, I received an immediate invitation to meet the Sultan alone one late afternoon on his houseboat, moored downstream from Temerloh. I found His Highness resting after a swim and dressed in his sarong. He was a tall well-built man with twinkling eyes and a huge smile. He talked to me in Malay and I did my best to reply in rajah Malay – slipping in the required honorifics, such as referring to him politely by the charming Malay word *Tuanku*, when I remembered to. We were waited upon by his third wife, a young Malay girl who listened quietly to our conversation. The Sultan agreed to issue a three-week amnesty to any Malay who admitted helping the terrorists; he said he would get together with me after Ramadan, the Muslim fasting month, to discuss detail. I stayed for a light meal of rice and vegetables (eating with my right hand) and left late at night for my return trip by boat against the current and by moonlight.

Little did I know that the next day was to be so fraught with unexpected excitement. Mr Grieve, the co-operative and friendly District Officer Kuantan on the east coast north of Pekan, and his wife, came to lunch with Jock and me, on their way to spend part of their leave in Kashmir, before flying on to England. During lunch, I received a call on our wind-up telephone from the Indian stationmaster. He was very excited and said that the armoured train from Negri Sembilan had been stopped by terrorists five miles down the line. Three of them had boarded the train. It was due to arrive at any moment. He understood that they wished to surrender; but, he warned, it might be a trick. I asked him to divert the train to a siding in Mentakab station.

I said hurried farewells to the Grieves, telephoned one of my Chinese inspectors to warn him that something was afoot; and hurried down a short cut to the railway line, just in time to climb aboard the train as it stopped. There was an air of excitement among the thirty or forty passengers – mainly Asian visitors to the small rubber estates either side of the line further north. I found the train's police escort, armed with rifles and a Bren gun, commanded by a young Malay police sergeant. They produced two long-haired, very pale, young male Chinese in dirty jungle green uniform, together with a thin, angular, much older Chinese lady also dressed in well-worn jungle green. Apparently, they had stood on the railway line and signalled the train driver to stop. Ignoring strict government orders to the contrary, he did so with a screeching of brakes and a jerk. The three persons retrieved their large packs from the jungle edge and handed over to the train's escort a loaded pistol, two carbines and two primed hand grenades. They spoke in broken Malay and asked the driver to take them to Mentakab. He had passed on the information, via his mobile radio, to the stationmaster.

When I boarded the train, I discovered that the two male Chinese were Hakkas (a Chinese race) and knew no Hokkien. But one of them made repeated urgent references in English to a 'Captain' which did not seem to make sense; the Chinese lady had nothing to say and seemed to go along with whatever her companions decided. I thought, therefore, that one of them might be a senior Communist leader; though their obvious youth seemed something of a paradox. The escort sergeant unloaded the pistol and carbines and I de-primed the two hand grenades. The main thing was to get them off the train unrecognised – there were a few idly curious people on the siding platform. I asked two of the escort guards to dress up as sloppily as possible, remove their heavy boots, put on their gym shoes and try to look like Malay bandits, with handkerchiefs tied across the lower halves of their faces. I told the rest of the escort to handle them fairly roughly and march them off to the police station. I asked the stationmaster to suggest to any enquiring people, that they were much-wanted Malay robbers and would be dealt with accordingly. I also asked him to telephone my inspector and arrange for him to meet me at a certain crossroad between Mentakab and Temerloh.

Meanwhile the relieving escort boarded the train, passengers came and went, and the three Chinese and I climbed down unseen from the other side of the train. We made our way to my garage, which was up a nearby hill out of sight of the station. So far so good; I tried out my Hokkien again on the three Chinese but I did not get very far. Speaking in Malay was a bit more successful and they agreed to accompany me, though, once again, the word 'Captain' continued to be emphasised. We got into my car and I picked up my inspector at the crossroads; we drove to a safe house (a quiet secluded hut on an abandoned smallholding), where we could carry out an immediate tactical interrogation. I had three developments on my mind. The first was to see if one or more of them could be persuaded to go back into the jungle and work long-term for us; the second was to examine the possibility of attacking

186

their camp, the third was to obtain operational information which might lead to a capture or a kill by ambush. These points were churning through my brain as we drove to the safe house. On arrival, I used the inspector as my interpreter. He spoke excellent English, Hakka, Cantonese, Mandarin and Malay.

A rude awakening came immediately as the three packs were dumped on a table in front of me. The largest one had dried blood outside and strands of tangled black human hair dangling out and down the sides. Without doubt, it contained a human head! The younger of the two Chinese undid the straps and, with a flourish, lifted out the head by its hair and turned its face towards me. I felt very much as Herod must have felt when Salome produced the head of John the Baptist. At last the penny dropped, here was the Captain! This was confirmed by the smiles and nods of the two young men. It turned out that the Captain's name was Ah Kuk. He was an important Central Committee member of the Communist Party of Malaya and Representative of Johore state. He also held the rank of regimental commander. The two young Chinese were his bodyguards.

The group of four had left Johore in 1952 to attend an important Central Committee meeting of the Communist Party in Pahang. They arrived too late to meet Chan Peng, the Secretary General, who had already begun his move north to the Thai border. They were on their way back to Johore, having collected the latest political directives and communication plans from South-West Pahang Communist regional headquarters. The two bodyguards had become fed up with Ah Kuk's overbearing and bullying nature and one day, while passing by a Chinese resettlement village on the jungle fringe, they had seen a poster offering a huge reward for Ah Kuk, dead or alive. Neither of them were Communist Party members – both were long time probationers – and they were sorely tempted with the first option. They seized their opportunity while Ah Kuk was asleep, cut off his head with a *parang* (long knife) as evidence of their deed, and made their way into civilisation, taking the Chinese lady with them, together with the grizzly head and a treasure trove of documents. Meanwhile, the lady kept silent and was completely ignored by the other two. I paid little attention to her. After an hour or so, we decided to believe their story and, because they did not know our area and were only passing through and were unwilling to work for us in the Johore jungle, we concluded there was no obvious tactical advantage to be gained.

I arranged for them to be given temporary accommodation in another safe house, food from the Chinese shops and fresh clothing. I asked Ah Soo, the civilian wife of a Chinese Sutton Boy police constable to act as companion for the female. On returning home, I used our radio link with Kuala Lipis to inform an incredulous David Henchman what had happened. He arranged for the documents to be sent to Kuala Lumpur for translation and assessment, and for photographs of the head to be examined by reliable senior Communist Party members working on our side. Having made my peace with the 'arrested' members of the train escort, I returned to the safe house. I saw Ah Soo wringing her hands. She was in a frightful state. She told me that the Chinese lady had gone into another room to change her clothing; and had slipped out through the back door and disappeared, leaving her fresh clothes neatly folded on her bed. I felt responsible, as indeed I was. Who was she? Where had she gone? The two bodyguards said that she had accompanied Ah Kuk throughout his journey; but was not his wife or girlfriend. Fortunately, I found her sitting under a lantana bush in the garden, crying. She admitted she was too tired to go back into the jungle. We then put her under 'house arrest' with a formal guard and treated her as a captured terrorist. It took two days to produce from Kuala Lumpur a qualified female interpreter. The 'old' lady turned out to be in her mid-thirties, was a university graduate and the Communist Party District Committee Secretary of North Johore, in whose area Ah Kuk had been based. She eventually gave us the equivalent of her name, rank and number but nothing else. It was fifteen years before I saw her again.

The documents brought in by the two bodyguards were most interesting. They outlined in great detail the reasons why the Communist Party of Malaya's politburo, under Secretary General Chan Peng, had decided recently to move to the Thai border. The original policy on 'liberated areas', and the armed struggle from within the jungle, was to give way in importance to the need for a return to 'outside' subversion within the trade unions, schools and political parties: a fresh development which enabled the government to prepare early counter-measures on a national scale. Chan Peng wished also to secure communications with China and the outside world and had decided to move to the Thai border area, where this would be easy, and comparatively safe from Malayan security force attacks. One of the other packs contained a battery-operated radio receiver and a transmitter, together with wavelengths to be used and a simple code. The receiver was similar to the Force 136 machine which I had found disused on a col off the Kuala Lumpur-Rawang road in 1948. The two young bodyguards were given their enormous rewards and eventually set up a coffee shop near Ipoh in Perak. They remained friends and came to see me years later on their way to China under assumed names. I heard that one of them died at sea on the journey home to China.

After this excitement, my relationship – indeed friendship – with the Sultan of Pahang grew apace and I visited his palace in Pekan frequently. Norman Bewick was an engaging companion and the three of us had many great times together, trekking around the countryside and meeting many of his 'subjects'. I think our combined efforts, led by the Sultan's energy and good humour, went some way to prevent any further significant support for terrorists within the loop of the Pahang River. When entering his palace in Pekan, I never failed to be impressed by a life-size portrait of His Majesty King George VI (later to be replaced by Queen Elizabeth II) before which, when passing by, he always paused, turned and solemnly bowed.

An interesting side-development of my researches into the history of the Pahang Wars enabled me, by trial and error, to decode jungle courier messages between the Malay terrorists operating around the loop of the Pahang River (Bahaman 1 District) and the Malay terrorist organisation to the east on the Raub/Kuala Lipis border (Bahaman 11 District). The keyword used was the seven-letter word Bahaman; once discovered and allowing for the three letters A, I found it possible to decode every message in detail. I confess that I achieved no financial success with my completed *Straits Times* prize crossword puzzles, but this decoding was quite original and, even though it was so simple, I felt pleased with myself. And, of course, it gave us an exploitable window through which to deduce what was going on in these two regions.

Of a visit by General Templer to Temerloh, I wrote home, 'Jock Neil and I were given twenty four hours' notice to clear his visit with the Malay Assistant District Officer (the British District Officer was on leave) and to arrange for the general to talk to the

189

Malay *penghulus* (village leaders) and the Imams (mosque officials) and any other Malays we thought he should meet. The Malay Assistant District Officer was most co-operative and he produced a good turn-out. The general arrived, unaccompanied by the British Adviser who had taken a wrong turning and had lost his way. We were left with the general, his driver, a tin trunk and some fifty Malay leaders from the Pahang riverine kampongs, most of whom were dressed up to the nines, in full clerical garb with Arab-type headdresses. The general commandeered a bedroom in the rest house and off he went accompanied by the driver and the tin trunk. The Malay officials and the Muslim clerics assembled at one end of the adjoining public room. Some of them could speak good English and all were agog, and a little fearful, at what would happen next. The general told us that he thought his army uniform would create a better impression than his thin crumpled civilian suit. He fished it out of the tin trunk and began to change. Jock and I joined the throng outside.

'The rest house rooms had swing stable-type doors and we could see him undressing and dressing – or rather we saw his head above and his legs below the swing doors. Down came one pair of trousers revealing two thin white legs, up came the other pair with a pull here and a tug there, then the head disappeared and two hands appeared to tie the laces of his highly polished shoes. Up came the head, a brush flicked about and on went the general's beribboned hat. Then he disappeared. The watching crowd became silent. Suddenly, the swing doors opened and a uniformed general of the British Army emerged with a flourish, exclaiming, 'Bring in the Camel Corps!' A massive intake of breath was the immediate reaction, so I clapped my hands and so did everyone else. The ice was broken, the general laughed, so did everyone else. The Assistant District Officer interpreted the pep talk which I had drafted for him the day before. He stuck closely to that, and the subsequent intermingling went down very well.'

On 19th May 1953, to my great surprise, I was transferred on double promotion to Kuala Lipis to be second-in-command of the Pahang Special Branch in an appointment quaintly called Communist Co-ordinator, shortened to ComCo. I soon discovered that my predecessor in Kuala Lipis, a much-experienced senior Chinese police officer, had gone into hospital suffering from overwork and stress.

I handed over to my deputy in Mentakab and left a very cross Jock Neil alone in the bungalow. I had enjoyed my short time in Mentakab and had extended my experience on the ground. In particular, I had been thrilled to practise my Hokkien in the comparatively remote Triang area where there was quite a large jungle-fringe Hokkien community. I greatly enjoyed seeing the surprise appearing on people's faces when it dawned on them that I was talking directly to them in their mother tongue – their smiles were genuine and, after a bit, many overcame their natural reluctance to talk to a stranger: I found their views of life, the Emergency and resettlement of enormous practical interest and that, with tact and patience, I could gently exploit them professionally. On quite another front, I thought I had started something positive about the Malay problem within the loop of the Pahang River, and I had secured much willing support and good will from the Royal Palace in Pekan. My wanderings on official visits had taken me by boat up and down the Pahang River, deep into the jungle on foot round the Tasek Bera (a large unfriendly swamp) to the south and I had made many good friends among the police, the army – especially the 4th Battalion of the Malay Regiment – and the European planting community. I was very sad to leave; but I was determined to continue my work from a different angle in Kuala Lipis.

On arrival in Kuala Lipis, I moved into the rest house and discovered that the Chinese Hailam cooks there were from one family and could produce excellent Chinese or European food, often to order if given sufficient warning. Kuala Lipis was a mainly Chinese town above the steep banks of a swiftly flowing river. It was surrounded by Malay kampongs and a small Malay community lived on rafts along the steep river bank below. My boss, David Henchman, and his wife were friendly and welcoming. David had undertaken a lot of extra work during my predecessor's illness, and departed on a month's local leave soon after I arrived. My takeover took place in Kuala Lipis Hospital. It was obvious to me that David and I had a lot to do if we were to get on top of the Emergency.

We had some outstanding Circle and District Special Branch officers, including a convivial Irishman in Kuantan on the east coast

DIAGRAM 2

Simplified chart showing the integration of intelligence planning and security force operations during the Malayan Emergency 1952–1960 following the appointment of General Templer as High Commissioner and Director of Operations

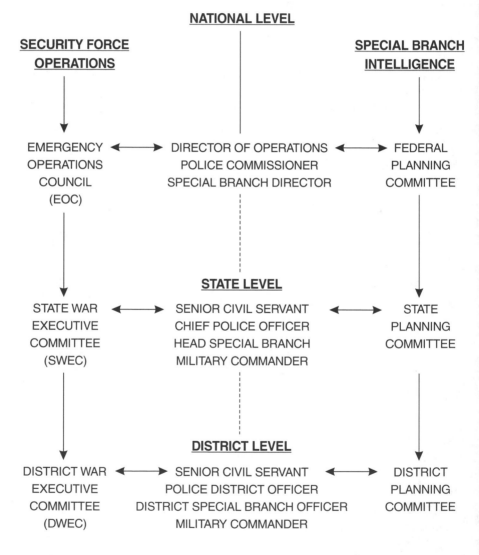

NATIONAL LEVEL

SECURITY FORCE
OPERATIONS

SPECIAL BRANCH
INTELLIGENCE

EMERGENCY ◄──► DIRECTOR OF OPERATIONS ◄──► FEDERAL
OPERATIONS   POLICE COMMISSIONER   PLANNING
COUNCIL   SPECIAL BRANCH DIRECTOR   COMMITTEE
(EOC)

STATE LEVEL

STATE WAR ◄──► SENIOR CIVIL SERVANT ◄──► STATE
EXECUTIVE   CHIEF POLICE OFFICER   PLANNING
COMMITTEE   HEAD SPECIAL BRANCH   COMMITTEE
(SWEC)   MILITARY COMMANDER

DISTRICT LEVEL

DISTRICT WAR ◄──► SENIOR CIVIL SERVANT ◄──► DISTRICT
EXECUTIVE   POLICE DISTRICT OFFICER   PLANNING
COMMITTEE   DISTRICT SPECIAL BRANCH OFFICER   COMMITTEE
(DWEC)   MILITARY COMMANDER

'War by Committee' ensured that Security Force operations at all levels would be efficiently co-ordinated and would be based on Special Branch intelligence.

T.E.H.

192

of Pahang, who had pre-war experience in China and Hong Kong. Two graduates of my recent Hokkien course had just been posted to Bentong and Raub respectively; there was also the District Special Branch officer in Jerantut who had just married the leading lady of the London Windmill Theatre ('We never closed!'). She improved the tone of our social life no end. There were also three excellent Military Intelligence officers stationed in Pahang, responsible to me for providing the security forces with operational information. All these people, together with our efficient loyal Chinese, Malay and Indian inspectors and detectives, were brilliant colleagues.

It turned out that my successor in Mentakab did not have sufficient experience to deal eighteen hours a day with the Emergency. He was unable to speak Malay, so a more appropriate appointment was found for him on the administrative staff in Kuala Lumpur, where his extensive police experience in India could be put to better use. David Henchman and I set about double-checking all aspects of our work. He reorganised the registry, helped by our newly appointed registrar. They restored order out of chaos by introducing a system which enabled us to keep close control of agent-handling, intelligence projects, obtaining value for effort and proper accounting of the secret service fund.

I set about getting to know the Special Branch officers in the rest of Pahang State and also to meeting and talking with the various heads of state departments in Kuala Lipis. One of General Templer's innovations was the introduction of war by committee. We had the Pahang State War Executive Committee in Kuala Lipis and District War Executive Committees at District level (see Diagram 2 on page 192). The most influential people were John Clifford, a direct descendant of former governor Sir Hugh Clifford, who was the avuncular pipe-smoking approachable secretary of the State Committee; and Brigadier Frank Brooke (later General Sir Frank), Commander of the 1st Malay Infantry Brigade.

The British Adviser (BA), a benign but remote figure, was the chairman of the State War Executive Committee – all I remember about him were excellent dinner parties followed by 'Up Jenkins' and 'Hands On the Billiard Table'; the last guest to take hands off the side of the table when a billiard ball was hurtled along the green, either had squashed fingers, or was praised for his or her nerve. When General Templer visited us, he promised us some

Hussars, (whose armoured vehicles were supposed to deter ambushes on the grand trunk road running west to east through Central Pahang). On hearing this, the BA whispered to me, 'It's all very well, but where are they to find fodder for their horses?' Luckily for his career, he spoke quietly, and the general did not hear.

I listened to the coronation of Queen Elizabeth in a friend's room in the rest house at 7.00 p.m. on 2nd June 1953, with the rain coming down outside. I moved into my new home on 6th June. It had two bedrooms and I shared with a former Indian Police inspector. Rather like my house in Kuala Selangor, we had to climb thirty-nine steps before we could enter our front door. Our small garden could be recognised from afar by the presence of a rare three-branched palm tree. Most unfortunately, my companion developed an ingrowing toenail and it had to be treated in hospital. His leg became infected with a ghastly bug and the surgeon took off his foot from below the knee – he was in very considerable pain before and after the operation. It really was a frightful disaster for him. The Public Works Department found him suitable temporary accommodation on level ground, and he was later transferred to an administrative post in Kuala Lumpur. His place was taken by an officer whose home was in the Channel Islands. He proved a very pleasant and amusing companion.

Soon after I arrived in Kuala Lipis, whilst David Henchman was still on leave, a terrorist arrived on the Raub-Kuala Lipis Road and surrendered to a small army convoy returning Frank Brooke in his brigadier's mess dress from an official dinner. Some of us had been at a formal party in the club and were in dinner jackets too. We all congregated in the local Special Branch office so that the first Europeans the terrorist saw, after several years in the jungle, were dressed exactly as depicted in Communist cartoons of the period – capitalists and colonialists in full gear, but minus their top hats. He told me later that he was not the least surprised though we all thought – quite mistakenly – how incongruous we must have looked to him. He claimed that, just before leaving the jungle, he had shot and killed a Central Committee member and most of the North Pahang State Committee membership, all extremely important members of the Communist Party of Malaya.

He had not stopped to check who was left alive. Next day at dawn, I went out with him and the local Special Branch to verify the facts and we located a number of graves with wreaths on top and uniformed bodies inside. Nothing else was around and, sadly, no documents. We sent the wreaths to Kuala Lumpur for further examination and, next day, Guy Madoc, the Director of Intelligence, phoned me to say, somewhat testily, that the wreaths mourned the recent death of Stalin and we had been guilty either of wishful thinking, or naivety in the extreme, or probably both. It was with great difficulty, and after dodging a bottle of ink thrown at me, that I was able to convince Guy the next day that his experts were quite wrong and we had an unplanned, but exceedingly fortunate, development to exploit. The tock tock birds were very active on the road as I returned to Kuala Lipis later that evening.

On the day David returned from leave, rather annoyed to have missed the fun, the manager of Mentakab estate was murdered by a group of ten terrorists. I knew him quite well and his death was a great shock. A year or so later, a surrendered terrorist from the same gang took me to a jungle cache where we found the manager's wallet intact; I handed it over for dispatch to his next-of-kin. At the request of the Chief Police Officer, Kerr Bovell, I gave lectures in Malay to all the *ketua kampongs* (Malay village leaders) in Pahang over a period of one year, and I gave civics course lectures in both Malay and Hokkien to meetings in all the towns of Pahang. I also talked to the Malayan Chinese Association, the Hakka Association and to the state committee members of the United Malay National Organisation. I also discovered that Inche Sallehuddin, a settlement officer in Kuala Lipis, was another knowledgeable direct descendent of Bahaman and I was able to update my original paper. I was even able to go through my revised paper, paragraph by paragraph, with the British District Officer Temerloh, who, until then, had been very stuffy on the subject, and I obtained his enthusiastic support for my recommendations. The latter included allowing the new local District Special Branch officer Mentakab, to proceed with his own plans, free of security force activities, to penetrate and influence Malay Communist District organisations in Bahaman 1 and 11. He managed this brilliantly and eventually all the remaining members of the Communist 10th Regiment surrendered in the Mentakab/Temerloh area personally to him.

195

On 10th July 1953 General Templer visited Kuala Lipis and found time to call David and me in for a five-minute chat, saying how very pleased he was with our results.

Generally speaking, my time was spent touring the state and attending project co-ordination conferences in Kuala Lumpur. Very occasionally, I was in charge of Special Branch operations involving two districts, or I organised interesting missions. On one of these occasions, we had two recently surrendered terrorists, who had volunteered to lead us back to their former operational area and meet three high-level couriers in a certain Chinese-owned rubber estate, between Bentong and Raub. Six of us went down in a commandeered Chinese lorry to another estate nearby with a view to capturing the couriers early next day. That night the tock tock birds went hard at it and made sleep difficult. Suddenly, one of the surrendered men decided to commit suicide. He shot himself in the mouth, covering Inspector Cheah Seng Fatt with blood and deafening me, trying to sleep in the cab. I thought he had murdered Seng Fatt, but by the time I had loaded my carbine, Seng Fatt's language indicated he was very much alive. Everyone was in a state. I decided to call the whole thing off – a delicate operation such as ours was no longer feasible. Suicide in such circumstances was not entirely unknown, but for a long time afterwards I thought, perhaps, I should have included the possibility into our plans beforehand. I later passed information about the same couriers to the 2/7th Gurkha Rifles and they killed them after flying into deep jungle and laying an ambush on a dead letterbox (actually in a cleverly constructed hole in the trunk of a large tree).

I have often been asked what was my worst experience during the Malayan Emergency. I have no difficulty with my answer. It took place on a remote Chinese-owned rubber estate in 1953. Early one morning, Communist terrorists had entered the estate *kongsi* (a long shed where rubber tappers lived in family rooms). They rounded up the occupants and accused them of not paying subscriptions to the Communist Party and of not providing their quota of food supplies. They murdered all the men in front of the assembled families and left taking with them as much clothing, food and cash as they could carry. A twelve year old girl ran after them shouting and crying. She too was taken away by the terrorists. I happened to be in the local police station when two red-eyed Chinese ladies rushed in to make a report. I joined the armed investigation party.

On the way, we reached a clearing near the *kongsi* where there were some wintering rubber trees. Suddenly we heard a faint cry coming from a shallow irrigation trench filled with dried leaves. We quickly cleared away the leaves and saw the body of a small child lying in a pool of half-dried blood. Her clothes were nowhere to be seen so we wrapped her up in my vest and carried her back to the road, followed by her distraught mother and took her to the district hospital. The Polish doctor there told me that she had been stabbed 22 times – but was alive. I kept in touch with the estate owner and later I was told that she had recovered physically. But I feared greatly for her inner state of mind.

In the spring of 1953, Colonel Arthur Young, who had replaced Nicol Gray as Commissioner of Police, arrived in Kuala Lipis, without any warning, accompanied by a huge armed escort. He announced that all gazetted officers and police lieutenants should attend a meeting the same day – for some strange reason, inspectors were excluded. This was at a time when almost everyone was involved on work of operational importance and many simply could not get away. He was cross when only about a third of us turned up. He then amazed everyone by saying that the police service (he called it 'police force') was overstaffed in comparison with police forces in other 'colonies', and would have to be run down to half its size immediately. We were expecting to hear his views about the Emergency and, maybe, a word of praise too. His talk lasted about ten minutes and quoted a lot of facts and figures. He would not take questions. Then off he went leaving us open-mouthed with astonishment. Morale collapsed throughout the state as a result of his ill-chosen words. The District Planters' Association, most of whose members were honorary inspectors and proud of their membership of the Malayan Police Service, wrote him a strong letter of protest. I never saw him again, and nothing much changed. Our battle against aggressive militant Communist terrorists on the ground continued. The Chief Police Officer Pahang State, Kerr Bovell, struggled hard to restore morale and the tock tock birds continued their nightly tocking.

As 1953 progressed, David Henchman and I realised that although operations against the Communist terrorist organisation in Pahang were quite successful – often against high profile targets such as the two Communist regiments (Numbers 6 and 11) and the independent platoons – terrorist recruitment still went on, casualties were replaced and there was little real change in overall terrorist numbers or their domination of the jungle fringe. We argued that, unless security force operations were planned and carried out with vigour against stable party infrastructures (i.e. their permanent district organisations) on a longer-term basis, the Emergency could last for ever. Following General Templer's reorganisation plans for Special Branch, we had collected in Pahang State a talented headquarters' staff, a group of really good District Special Branch Officers and some very brave and experienced Malay, Chinese and Indian inspectors and detectives As 'Communist Co-ordinator', I was confident that we had reached the point where we could launch a completely fresh initiative. We discussed our ideas with Frank Brooke and won his personal interest and tentative support. I prepared a paper for the Pahang State War Executive Committee outlining the need for a complete change of strategy and then proposed, firstly, that a Communist District organisation should be the next State target and that it should be of great strategic importance to the Communist Party; secondly, it should be in an area of our (Special Branch) choice where we were confident of success; and, thirdly, the smashing of the target should provide the likelihood of good operational leads into an adjoining District or Communist military formation. We concluded by recommending that the Communist District organisation in Bentong, which until recently had supported the Central Committee in the hilly jungle nearby, fulfilled these requirements admirably. It was self-contained, well-led by a female District Committee secretary, specially chosen by the Communist Party's Central Committee; and was the centre of both jungle and outside courier organisations with tentacles extending throughout Malaya and into China.

After prolonged discussion, the State War Executive Committee agreed, thanks to strong support from Frank Brooke and John Clifford. We crossed our fingers, hoped for the best and set about organising Phase One of Operation Agile in Bentong. Our aim was straightforward – to build up medium-term intelligence, and provide the security forces with first-class operational information when Phase Two was reached. As ComCo, it was my task to come up with original ideas, produce the intelligence plan, co-ordinate our efforts, evaluate the risks involved and encourage and support the Special Branch officers on the ground, who were very much at the sharp end.

The local Military Intelligence officer's responsibility, under my direction, was to research and bring up-to-date the enemy order of battle at District and Branch level; including armed work forces, independent platoons, jungle courier networks, printing presses, deep jungle cultivation units etc. He would also prepare an area survey showing previous security force clashes with the terrorists, their abandoned camps, terrorist incidents and food dumps; rubber estates with names of managers, telephone numbers and airstrips; forestry concessions with logging tracks; rivers, ferries and places liable to flooding; landing zones for helicopters; padi fields with harvest dates; whereabouts of *Jakun* (*Sakai* or jungle dwellers) in fact anything of interest to security force operational planning. His sources would include our operation-room maps; surrendered and captured terrorist statements; forestry department records of logging concessions; the Protector of Aborigines information on the location of aboriginals; and sightings reported by Malayan Airways and Army Auster pilots, as interpreted by the photo reconnaissance section staff in Kuala Lumpur.

One of our Special Branch headquarter sections in Kuala Lipis would prepare dossiers on every Communist terrorist known to have operated in the state since the beginning of the Emergency, outlining all that was known about him or her, e.g. nicknames, hobbies, weaknesses (smoking, drugs, sex), personal relationship with comrades, schools attended, medical history, party membership, physical and any other peculiarities, hobbies, specialisations such as armourer, explosives, medical (eastern or western), and weapons carried. At the same time, another section would produce detailed charts of the outside Min Yuen and Communist cell system, indicating the party member responsible and whether or not their party loyalty was suspect; also the whereabouts and details of all known terrorists' relatives and contacts. They would prepare detailed diagrams of the various Communist-controlled subversive organisations in Pahang such as the Little Devils' Corps (in Chinese primary schools), the Students' League (in Chinese middle schools), the Anti-British Farmers' Union (in new villages and resettlement areas) and the Underground Rubber Tappers' Union.

Of vital importance was what we were to call our strategic supplies chart. This indicated, as accurately as possible, exactly how the Communist Party was able to live, work and survive in the jungle. Printing presses, which were so important for Communist morale and communication, existed on the supply of ink, stencils, typewriters, stylo pens, stencil plates etc. We listed all the shops where these were available and either watched them, or opened a shop ourselves. Similarly, terrorists sometimes stole, or forced employees to hand over, explosives such as dynamite, gelignite and detonators from public works department stores, and from commercial quarries and from tin mines. Jungle clothes and uniforms were made up, altered and repaired on the ubiquitous Singer sewing machine; these often broke down and needed spare parts from local shops. Terrorist cash was invested in pawnshops and gold jewellery (there were no less than nineteen licensed gold shops in Raub town, some of which thrived on stolen gold from Raub Australian Gold Mine). The supply of medicine was an ongoing requirement for use in the jungle, especially penicillin, M and B tablets (which could be traced via serial numbers on the packaging), bottles of highly popular Scott's Emulsion and even Tiger Balm, all of which were freely available either from District Hospitals or chemist shops. Battery-operated small wireless sets, especially the baby Philips model, were very popular in the jungle and so were the services of watch-repairers and dentists. We found, listed, examined, located and exploited all these avenues into the terrorist supply organisation throughout Phase One. We were doing this for the first time on an organised and fully documented basis. We went to a great deal of trouble to brief civilian members of the State War Executive Committee, some of whom, at first, were suspicious of our motives. A succession of senior army commanders were fascinated by our work, and could not believe their eyes, when they examined the useful visible detail we had amassed. All this encouraged mutual trust and a friendly understanding of our often dangerous work.

Towards the end of Phase One in Bentong district, some three months after the start, we found we could close down 90% of the identified supply lines into the jungle, and leave about 10% to operate more or less under our control. Our aim was to force the Communist terrorist organisation to limit their activities willy-nilly to the areas which we chose. We prepared lists of those to be arrested on D-Day of Phase Two. We were able to turn two wavering terrorists, unknown to each other, and put them back

200

separately into different Communist branch organisations in the jungle: thereafter, they communicated with us by a series of dead letterboxes and, later on, by physical contact on the jungle edge. These two enabled us to penetrate successfully the local inside jungle courier organisation and we were able to monitor enemy plans throughout the following year.

We arrested one hundred persons under the Emergency regulations on D-Day of Phase Two. Sixty-six of those detained, including some of our own agents, were released after a few days. The remainder had strong cases against them and were sent into detention elsewhere, with their case files previously prepared in detail. Among those released we managed, after interrogation, to recruit six new informants who gave us some excellent unexpected coverage.

Phase Two of Operation Agile started in July 1953 and ended a year later. The result was that the hitherto important Bentong Communist District was reduced in strength from seventy terrorists to twenty-two. They were unable to regroup or recruit replacements and their courier organisations were either smashed or penetrated by us. Five months later, the number of terrorists was reduced to thirteen. In early 1955 the party abandoned the district altogether and the government declared Bentong District a 'White Area', free of armed terrorists. We did not appreciate it fully at the time; but, as will be seen later, it was a significant military defeat for the Communist Party of Malaya.

Phase One of Operation Hawk was mounted against the neighbouring Raub Communist District (next to Bentong District) in September 1953. Phase One lasted four months and Phase Two concluded in November 1954. A total of seventy-four terrorists were killed, captured or surrendered; the Party's North Pahang base (previously designated as a 'Liberated Area') was closed down, never to reopen; 32 Independent Platoon was routed by the 6th Battalion of the Malay Regiment; and 3 Independent Platoon, which was responsible for ambushing and killing Sir Henry Gurney in 1951, was also destroyed. The Communist Party regrouped and attempted to build their supply organisations on three occasions, to no avail. The last terrorist surrendered in October 1955 when the government declared the Raub District a White Area, thus doubling the size of White Areas (free of Communist military activity) in Central Malaya.

201

Operation Apollo against the two Communist Districts around Kuala Lipis, which were themselves adjacent to Raub District, started in January 1954. Phase One lasted five months and Phase Two seven months. A total of eighty-eight armed terrorists were accounted for, and the Malay and Chinese sections of the Communist Party of Malaya's Unity Press were captured intact. We had been intercepting, and decoding, rolled slips for several months and it was clear to us that the party's Department of Malay Work was not contemplating any military activity. Members of the department in North Pahang had been reduced to subsistence living, mainly on bananas and tapioca stolen from Malay-owned orchards near the jungle fringe. It came as no surprise, therefore, to receive directly an offer of surrender. Our immediate reaction was to use them to stay inside the jungle and act as a bait for any other Communist terrorists who might pass through their area. However, our operations had proved so successful that there was little point in keeping this group under our control. Therefore, we gave the District Special Branch in Kuala Lipis permission to obtain their willing surrender, providing they agreed to bring out all their arms, ammunition and documents. When they emerged they were thin, emaciated and their pale skin was yellow. The wooden butts of their .303 rifles had been eaten away by termites and they could hardly walk.

Their leader, who was Chinese, spoke fluent English, Malay, Cantonese and Japanese. On leaving school, he had been recruited by the Japanese and trained by them as a spy against the Malayan People's Anti-Japanese Army. After the Japanese surrender he went into politics and joined the Communist Party of Malaya where his linguistic abilities attracted attention. On taking to the jungle in 1948, he joined the Battle News Press as a translator from Chinese into Malay and English; but he produced very little original work of his own. He later became the District Committee secretary of the party's Department of Malay Work in North Pahang and editor of its Unity Press. In addition to his translation work, he also played a leading part in the atrocities committed by the party's 10th Regiment on the Malay civil population. He was wounded in the leg at this time. Although he was an impulsive leader and unpopular with intellectual Communists, he had a winning way with the simple Malay village boys, many of whom had joined the Communist terrorist organisation for excitement, rather than for political reasons. After his surrender, he achieved greater fame later with European authors and journalists than he achieved earlier among his Communist superiors, who regarded his Japanese connections with suspicion.

In the Kuala Krau area of Mentakab District, which adjoined Kuala Lipis and Raub Districts, Phase One of Operation Stockade got under way early in 1955; but, by then, our intelligence was so detailed and so complete that, on our advice, SWEC decided to invite the 1st Battalion the North Rhodesia Regiment to enter the fray at once. This resulted in the whole party organisation being destroyed militarily within a fortnight, chiefly by way of capture and surrender of some thirty-nine terrorists.

As has been seen, our Special Branch directed operations in Pahang enabled the government to declare a White Area over most of Central Malaya by the end of 1955 (see Diagram 3 on page 204). This split the Communist armed forces in Malaya into two widely separated halves – Negri Sembilan and Johore to the south and Perak and Kedah to the north. My operational orders, i.e. the original intelligence plans, were requested by the police and the army for study by their respective staff colleges 'as soon as security is downgraded'. I was also asked to prepare a draft 'director of operations instruction' on Special Branch operations in support of the security forces, and another draft instruction on food denial operations. The latter eventually became mandatory for security force operations elsewhere in Malaya.

Whilst these operations continued, David Henchman left to go on long leave to the United Kingdom in August 1954. Meanwhile, after the declaration of the White Areas in Pahang State, I stayed put and slowly began to work myself out of a job. In course of time, as the Emergency situation continued to improve, most of our ranks were downgraded except mine. This was because the new chief police officer in Pahang wrote to our federal head-quarters in Kuala Lumpur, 'Tim Hatton has held the post of acting superintendent since 19th May 1953 and in view of his excellent work ... I write to enquire whether it is possible not to downgrade his post until after he goes on leave on 4th May 1956 ... such a step would indicate appreciation of his work and in some measure would ease a feeling that certain officers are working towards their own individual reduction in rank.' This was a really courageous thing to say, given the Commissioner's known views on such

DIAGRAM 3

Indicating how Special Branch directed food denial operations in 1953–55 resulted in Central Malaya being declared a White Area free of Communist terrorism

matters, and I regarded his intervention as a huge compliment – even more so, when it was immediately approved.

I had very little time away from work during 1953 and 1954 though I managed to play bridge occasionally with the hospital staff in Kuala Lipis. I continued my regular studies of Hokkien, sitting my follow-up examination in the Chinese Secretariat at Kuala Lumpur, passing with Great Credit and obtaining a modest financial 'bonus'. The written part of this exam involved a translation of the annual federal budget, announced that very morning, and my comments were requested in the vernacular on recent increases in customs duty – as usual, not a word about the Emergency situation!

7

All good people agree,
And all good people say,
All nice people like Us, are We
And everyone else is They:
But if they cross over the sea,
Instead of over the way,
You may end up looking on We
As only a sort of They.

RUDYARD KIPLING, 'A FRIEND OF THE FAMILY'

Having completed my final Hokkien exam, I put in for six weeks' accumulated leave and sailed from Singapore on the SS *Patroclus*, a 10,000-ton Blue Funnel cargo ship carrying thirty passengers, to Otaru in Hokkaido Island in North Japan. My spending power was limited to just £25 because Japan was outside the sterling area. We sailed via Manila, where I had time to explore the remains of the American and Japanese defences of Corregidor and the Bataan Peninsula, and then on to Hong Kong. I wrote home, 'Manila is exactly what I would expect an American west coast city to look like. Lots of skyscrapers, huge American taxis and traffic cops all looking like benevolent Eisenhowers. The shops are full of food and shoes. The countryside is flat. The city is divided into two by a river, with the old walled city on one side, and its modern counterpart on the other. The former was built by the Spaniards in the seventeenth century, on a massive scale, and remained more or less intact until 1945, when the Americans bombed it to smithereens. No one has cleared away the debris since then and the locals have built a shanty town all over the place, pulling down the stone and masonry as they please. I walked round the circumference identifying bastions and small fortresses jutting out from the wall. I noticed three ruined churches, the remains of the governor's palace and two or three large army barracks. A great shame to see such devastation. I saw the relics of Jose Rizal, the national hero shot by the Spaniards sixty years ago, and was shown a bit of his fibula pickled in alcohol.'

On arrival at Otaru, I was horrified to find the place under very deep snow, so that I had to climb down steps of frozen snow into the shops. However, I soon discovered that the Japanese railways had a wonderful system of snowploughs and were running frequent services. As I was about to go ashore wearing three vests and two tropical suits on my person, and carrying three half bottles of malt whisky in my suitcase, my cabin steward – a toothless veteran of many years' service with the Blue Funnel Line – said, 'Where do you think you are going, Sir?'

'Ashore,' I replied, adding, 'I'll meet you at Shimetzu in a month's time.'

'No you won't. You'll die of cold long before that. Wait here,' he ordered. He soon returned with two thick white Blue Funnel blankets, four huge safety pins and a Japanese kepi-type cap. 'Wrap these around you, put on your cap, eat rice and raw fish and everyone will think you are a Nip,' he said, placing the kepi firmly on my head, giving it a hard tug to one side.

I went to the railway station to buy a third-class ticket on the slowest night train to Tokyo. The stationmaster saw me and, discovering that I was an Englishman and not an American, took pity on me, refused to let me pay for a ticket and rang down the line warning his colleagues of my journey. I did not argue with him. I entered the train, sat down and away we went. It stopped at the next station where my thoughts were rudely interrupted by a hard whack on the head. I looked up and saw a little old Japanese lady, in a black kimono, waving a small umbrella and pointing at my seat; the penny, or more likely the yen, dropped – the tiny wooden seat was designed for two Japanese adults, and she intended to occupy the other half. I moved over, she sat down, we proceeded without a word.

The train really was a slow one and I was met by many station masters along the track in Hokkaido Island. Most Japanese railway officials seemed to have completed, before the war, their basic training in England; they had a great affection for the English. But they all hated the Americans. I was unable to pay for any railway ticket and no one would accept a tip. I stayed several nights in beds set up for me in the middle of waiting rooms, efficiently heated by a large wood-burning contraption beside me. On the way, I was given an introduction to the King and Queen of the Ainus, said to be the original inhabitants of Japan, in the middle of nowhere. I was entertained royally in their palace, actually a small hut in a village high street, and they insisted on presenting me with a small, delightful, unpolished wooden carving of a bear catching a fish. It had just been made by the King himself in readiness for the arrival of the summer tourists. In return, I gave them both a few wee drams from my whisky bottle.

I spent two days exploring the thermal springs in South Hokkaido; and then crossed by a four-funnelled ferry from Hokkaido to Honshu, and boarded the train for Tokyo. Here I stayed one gloriously comfortable night in the cheapest room of a large hotel. I wrote home, 'Otaru on Hokkaido Island in North Japan is like old pictures of Siberia. Some Japanese travel on sledges pulled by horses or dogs, others whiz around on little skis. They look like woolly Eskimos in their traditional clothing. Children wear gaily coloured jerseys, coats and stockings whilst babies are wrapped up snugly on their mothers' backs – extremely quaint but very pretty and quite out of this world.'

It was springtime in Central Japan and pink blossom was everywhere. I was reminded of my mother's sketches when my parents visited Japan in 1923. Their visit was curtailed by the earthquake and they decided to cross the sea to China for a year's exploring. I had less than a month to explore Japan. I found Tokyo just another bustling eastern city, so I decided to go on a pilgrimage to Hiroshima, further to the south, by bus and by train through the mountains. I did not see the summit of Mount Fuji so, if the legend is true, I shall never return to Japan.

I suppose I was not fully prepared mentally to assess the effects of the atom bomb dropped on Hiroshima ten years before. The surrounding hills were home to many hospitals, where its victims were living out what was left of their unfortunate broken lives. The area down below was a shanty town and had not yet been developed or built upon. A former municipal building, with the remains of a dome on top, still stood gauntly in the middle of this desolation. A small temporary museum nearby showed bizarre exhibits. I shall never forget the shape of a man, riding his bicycle, incinerated in outline on a brick wall, the moment when the bomb exploded. I found the local stationmaster and we talked about the bomb and its after-effects; his own family lived in Osaka, but he had lost some relations in the holocaust, and three more were in a hospital on the hills. He recommended an inn on Miyojima island, near the sea, among the cherry blossom and seaside-shrines as an antidote to the horrors of sightseeing in Hiroshima. I went there and moved in. However I did not like the food in the inn – mainly uncooked fish. The only food I found palatable were huge, coarse strawberries the size of my fist. I soon tired of these and went by train to Kyoto where, once again, I stayed in the cheapest room of an expensive hotel. Kyoto was every bit as exciting as the tourist brochures claimed. I went to three Japanese plays in the evenings and visited temples and gardens by day.

I left Kyoto by train for Osaka and Kobe; sitting opposite me were a young Japanese mother and her two small children. They made a complete zoo on the table between us, using origami paper. The mother spoke a little English and it turned out that she was a past 'prima donna' of the Takarazuka All Girls Opera Company. She presented me with tickets for Madame Butterfly performances in her hometown and in Kobe. Both were given by different troupes of the same company; I saw them and found them most enjoyable. I called in at Shimetzu to see if the *Patroclus* was in port and, to my relief, the first thing I saw as I left the station was a familiar blue funnel, clearly visible over the wooden roofs in front of me. I boarded the ship tired and broke. It had been a wonderful holiday, limited only by my £25 spending power. Nevertheless, I managed to acquire several small inexpensive antiques as souvenirs. On my arrival, my steward confirmed he had worried a lot about me.

On leaving Japan, I wrote home. 'Looking back on my stay in Japan, I was impressed by the punctuality, efficiency and friendliness of the railway system; Japanese hatred of Americans generally; the wonderful array of loudspeakers on buses, trains and in hotels, parks and streets; the absence of beggars, except a few wounded war veterans whom the police were reluctant to move on; the schoolboys who look like little Victorian sailors with a single row of brass buttons on their severe black uniforms and peaked naval kepis; and the schoolgirls who wear a dark blue or black coat, skirt, stockings and shoes with a sailor's square around their necks. Babies are taken to school as soon as they can walk and they are taught to sing, draw and make things with their hands and fingers from a very early age. Bus conductresses entertained us singing tunes from the musical *Kismet*. I was told that the modern Japanese lady is undergoing a major physical change so that she may wear smart western clothes (American) to advantage – not sure what this involves; but I suppose it is rather like Chinese females across the water who gave up binding their feet fifty years ago and had to learn to wear shoes. Countrywomen, and most of the older women in the city, wear the kimono and they really do shuffle along as they do in *The Mikado*. Office girls, however, wear western clothes and look very sophisticated. A great period of change is going on and it is the Americans they wish to imitate.'

On my way back to Singapore, we called in at Hong Kong again and I much enjoyed sitting on the Star ferry watching the office girls from Kowloon crossing over to work on the island – every single one an Audrey Hepburn lookalike. We left Hong Kong harbour late in the evening, surrounded by twinkling lights of every description, with great neon advertisements as large as houses extending up the hill and along the top of Victoria Peak. The night sky was rather cloudy and a full moon shone between the clouds, casting large black shadows on the sea. As we steamed out of the harbour, the lights gradually faded into the distance. Suddenly, a fleet of fishing boats glided closely by in the opposite direction and it seemed to me they were floating on air because the colours of the sky and water had merged seamlessly together, and they made no noise at all.

I reported back for duty on 12th April 1955 and found that my latest companion at home had moved in while I was away. He had been approached by the Public Works Department engineer, who wished to surprise me, and I found we had modern sanitation instead of my thunderbox, a new coat of paint throughout and a brand new 'Dover' stove for cookie. Unfortunately, my new companion was one of many who, as a staff officer in Kuala Lumpur, had not passed his exams. His salary increments had been frozen and he had been given a year to complete his exams in law and Malay. Evidently he had been posted to Pahang where, theoretically, there would be no distraction from his studies. He thought everyone was against him, hit the bottle and became extremely

210

morose in the evenings. He stayed with me for five months, until his wife and child came out, and they moved into a modern bungalow. He was by no means the worst of my companions; one of the others decided that cookie cheated on the monthly accounts which we shared. He began to check everything and queried cookie's every move. The result was that cookie resigned four times and disappeared twice; the little social life we had became somewhat strained. Of course cookie cheated; but it was within reasonable limits, and his cooking was the envy of my married friends.

During my last year in Kuala Lipis, I concentrated on clearing up after our major Special Branch operations; preparing coverage on the ground to counter any fresh Communist attempts at subversion outside the jungle; and advising the State War Executive Committee on small operations in areas where the Communist terrorist organisation was still active. My old hunting grounds in Temerloh and Mentakab Districts, which later had been the scene of great exploits by the District Special Branch Officer, were declared a White Area free of militant Communism, together with the Kuantan area on the east coast of Pahang. Thus the whole of central Malaya had been declared White and was accompanied by a relaxation of most of the Emergency regulations.

One of those captured by the North Rhodesia Regiment in Central Pahang was Ah San, a Central Committee member of the Communist Party of Malaya. Before the government's declaration of the Emergency, he had been responsible for the Party's Indian Department, which operated within the Malayan trade unions. Not many Indians went into the jungle in 1948, though there was a strong Tamil armed unit in Johore and I had come across some aggressive Tamil terrorists in the Batu Arang and Sungei Tinggi area of North Selangor. These Tamils were utterly fearless, quite ruthless and excelled in jungle warfare. Sambanthamurthi, a really brave police officer, persuaded his superiors to allow him to be recruited into the Johore terrorist unit under cover. His subsequent adventures were rewarded with an extremely well-earned George Medal.

The Federal Interrogation Centre told me that Ah San was of no interest to them, so I was given a free hand to obtain his legal reclassification to that of a surrendered person, and to interrogate him. He was English-educated and had been left behind in Pahang by Chan Peng when the latter moved north. He was a genuine English-speaking academic Communist and was of enormous interest to me, but he had no information of operational use, his capture was widely known and he was severely wounded. I had him admitted to Kuala Lipis District Hospital and persuaded the surgeons there to operate. This entailed eight weeks in traction with his leg sticking up in the air. He became very despondent – his new life in hospital outside the jungle was certainly not of his choosing. At first all he wanted to do was to die, and he declined to speak to me. Eventually, he had to talk to someone and I was his only visitor. I lent him Somerset Maugham's *Writer's Notebook* which amused him. I followed this up with *Down with Skool* by Geoffrey Willans and Ronald Searle; and *The British Character*, by Pont of Punch, with an Introduction by E.M. Delafield – not at all the sort of books one would be expected to give a captured Central Committee member of the Communist Party of Malaya.

He softened up considerably and began to discuss his thoughts with me. He said that his belief in international Communism, i.e. Marxism, Leninism and Stalinism had never faltered in the jungle, despite the party's failure to establish liberated areas and its failure also to capture the towns and cities. Occasionally, on a hill at night time, he said, he would look up into the clear night sky and think of Communists around the world, engaged in social revolution under the same night sky, the same moon and the same stars. It gave him a great sense of belonging to a worldwide revolution. At this time, I was reasonably sure he would remain a Communist and would continue to believe in his definition of socialism. Our conversations took place before the death and debunking of Stalin, the collapse of monolithic world Communism and the 1956 Russian invasion of Hungary.

I was determined to find out all I could about Chan Peng's move to the north, and especially about the people he took with him. We already knew quite a lot from our successes in Operation Agile in Bentong; but I wanted more and I enlisted the help of Cheah Seng Fatt. Seng Fatt was considered by police headquarters too old to join the permanent ranks of what used to be called the Asiatic Inspectorate; but he was both Chinese and English-educated. He had a fund of risqué stories, an inquisitive mind and was great fun to work with – a most entertaining companion when we broke off for meals in Chinese coffee shops. He proceeded to build up a handwriting index of everyone concerned in the move north. This enabled us to identify masses of hitherto disregarded documents and learn a great deal more about important writers and recipients. A side-benefit of his index arose when we intercepted a letter from Singapore, saying that the writer was about to sail to his home in China via Hong Kong. Seng Fatt said he was certain that the handwriting was that of a high-ranking Pahang Communist fleeing from the jungle. We arranged for a reception committee to welcome his arrival in Hong Kong. He turned out to be a notorious and much-wanted Regional Committee member from North Pahang who had escaped the fate of his comrades, recently murdered by one of their bodyguards.

I decided, as a sort of hobby, to write a detailed paper, with personal descriptions, on the three groups which accompanied Chan Peng, Siew Ma and Siu Cheong from Bentong to the Thai side of the Malaya-Thailand border in 1952–53. I also put up a similar paper on the small group of Malay terrorists, who went north with the politburo; their presence serving to retain a semblance of Malay participation in the party hierarchy and would be available, if considered politically wise, to influence Malay irredentism in South Thailand. This labour of love became the authoritative work on the subject for some time.

Unfortunately, Seng Fatt's system for classifying Chinese handwriting by analysing the writer's handwriting idiosyncrasies when communicating in Chinese characters, could deal only with the handwriting of about 800 people. Although we found it helpful and used it a great deal, neither the Americans nor the British security authorities expressed any interest in his work.

All the time I was in Kuala Lipis, I kept a Siamese cat called Poose and in 1955 I decided to try and breed from her. I acquired a male pedigree Siamese cat called Billi, but Poose did not take to Billi, until Cookie placed one of Billi's hairs in Poose's ear and vice versa – it did the trick immediately and soon we were blessed with six lovely kittens. I gave one to my Malay *munshi* who named him Cartoon after seeing a Disney film.

I developed my studies of Malay history in Pahang by collecting more than fifty short stories and local myths, remembered by elders of the Pahang Malay rural community. Almost every rocky outcrop, bend in a river, rapids and cave had its own story. The upper reaches of the Pahang River, and the great caves at Kota Gelanggi on the Jerantut road, were favourite weekend picnic spots for me and my Malay friends. The limestone formations were the setting of many stirring tales of wild beasts devouring pretty maidens, wedding guests being turned to stone and ancient battles fought between groups of Malay warriors, often with recognisable Hindu origins in the background. I think I must have struck them as being a little eccentric, for they elected me not only a member of the Kota Gelanggi Development Committee (for the collection of guano, the excrement of bats); but also wrote my name in lamp-black on the roof of the highest cave. I never discovered how they did it: I think they must have used long bamboo poles tied together with a smoking flame at the end.

Meanwhile, seminal political changes were taking place in Malaya which would dramatically affect everyone's lives. Those who read the English, Malay, Chinese or Tamil newspapers, or listened to the radio, began to follow developments with all sorts of mixed feelings. The first event occurred in June 1955 when Chan Peng, the Secretary General of the Communist Party of Malaya, offered to negotiate a peace settlement and called for a conference to agree ways of ending the war. The British colonial government, having consulted the leaders of the three main communities in Malaya, rejected the offer as a cunning Communist plot. In fact, the offer was carefully timed to precede Malaya's first general election and was deliberately designed to influence subsequent political discussion. This election took place in the following month and the Alliance Party (comprising UMNO for the Malays; MCA for the Chinese; and MIC for the Indians) obtained 85% of the votes and won 51 out of the 52 seats in the National Assembly. Tunku Abdul Rahman ('the Tunku'), another of the hundred royal descendants of a previous Sultan of Kedah, became Chief Minister. The country was launched on the road to independence from colonial rule.

Some six weeks after the election the Tunku, wishing to seize the political initiative, offered the Communist Party an amnesty under which terrorists who surrendered would not be prosecuted for any offence committed during the Emergency, and would be freed after interrogation. Those who wished to go to China would be allowed to go. Chan Peng replied a month later suggesting that an immediate ceasefire should be declared by both parties. He would send his envoy to arrange a meeting between his representatives, and representatives of the Chief Minister, to make formal arrangements for discussions on a political end to the war. The Tunku's hand was immeasurably strengthened by the British decision that the granting of independence would no longer be contingent on the successful military conclusion of the war. As requested by Chan Peng, the Tunku replied by code on Radio Malaya stating his agreement for a preliminary meeting between representatives of both parties.

The Communist representatives were led by Chan Tien who had attended the Communist conferences in Prague, London and Calcutta during the late 1940s and had been one of the Malayan People's Anti-Japanese Army leaders who took part in the Victory Parade in London after the war. The Malayan representatives comprised Colonel John Davis DSO, a pre-war Malayan Police Service officer who had transferred into the Malayan Civil Service; and Ian Wylie, the Deputy Commissioner of Police. Both these officers had relevant backgrounds.

During the Second World War, John Davis had landed in Japanese-occupied Malaya by submarine in August 1943. As leader of the British-organised Force 136, his aim had been to contact the Anti-Japanese Army, set up radio contact with the Allied Command in South-East Asia and arrange for the supply of British arms and equipment to be parachuted into Malaya. He made contact with Chan Peng, then in charge of the party's armed forces in Central Malaya, and worked closely with him for the next two years. He was soon joined by Ian Wylie. Altogether, one thousand air-drop sorties delivered 510 men and a very large amount of supplies and equipment. Fortunately, the Japanese in Malaya surrendered following the dropping of atom bombs on Hiroshima and Nagasaki; neither Force 136, nor the MPAJA, were needed for the planned guerrilla offensive to coincide with a full-scale Allied landing on the coasts of Malaya. Lord Louis Mountbatten deputed John Davis to take the surrender of the Japanese forces in Malaya, and ordered Force 136 to take over important areas, hurriedly abandoned by the Japanese army.

I met John at various times during the Emergency in Malaya

and was hugely impressed by his shock of unruly hair, his friendly blue eyes and his complete lack of pomposity. He and Ian Wylie were the sort of men whom the Tunku not only trusted and respected, but liked as well, and with whom he could be fully at ease. They were absolutely the right persons to gain the confidence of Chan Peng and Chan Tien and could be relied upon to produce an appropriate background for political discussions. (I met John again years later after my retirement from Malaya, when I was a Principal in the Development Commissioni and he was the exceedingly efficient and popular Chairman of Kent's Voluntary Services.)

So it was, at the Tunku's direction, that Ian Wylie met Chan Tien three times on the jungle fringe. They agreed, and set up, the administrative detail for negotiations between the Malayan and Communist delegations, to be held in converted school premises at Baling, in North-East Kedah, close to the border with Thailand. While all this was going on the world was astonished to hear Chou En Lai, of Communist China, preaching coexistence between Communism and Capitalism at an international conference in Bandung, Indonesia. This was another development which Chan Peng brought cleverly into play in his future relations with the newly elected government of Malaya.

John Davis became the conducting officer and met Chan Peng along the road near the Thai-Malayan border, between the small town of Klian Intan and the huge opencast Rahman Hydraulic tin mine. They shook hands, and John briefed him and his party on the timetable, arrangements for meals and sleeping accommodation. In their turn, Chan Peng's party asked for clean clothes, toothpaste, soap and towels, so that they could feel at ease and look respectable. The Tunku was accompanied by David Marshall, the Chief Minister of Singapore, and Tan Cheng Lok, who was the leader of the Malayan Chinese Association. Chan Peng was accompanied by Chan Tien and Rashid Maideen, one of the leaders of the Communist Party's Department of Malay Work with the rank of Central Committee member. It is amusing to note that, when Radio Malaya organised one of its regular phone-in programmes, a British soldier guarding the meeting asked for the song, 'When The Red Red Robin Keeps Bob-Bob-Bobbin' Along!' which some people thought was a serious security leak.

The Tunku's terms were exactly the same as before. Chan Peng agreed to disband his army and hand in their arms; but insisted that his party must be recognised as a legal political party after the independence of Malaya, saying, 'We must enjoy equal status with you so that we may pursue our policies by constitutional means. We will not be forced to give up our ideology.' Both sides remained adamant. Chan Peng ended up by saying angrily. 'Then the present situation suits us perfectly.' The meeting came to an abrupt end. John Davis escorted Chan Peng back to the jungle, sharing a tent with him that night as a former comrade in arms. They shook hands and the last thing Chan Peng said to John was, 'The British have let us down.' John declined an escort back and returned alone.

Having returned to his base in South Thailand, Chan Peng issued instructions for the Communist Party of Malaya to continue its armed struggle, and to step up the subversion of political parties, trade unions and schools. Malaya achieved full independence from the British on the 31st August 1957 by political means; but it was not until 1960 that the State of Emergency came to an end.

In my opinion, the stand taken by the Malayan politicians before, and during, the Baling talks with Chan Peng was in conformity with the wishes of the Malayan people. The British Government was not directly involved and, for the first time, the Malayans were acting on their own; though it is true that they were well aware that Britain was soon to grant Malaya its freedom (Merdeka) and independence.

Communal aspirations at that time tended to be expressed separately by each of the three communities. The Malays considered themselves the *bumiputera*, or sons of the soil, they looked forward to effective political representation and a better standard of living, especially among the farmers in the countryside. The Chinese were keen to get a tighter grip on the country's economy and make more money. The Indians were intent on using their membership of the Alliance Party to develop their newly recognised political rights. It was Tunku Abdul Rahman, the Chief Minister, who united these three communities into one highly successful, freely elected political party which spoke confidently, and with one voice, throughout the negotiations with the Communist Party of Malaya.

The year 1941 was a disaster for the Malayan people. Ordinary peaceful men, women and students on the five-foot-way or in the padi fields or in the factories were astonished and shocked when

217

the British were chased out of Malaya by the Japanese so quickly, so easily and so completely. They all suffered immensely during four years of the Japanese occupation (1942–45) from the cruelty of the *Kempei Tai* (Japanese secret police) as well as the brutal ruthlessness of the Communist Party. After seven years of the Emergency (1948–55), they had come to regard Communism as a wholly irrelevant, alien culture. By 1955, they had literally 'come of age', were politically astute and welcomed the forthcoming orderly departure of the British. There was no stopping them as they progressed expectantly along the road to independence, led by their own elected politicians and free from overt outside political interference.

Chan Peng and his military leaders had already been defeated on the battlefield and their current political ideals. based on old-fashioned Marxism, Leninism and Maoism offered no practical solutions to their problems. When the party decided to launch the armed struggle and took to the jungle, it lost political contact with the people and became increasingly isolated and unable to take part in, or frustrate, or exploit, the country's first democratic general election. Chan Peng, as the party's leader, had consistently underestimated not only the will of the British people and the Commonwealth to defend Malaya against militant Communism; but also British determination to grant independence to a freely elected government of Malaya as soon as possible. Furthermore, he underrated and misunderstood the feelings of the people. He made no attempt whatsoever to win their hearts and minds in a civilised and acceptable way. He had failed abysmally both as a military commander and as a politician.

I had enjoyed my three and a half exciting years in Pahang; I realised how fortunate I had been to have worked with such talented and dedicated groups of people. Many of the original Circle and District Special Branch officers had left to go on long leave; but their replacements had been equally good. My senior officers had given me a free hand and had allowed me to get on with the job. The Military Intelligence officers, sometimes a thorn in the flesh elsewhere, had been loyal hardworking and friendly. We had succeeded in creating a White Area, free of militant

Communism, from the State of Selangor on the west coast right across Central Malaya, and we were very proud of that.

During my first tour of duty in Malaya I was recommended unsuccessfully for the Colonial Police Medal for Gallantry in 1949, and I was awarded the Colonial Police Medal for Meritorious Service in 1954. I also received four Letters of Commendation over the same period.

One of the pleasures of professional success is to receive letters from one's friends and acquaintances. A very senior officer from General Headquarters, Far East Land Forces in Singapore wrote, 'I congratulate you on your newly won distinction and upon the continuous stream of successes we read with so much interest ... your operations are the most successful that I have ever heard of ... a very great deal of this success belongs to Special Branch, and particularly to you. Brigadier Talbot says you are going very strong!' Another letter from the Office of the Director of Intelligence, Malaya, said, 'Almost all I know about the Emergency I have gleaned from you. Similarly what success I have had was almost invariably the result of quoting your experience and advice ... sometimes, I am ashamed to say, as original.' A delightful Hokkien lady, who worked in my office in Kuala Lipis, ended her letter to me thus: 'Well, sir, I must thank you very much for being so kind to me when I was in your office. I really say in the world I can never find a boss so nice to me and I miss you. I wish to become Roman Catholic. I am studying Cathechism and I will be baptized in two months time. I just like to become RC. I am also having tailoring lessons.'

I shall always remember the time in Pahang State when, alone in my car one dusky evening, I came across a herd of wild elephant, miles away from anywhere, on the Jerantut road. This was not far from the remarkable one-car wooden ferry, worked by an old man using ropes and pulleys, expertly harnessing the power of the swiftly flowing river. The elephant appeared to be enjoying the evening sun, or perhaps liked the reflected warmth of the tarmac road; anyway, they slowly waved their trunks towards me in quite

219

a friendly greeting, but they circled round my car and prevented me from driving on. I soon became impatient. I blew my horn once to encourage them to clear a way for me to escape their unwelcome company. The largest elephant promptly sat heavily on the roof of my car with its four legs visible on my starboard quarter. I blew my horn again and a small elephant sat on what the Americans call the trunk of my car. It was getting dark. I began to worry when the dent on my roof started to deepen as the larger elephant rubbed itself, and shifted to obtain a more comfortable position. Just then, an open lorry came along full of Chinese loggers who jumped out, shouted and clapped their hands and away my elephants lumbered, leaving dents in my car, and in my pride.

I handed over to my successor in April 1956 and I boarded the 24,000-ton P&O liner SS *Chusan* on 4th May, bound for England. Among my friends on the ship were Keith Soon and his mother, whose Hokkien family I had known well in Penang, and two maiden aunts of Archie Kennedy, with whom I had shared many adventures at Pangbourne. I invited the former to my mother's house in Chipperfield and I have kept in touch with the Soon family to the present day. We spent two days in the Suez Canal and I combined a visit to Cairo, where I explored the magnificent museum, with a camel ride to the pyramids. We docked at Tilbury on 27th May and I bought a brand new 2.4 Jaguar motor car at a special introductory price of £995, which included later shipment out to Malaya.

8

I was not false, dear, when years ago
Thinking I loved you I told you so
Yet, my gift to you I live to see
Was not fair payment for yours to me

I first met Joanna Cristall Tarver in 1941 when my parents bought my aunt's cottage in Chipperfield, near Kings Langley, in Hertfordshire. She was the same age as me and we went to the same parties, played tennis and earned money together weeding gardens, pruning roses and picking fruit in our school holidays. People paid more per hour for girls' labour (one shilling and sixpence or 7½p)) than for boys' labour (never more than a shilling or 5p); presumably because girls worked harder, did not play around and were considered more reliable. I found it most unfair – definitely not politically correct in modern parlance – but it provided benefits, other than financial, and I liked Joanna's company.

Joanna's grandparents lived in a beautiful seventeenth-century cottage, half a mile away from Chipperfield. Her grandfather, Captain Malcolm Tarver, had served in sail after leaving school and, following his marriage, took ship to the Argentine, where one of his older brothers was high up in the Argentine railways, and bought a small farm for breaking-in ponies. He sold this a few years later, returned to England and went back to sea, became a master mariner, and commanded HM Hospital Ship *Maine* for many years till she ran ashore and was sunk, early in the Great War. He volunteered for mine-sweeping, was blown up three times, was severely wounded, transferred to Q-ships and was responsible for sinking the German submarine U23 for which he was awarded prize money by the Admiralty. On his retirement, he was elected a Younger Brother of Trinity House, published a number of articles on his experiences at sea and developed his hobby of woodcarving, achieving national recognition for making the most wonderful ship models. We still have his models of the four-masted sailing ship *Primrose Hill*, and the *Victory*, carved from the *Victory*'s original wood, rescued during repairs. He never recovered from the death of his only son, John, who was reported missing, believed killed, while flying as a lieutenant observer off HMS *Ark Royal* in 1941.

His only daughter was Joanna's mother. She married her second cousin, John Hyde Tarver, who had lost an arm in the Royal Flying Corps a few days before the Armistice in 1918. After university, he devoted his spare time to helping the Waugh family in their social work among the London poor. He joined later the Ellerman Line's offices in London, and was still working there when he died in a snowstorm during the cold winter of 1958. He had a great hook on the end of his arm, and frightened the life out of me when he attracted my attention by hooking himself on to the sleeve of my jacket. Joanna was their only child and the apple of their eyes. For years they had an ancient family car called 'Clackety Anne'; but it eventually conked out and had to be abandoned on a roadside in Devon. They replaced it with bicycles on which they went picnicking all round the open Hertfordshire countryside, before it was fenced off shortly after the war.

While Joanna's father liked conversation, and could talk knowledgeably and at length on any subject, her mother suffered from a form of *cacoethes scribendi*, an incurable urge to write, which took the form of compiling a detailed annotated family tree going back to the early eighteenth century. She wrote letters all over the world, following up family leads, and received replies from almost everyone.

The best-documented direct line of descent concerns an eighteenth-century forebear who is known to have dissipated his fortune gambling on the horses and, to escape certain incarceration in a debtors' prison, scooted off to Dieppe with his wife and children. Here, misfortune fell upon them at the start of the French Revolution, and subsequent wars between England and France. During a lull, he fled on an American ship to the United States, leaving his family stranded in France. Shortly afterwards, his wife managed to persuade a friendly captain of a fishing boat to take her, and all but one of her family, back to England. Unfortunately, young John Charles Tarver had just caught scarlet fever and had to be left behind with the Fèrals, a kindly French couple who, having no children of their own, treated him as their own son. He did not see his family again for over twenty-five years. Madame Fèral nursed him, sent him to school as soon as he recovered from his illness, and Monsieur Fèral made sure that he was bi-lingual in French and English – thus laying the foundation for his subsequent astonishing career. In common with his French contemporaries, he was called up for military service and opted to go into the French Navy. Although England and France were often at war during this period, the pre-postage stamp mail still operated sporadically between the two countries and he was able to keep in touch with his mother, who happened to tell him that his elder brother had become a lieutenant in the British Navy. After conscription, John Charles came to the attention of the French admiral at Toulon who gave him the rank equivalent to midshipman and made him Admiral's Secretary and Interpreter. We have a miniature of him, wearing his French uniform, sent home to his mother at that time. Meanwhile, the English fleet mounted a blockade outside the French Mediterranean coast and, in order to remain at sea, the English would, from time to time, arrange a truce with the French, so that they could come ashore and obtain fresh water. It transpired that John Charles's older brother was often in charge of these British landing parties. He wasted no time in contacting his younger brother, who passed on details of the French order of battle together with the projected comings and goings of convoys and individual French ships. This game of spying came to an end with Napoleon Bonaparte's final exile to St Helena in 1815, and the return of near-normal relations between England and France.

John Charles had great difficulty in acquiring an English passport; however, after many months of frustration, he returned to England, married his cousin Mary Cristall in 1819 and in 1826 was appointed French master at Eton College, where he remained until his death in 1851. In 1845 he published his seminal work, entitled *Royal Phraseological Dictionary* (English into French) dedicated 'by Gracious Permission, to HRH Prince Albert'. In 1850 he published the second part, French into English. It was a great success and is widely regarded as the best French/English dictionary of the nineteenth century.

*

Joanna's main wish in her schooldays was to get away from her parents and to live a life of her own. She seemed to like her father more than her mother, though she seldom agreed with him in their many disputations. Her mother had all the domestic qualities of a busy, faithful wife and, in particular, was an energetic piano player and a very good cook, dedicated to her kitchen range and the supply of free cakes, puddings, bread and biscuits to local fairs and fêtes. Joanna was a tolerable pianist, but never took her music seriously. She steadfastly refused to learn to cook because she thought she would never be smart enough to compete with her mother. Shortly after leaving school, she was left a small library of books on flowers, mostly illustrated and coloured by hand; and another relative left her the family collection of Joshua Cristall's watercolours and books on butterflies, moths and plants. (Joshua, 1767–1842 was founder, and frequent president, of the Old Watercolour Society.) She decided that horticulture would be the life for her.

However, it was wartime, and her family wanted her to go into the Women's Royal Naval Service. Unfortunately, the local recruitment office discovered her ability to draw and directed her to work in a government drawing office in Watford. She managed to escape from this dull repetitive work and was transferred to a farmer, who was greatly surprised by her efficiency and strength in shearing sheep. After the war, she successfully completed a four-year academic and practical diploma course at the Botanical Gardens in Cambridge. When I came home on leave in 1956, she was living in Sharnbrook, Bedfordshire, superintending the extensive gardens of Sharnbrook House.

During the next few weeks, I motored up to Sharnbrook and back a great many times. In addition to her responsibilities in the gardens, Joanna was busy entering her prize specimens into the various vegetable, fruit and flower shows, exhibiting in competition with the other professional gardeners. Her plants did very well, and on one occasion she herself was voted Sharnbrook's prettiest gardener! I proposed to her while we were sitting on the huge kitchen table in front of the Sharnbrook House boiler which we had just stoked – she accepted, even after I had explained details of my Spartan life in Malaya and showed her some rather gruesome photographs. Things began to move fast.

My mother had to be told first. We called on her unexpectedly the next day to break the news. She spotted us coming through the garden and met us, sherry glass in hand. Joanna said, 'We have become engaged, and you are the first to know.' My mother dropped her glass and it broke on the flagstones. 'Oh dear,' she said, 'come inside and we'll start again.' Our next port of call was Joanna's parents' house; they were both at home, and insisted that I should take a photograph of us all sitting on a garden seat. Having set the camera for a delayed action shot, I ran to join the others, sat down and the wretched thing collapsed under me. Fortunately I managed to balance myself and smile – the resulting picture showed nothing amiss.

Our biggest problem was where to have the reception, until our friends the Hays very kindly offered us their home in nearby Sarratt. All I had to do was to choose a best man, appoint ushers, purchase a wedding ring, admire the trousseau, make up my mother's spray of roses from her rose garden, collect the ice on the morning of the great day and book all tables for lunch at the nearby Two Brewers Hotel.

We were married in Chipperfield Church by the Reverend Gerald Lane on 13th October 1956. The church was full to capacity with our friends and relatives, and there was an enormous crowd of well-wishers and passers-by outside. Joanna wore a full-length white silk wedding dress made up from a length of silk brought back from China, for just this purpose by her uncle when his ship was visiting the Chinese Treaty Ports in the 1930s. Friends from the Cambridge Botanical Gardens decorated the church and the marquee in the Hays' garden. The speeches went off very well, even mine, and we left for our honeymoon in my brand new 2.4 Jaguar. We did not go far and, as soon as we dared, I stopped the car and removed various noisy pots and pans tied to the back and various rude notices. The inside of the car had confetti everywhere and we continued to discover little bits over the next four years. We motored on to Stratford-upon-Avon where we spent the first night of our honeymoon. We enjoyed a fortnight in Scotland, based in Fort William, exploring everywhere and revelling in the gorgeous colours of the Scottish autumn.

On our return we stayed with my in-laws who made over the modern extension of their cottage for our exclusive use. Fortunately, I located a friend from Malaya whose wife briefed Joanna on what clothes to take out to the tropics, and how to deal with extremes of heat and wet. We also had to pack up the majority of our wedding presents, leaving them in my mother's attic, not to open them again for ten years. Then we were faced with the question of how to return to Malaya. The Suez crisis was in full swing and no civilian planes or ships were allowed through, over or around the Mediterranean. I appealed for help to the Colonial Office and was told that there were no civilian flights to the Far East; it was up to me to find my own way back to Malaya by sea, round the Cape of Good Hope. I decided to approach the Blue Funnel Line, with whom I had travelled on leave to Japan, and they suggested we should sail in the *Perseus*, a sister ship of my old friend the *Patroclus*. I cleared this with the Colonial Office. Joanna and I and our Jaguar left Liverpool, bound for Malaya, in early November 1956, via an unscheduled four-day visit to Rotterdam; a day ashore at Dakar in French Senegal; a day in Cape Town where friends looked after us very well; and a long monotonous journey across the Indian Ocean to Singapore. We arrived on 12th December 1956. John Lawrence, my friend from the Hokkien course, met us on the quayside, presented Joanna with a huge bunch of mixed orchids, gave us a lovely wedding present and took us to a ball organised by the Alliance Française at the Raffles Hotel. We spent the remainder of the night at the Adelphi Hotel and next day collected our car and drove up to Kuala Lumpur.

One of the first things I found on my return was a letter from the Malayan Civil Service official responsible for government pensions. He wrote, 'Your return by sea was unauthorised by this office ... and you exceeded your approved travel leave ... the difference in the time taken ... unauthorised return travel by sea less the authorised return journey by air ... is twenty-eight days ... these twenty-eight days will be deducted from your final pensionable service.' I thought this was most unfair. We had travelled back with the agreement of the Colonial Office on the only means of transport available at the time. I appealed unsuccessfully, and was told somewhat testily that government regulations could not be changed to suit individual cases. We were given temporary accommodation in a chalet near the Kuala Lumpur racecourse and, a few weeks later, we were allocated a bungalow in Airport Road, near the Merdeka Stadium, which was then under construction.

On reporting to Special Branch HQ, I was told by the Director that he wanted me to become one of his senior staff officers in Kuala Lumpur. He said that it was time for me to obtain staff experience in an important headquarters appointment and he considered I had the right experience to make a success of it. I became responsible for the Communist terrorism desk in the Malayan Special Branch headquarters. My predecessor, Mike Day, yet another former officer in the Gurkhas, had just left the police service to join the Foreign Office and could not be spared for a handover. My staff comprised a lieutenant colonel, who was also head of Military Intelligence, and five majors responsible for South Malaya, Central Malaya, North Malaya and the Thai border. We were a very happy team. Our main task was to keep the civilian, police and army populations, individually and jointly, *au fait* with the security situation. In addition, I attended meetings of the Federal Intelligence Planning Committee and I co-ordinated short-term operational projects, involving the testing of inventions and other bright ideas. At the request of the headmaster, I rewrote and presented the standard lectures on militant Communism and subversion to students attending the Special Branch school; and gave regular lectures, by invitation, at various army training locations and to the sixth forms of English-language secondary schools. It entailed regular visits to all the states in Malaya, to Singapore and to the Thai border, sometimes at short notice, usually with one or other of my army staff officers. In addition, I became the editor of the Police Intelligence Journal (PIJ) off and on for the next ten years.

An interesting part of my job was this investigation into the many bright ideas submitted to the Director of Operations. One of these, the use of patchouli oil, was the pet idea of a very senior civil servant. His idea was that if patchouli was used to impregnate cloth bound for Communist-owned sewing machines in the jungle, the follow-up by sniffer dogs, who had no difficulty in recognising it, would reveal a terrorist camp. Eventually, a helpful Special Branch officer in the field produced a keen young impecunious informer, willing to deliver the impregnated cloth into the hands of the Communist terrorist organisation. A suitably briefed police Field Force platoon was trained, together with the sniffer dogs. The important man himself came to see the practical result of his idea. However, the result was not at all what he expected. Apparently, Tamil ladies used patchouli oil to keep their skins nice and smooth; and every female Indian tapper within a mile of the potential launch was made a great fuss of by the dogs, much to the amusement of the Field Force and the chagrin of the great man. A much more important project was Operation Squeaker.

Operation Squeaker involved the replacement of a valve in a baby Philips battery radio with a homing signal, which could be picked up by an Auster plane flying indirectly overhead and, again, by an extremely heavy monitor lorry on a nearby road. When I took over the project from Mike Day it was in the doldrums for two reasons. Firstly, because the Auster people appeared to have lost interest and no pilots were available at short notice: and, secondly, because Special Branch on the ground had not produced any operational projects to insert the radio via a reliable informer into the jungle. I was asked by the Director to do something about it. Fortunately, a new RAF member of our directing team, who had not been involved in the early stages of the practical side, was Wing Commander Dickie Wakeford (later Air Marshall Sir Richard), and we immediately hit it off. We soon discovered that the weakest links were indeed the extremely busy Auster pilots who had insufficient time to carry out the necessary training. During practice runs, it had been found that many pilots were slightly deaf and the Squeaker was difficult to hear above the noise of the engine; its signal was weak because the flight path had to be far enough away not to alert the target on the ground. Talks in their mess revealed one pilot whose hearing was perfect but, it was said, he was at his best before lunch, preferring to do his administration in the afternoons. He was a splendid man and Dickie took note of him. My next responsibility was to ensure our technicians produced the Squeaker and that its bench tests were in order in the lab, and in the field, in conjunction with the Auster pilot and the monitor lorry. This was a matter of simple trial and error and presented no insuperable difficulties. My other much more difficult task was to find an ongoing short-term Special Branch project which would produce a worthwhile target. My travels produced possible targets in Kelantan (but there was no main road for the heavy detector lorry); Perak (long-term projects at that time precluded a short-term strike) and Johore (little enthusiasm from the State War Executive Committee). But we 'struck oil' in Negri Sembilan, where every effort to kill, capture or subvert a notorious high-ranking Communist called Tang Fook Leong (widely known. of course, as 'Ten Foot Long') had proved annoyingly unsuccessful. The local District Special Branch Officer, whom I had known well in 1953, was able to produce a good informer capable of doing exactly what we wanted. I discovered to my delight that high up on his shopping list from the Communist Terrorist Organisation was a request for a portable Philips radio.

Our pilot was achieving a 25% success rate in field tests of Squeaker. He was our only chance and we had nothing to lose. Ten Foot Long was not only a State Committee member of the Communist Party, but ruled his area mercilessly, slaughtering any comrade who opposed him and carrying out a vicious series of murders – men, women and children – to enforce his domination of the local Chinese rural population, in order to compel their support. He was a bad lot and his gang were all of the same ilk. Dickie Wakeford alerted the RAF to stand by for a confirmed six-figure map reference air-strike in the deep jungle of north Negri Sembilan. Then, one day, everything fell into place. The informer said he had arranged to hand over the Philips radio in three days' time. We gave it to him with the Squeaker switched on secretly; Ten Foot Long's man took it across the jungle fringe; the monitor lorry proceeded to its position at the highest point on the Kuala Lumpur-Seremban road and received a really good signal; our pilot had an on-day receiving a fairly strong signal, two fixes were obtained and an accurate six-figure map reference was achieved. Dickie called in the RAF who came straight over and bombed Ten Foot Long's camp accurately, and without prior warning, killing everyone inside except one bodyguard who was washing in a nearby stream. He surrendered the next evening, quite deaf, and in a very nervous state. Squeaker and other similar projects based on our success were developed elsewhere, but I was not involved with them.

Joanna was taken seriously ill on 23rd May and I took her directly to Bungsar Hospital where a ruptured ectopic gestation was diagnosed. She only just survived, thanks to the excellent operation carried out at once by the surgeon who, for good measure, removed her appendix too. She stayed there a week and then we went on ten days' leave to the Cameron Highlands Hotel, where I had stayed during my Hokkien course. I described our return in a letter home. 'We left the Cameron Highlands Hotel in the morning and arrived back here in the early afternoon to find quite a reception party on the doorstep. The *kebun* (gardener) and family produced a huge bunch of flowers, *amah* was very excited and sung a little song, little (eleven-year-old) Ah Peng was jumping up and down. Although cookie was fast asleep, he came along a few moments later to supervise the unloading. He produced yet another wonderful bowl of flowers, baked a large, intricately decorated, chocolate cake and as *"chef d'oeuvre"*, some light, tasty, almond meringues, especially for the occasion. The house had been spring-cleaned and the rather tatty woodwork carefully cleaned – *pace* those who say a new wife should never employ her bachelor husband's former cook!'

Joanna said she wanted to learn Malay soon after we arrived and we employed a *munshi* (teacher) twice a week, so that she could take the Government Standard 1 Malay examination in Jawi script; which she did within the year. She also became unpaid assistant secretary of the Malayan Nature Society, and unpaid adviser to the committee running the Lake Gardens in Kuala Lumpur. She took up ikebana (flower arranging), run by enthusiastic wives of diplomats in the Japanese Embassy, and also started learning how to paint on rice paper for producing Chinese scrolls. She spent several years painting bamboo leaves before being allowed to go on to landscapes, animals and birds. Eventually, with her teacher's encouragement, she sent her best results for stretching and mounting to Hong Kong for occasional submission to exhibitions in Penang, Kuala Lumpur and Singapore. We gave the local driving school fifty dollars for an unlimited number of lessons and a guaranteed pass. Joanna passed at her first attempt.

Immediately behind us was a small hill on top of which was a rambling wooden Malay palace among some beautiful casuarina trees. This was the home of HH the Sultan of Selangor's second son Tunku Laksamana (which, translated, meant Lord High Admiral), or Number Two, as I called him. He was a jolly man and appeared to be the only male adult among a cohort of wives, sisters and daughters. One day a large Humber Supersnipe car pulled up in our short drive and out popped Number Two and no less than eight comely young Malay ladies. They declared they had come for tea. Number Two and I sat in our large sitting room and Joanna and her group squeezed into our small dining room. It transpired that Number Two wanted to talk to me about anything at all; his English was perfect, and he rather hoped Joanna would teach English to his ladies on a regular basis in two groups, each of four very eager students. We felt unable to say no, but we made the point that, although we would not teach them, we would be delighted to converse weekly with the students together in the house if it rained, or during walks round about if it was fine. This arrangement suited us all, and in addition we joined Number Two and his family on monthly expeditions and picnics all over the state. He usually brought his youngest son, called Lot Pi, who was eight years old and very shy at first. We much enjoyed these trips.

I was directly involved in the Merdeka (independence) Celebrations as an extra ADC-cum-bodyguard to HRH Prince Henry, Duke of Gloucester throughout his visit, except for the handing over of the Constitutional Instrument at the Merdeka Stadium on 31st August 1957, when, for some reason, I was given the day off. I received a surprise note from Tunku Abdul Rahman himself saying that he understood we did not have personal invitations to attend the ceremony, and he enclosed three tickets. I think his office had been put up to it by a group of old Kedah friends. We attended, taking cookie's daughter with us. It was a very impressive occasion with all the Sultans and their courtiers dressed in Malay ceremonial clothes under large picturesque umbrellas.

The Duke of Gloucester was in a frightful mood, suffering intensely from the heat in his Gilbertian uniform and rather heavy suits. 'It's bloody hot,' and 'Is it always like this?' he complained loudly. The Duchess, on the other hand, was impeccably dressed, cool as a cucumber and won the hearts of everyone wherever she went. Prince Henry gave me a gold tiepin as a memento.

The irrepressible Harry C.C. Too was the head of Malaya's Psychological Warfare Department. He set about the exploitation of Malaya's independence among the Communist terrorists still at large in Perak and Johore. With our help, he accomplished this with typical enthusiasm and flair, producing some excellent pamphlets which we arranged to distribute both inside and outside the jungle. The first result of this came in Perak where, almost without warning, a senior Communist leader surrendered and persuaded 118 terrorists to accompany him. This was handled by the Perak State Special Branch in the greatest secrecy and, quite naturally, they were extremely protective of their good luck. Unfortunately, it coincided with a change in Military Intelligence leadership, following the departure of its hitherto utterly reliable and extremely efficient colonel.

Harry Miller, editor of *The Straits Times* newspaper, came to us and said he had been told by a military source that a large number of Communist terrorists had surrendered in South Perak; he asked to be given the details for publication. We had a press division responsible for press releases; but it fell to me to have a word with Harry Miller. It was only through his loyalty to us, and his influence over the press, that I was able to prevent a serious leak which other hard-core terrorists in Perak would certainly have exploited to the full. The miscreant was the new chief of Military Intelligence and, although he admitted his indiscretion, life would never be the same. At the request of the GOC, he was omitted from all our planning committees and secret operations. This was unfortunate for me as I had always relied on his predecessor as a buffer in our relations with the GOC; from then on, I had to brief the general myself. The GOC, General Sir James Cassells (later Field Marshal), took an abiding interest in the details of what was going on and always referred to surrendered persons as 'Sputniks'. I forgot to bring a pointer with me on the first occasion I briefed him and he lent me his 'swagger-stick'; this became a regular habit, but when he became a field marshal I had moved off his stage and could not enjoy the use of his field marshal's baton. After Merdeka, the general always invited the prime minister (Tunku Abdul Rahman) and the defence minister (Dato Abdul Razak) to our briefings.

Earlier on, Joanna's mother had given us the names and addresses of two of her close friends living in Kuala Lumpur. The first was a senior entomologist at the Institute of Medical Research (IMR) and a world expert on the anopheles mosquito. The second was the British Deputy High Commissioner to Malaya. The former introduced us to the strange world of the IMR and the latter brought us up to date with life at the top. These two families, together with the wives of my army staff officers, proved enormously helpful to Joanna. Meanwhile, Joanna's interest in ikebana brought us into the world of expatriate Japanese and American ladies; while her scroll paintings

232

brought us into the orbit of a wide range of Chinese painters in Kuala Lumpur and in Singapore.

Joanna's mother came to stay with us in February 1958. Soon after her arrival, I received a telephone call from a neighbour of hers in England to say that her husband, Joanna's father, had died of a heart attack while caught in a blizzard on his way home from his office in London. She decided to fly home at once. Joanna could not accompany her because she had just become pregnant with our first child, and our doctors advised against flying.

During March, after my permanent promotion to superintendent of police appeared in the Gazette, I received a letter from Sir Kerr Bovell, my former boss in Pahang, now Commissioner of Police in Nigeria. He wrote. 'What are you doing in Malaya? ... Presumably you are in Federal Special Branch Headquarters in Kuala Lumpur ... the real spider in the web ... our best wishes to you and Joanna.'

In April 1958, Hor Lung, a senior Communist terrorist in Johore, surrendered, bringing with him approximately 180 armed men and women.

Once again, C.C. Too's psychological warfare people reported that the main reason given for this mass exodus from the jungle was Malaya's independence from the British, and the futility of carrying on with the armed struggle against a freely-elected national government. After talking to a cross-section of those who had surrendered in Perak and Johore, it became obvious to me that party members regarded their decision to give up their part in the armed struggle as very much in line with party policy to run down the military aspect, and to develop, once again, a more popular 'revolution' on the political, labour and educational fronts. The great majority seemed to me to be hard-core Communists and certainly did not regard their exit from the jungle as a military defeat – merely a change of tactics. They kept their dignity; some found it very difficult to give up their Communist beliefs and had to be detained for the time being. Others, tired of the jungle war, opted to go to mainland China with their families.

It seemed likely that the armed struggle of the Malayan Communist Party in future would be limited to operating from bases in South Thailand, opposite North Perak. It was also likely that, once again, I would soon be out of a job. This is exactly what happened. I was told to hand over my current responsibilities and was promoted to the acting headship of the local Selangor State Special Branch. I spent the next fortnight touring my old stamping grounds in Kuala Selangon, Sekinchang, Rawang and Kepong. Then I sat my last and most difficult Chinese character and Mandarin examination at the Chinese Secretariat in Kuala Lumpur. It took place over two days. I passed with Great Credit.

There were still a few Communist terrorists in Selangor but they were not very active and I had long talks with Colonel Deane Drummond of 22 SAS concerning the best way of dealing with them. These terrorists were operating from deep jungle areas, familiar to me nine years before, and it was interesting to see how little the terrain had changed since then. The SAS were superbly fit, and were continually training; I did my best to ensure that Special Branch on the ground gave them good operational information. However, I was not really involved with the detail.

Much more important, however, was the long-term danger posed by the formation of some well-led, well-organised, subversive Communist organisations among the Chinese middle schools, of which the Selangor National Independence League appeared to be the largest and most dangerous. Selangor Special Branch was still closely geared to the Emergency and little had been done about the subversive organisations outside the jungle. Clearly this would have to be a priority so, once again, we had to start afresh, retrain our personnel, win the confidence of the public, recruit an entirely different set of informers and build up new resources to solve new problems.

My immediate task at this time was to tackle accepted opinion among some of my immediate superiors. For them the end of the Emergency was in sight, following the surrender of such large numbers of Communist terrorists in Perak and Johore. Communist penetration of political parties, schools and the labour force was negligible, they said, and the run-down of the Special Branch, its personnel and its facilities could proceed apace. Large sections of Special Branch registries, containing vital records, were being closed and files destroyed on a non-selective basis. I explained my worries to Desmond Palmer, then the Acting Director of the Malayan Special Branch, and, at his suggestion, I started on the production of a working paper on *hsueh hsih* (pronounced 'shir sheh'), the Communist method of indoctrination. I had already studied this in depth with Ah San, the English-speaking Central Committee member captured in Pahang a year or so ago, and I had put up a preliminary paper explaining its use by the Communist Party, both inside and outside the jungle. I brought this up to date by reference to Special Branch Singapore's paper on the spread of Communism in Singapore Chinese middle schools' students' union. A final version was edited a little later on by Chan Chee Chung, the extremely bright head of our Analysis Section, in 1959, following our experiences in Selangor.

My aim was not only to use the paper as a basis for lectures in the Special Branch school; but also for lectures and talks to sixth-form students, politicians, journalists, trade union leaders and, at the suggestion of Sir Claude Fenner, I included the 'further education' of senior government officials. One day, I even talked to a very senior British judge who asked lots of penetrating questions. When I finished, he leaned forward in his chair and said it was one of the most interesting and important hours he had spent in the last ten years! Of course my real intention was to ensure that as many influential people as possible would be able to recognise hsueh hsih in all its forms.

The term hsueh hsih derives from the first sentence of the *Book of Discourses* in the third volume of *Four Analects* by Confucius. It reads. 'Confucius said, "How delightful it is to study and practise frequently."' Its literal meaning is, therefore, to study and practise often and, extended further, to study hard and emulate the good example of another person by constant practice. To the classical Chinese mind, it had a respectable connotation implying hard work, diligence and a desire to study deeply.

Traditional Chinese scholarship emphasises the need to study books, i.e. to *hsueh*, but the art of practice, to *hsih*, was largely neglected. This neglect, and exact meaning of the two words became a favourite, and exceedingly complicated, topic amongst Chinese philosophers through the ages. It did not appeal much to the Chinese as a popular phrase, and was seldom in use until the Communist Party deliberately resurrected the words and used its respectability, and its association with ancient Chinese scholarship, to conceal their own sinister interpretation. It was, therefore, very important to understand clearly what this Communist interpretation really was. In fact, it was none other than the straightforward teaching of Communist ideology.

By means of the hsueh hsih system, Communists sought to explain the materialist philosophy of Communism. It was the exact opposite of idealism, and taught that all human ideas and history were the reflections of the material environment and, particularly, of the economic environment. Ideals, religion, art and independent thought were of no value and did not exist, except as reflections of the material interests of the class from which they arose. Communists believed in the historical inevitability of the masses coming to power so that all intellectuals, all art and all economic theories must conform with the wishes of the proletariat for whom they claimed to speak. Anyone who went against this theory was denounced as a traitor to the masses.

During 1955, groups of male and female subversive students from Singapore middle schools toured Malaya. They succeeded in indoctrinating considerable numbers of Malayan Chinese middle school students, especially in Kuala Lumpur, Klang and Penang. Furthermore, many Malayan-born students studied in Singapore middle schools and in the Nanyang University, where they came into contact with subversive students and were accepted into Communist satellite organisations, often rising to important positions. On their return to Malaya during school holidays, or when they completed their studies, they were able to contact embryo illegal Communist organisations and were able to give direction and advice, and organise a regular supply of subversive literature.

In order to hsueh hsih collectively, uniformly and to expand Communism and Communist organisations rapidly, it was essential for the organisers to have access to Communist literature. They had to have the necessary pro-Communist books with which to sow the seeds of 'socialism' in young receptive minds. They had to follow this up with extracts from the more readable works of Marx, Engels, Lenin, and Mao Tse Tung. Thus they were enabled to embark on the indoctrination of Communist theory and the important principles of materialist philosophy and so on. They had to relate these principles (study) to present-day economic, political, educational and cultural conditions (practice), in what they termed a semi-colonial society. There was absolutely nothing Malayan about it at all; it was an alien teaching aimed to corrupt the minds of young people on orthodox Communist lines.

The experienced Communist organisers appreciated that the

vanguard of a Communist return to Malayan politics would have to stem from efficient Communist underground organisations in the towns and villages, which would supply the driving forces behind an eventual Communist-dominated united front of political parties. To prepare for this return to legal politics, they regarded their most urgent task to be the introduction of long-term hsueh hsih study groups in primary and middle Chinese schools, in youth clubs, in political parties and among the work forces of Malaya.

At the request of Desmond Palmer, the Deputy Director of Special Branch, I agreed to join him in regular briefings of the Malayan cabinet. He talked about the security situation on the Thai-Malayan border and the threat to Kedah, Perlis and North Perak; and, in an entirely fresh capacity, I talked about the threat posed by the Selangor National Independence League and the dangers it posed to legal organisations. I quoted verbatim from recent Communist policy documents, which emphasised the need for the revolution to be stepped up in the political, labour and education fields by the widespread use of hsueh hsih. Among those attending were Tunku Abdul Rahman, (the Prime Minister); Dato Abdul Razak, (the deputy prime minister and defence minister), ministers Sardon Jubir, Tan Siew Sin, Ong Yoke Lin and Khir Johari. Some of them were taken completely by surprise at the detail we gave them and the extent to which this was taking place. All became attentive listeners, asking a great many relevant questions.

I handed over the headship of the Selangor State Special Branch to Hussain bin Haji Mohamed Sidek, fresh from long leave in the South of France with his favourite wife, on 21st May 1958. He fell in completely with my views, or rather his coincided precisely with mine. We talked together for three days on end, bouncing ideas off one another, and decided to give equal priority to retraining the staff and to launching an operation to penetrate and destroy the Selangor National Independence League. 'Huss' became personally responsible for retraining the staff and put aside one whole day a week for this.

I set about improving the welfare of our staff, achieving much success in persuading young married couples to buy their own houses in the burgeoning satellite town of Petaling Jaya, adjoining

Kuala Lumpur. The interest and return of capital on the money borrowed by way of a mortgage could be funded by judicious lettings. To my surprise and pleasure, police headquarters had no objections and allowed them to do this and remain in government quarters. My main task, however, was to build up our resources of men and material and we worked together on Operation 'Bomoh' against the Selangor National Independence League. We decided to launch the operation on the night of September 30th and October 1st. I had given myself four months to sort things out and launch our strike.

Penetration of the League was no easy task and quite different from winning over members of the Min Yuen on the jungle fringes. The carefully set up Communist cell system in city areas tended to make our task a long hard slog. It was within their communication system that we found the weak links between the party member and the cells he or she controlled. We concentrated on this link using all the tools available, including interception of letters through the post office; bookshops selling illegal propaganda from China; music shops selling illegal sheet music published in China or copied in-house; cheap jewellery hiding Communist emblems, and so on. All these items were highly treasured by many young Chinese, following Mao Tse Tung's victory in China during 1949, and it was with these aids that the party members could interest, influence, recruit and even reward their cell members.

We soon found that the league's leaders were very security-conscious. They did not have permanent addresses but moved frequently from one place to another. This meant we had to train up our own small surveillance sections (we called them 'dancing teams') using a variety of nationalities, depending upon where the targets were located. We trained our people in the use of cameras for surveillance and for photographing documents passing through our hands, and also in the use of microfilm. While none of our targets used motor vehicles, they did use trishaws (pedal-driven three-wheelers) and bicycles and we had to teach our own cyclists how to protect their own security. Our records had to be completely reorganised not only to produce strong cases in advance for keeping people in detention, but also to cross-refer vital evidence obtained from informers, casual sources, security aids. and from statements made after an occasional arrest took place. It involved a complete reorganisation of our registry. Huss also insisted that we should both make a careful record of every aspect of our retraining, and preparations for the launch of our operation, so that the Special Branch school, and other states in Malaya, could learn from our experiences and mistakes.

On the night of 30th September we launched Operation Bomoh against the Selangor National Independence League. The dancing teams had identified the temporary houses of seven of the eight leaders we wanted to arrest. Their houses were searched, documents recovered and all were detained for interrogation. A total of 110 men and women were brought in and we detained 68, releasing the rest as cover for our regular and newly-recruited agents. We recovered a mass of really high-class documents, illustrating overall Communist direction, partly from the Communist Party of Malaya in the jungle and partly from Communist cells in the Singapore Chinese middle schools. Much of the latter originated from China and had been conveyed by travellers via Hong Kong. All the leaders wanted by us had been operating under pseudonyms; we were intrigued to find many were mature university-educated cadres from Singapore, Hong Kong or China. All had been using identity cards with different names. We succeeded beyond our wildest dreams; but, on sober reflection, we realised how little we had known, six months before, about the League and the ingenuity and the quality of its leaders.

I took Joanna to Bungsar Hospital in the middle of Operation Bomoh, and John was born at 8.40 a.m. on 1st October 1958. I reported to the expectant grandmothers, 'Everything went well, with Llewellyn Jones and an Indian doctor in the background and two Chinese nurses, called Hunky and Woo, on hand. John has a complete head of hair and lively blue eyes. Joanna is sharing her ward with the English wife of an Italian rubber planter, whose family have lived four generations in Denmark. Next door is the Eurasian wife of an English planter sharing with a Chinese girl also having her first baby. They all collect together in the evenings, shoo away the chickens which stray around the hospital wards, and tell each other dreadful stories.'

All this took place during the final phase of our operation. Fortunately, as the director of the operation, there was little constructive work that I could do once it started, and my uninterrupted presence was not required. Four times I slipped off a mile away to Bungsar Hospital to see how things were going on; but even there, I found that I was a passenger too. Next day, despite working through the night, it seemed everyone wanted to go with their families and see Joanna and John in the hospital. Huss immediately nicknamed him 'Bomoh', a name which stuck to him throughout the rest of our time in Malaya. John was baptised in the Anglican church in Kuala Lumpur on 21st February 1959 by Canon Chiew Ban It, in the presence of his proxy godparents Mrs Hunt, Mrs Reid, Major Clinton Robinson and Major Byrd, with the Director of Special Branch Harvey Ryves, Harry Too and Huss as valued supporters.

One of the surprising and unforeseen results of Operation Bomoh was our discovery of another, hitherto undetected, Communist Party subversive organisation called the Malayan Races Liberation League, formed two years before. Its aims were to develop the revolution outside the jungle, independent of the armed struggle. It was organised and directed by a different group of Communist Party members, most of whom came originally from Singapore. It was obvious that some of the Liberation League leaders were aware of the identity of some of the Independence League leaders; but they operated in conditions of the greatest secrecy in different areas. The Liberation League was strongest in the Chinese middle schools outside Kuala Lumpur, notably in Klang, and had connections extending down to Negri Sembilan to the south.

Thus the Malayan Races Liberation League became a prime target and we gave ourselves four months to obtain sufficient intelligence to identify and arrest its leaders. We used the same tactics we had used against the Selangor National Independence League and applied the many lessons we had learnt. By the end of February 1959, we were ready to launch our attack. Identification, descriptions and backgrounds of those to be detained were given to the arresting teams, the interrogators and to the translators. The dancing teams, which had already located their targets, set off to confirm details and a total of 68 people were arrested. Of these, 28 were detained under the Emergency regulations and the remainder were released. This time all our main suspects were located and arrested and, in addition, we found two pistols, some ammunition, two modern underground presses used for printing hsueh hsih material, and a most interesting haul of documents, most of which originated from mainland China.

Huss was taken seriously ill during the night and had to go into hospital with a highly suspect liver; so, in addition to directing the operation, I had to keep him informed of progress. He was very angry with himself and gave the nurses a hard time – but they saw through him, and looked after him very well, greeting his impatience with cheerful banter. I also had to brief the Director of Special Branch, the Commissioner of Police, our minister (Dr Ismail) and certain cabinet ministers, because not only did we find more strong evidence of Communist activity in the schools, but also several disturbing and successful examples of Communist penetration of the legal Labour Party of Malaya. This was political dynamite. I had to be very careful about what I reported to the Malayan cabinet. The evidence had to be clear, overwhelming and irrefutable. Some of those arrested agreed voluntarily to be interviewed by a government minister; later I was asked to arrange for these detainees to talk to political leaders of the Labour Party. If there was any doubt about the activities of the Communist Party outside the jungle, our operations against the Selangor National Independence League and the Malayan Races Liberation League dispelled them for ever. Harry Too, who was universally respected, became a strong influential supporter of our efforts and spent a great deal of time convincing the diplomatic community that we were not becoming a police state intent on crushing the political opposition!

Nevertheless, a feeling that the danger from Communism had ended with the surrenders in Perak and Johore gained momentum within the mostly Malayanised civil service, international journalists and the intelligence community in Kuala Lumpur. In particular, the British and the American representatives, many of whom had arrived recently, openly shared this belief. Fortunately, Dr Ismail, our minister, and Dato Nik Daud, our permanent secretary, did not take this view and, with full cabinet support, they decided to emphasise the need to counter Communist subversion by explaining in detail to many influential people in Malaya exactly what was happening. This involved me in the production and setting up of more lectures to civil servants, politicians of all hues, journalists and even the diplomatic corps. This was not too

241

difficult because we had obtained plenty of visible evidence; but it took up a great deal of my time.

Exploitation of our highly successful attacks on the Selangor National Independence and the Malayan Races Liberation Leagues continued to occupy our minds, and Huss took a strong personal interest from his sickbed. Dr Ismail's instructions were to smash all subversive Communist organisations and not to encourage any to exist. This meant we could not penetrate a subversive group for any length of time. The acceptable alternative was to leave 'sleepers' around to warn us of any attempt to rebuild the cells. We also haunted the Singapore Special Branch registry of missing subversives and were helped, to a large extent, by Duggie Farnbank who, at that time, was the Federal Special Branch liaison officer in Singapore. As a result, we were able to identify and pick up quite quickly most of the replacement leaders sent up to Kuala Lumpur. It became a war of attrition.

Huss never came back as head of Special Branch Selangor and eventually Sharif bin Mohamed took over from me. Sharif and his wife, Che Bee, a small, plump, jolly, bubbly person, became good friends and we often visited each other's houses. John loved being picked up and carried around by Che Bee and we always looked carefully to see if he had been borrowed by her when she returned home. Another friendly visitor was Saleha, the teenage daughter of a retired Malay diplomat who lived next door to us in Airport Road. She told us that she had a Circassian grandmother with red hair, and that her father had Siamese and Dutch blood in his veins. She used to wander in at all hours and ask to look after John – all quite harmless and an interesting visitor.

We left Kuala Lumpur for three months' home leave on 8th June 1959, travelling by train to Singapore and by two taxis to the Adelphi Hotel. We spent a full day buying presents at C.K. Tang's large oriental store, Thai silk shops and Helen Ling's delightful shop in Orchard Road. Next day we boarded the MS *Oranje*, a 20,000-ton modern Dutch passenger liner, and discovered that the Raja Muda of Selangor (the eldest son of the Sultan), his first wife and eighteen-month-old daughter, were travelling on the same ship. He was the older brother of Number Two, our friend the Tunku Laxamana. Joanna and John spent a lot of time in their company. We had heard that the *Oranje* was the best ship on the Singapore run; and so it proved.

242

We arrived in Southampton on 29th June and went to stay with Joanna's mother at Chipperfield in Hertfordshire. We borrowed her motor car and showed John off to friends and relatives. Half our leave was spent with one grandmother, and half with the other grandmother, to ensure that there would be no jealousy between them.

9

And falling and crawling and sprawling,
And driving and riving and striving,
And sprinkling and twinkling and winkling,
And sounding and bounding and rounding,
And diving and gliding and sliding,
And trumping and plumping and bumping and jumping,
And dashing and flashing and splashing and clashing.

ROBERT SOUTHEY

We left England by plane for Malaya at the end of September, and on arrival in Kuala Lumpur we were met by Malay friends and taken home. Cookie baked a cake, amah sang a little song for John in Chinese (it sounded like 'Little Brown Jug') and the gardener's daughter had placed flowers in every room. The Public Works Department had painted the place throughout and replaced every bit of worm-eaten wood, including brand new windows and polished floorboards. We were very sad to hear that our next door neighbours, the Palmers, had retired to England via South Africa. They had been a great help to us, both in the office and at home. Whenever I had a difficult problem I could always discuss it with Desmond Palmer and we spent many an evening together discussing the progress of our various projects.

Soon after our return Harvey Ryves, the Director of Special Branch, told me that I was to be posted to Alor Star as head of the Kedah State Special Branch. My main task would be intelligence planning against the Communist terrorist organisation in South Thailand and in parts of North Kedah and Perak. This would be my first appointment as an independent head: Joanna was pleased to go to a country area where she could take John for walks. We decided not to take cookie and amah with us and Joanna found good jobs for them both with newly-arrived friends of ours. We confirmed also a place for Ah Peng, their younger son, in the Methodist Boys' School and found Ah Kuk, their elder son, a permanent job as a hotel lift attendant. We loaded our possessions into a railway wagon and set off by car, spending a night at the Station Hotel in Ipoh, and arriving at Alor Star Rest House on 23rd November.

Alor Star Rest House was originally built by the Japanese in 1943 as an ice factory and was converted into very small apartments by the State Public Works Department in 1952. The walls were very thick and had tiny windows; we were allocated two rooms which were small and dark. Early the next day, I had to fly to Songkhla in Thailand for a meeting of the Thai-Malayan Border Operations Committee, and was lunched well by the Thai's 5th Regiment Combat Team under General Charn at Haadyai.

I toured Kedah State and showed Joanna my haunted house in Kulim. Tunku Farid, my great Malay friend in Kulim days, had always kept in touch with us. He had sent us a wedding present on our marriage and delicious little parcels of Malay food when John was born and, again, each time we returned from leave. When he heard of our arrival in Alor Star, he and his wife hurried up from South Kedah, where he was an Assistant District Officer, to welcome us. Again, they spoiled us with Malay food in their family home and took us round the various Malay historical sites. The Military Intelligence Officer in Kedah was a White Russian with a vivacious Austrian wife. He was an enormous asset and was popular with the police, the army (1st Battalion of the Malay Regiment), the civil authorities and the Thais. I began to like service life in Kedah. I bought a set of golf clubs from the Malayan Police bandmaster who was about to retire and, urged on by the young Sultan of Kedah, I started to learn to play ... alas, not very well.

I took every opportunity to visit the Thai Border Police who were a cut above the Thai provincial police. They had better jungle uniform, up-to-date weapons, their own modern transport and claimed to carry out aggressive patrolling against bandits, Communists and smugglers. I made a point of talking to the English-speaking officers and travelling with them around South Thailand. I soon discovered that there were no-go areas, said to be dominated

245

by the Communist Party of Malaya, into which their Bangkok headquarters would not allow them to go. It became obvious that for their own political reasons they did not wish to stir up a hornet's nest. We tried hard to get them into these areas and on one occasion a fusillade of shots were fired at us. No one was hurt, but our jeep was hit, crashed and rolled over into a flooded ditch. I was unharmed but the driver and the Thai general were both crushed underneath. The two escort soldiers and I managed to free them before they drowned. During a subsequent celebration, the general gave me his swagger-stick, and the driver gave me his cap badge, as souvenirs of our adventure. Joanna was not at all favourably impressed when someone else told her of my adventure.

Kedah State was very forward-looking, protected its historic places and preserved and celebrated its ancient traditions on all possible occasions. Over the Christmas holiday, I wrote home, 'We saw a crowd of Malays near the river and on joining them we noticed that the local political party, the United Malays Nationalist Organisation, was organising boat races to honour and enjoy a visit by the Prime Minister who is a prince of the Kedah royal house. We watched for a while and saw six long boats, each with twenty-eight paddlers, racing against one other. They went very fast indeed and one could distinguish the crews, who came from various districts, by the coloured kerchiefs worn as headbands. Suddenly, some of the officials noticed us, brought chairs for us to sit on and cleared people from in front to provide us with a clear view. As we were the only non-Malays there, we felt rather embarrassed, especially when we discovered that we were next to the Prime Minister's party. However, no one else seemed to mind. The Tunku recognised us and joined us for about twenty minutes to explain what was going on. He said he was very surprised to find us in Kedah.'

We moved into a comfortable government chalet on New Year's Day and John became friendly with several Chinese children round about, of whom a pair of twins were called Coro and Nation respectively, having been born on Queen Elizabeth's coronation day! We acquired a Hokkien-speaking amah to do the chores and we all got on very well together. Our stay in Kedah would not last very long.

On 12th April 1960, a strange letter came from Huss, who had just taken over from Harvey Ryves as the first Malayan Director of the Malayan Special Branch. Extracts from his long letter read as follows: 'I should have written earlier to inform you of my plans to move you to Kuala Lumpur as Head Special Branch Selangor vice Sharif who has not proved successful and is to go to uniform branch ... (the Ministry of Home Affairs) has agreed ... these moves are firm and definite ... I would like you to take this transfer back to Kuala Lumpur with serene and bright prospects to follow. I mean future days, I am a bit worried about your wife in particular, please explain things to her. In respect of these changes, I have had to face bitter criticism and plenty of "talks" which are unpalatable and unpleasing to stomach BUT I am determined ... It is my wish to have you near to me for many reasons and I have won my day to bring you back to Kuala Lumpur at the expense of some displeasure ... which I had to fight back. If I may say so ... please discuss with Joanna who has been in the forefront of my heart when the transfer was first mooted ... I want a real friend who I can trust in my future difficult task and this I can always find in you, with Joanna providing support and encouragement. The "unity" which will be forged by us together would make us all happy and efficient in our respective lines of duty ... I hope this two-page letter will explain the feelings I have been harbouring ... good luck to you, Joanna and Bomoh ... yours very truly, Huss.' The tock tock birds in Kedah were every bit as busy as elsewhere in Malaya; but I no longer played cricket with the tocks.

Huss followed this up, three days later, with a long telephone call. He said that the Prime Minister, Deputy Prime Minister, the Minister for Home Affairs and Claude Fenner had, from the beginning, warmly supported the combination of his appointment and my return to Kuala Lumpur. I was to have no worry about political support and the other difficulties would soon disappear. Claude Fenner also telephoned me to say that he strongly supported my move back to Kuala Lumpur and urged me to accept.

I had always liked Huss and our many long conversations – sometimes disputations – had been enjoyable, invigorating and always highly productive. I had no idea he felt so strongly about our professional relationship and it was some months later that I discovered from the Malayan Commissioner of Police, Tan Sri Mohamed Salleh, that Huss's battle fought over my appointment, and its future implications, was because I was not the most senior of the British officers available and some long noses had been put out of joint. Of course, we accepted the transfer with the good grace requested; although it involved our fourth move in under a year. We were both genuinely sorry to leave Kedah. I handed over to my deputy and we said farewell to our newly acquired friends, especially the Thai Border Police and members of the Border Operations Committee. The Sultan of Kedah and his Sultana gave us a private dinner – a great honour. We retraced our steps to Kuala Lumpur with our baggage travelling by rail.

Three days after we arrived in Kuala Lumpur, we moved into 4, Maxwell Drive. We were joined by Ah Loy, a female cook, aged thirty-nine, who was the mother of eight girls and two boys; and Ah Kim, wash amah, who was Ah Loy's youngest sister, aged twenty-two. Ah Loy parked her family elsewhere; but we persuaded her to bring her youngest son, aged five. He proved a wonderful playmate for John. Of our new ménage, I wrote home, 'Ah Loy's husband is a cook on the mail train. He spends one night in Penang, another night in Singapore and comes home to us every third night. We can just see the railway line half a mile or so to our left and, as his train passes by, the driver gives a toot on the whistle from the front and Ah Loy's husband waves to us from a large window at the back of the train. Ah Loy learned to cook by paying for cookery lessons when she was nineteen years old, her last employers were Swedish so we have great variety in our food.'

Huss was the previous occupant of No. 4 and when we arrived it was inhabited by two of his wives, their ten children, and eighteen miscellaneous relatives; we counted at least twelve cats. It had two storeys, a wide porch and was much larger than 5 Airport Road. There were four very large bedrooms with spacious dressing rooms, and a long row of servants' quarters at the back. All the children were of school age and, every morning, Huss had to drop them off at four different pickup points for arranged onward transmission to their schools. The reverse happened every evening. Huss's third wife, number two in the pecking order, was the headmistress of a large school, and we were never sure where number four wife was located. All the adults lived happily together and we were very glad to see them again.

The Huss family were delighted to leave 4, Maxwell Drive because a four-carriageway road was being constructed through the jungle valley, opposite the house, to the Lake Gardens, where the new houses of parliament were being constructed. The jungle had already been cleared before our arrival; but eight huge bull-

248

dozers were working all day levelling the ground. On dry days, red dust blew into the house and, on wet days, the place became a quagmire. We could not use the telephone by day because of the noise made by tractors. It made no difference to the tock tock birds – if anything, their nocturnal adventures became even more exciting.

In the short time we had been away, we found social life in Kuala Lumpur among the expatriate civil servants had changed considerably. Many people knew, or had good reason to believe, that their contracts would not be renewed by the Malayan Government. There was an air of *laissez faire* around and the work ethic suffered accordingly. With the ending of the Emergency, the security forces had been run down, military headquarters had been disbanded and many units had returned to their home countries in the Commonwealth. The staff in the British High Commission were of quite a different calibre; few, if any, could speak Malay and they tended to congregate with their expatriate friends in the commercial houses. Little or no attempt appeared to be made among these diplomats to communicate with the Malayan Government representatives, or even to mix with local people, and there were very few exceptions to this practice.

Naturally, local people noticed this with misgiving. A minor example of an unnecessary *faux pas* was the occasion at which a senior British diplomat's wife wore a bright yellow dress at an important royal function, not knowing that yellow should be worn only by Muslim royalty in an Islamic country. This did not go unnoticed. Other slights, real and imagined, occurred from time to time and silly tales against members of the new government became an unguarded feature of the cocktail party circuit. People in the British High Commission, and in some of the British commercial houses, were accused by the Malayans of rudeness, taking local people for granted, and expecting senior members of the administration to be at their beck and call. European politeness and ordinary good manners seemed to have evaporated in the hot climate. Gradually a wall of distrust began to appear. Occasionally, things would improve a little when a new High Commissioner arrived, but the general atmosphere – so friendly and so open during the Emergency – continued to deteriorate and caused much unnecessary friction. Some of us tried to improve matters by talking privately to those in authority in the High Commission. Our representations were politely received; but it seemed that the High Commission worked in tight little boxes and resented advice from colleagues whose responsibilities differed from their own. Exactly the same affairs existed in the commercial houses, whose *tai-pans* (directors) had always been a law unto themselves and had no intention of changing.

Social life for us soon evolved around our Malayan friends. Joanna became pregnant for the second time and had a difficult and uncomfortable pregnancy. Despite this, she continued to do voluntary work for three half days a week in a government clinic for spastic children, kept up with her Chinese scroll painting, rejoined her ikebana group and made herself useful among the police depot families. I joined the Selangor Stamp Club and became its second vice-president for many years.

Selangor State was important from a professional point of view because its capital, Kuala Lumpur, was the centre of federal government. Parliament buildings were under construction. The large satellite town of Petaling Jaya, and other suburbs, were growing fast and the population was increasing by leaps and bounds. Foreign embassies and consulates, and many skyscraping hotels, were springing up everywhere and vast sums of money were being spent on the infrastructure. Malayanisation of the civil service was nearing completion and a feeling of national pride abounded. Malay became the national language; a most effective way to ensure people used it was to introduce it in all government offices slowly, but surely. One day a week, one week a month, one month a year – then Malay became the official language of government.

I took over as Head Special Branch Selangor from Mohamad Sharif. My first task was to bring myself up to date with what had happened since I left six months previously. I found that none of the secret service funds had been checked; so I did this personally throughout the state and then either I, or my deputy, Raja Adnan, continued to do this regularly. I changed all our safe houses (private houses, flats or apartments used for secret operations) because I thought most would have been compromised. I arranged for confidential reports to be completed on all our detectives and inspectors and later, by arrangement with the Chief Police Officer Selangor, transferring some to uniform branch and replacing them with men and women who either had language qualifications, or a higher education. This game of musical chairs took a year to complete; but our efficiency and energy greatly improved.

Another weak point was the standard of our detainee case files. During the Emergency, it was comparatively easy to gather strong evidence of association with the Communist terrorist organisation, and to obtain reliable corroboration from several reliable sources. But Communist subversion was more difficult to prove and the cases much more complicated. A number of important detainees were being released by the judicial authorities, quite rightly in my opinion, either because the case was poorly presented or the gap between legal socialism and illegal communism was not properly explained in the summaries which accompanied each file. In other words, independent, fair assessors, who decided whether or not a person should continue to be detained under the Emergency regulations, were becoming increasingly critical of our work.

Huss had already anticipated this months ago so I re-instituted his weekly training programmes; but divided them into subject groups, rather than general sessions. Raja Adnan and I shared this and slowly our written work improved and the likelihood of disastrous cases receded. I continued to spend a large part of my time lecturing in the Special Branch school, to the Malayan armed forces and to various gatherings of civil servants. I did my share of taking passing-out parades at the police depot, wearing my uniform, and endeavouring to speak to the parade in Hokkien, Mandarin, Malay, Urdu (if there were any Sikhs or Punjabi Muslims on parade) and English. My theme was always the three Cs: Corruption, Communalism and Communism, in that order.

Our second son Richard was born in Bungsar Hospital at ten minutes before midnight on 2nd July 1961, and I was able to visit Joanna regularly till she came home. Once again our Asian friends streamed in to admire Richard's long hair, his blue eyes and unwrinkled skin; once again the Malay and Chinese nurses were kind and helpful.

I handed over to Raja Adnan on 4th August and the next day we flew to the UK on fifty-six days' leave. We stayed with my mother in Chipperfield and Richard was baptised in the church where we had been married. We flew back to Malaya on 4th October and I resumed where I had left off.

I was awarded Membership of the Most Excellent Order of the British Empire (MBE) in the 1961 Birthday Honours and received

251

many nice letters from officers with whom I had served in Selangor, Pahang, Negri Sembilan, Kedah and Federal HQ in Kuala Lumpur. Letters from England included one from the Chief Constable of the Lothian and Peebles Constabulary; I had never met him and it was a pleasant surprise. Then, right out of the blue, I received the award of Pingat Jasa Kebaktian (PJK) in March 1962 from the hands of His Highness the Sultan of Selangor and, a year later, I was awarded the PKS on the coronation of his son. Joanna and I were received by the Sultan on several occasions thereafter, and we much enjoyed renewing our friendship with relatives of the royal family. They all lived in quite another world – very old-fashioned by today's standards – there was little evidence of great wealth, the womenfolk were still separated from the men on social occasions; but these ladies were always relaxed, friendly and full of curiosity. Overcome by the latter feelings, they always ran up to Joanna, who had been siphoned away from me into their cushioned quarters, and would feel her tummy to see if there was another one on the way!

I continued as the Head Special Branch of Selangor State for the next eighteen months, though I was frequently called in by the Prime Minister or Huss to take part in the preliminary discussions leading up to the formation of Malaysia. My opinions were sought on every conceivable subject and were not limited to professional or administrative affairs. During this period, I came to know the leaders of Malaya really well. It was for me a most exhilarating and exciting time.

Major objections to the talks leading up to the formation of Malaysia came from the Indonesian Government, which feared the creation of a Far Eastern rival to its own political and commercial aspirations. Another factor was the Sultan of Brunei's decision not to take part in plans for the formation of Malaysia. His was a very rich state, with a fast developing economy based on the export of oil. The Sultan thought it should exist as an independent country, enjoying its own considerable wealth and not having to share it with anyone else. However, it had a vulnerable land frontier with Indonesia. In December 1962, when it was clear that Malaysia would be created, an armed revolution egged on by the Indonesian Government was launched from the countryside against the Sultan. Azahari was the rebels' inexperienced military leader. He might well have succeeded were it not for the bravery and initiative of the forces sent in by the British, at very short notice, to come to the aid of the hapless Sultan. Interrogation of prisoners, and documentary evidence, confirmed that Azahari and his followers were supported wholeheartedly by the Indonesians. With the benefit of hindsight, this local war signalled the start of Indonesia's Confrontation ('Konfrontasi') with Malaysia.

One of the after-effects of the rebellion was the Sultan of Brunei's wish to build a palace in Kuala Lumpur to secure the safety of his eldest son and other relatives. As Head of the Selangor Special Branch, my responsibilities included the security of Kuala Lumpur and, of course, this included the site of the proposed palace. I had many friendly arguments with the Sultan's representatives trying not to make the place look like a prison, with armed security guards skulking in minarets on the corners. We reached a compromise quickly, because the contractors had to design and build the palace in one month. Never did a building go up so quickly.

When the Sultan's son arrived, he proved to be a very reserved little boy quite overcome by his change of address, and had few toys to play with. No one seemed willing or able to help him settle in; so we gave him our television set, an old wireless set and a tape recorder, together with a large number of jazz and pop tapes which he played all day long.

In early August 1963, Huss asked me to work alongside him full time during the weeks prior to the formation of Malaysia. I joined him, Claude Fenner, whose appointment at that time was Director of Police Affairs; and Richard Buxton on temporary attachment from our interrogation centre. We worked day and night with the Prime Minister, Deputy Prime Minister, our Minister, their officials and the constitutional lawyers. Every detail of the proposed amalgamation of Malaya, Singapore, Sarawak and North Borneo was closely studied: and Richard and I prepared papers on every subject under the sun. Where I was ignorant, I had to locate and persuade the relevant experts to fill the gaps, usually at very short notice. Almost everything we did had a high security grading. We were all under enormous pressure from local and foreign journalists, the Americans (CIA), the Australians (ASIO), the British (MI5), the Indonesians, the Taiwanese and hosts of others, to tell them what was going on.

It all worked out surprisingly well. The new constitution emerged like a butterfly from its chrysalis. The organisation and administration of a new country within the Commonwealth, called Malaysia, came into being on 16th September 1963, six years and sixteen days after Merdeka (the granting of independence to Malaya by the British).

The constitution was designed to ensure the existence of a strong federal government and also a measure of autonomy for the State governments. It provided for a constitutional Supreme Head, called the Yang-di-Pertuan Agong or King and a Deputy Supreme Head, to be elected for a term of five years by the Rulers of the Malay States from among their number. The Federal Parliament would comprise two houses: the Senate and the House of Representatives. The Senate would be made up of some members to be elected by the Legislative Assemblies of the States, and others to be appointed by the Supreme Head. The House of Representatives would consist of members elected by universal suffrage with a common electoral roll. Islam would continue to be the official religion and the constitution guaranteed religious freedom for all. So, in my opinion. it was as democratic as it could possibly be.

Our ministers were extremely open about their personal views and the sort of constitution they wanted to emerge and were more or less at one on this. Tunku Abdul Rahman summed it up during a relaxed conversation with me one evening. 'I want a constitution which meets with the wishes of the Rulers, and the inhabitants of the four component parts. Islam must be the official religion but I have no objections to other religions providing they do not go around the country converting Muslims to Christianity. We need to help the *bumiputra* (sons of the soil, Malays) because they are so behind on commercial and industrial matters. We must have universal suffrage and free elections. I am worried about the activities of Lee Kuan Yew in Singapore – he goes to bed with Communists, I do not trust him and he has eyes on winning the Chinese vote in the peninsula. We need to watch him, I think.'

When I handed over to a Malaysian in September 1963, I was the second last British officer to serve in Selangor State and I was the last Englishman to be a State Head of Special Branch. I bought the largest sterling silver cup I could find in Singapore, and presented it to the Selangor Police for an annual Sepak Raga Jaring Competition (a game rather like badminton, but played with the foot!) I joined the about-to-be-formed Malaysian Police Headquarters on 3rd September 1963, as the provisional deputy to Huss, who was the provisional director of the provisional Malaysian Special Branch. We were both confirmed in our appointments two weeks later. Richard Buxton and I were promoted to the rank of senior assistant commissioner by joint agreement of Dato Razak, Dr Ismail and Claude Fenner. The next task for Huss and me was the selection and appointment of officers and staff to work in our new headquarters; and then to hold meetings with the director of the Singapore Special Branch and the Heads of Special Branch in Sarawak and North Borneo. At the same time, I drafted our own responsibilities to the enlarged Ministry of Home Affairs and to Claude Fenner, soon to be knighted by Her Majesty the Queen and appointed Inspector General of the Royal Malaysian Police Service.

Joanna became pregnant with our third child at this time, but unfortunately she had to have a termination, because our Australian lady doctor discovered something seriously wrong. We never found out exactly what it was. Joanna was admitted to the General Hospital at once and had an immediate operation. There were no beds available afterwards and she had to stay on the operating trolley in a draughty passage, while I slept in a deckchair beside her. During the night she was taken seriously ill and, after a long search, the duty surgeon appeared and operated on her at once – just in time, because the previous surgeon had failed to remove the placenta. It was all a ghastly muddle. Joanna was very lucky to have survived. Although she denied it, I think this dreadful experience affected her for years afterwards.

It took a month of frantic building to construct the new Malaysian Police Headquarters at the top of Bluff Road. We moved in on 10th October 1963, next door to Claude Fenner's office. I spent a good deal of time with the Minister of Home Affairs and his staff; and Huss and I shared the entertainment of visiting officials from abroad. The Fenners took the really important ones; and it was great fun comparing results and impressions afterwards.

It was, I think, the British officials in MI5 who introduced us to Douglas Hyde, former editor of *The Daily Worker* newspaper and well-known British Communist Party member. He had left the Communist Party following the invasion of Hungary by the Russian Army in 1956 and had replaced his political beliefs by joining the Roman Catholic Church. After detailed negotiations, he was given a contract to work full-time interviewing and assessing hard-core Communist detainees still held by us under the Emergency regulations. We suspected that many of them were finding their previous Communist convictions to be transitory or flawed and we were keen to reduce the number of detainees as fast as possible. Our problem was to find a safe way to help them replace Communism with an acceptable, attractive and permanent alternative. Douglas Hyde not only spoke the language of international Communism; but he had, himself, also gone through the process of becoming disillusioned and discovering an intellectual replacement which would give him a good reason to want to live. As far as I was concerned, I had never forgotten the surrendered person who shot himself while under my protection ten years ago – all our efforts at that time were aimed at persuading people to surrender and then to work for us. We did not have the time, or the expertise, to give these people a fresh intellectual life to replace years of Communist indoctrination.

Douglas Hyde was my responsibility and became a valued friend. I saw at once that he was ideal for this sort of work and he approached it with enthusiasm, patience, understanding and determination. After three months or so, we were able with confidence to reduce the number of so-called hard-core Communists to a handful and we were able to release safely a large number of less dangerous detainees. We managed to keep in friendly touch with most of them over their first year of liberty. Whilst he was very successful with Chinese males, he was not quite so successful with Chinese females. The reason for this might have been his gender, or the inexperience of our female interpreters. Be that as it may, it had for long been my opinion that. in the prevailing circumstances, the ladies were guided much more by their emotions than the men, and were content to let their hearts rule their heads. Expressed simply, if they wished to come over to our side, betray their comrades and live with themselves afterwards, they would do so with little encouragement from us. However, if they did not want to do so, there was little anyone else could do unless there was an emotional key to be found and, usually, we did not know where to find it. For political reasons, I did not encourage Douglas to try and influence our few Malay Communist detainees, though he liked talking to them in a general way.

On one occasion, we had great difficulty talking positively to a particular person who had been captured some time ago in the jungles of North Perak. We could win most of the intellectual arguments with him about Communism and socialism; but he could not accept the existence of socialism in a capitalist society and would not be moved on this. Someone came up with the idea – it was probably Douglas himself – of flying out an ordinary low-level partner of John Lewis's departmental store (where the employees own the company) to explain how socialism really could coexist in a capitalist society. This person was given the minimum briefing by us and we put them together with an interpreter. They talked enthusiastically for hours and we ended up with a very different person in our hands.

One of our most interesting detainees was Ahmad Boestamam, quondam chairman of the extremely left-wing pre-Emergency Partai Rakyat (People's Party), a Malay politician who had spent some years in detention. Although certainly not an intellectual, he strongly favoured armed revolution in Malaya as a means to secure what he intended to be a free socialist society. There was some evidence that he joined the Malayan Communist Party pre-1948 and, in his words, he strongly supported from afar the Malay Communists Abdullah C.D., Rashid Mahidin and others, most of whom came from Pahang. In 1948 these people joined the Communist Party of Malaya's Department of Malay Work in the jungle and, eventually, went up north to the Thai border in 1952–53. Boestamam told me he often wished he had accompanied them into the jungle in 1948; but he felt he was much too soft to survive life in the jungle. Whilst in detention, he wrote a long autobiography. It provided a vivid description of the problems facing Malay Nationalism in the face of colonialism on the right hand, and Communism on the left hand. Strangely enough he was living comfortably, under 'house arrest', in one of the smaller police stations in the Kuala Lumpur area, where he had been given a room to himself. I had made friends with him some years ago, had visited him occasionally and lent him non-political books to read. I was quite unable to persuade our minister to release him, even though I said I thought he was no longer a danger to the country's security.

However, in a convivial mood one day, Tunku Abdul Rahman said to me, 'Go and talk to him and do a Douglas Hyde. Boestamam is so stupid that I think he will be a great deal of help politically to me if he is given his freedom and let loose on the public.' Mohamed Suffian, later a Tun (or life peer), was present and remarked. 'I think he should be released at once, his politics are so out of date, he is absolutely harmless.' I said, yet again, that in my opinion he was no longer a threat to security and I am glad to say that shortly afterwards we were told to release him. He later said in a letter to me. 'My views have not changed, you know!' Suffian was a judge in the High Court at the time and pro-Chancellor of the University of Malaya. He later became Chief Justice of Malaysia. He wrote a number of books on Malaysian law and told me he had brought up to date the works of à Beckett Terrell, my pre-war family connection. Suffian's wife was English and was born in Norfolk and was always known as 'Bunny'. They were both extremely good company and loved to spark off one another. Supper at Suffian's was a huge delight.

10

The rain, it raineth on the just
And also on the unjust fella:
But chiefly on the just, because
The unjust steals the just's umbrella

LORD BOWEN, 1835–94

The architect of Indonesia's Confrontation with Malaysia, which began in 1963, was President Sukarno. His dream of reviving the ancient 'Malay' empires, based on Java and Sumatra, originally came to light in 1944–45, towards the end of the Japanese occupation of the Netherlands East Indies. At this time, the Japanese were attempting to win popular support from their vassal states on the fringe of their so-called Co-Prosperity Sphere. During negotiations with the Japanese, Sukarno launched the idea of a Greater Indonesia comprising the Philippines (with its large Muslim population), Indonesia, North Borneo, Sarawak, Brunei, Labuan, the British Straits Settlements (including Singapore) and the Federated and Unfederated Malay States. But while the Japanese were willing, for their own reasons, to grant a limited degree of independence to Indonesian Nationalists in the former Netherlands East Indies, they refused to go along with the suggested enlargement.

Another, quite surprising, variation on the regional theme of empire came from the Philippines Government after the election of President Macapagal in 1961. He registered a territorial claim on behalf of the Philippines to the territory of British North Borneo: expanding his ideas, later, by proposing a regional alliance comprising the Philippines, Mainland Malaya, Singapore, Indonesia, British North Borneo, Sarawak and Brunei. This proposal aroused very little enthusiasm, especially among the countries

259

most affected; but it may have encouraged Sukarno seriously to consider that the time was right to embark once more upon his own empirical ideas. Nagging echoes of Macapagal's proposals; the failure of Azahari's Brunei rebellion in 1962; and Tunku Abdul Rahman's clear intention to go ahead with the formation of Malaysia in September 1963: all combined to bring President Sukarno's dream of imperial grandeur into sharp and immediate focus.

Most of us in Malaysia who were responsible for assessing what was going on in Indonesia, regarded President Sukarno as a skilful political juggler; a survivor in extremely dangerous times. He balanced carefully the conflicting aims of competing political parties, who were still trying to work within his pancasilas programme; and the need to keep his army generals on side, and their soldiers fully occupied. The trouble was he was ageing; moreover, he was not very well and he was over-indulging in exotic pursuits. His decision-making became harder and harder to predict and we observed with increasing dismay his tolerance of the Communist Party of Indonesia (PKI), which was itself moving away from the somewhat gentle guidance of Communist Russia to the more lively and dangerous influences of the Communist Party of China. We were all wondering, 'What next after Bung Karno?' and 'Would the PKI attempt to take on the generals at their own game?'

We assessed that President Sukarno was coming under the influence of Dr Subandrio, Indonesia's Foreign Minister; a number of generals in the Tentera National Indonesia (TNI, the Indonesian Armed Forces); and D.N. Aidit, the young and brilliant leader of the Indonesian Communist Party. All had their own reasons for strongly opposing the formation of Malaysia. He soon realised that, whatever political action he might take, he could not possibly prevent the formation Malaysia. Indonesia was becoming increasingly isolated on the world stage. It was obvious to him that Tunku Abdul Rahman, with strong support of Britain and its colonial territories in South-East Asia, was most likely to succeed in his plans. President Sukarno, tight-rope walker *extraordinaire*, suddenly lost his composure and shouted '*Ganjang Malaysia! Ganjang Malaysia!*' (Crush Malaysia! Crush Malaysia!) from his palace in Jakarta. His cries were echoed by the army, almost the whole population of Indonesia and politicians of every description. There was no doubt that the idea of *Konfrontasi* was a popular one in the early stages; though few Indonesians had any idea of how it would be implemented, or how long it might last.

President Sukarno himself issued a statement explaining his reason for confronting Malaysia. In simple words, it was to frustrate British neo-colonialist plans. The idea behind the formation of Malaysia, he said, was to create a long-term safe haven for British interests in the rubber, tin and oil industries. He considered that it was Indonesia's duty to prevent this happening and to put an end to European exploitation of the region's natural resources. Soon after this, came a number of armed infiltrations by the Indonesian army across the borders of British North Borneo (soon to be renamed Sabah) and Sarawak. Promises of moral support came from the Communist Government of China. The Communist Party of Indonesia rallied massive public support for Sukarno from among the Indonesians and the Chinese living in the countryside. The Communist Party of Malaya was in no position to increase its own political or military activity: but in Sarawak there was already a well-organised and well-led militant Communist organisation, quaintly called by the Sarawak Government the 'Clandestine Communist Organisation' (CCO), fighting against the government from jungle bases on the frontier with Indonesia. The CCO increased its militant activity and its political work among the population, tying down a sizeable proportion of the government's security forces. Within Indonesia itself, the British Embassy was stormed by the mobs, said to have been enraged by the playing of a Scottish bagpiper on the embassy roof! Many Malaysian and British-owned commercial properties were attacked and destroyed by the mobs. Union Jacks flying in the breeze were hauled down by the rioters, burnt and replaced by the red and white flag of Indonesia. The Indonesian Government expelled the American Peace Corps and allowed the mobs to burn US information offices and libraries. As far as we were concerned in Malaysia, the Indonesians started to infiltrate small armed units, and groups of saboteurs, into Singapore and along the west coast of Malaysia. These were detected and arrested within days of their landing. There was no support from the local population. The largest of these incursions into West Malaysia took place when the Indonesian Air Force dropped 96 paratroopers into North Johore in September 1964. All were either killed or captured.

Malaysia was accepted as a Member of the United Nations in

late 1964 and soon became a non-permanent member of the Security Council. Indonesia's response was to withdraw forthwith from the United Nations Assembly.

On 1st October 1965, units of the Indonesian National Army launched a coup in Jakarta. They seized a number of 'Centrist' Indonesian generals; six of whom, including General Yani, the army's Chief of Staff, were murdered. General Nasution, the armed forces Chief of Staff and Minister of Defence, appears to have been warned just beforehand. Pushed by his wife, he jumped over his garden wall into the grounds of the Iraqi Embassy, breaking his leg in the process and was *hors de combat* for some time. President Sukarno was unharmed and was allowed to continue as head of state. It was agreed unanimously by the leader of the coup that Confrontation should continue. During subsequent discussions and power struggles within the army, General Suharto emerged as the next strong man in Indonesia. He does not seem to have played an overt part in the coup, but troops loyal to him restored order, more or less, throughout the country. Internal peace within Indonesia did not last for long.

The Malaysian Special Branch was the country's Intelligence Service and it was our view that General Suharto would not only support Bung Karno in his declining years, but would succeed him eventually as president. We did not think the Communist Party of Indonesia was responsible for the coup behind the scenes; though, of course, it would exploit the post-coup situation as opportunities occurred. However, we were greatly surprised to hear that, on the same day as the coup, the Communist newspaper *People's Daily* came out strongly in support of the coup. This really put the PKI cat among the TNI pigeons! The newspaper and other Communist publishing houses in Jakata were closed down at once, and leading Communists were arrested. Waves of suspicion, leading to out- breaks of unrest, quickly swept throughout the length and breadth of Indonesia. Manhunts became purges; old scores were settled by one community on another community. The army, now firmly under popular right-wing General Suharto, sorted itself out, then took a ferocious lead in 'restoring order'. Unbelievably large numbers of civilians were killed on suspicion that they were either Communist, non-Muslim or were said to be willing to overthrow the president. D.N. Aidit, the Communist Party leader was dis- covered in his hideout and was among the million men, women and children, said later by Indonesian Government investigators, to have perished in this holocaust.

As we debriefed our sources operating in Indonesia, we realised the terrible things taking place in our neighbouring country. Even now, it seems impossible to blame any particular person or any particular party or any particular policy. The mass killings on such a huge scale had simply got out of control – like a child playing with fire, or a river overflowing its banks and flooding the countryside in minutes, or like the unstoppable powers of an avalanche or volcano eruption. I had seen this on a smaller scale in Malaya – fighting between Malays and Chinese. I had experienced it before in India, between Hindus and Muslims, where hundreds of thousands of innocent men, women and children had been killed in Bengal and again in the Punjab. Now it was happening all over Indonesia from Atjeh in the west of Indonesia, to the islands in the Eastern Seas. Even Bali, lovely island jewel, the home of ancient Hindu religion and customs, was racked by mayhem and murder, carried out by the Indonesian Army and recently arrived Javanese immigrants against the mainly Hindu inhabitants. Some 100,000 Balinese were killed, according to official Indonesian Government records issued after peace returned to the island.

None of this effected President Sukarno's wish to pursue Konfrontasi with Malaysia. It continued, though in a rather desultory fashion – at least for those not actually engaged in running battles along the East Malaysian-Indonesian Kalimantan border, or on the Island of Singapore and the west coast of Malaysia.

On 4th May 1963 my friend Mike Day, who had left the police service and was serving in the office of the Commissioner for South-East Asia in Singapore, was travelling in a Belvedere helicopter in Sarawak. It suffered a mechanical failure and crashed in deep secondary jungle killing all nine occupants. A memorial has since been built by the Trusan Memorial Project, at the nearest accessible site, and is maintained by the local devout Christian Muruts; so that friends and descendants of Mike, and his colleagues, may visit the place and pay their respects.

I bore this terrible accident very much in mind when, next month, I started on my first tour of Malaysia. I left Kuala Lumpur by plane for Kuching, the capital of Sarawak, with two Malaysian colleagues, one of whom was Abdul Rahman bin Hashim, then junior to me in the Special Branch hierarchy. We were met by Roy Henry, the Commissioner of Police, whom I had visited years ago in Tanjong Malim. We stayed the night in the Aurora Hotel. I wrote home: 'I have explored the town and managed to spend several hours in its most interesting museum. Everything is very colonial, life moves slowly and the other two members of my party are shocked by the complacency everywhere . . . they have a serious armed Communist problem in the countryside; but, apart from the security forces, no one else appears to be involved seriously, rather like Malaya in the early days of the Emergency. Kuching is on two sides of a fast-flowing river, the western bank includes the Rajah's palace and the houses of government officials and a splendid police officers' mess. The town proper is on the east bank and is well laid out, completely flat, but liable to flooding. No one really likes it here and old Malaya hands say that they would much prefer to be in Malaya.'

We spent three days in Kuching and then flew to Jesselton in North Borneo, via Brunei where I had an interesting talk with the acting head of the Brunei Special Branch. Then on to Jesselton where we were met by the head of the North Borneo Special Branch. We stayed at the Brunei Hotel where prices were twice as high as at hotels in Kuala Lumpur. I wrote home: 'Jesselton is really very nice indeed. It is on a sandy coast with pine trees everywhere and a wonderfully blue sea. Cool winds all day, islands in the sea, marvellous bathing and all very clean. It was flattened by the Allies during the war and has been completely rebuilt. I have come across an astonishing thing. A certain government official keeps a large hornbill as a pet. This man goes to his office every morning at 7.30 a.m. on a motor scooter and his hornbill flies with him. It is a strange sight watching the magnificent bird flying majestically a few feet above his head, providing shelter when it rains!'

We flew to Tawau on the borders of Indonesia two days later and were met by the local Special Branch officer and stayed the night in the Tawau Hotel. I wrote home, 'Tawau is one of those very modern concrete, characterless, Chinese towns which seem to have sprung up round the Far East since the war. Its prosperity is based on the barter trade with the Philippines and Indonesia. Cigarettes, watches and luxury goods are traded for rubber, copra, spices and pepper. A favourable rate of exchange cements some very good bargains for the local participants who, of course, are Chinese. Our hotel cook is a convict who is serving a life sentence in the local prison for murder. He's let out in the mornings and admitted back into the prison in the evenings; sometimes he returns too late and they won't let him in, so he has to sleep in the room next to mine!'

Most of the European civil servants we met in Borneo were highly critical of the formation of Malaysia and said that Britain had sold them down the river. Rahman bin Hashim, in subsequent personal reports to the inspector general and our minister, was scathing of them and recommended that all except one or two should be encouraged to retire early. My report, which concerned the organisation of the Sarawak and North Borneo Special Branches and, especially their knowledge of the Communist organisations and the Indonesian forces on the borders of both States, strongly recommended that the small number of Special Branch staff should be trebled in Sarawak and doubled in North Borneo (Sabah). I recommended that many more women should be recruited into Special Branch; and that the two Special Branch registries should be modernised and properly linked with those in Federal Police HQ Kuala Lumpur. I also urged that all Special Branch personnel in the Borneo territories should complete a course of retraining at the Special Branch school in Kuala Lumpur as soon as possible.

We left Tawau by plane landing at Lahad Datu, Sandakan, Jesselton, Brunei, Kuching and Singapore for talks before returning very late to Kuala Lumpur. Whilst in Jesselton, I saw Arthur Jacobs, the American CIA's representative in Kuala Lumpur, fast asleep in the bar of the Nan Heng Hotel. I woke him up and we had an amusing time trying to find out what the other was up to.

Joanna gradually recovered from the loss of her third child and we began once more to entertain our new friends. We gave three cocktail parties as our share in welcoming visitors from what was now called East Malaysia, of which the last was for sixty people. This was much too large for us to manage so we asked the Singapore Cold Storage to do it for us and, for once, we enjoyed our own party. We began to be invited to small formal parties given by Tunku Abdul Rahman, Dato Razak and our own minister, Dr Ismail. These usually involved staying on afterwards for an al fresco meal when the guests had departed. Sometimes, we had to take Huss's place at formal state dinners and, on one of these occasions, I found myself sitting next to Lee Kuan Yew, the Prime Minister of Singapore. He held the stage throughout the evening expounding his own often amusing views. He told me that he welcomed the formation of Malaysia; but he thought Tunku and the British had missed the bus by not persuading the Sultan of Brunei to join, adding, 'Brunei's oil revenue will increase enormously in the near future and I guess it will be wasted,' and later, 'I wonder whether the Peninsular Chinese will continue to support the Alliance – their leaders are very old hat. Templer said that hearts and minds mattered; but, this time round, it will be politics and purses.'

My work included going over with the Prime Minister, Dato Razak and Dr Ismail their public and parliamentary speeches on security and defence matters. Claude Fenner used to do these; but on my arrival he passed this chore to me. They would often invite me to listen to their speeches in parliament and, sometimes, I was able to take Joanna with me. Neither the government with its huge parliamentary majority, nor the ministers, always had it their own way. Members of Parliament were often quite critical and I noticed that, to be successful, my ministerial friends had to learn to be patient and polite, study their homework properly, and acquire a friendly sense of humour – some took longer than others to acquire these qualities, others developed quickly a knack of effective repartee worthy of the Mother of Parliaments!

Joanna was admitted to the Templer Hospital in January 1964 with a painful quinsy and the doctor kept her there for a fortnight. We had all suffered quite severely from coughs and colds over the last two years. Our doctor kept telling us that it was due to the clouds of red dust, which drifted into the houses bordering Maxwell Drive all day long, whilst the tractors were levelling the ground outside. Fortunately, the government ran out of money and imposed a delay on completion of the road works. After that, we had an enjoyable respite from this pollution for the next two years and the health of our neighbours and ourselves took a welcome turn for the better.

We flew to England on home leave in March 1964, and stayed in a bungalow recently built in Chipperfield by Joanna's mother for her retirement. Unfortunately, Mrs Tarver had become seriously ill before she could move in and was permanently in hospital throughout our leave. We stayed in her bungalow with the boys, and made a number of day trips to her and to friends and relatives.

While on leave I received a strange message from Huss, via one of his United Kingdom student relatives, which said that he was arranging for a secret operation to take place in London, and he asked me to make sure it went off smoothly. It involved the defection of a senior Indonesian diplomat in Europe and his onward despatch to Kuala Lumpur by air. The British security services would be represented by a man with a watching brief from the London Special Branch. Apparently neither MI6 nor MI5 wished to be directly involved. I had no difficulty clearing with him that what we were planning to do was legal. I duly met the diplomat and discovered that, for security reasons, his family had been routed via another airline and another country, and would arrive two days later. I managed to change all their onward flight bookings and was left with him hanging around for two days. The London Special Branch man was a junior official, he was not the least bit interested and he persuaded me to let him go home. I decided to take two rooms in a London hotel and find out what the diplomat had been doing in Europe. It was lucky that I did. He spoke quite good English, and my Malay was acceptable. It turned out that he was the linkman between the Indonesian Communist Party and Lumumba University for overseas students in Moscow. In particular, he gave me the names of the couriers and agents responsible not only for vetting and recruiting the students from South-East Asia (including Malaya and Singapore), but also for the return of the students, and liaison with Communist controllers in their countries of origin.

I had to get this detailed information back to Huss as soon as possible, because I believed immediate action was needed to launch a turning operation within the next batch of recruits. It all worked very well; another of Huss's relations was delighted to return home for a few days, the diplomat was united with his family, they were all given permission to reside in Malaysia and Huss enjoyed himself hugely with some very fruitful follow-ups.

*

We returned on 8th July, and found that the Public Works Department had completely repainted the house, and installed bars on the upper windows to prevent John and Richard falling out. Work had not restarted on the road building project opposite and all was comparatively peaceful.

Joanna decided to accept an invitation to become a committee member of the YWCA, and Huss decided to go on leave in September and again in November. Much to my surprise, I was asked to take over as acting director in his absences. Malaysia having achieved independence, it would have been natural for another senior Malay to take over from Huss, but Dr Ismail and Claude Fenner asked me to step in. In fact, I was to act as director on five occasions in the next three years, with the acting rank of deputy commissioner, whilst Huss and later Rahman bin Hashim were away for long periods serving with the Malaysian delegation at the United Nations Assembly. My first task in September was to prepare Malaysia's case against Indonesia to be presented at the United Nations Assembly, with no help forthcoming from the embryo Malaysian Foreign Service.

I had always been extremely fortunate to have been served by some excellent secretaries. They did not have a cushy time. I considered myself to be somewhat critical of other people's work, a perfectionist with my own and a bit of a slave-driver. Moreover, when I am in a hurry my handwriting sometimes deteriorates almost to the point of illegibility – a form of ogham, (an ancient Welsh script), some said. Sally Lim in Pahang, who had a cheerful, calm and unruffled personality, married a civil servant and eventually they came to Kuala Lumpur and lived in our old bungalow at 5, Airport Road; Mrs Ong in Selangor looked after me with endless patience and unflagging loyalty, and often worked long hours without complaint; Miss Khoo, who was intelligent, forward-looking and practical, later married to become Mrs Gunn Yew Thai and looked after me with cheerful abandonment of her social life at home. Other people seemed to change their secretaries frequently but I was lucky and obtained enormous benefit from continuity, familiarity with the work and a practised way of dealing with awkward customers.

The basic salaries of the Service were reviewed at about this time, not having been increased since 1952, over ten years earlier. The moving spirit behind this, and behind the favourable retirement terms eventually agreed between the British Colonial Office and the Malayan Government after Merdeka in 1957, was Dato Razak, the Deputy Prime Minister. Colonial Service and Overseas Civil Service officers serving in Malaysia after 1957 owe an enormous debt of gratitude to Dato Razak, who agreed much more favourable retirement terms for us than those first presented by the British Government.

When I was asked by Huss to join Tan Sri Salleh, the Commissioner of Police, and his personnel chiefs in discussions about the future of the Malaysian Police Service, I stressed the need for the recruitment of honours graduates from the University of Malaya directly into the Gazetted ranks. I said that they should be eligible for properly planned fast-track promotion to the senior ranks. Similarly, where we already had outstandingly successful officers – and most of us knew whom we were talking about – they too should be earmarked for fast-track promotion. I believed we had far too many over-promoted officers who were out of their depth, or just coasting along or were plain idle (Huss called them 'Peter Simples'). It was a matter of urgency to ensure young, energetic and talented people were not allowed to rust away in routine jobs, having become irretrievably burnt out when their turn came to be considered for senior posts.

Huss's own reaction was typical. I was given a young personal assistant, called Mohamed Hanif bin Omar, and I was told to train him up, give him responsibility, work him hard and to get rid of him if he failed to impress. It did not take me long to discover that Hanif was one of a very few exceptionally talented university graduates who could well become one of the country's leaders in a very few years. Eventually, I had to write my report on Hanif. I had no hesitation at all in strongly recommending him for accelerated promotion into an entirely different sort of job in uniform branch, which would add to his experience and qualify him for further promotion. My faith in Hanif, together with Huss's original judgement, came to fruition a few years later when he became Inspector General of the Royal Malaysian Police Service and was rewarded with the high Malaysian title of Tun. After his retirement,

Tun Hanif became a director of Genteng Berhad, probably the largest commercial business in South-East Asia.

At various times after 1963, I became a member or chairman of eight Malaysian Intelligence and Operations Committees. I continued to draft and prepare most of the Malaysian position papers for the United Nations and the Malaysian side of the Joint Intelligence Committees with the British. I worked with the CIA representatives, including the somnambulant Arthur Jacobs (like most CIA officers he was an astute lawyer, but he was a dead loss at dinner parties). A representative of the Rand Corporation attempted to recruit me to work in the Middle East; and, on my refusal, offered me a mature student's free place at Berkeley University in California which I also declined. I suggested he should approach a colleague who, though having no intelligence experience, certainly had the gift of the gab and might prove of value to the Americans. Other interesting people who spent some time with us were Lieutenant General Thornton, the New Zealand Air Force Chief of Staff, US General Wienecke and a host of Australian army officers and politicians, of whom Gough Whitlam was by far the most popular and respected by the Malaysians. Nearer home were two senior officials of the Vietnamese Ministry for Pacification who were extremely envious of our centrally controlled intelligence organisation. Nearer home still was Brigadier Wyldebore Smith, who had come up from Singapore on a visit; I introduced him as Brigadier Smoothbore Jones to the Prime Minister in a moment of forgetfulnes, producing from the brigadier friendly silence and a raised eyebrow – not at all the sort of mistake a former ADC should make.

I briefed and had formal discussions with the Rulers' Conference, the Malaysian Cabinet and the senior staff of major foreign embassies. Apart from all this chattering, I had not a great deal to do with running the field intelligence side of Konfrontasi. Our own staff under the brilliant and tireless Mohd Amin bin Osman (later to become a Tan Sri, the Malayan equivalent of a knight) were excellent at this. Their operations against the Indonesians were extremely successful and produced a great deal of accurate intelligence of Indonesian military intentions. Similarly, our relations with George Bogaars, Director of Special Branch Singapore, were close and friendly. Joint intelligence operations with the Singapore

Special Branch southwards into the Indonesian Rhiau Archipelago were remarkably successful and productive.

My main interest concerned the penetration of courier links between the Communist Party of China and other Communist Parties in South-East Asia. The Communist Party of Malaya was based in South Thailand, whence its leaders could travel to China as they wished and we were quite successful in the interception of their correspondence. Richard Buxton, who was responsible for the servicing of our important projects and for the invention and supply of technical aids, had directed some extremely successful operations both against the Communist Party itself and the Indonesians. These gave us pretty good coverage of what was going on within Indonesia; and we were able to add considerable detail to the general information supplied by the British. Americans and other friendly intelligence services.

I did not always agree with Huss. We had long talks after our meetings, especially if either Huss or I had a difference of opinion with our political bosses. I think that by far the most difficult of our problems was the widespread, strong political antipathy felt in mainland Malaysia towards Lee Kuan Yew and his People's Action Party (PAP); and what was perceived as the PAP's overzealous one-party politics in Singapore, and their expansionist activities northwards. Moreover, some influential European observers thought that a Singapore political takeover of Malaysia would create a much stronger, better led country, less dependent on British support, which would balance Indonesia's growing influence in the area. Lee Kuan Yew's decision to encourage his Peoples' Action Party to contest seats in Malaya's 1964 election really worried his political opponents in Malaya. It seemed to us, at the time, to make inevitable Singapore's secession a year or so later. It was clear to Huss, and to me, that it was only a matter of time before we would part company with Singapore; so we did our best to ensure that the closest possible relationship with Singapore Special Branch would continue.

At about this time, I was admitted into the Templer Hospital to have a hernia sewn up. I went into the public ward which seemed to be full of snoring Sikhs. Huss visited me – a strange reversal of roles – every day and we talked shop for hours and hours. On leaving the hospital I was given two weeks' sick leave at home.

On return to work, I saw our minister on a daily basis, flew to Singapore for conferences in a Malaysian Air Force plane twice a month, visited the Borneo Territories once a month and Thailand every two months. On one of the latter visits, I was approached by the CIA who were sponsoring a photo research team from California. They had developed a secret process for identifying human beings from the air by the warmth of their blood. We arranged for the team to check a suspect jungle area north east of Kedah, just west of the Betong Salient in South Thailand, hoping to locate one of Chan Peng's camps. The team duly flew over the area, courtesy of the RAF, and, two days later, came up with a wonderfully annotated map showing the movement of busy human beings who created a distinct pattern of activity in the thick jungle below. The team leader indicated to us a central camp for an estimated one hundred terrorists, bathing places in a nearby river and a series of sentry posts. The RAF liaison officers were ecstatic: however, our jungle fringe intelligence gave us no supporting leads of any kind. Nevertheless, we agreed to allow the RAF to bomb the area. The bombing, which was accurate and concentrated, resulted in the destruction of hundreds of trees and the discovery of many dead bodies of jungle pigs!

The cocktail circuit in Kuala Lumpur was taken completely by surprise when its constituents woke up on 9th August 1965 to discover that Singapore had seceded from Malaysia. The British High Commission was bombarded by signals from London and officials were running around chasing their tails, moaning, 'No one tells us anything.' An explanation soon came from the British High Commission. It stated that Tunku had lost a game of golf with Lee Kuan Yew and had got his own back by kicking Singapore out of Malaysia. There may or may not have been an element of a half-truth in this, but it meant a great deal of extra work for me.

Claude Fenner called in Richard Buxton and me to join him once again in putting up the constitutional drafts, the separation of responsibilities, the temporary extension of existing law, and a host of other unforeseen administrative matters, which kept arising as the days went by. Whereas the formation of Malaysia had been planned beforehand and, apart from frantic interventions by Indonesia, time had been more or less on our side, we now had a *fait accompli* to deal with as expeditiously as we could. We did not talk with Lee Kuan Yew himself because he said he wished to keep his mind clear of detail, but we liaised with members of his provisional cabinet. Not knowing how strongly people felt about secession, it was certainly comforting to hear Mr Goh Keng Swee, Singapore's provisional Defence Minister, say, 'Please bear with me, the only military experience I have had was as a stretcher-bearer in the last war.' Hard work, long hours, friendly compromise and a sense of humour among all those taking part, on both sides, ensured a smooth transfer of power; and an agreed position from which the constitutional lawyers could complete the task in their own time.

Whilst our attentions were directed elsewhere, a certain group of Malaysian politicians and civil servants, with help from abroad, decided on a trial of strength and started planning their own intelligence organisation, to be based on Malaysian embassies in foreign countries. Their machinations came to light when they demanded a brand new headquarters in Kuala Lumpur. Whilst the arguments were going on, news came that the Indonesians had sunk a boatload of armed Malaysians, killed all the occupants and captured intact their wireless equipment. We first heard about it from our own Special Branch sources in Indonesia. It was a ham-fisted effort, cost lives, gave the Indonesians a welcome present and caused consternation among our own agents operating in that area. Tunku Abul Rahman and our minister were furious and wanted to 'carpet' a number of Malaysian Foreign Office officials; and to make certain over-enthusiastic expatriate individuals *persona non grata*. Both politicians had every reason to suspect dirty work at the crossroads and wanted to show their extreme displeasure. I said that expelling people would not help matters; they had learned their lesson, and would now be keen to make amends. It would be better to order them not to initiate this sort of ill-planned skulduggery and to persuade the Malaysian Foreign Office to stick rigidly to their non-executive security responsibilities. My masters agreed most reluctantly not to expel anyone, but they made their displeasure felt among those concerned.

Huss and I continued to believe strongly that there should be only one central intelligence organisation throughout Malaysia. It should remain under the Minister for Home Affairs and the police service should be responsible to him for its performance. We made this point strongly with visiting British MI5 chiefs, and their

273

advisers, who landed on us from time to time. We had seen in Vietnam the effect of numerous intelligence organisations operating there, in competition with each other, and the lack of central control and forward planning. Our views were opposed by those who were pressing for two independent security services, one external and one internal. We took a strong line with government, vigorously supported by our own minister. In the end, the status quo was agreed and we were able to restrict the new intelligence service, run by the Malaysian Foreign Service, to the non-executive collection of intelligence from embassies abroad, and the formation of yet another joint committee to assess the information received.

When Air Marshall Ky and his beautiful wife visited us from South Vietnam for talks we agreed to increase greatly the number of South Vietnamese students attending our Special Branch school. I was invited to fly at once to Saigon and make the necessary arrangements. I was soon to discover that my first major task in Malaysia, and also during subsequent visits to South Vietnam, was to persuade South Vietnamese intelligence officers to stay alive, by putting into practice all the things they had learnt from us while at our school in Kuala Lumpur. I was horrified when I discovered that 20% of students going back to South Vietnam, after their courses in Malaysia, were murdered by the Vietcong in the first three months of their return. I lectured on this myself during their courses with us, emphasising the need for personal security, on and off duty, to be in the forefront of their minds, twenty-four hours a day. It was comforting, later, to see a much larger number of former students at the course reunions I attended in Vietnam.

The fifth of January 1966 was a curious day. Claude Fenner and I had informal talks with Mr Edward Heath, the British Conservative politician, in the morning and I found him interested, cheerful and a very good listener. That afternoon, I went to the local blood transfusion unit to donate my blood, accompanied by all my staff, but leaving Huss behind to hold the fort because, he said, his blood would be of no use to anyone. I was voted unanimously to be the first one to go in. Then something went horribly wrong. The tube slipped out of my arm and my white shirt was covered with bright red blood. When I emerged, the girls shrieked and scampered off; the boys' faces went as white as sheets and the hospital staff had to use all their wiles to persuade them that I was unharmed; and that it was their duty to stay put and donate their blood. People recalled that incident for a long time afterwards, and forgot many much more important ones!

One day in February 1966, Huss came to see me at home and asked if Joanna would spare me for a holiday in Cambodia. This approach did not fool us and he went on to explain that he would like me to meet a certain high-ranking Indonesian who might wish to defect to the Malaysians. This person had asked to negotiate through a third party who should not be a Malaysian. Apparently no one else was available. Dr Ismail, our minister, said that I should go and find out what it was all about. I managed, by chance, to join a Singapore University study seminar group at the last moment and was given an up-to-date briefing on Konfrontasi by Mohd Amin bin Osman in Kuala Lumpur and by George Bogaars in his Singapore office. I left Singapore by Air Cambodge for Pnom Penh, the capital of Cambodia, and then flew to Siem Riep, the provincial capital. Just before landing we had a glorious view of the quincunx ruins of Angkor Wat in the evening sun.

We were an odd group. Our leader was described as the Curator of Singapore University Arts Faculty, and the membership of our group comprised mainly horticulturists who collected flowers and entomologists who collected bugs. There were also two Chinese males and four young female British staff from their Phoenix Park Headquarters in Singapore, whose high spirits and energy made our expeditions and post-prandial evening lectures extremely enjoyable. We studied the ruins in chronological order climbing all over them like mountain goats. I wrote to my mother, 'I got really frightened when I climbed up the ruins carrying an air travel bag full of my heavy photographic equipment; it kept slipping sideways at the most awkward moments and I almost lost my balance. The worst time was when I climbed alone to the top of one of the towers of Angkor Wat itself in moonlight. I started off when the moon was bright, and the atmosphere enthralling, with the whole temple looking dark and mysterious in the moving light and shadows down below. Suddenly a wind got up, clouds covered the moon and it began to rain. The very steep stone steps on the edge of the tower became slippery and impossible to see as I descended slowly – each step requiring a decision to stretch out my free leg downwards into the unknown. I was in constant fear of losing my foothold and crashing down to the bottom. Worse still, it became very cold, my fingers were numb, I could hardly hold on and my

275

thin clothing became soaked by the rain. However I survived, but that was the end of my nocturnal mountaineering.'

I did not tell my mother that some of the photographic equipment was used to record the documents carried by my Indonesian friend. We met up, as agreed, in the foyer of a certain hotel and we spent a whole day getting to know one another. It transpired that he was a senior general and represented a majority group within the Indonesian Government. He was very anti-Communist (which I already knew) and did not support (or perhaps no longer supported) Indonesia's Confrontation with Malaysia. He wished me to inform the Malaysian Government of his country's wish to end Confrontation and, meanwhile, he said Indonesia would cease major action against Malaysia on land, sea and in the air. He gave me a copy of the latest intelligence on the PKI (the Indonesian Communist Party) and the names of the Indonesian hierarchy who would actively support the cessation of Konfrontasi. As a side issue, he wished to discuss the fate of the Indonesian paratroops who landed in Johore State in mainland Malaysia on 2nd September 1964. I had already been told by the Malaysians to expect this, and I had been given permission to quote freely from the Malaysian External Affairs Ministry's report to the United Nations on this subject.

In fact, the original Indonesian force comprised 151 paratroops and 41 Malaysian Communist Chinese in four aeroplanes. The first aircraft with 48 men failed to take off from its base; the second aircraft almost certainly crashed into the China Sea; and the third and fourth aircraft carrying 75 paratroopers, together with 21 Malaysian Chinese, crossed the east coast of mainland Malaysia in a thunderstorm. One of these aircraft failed to locate its dropping zone; its complement of parachutists were decanted over five miles of comparatively open countryside, losing all their supplies of food and ammunition. The remaining plane dropped its troops into high trees and ropes had to be used to descend. They, too, lost all their supplies and their leader became separated from his men. Malaysian forces made contact soon after the landings and killed 33 and captured 61; the remaining two persons were presumed dead. My Indonesian general was particularly interested in the fate of the aircraft lost at sea because its pilot was the son of the Indonesian commander-in-chief, and was a friend of his. He was devastated to hear for certain that he had not been captured.

We continued to meet over the next few evenings and we worked out a method of contacting each other by wireless and by mail. As agreed before I left, I had to return to Malaysia on the next commercial flight which would be in a fortnight's time. I spent the next few days exploring the ruins of Angkor Wat and surrounding countryside.

All that was left of the original Khmer civilisation were the enormous stone edifices deep in the dry, teak jungle. We explored the primitive, classical, baroque and decadent periods dating from AD 800 to 1250, (about the time that the Anglo-Saxons ruled much of England, the Normans succeeded them and Westminster Abbey was rebuilt). No inhabited buildings, which would have been constructed in wood, had survived from those days – just the mausolea, monuments and steles of the Khmer kings and their relatives, which often contained delightful stone carvings depicting the story of the Ramayana and the Mahabharata. The whole site, covering many square miles, was under active conservation by French far-eastern archaeologists and was a most exciting place to explore. Although I did not climb Angkhor Wat again by night, I did visit some of the other ruins at night time and it was an unforgettable experience to come across, suddenly and without warning, the huge heads of Buddha high up on the walls of the Bayon, looking curiously at one with the moonlight emphasising their half shut eyes. The smaller ruins at Bantei Serai some twenty miles away had been beautifully preserved and lived up to Sacheverell Sitwell's marvellous descriptions in *The Red Chapels of Bantei Serai.*

We flew from Siem Riep over the barrages of water below to Pnom Penh, where I made friends with our two Chinese colleagues. The first was a doctor, trained in both Western and Chinese medicine, who immediately cured my funny tummy with a Chinese herb from the market; the second was a Malaysian Chinese manager of the Bank of China. I was very pleased to meet the latter as the few Bank of China employees I had come across previously were inscrutable, unapproachable, mainland-China appointees. He explained to me the complicated system used for registering Chinese companies in the Far East, and how it was possible to trace clan and family ties and ownership within these companies. Fascinating for me, and very useful in my professional work. Having returned to Malaysia, I reported on my talks with the Indonesian general directly to the Prime Minister.

277

On arrival back in Kuala Lumpur, I reflected on the impending end of Confrontation and my thoughts turned to the ending of wars in general. The winning side would celebrate and the military would fire their guns in the air, let off fireworks, don their best uniforms and march around the streets to the cheers of the populace. Whilst the victorious troops enjoy themselves, revenge sometimes takes over. For example, in 1945, after the Japanese surrender in Malaya, very large numbers of murders took place throughout Malaya and scores of debts were settled by the bullet and the *parang* (large knife). Not so in 1960. The end of the Emergency was declared by the independent government of Malaya and the largest parade ever seen in the country was held in Kuala Lumpur. The Malayan Armed Forces, the British Forces, Commonwealth contingents, the police and a host of civilian organisations, accompanied by their respective bands, took to the city streets. They marched past the Selangor Club and the moorish pinnacles of the Secretariat, over the hill and down to the turrets and towers of the railway station and government offices, and on beyond. The crowds of Malays, Chinese and Indians cheered and cheered. Everyone appeared to be in a carefree holiday mood. I stood alone and watched the passing scene from beside the bust of King Edward VII, lately moved on its plinth from a more prominent position in front of the Secretariat building to a pleasant, shady, and less conspicuous spot close by.

A crowd of Malays dressed in their best sarongs and *songkoks* (hats) came slowly out of the nearby mosque and stood beside me. One of them climbed up and gently sat upon King Edward's head. I did not feel that either of them were the least bit out of place. My mind was elsewhere, dreaming about the twelve years of the Emergency and how it had affected so many lives. Suddenly, I saw a tall lean European, dressed in a white shirt, white cricket flannels and wearing a white linen haji's cap, marching along the road on his own and looking most distinguished. I asked my Malay companions who he was. 'Don't you know?' they said, 'That's Haji Mubin Sheppard.' Then I realised that he had been my host when he was the District Officer Klang, and my opponent when he was the British Adviser Negri Sembilan, whose decision I had overturned with the help of General Templer. ff. Sheppard was a very rich man and the owner of a large castle in Ireland. I remembered also attending a Christmas party at his house in Klang, where arriving guests had to discover the identity of names pinned on their backs. Mine was 'Simon, the Cat' (which dates the party to 1949, and the cat to HMS *Amethyst* which had just escaped downriver in China). On his retirement, Mubin Sheppard stayed in the Far East, completed his haj to Mecca and lived as a Muslim in Malaysia.

Seeing Mubin striding by, reminded me of my disputations with him on the beliefs and practices of Islam and my wide-ranging talks with other European friends who had decided to become Muslims. I also reflected on my lengthy discussions with Tunku Farid and my Malay friends. I was told that Muslims believe that there is no God but Allah and that Mohamed is his messenger and prophet; and that the Qu'ran is the language of Allah, as revealed to Mohamed some six centuries after the birth of Christ, and reflects the conditions in Arabia which existed at that time; it is neither a legal document nor a textbook of science, but a guide to personal behaviour. Islam means 'submission' and 'perfect peace', implying the surrender of one's will to Allah and the striving for a state of friendship, harmony and concord within one's community. My European Muslim friends considered that they had reverted rather than converted to Islam. Muslims, I understood, believe Islam to be a way of life based on five pillars of faith, and five pillars of observance.

The first five pillars are belief in one God, who is powerful, gracious and merciful; belief in the angels to whom Allah had assigned certain duties; belief in their prophets, the first of whom was Adam and included Noah, Lot, Abraham, Moses, David, Jesus and Mohamed, who was the greatest of them all; belief in the Day of Judgement, Paradise and Hell; and belief in the timeless knowledge of God, who has given men and women the power of choice in their decisions and their actions. The five practical observances are Shahada (the declaration that God is indivisible and Muhammad is his prophet); Salat, the five compulsory daily prayers which are said at dawn, midday, afternoon, sunset and at night; Zakat, the obligation to regard almsgiving and charity as acts of worship; Siyam, fasting by day during the month of Ramadan (self-discipline); and finally, Haj, the pilgrimage to the Holy Shrine at Mecca unless prevented by illness or poverty.

The two chief Muslim groups are the Sunnis who form 90% of Muslims; and the Shi'ites (from the Arabic word for 'sect') who form the remaining 10%. The former are orthodox disciples of the

279

Prophet Mohamed and follow the historic teaching of academics based in Al Asar University, Cairo. The latter are the followers of Ali, a relative of the Prophet Mohamed whose elected leaders are direct descendants of the Prophet and, nowadays, live mostly in Iran and south-east Iraq. Some common distinctive features of Islam are the equality of sexes, the protection of women, limitation on polygamy, a strong sense of community, an absolute ban on the consumption of alcohol, the rejection of pork in all its aspects, the avoidance of dogs and a belief in the prophets of other religions such as Krishna, Buddha, Confucius and Zoroastra. Muslims are told to regard faith without virtuous intention and action to be worthless; people are responsible for their own actions and by these they will receive final judgement. No regard is given by Allah to a Muslim's ability to acquire money or power. The charging of interest is a sin (but, now, frequently ignored).

The main Muslim disagreement with Christianity is based on the first and most important pillar of their belief – the absolute oneness of God. The belief that God is virtually a physical father, that Jesus is the son of God and worship of the Holy Trinity are all unconditionally rejected by Islam as fundamental departures from the Truth, which had been divulged directly to the Prophet Mohamed by God fourteen centuries ago.

It seems to me that, while the majority of Muslim countries may be considered traditionally Islamic, Islam may also be separated into political groupings such as Revolutionary Islamic in Iran; Islamising Military in Pakistan and Bangladesh and, possibly, parts of the Sudan; and Nationalist Islamic (essentially secular) in Egypt, Iraq, Palestine, Turkey, Indonesia, Brunei and some states in North Africa especially Morocco. In most of the latter the Nationalist Islamic governments face internal security problems from their own fundamental revolutionary Islamic groups.

In my opinion, it is vitally important for people living in non-Muslim countries to understand and appreciate what is happening in the Islamic world. The great majority of Muslims are peace-loving; but 'fundamental' Islamic pressures on them, especially among the young, are becoming increasingly difficult to contain. This will continue relentlessly until the Israelis and the Palestinians resolve their differences. If they do not, I think global terrorism, especially al Qaida, will seek out and exploit local Muslim discontent wherever it exists.

My thoughts also went to the future. Although the official end of the Emergency had been declared, there were still several hundred Communist terrorists on the Thai-Malaysian border and they had the ability to return to North and Central Malaysia, should they wish. Moreover, subversion of the legal political parties, schools and trade unions was very much the order of the day. I remembered with a heavy heart that we still had an enormous amount of work to do after the celebrations and the farewells.

And now confrontation between Indonesia and Malaysia was about to fizzle out. General Suharto took over from President Sukarno in 1966 and was appointed president in 1968. The thoroughly disgraced army stayed within the borders of Indonesia and began to reassert its authority through its political arm, the Golkar Party, which soon became the strongest elected political party in Indonesia.

It was with great relief that we witnessed the fall of the Communist Party of Indonesia from its position of considerable political power a decade before, and its subsequent inability to recoup the loss of its leadership and return to meaningful politics. Although I knew that the Malaysian standard of living and its infrastructure would change dramatically as the years went by, I did not foresee the huge influx of cheap labour from Indonesia into Western Malaysia which was required to make this possible; nor the social problems this would cause. But this would be a long way into the future.

11

'I'd rather have your family in the front boxes than all the Lords and Commons! I like you all, I like your looks, I like your manners. I'm tempted to run away with all of you one after another!'

THE ACTOR DAVID GARRICK TO THE VERY YOUNG
BURNEY SISTERS, 1762

During the years prior to the end of my service in Malaysia, I used to visit South Vietnam, mainly to give lectures and to renew South Vietnamese, American and British friendships. Thirty years later, in 1998, I decided to fly to the Far East on a month's tour of both North and South Vietnam and to spend three days in Kuala Lumpur on the way. I contacted my old comrade Mohamed Amin bin Osman who, having retired as a senior officer in the Royal Malaysian Police Service, had become a successful businessman. On arrival at Kuala Lumpur's huge brand new airport, completed a few weeks previously for the Commonwealth games, my second wife Sarah and I were bowled over by what we saw. The airport itself and the surrounding area had been familiar to me, but there was nothing left of the hills – all had been sliced off and the valleys filled in. Oil palms had replaced rubber trees and the surrounding jungle. Inside the main building was a huge atrium of enclosed jungle vegetation, there were fountains round about and there were many modern international shops. However, the place was almost empty following the departure of the athletes and the multitude of trainers, journalists, spectators and hangers-on.

I recalled the day, it seemed a century ago, when the old international airport at Subang was opened; it was the first time that large areas of glass were used to divide the various halls. Malay villagers from all over the State of Selangor were given free transport and invited to see the new building. They came by bus, bicycle and by foot, thousands and thousands of them dressed in their Friday best. No one had warned them to be careful of the newly-installed, squeaky-clean acres of glass. Hundreds of men, women and children involuntarily crashed into the glass – concussed people and blood all over the place – the arrival and departure halls looked like battlefields. Ambulances, doctors and nurses were summoned from hospitals in Kuala Lumpur and all over Selangor State.

Amin took us in his large chauffeur-driven white air-conditioned Mercedes Benz out of the city through my old District of Kuala Lumpur North where every corner, crossroad and bend in the road whispered to me its story of Communist terrorist ambush, counter-ambush and road accident. Our destination was the Genting Highlands. I had learnt my Hokkien in the cool climate of the Cameron Highlands and I had spent delightful weekends at nearby Fraser's Hill and at Maxwell's Hill near Taiping. I had crossed over the Genting Simpak Pass several times on foot in the jungle, and by car along the narrow steep road. But I had never heard of the Genting Highlands. Then, of course, I realised that the recently named Genting Highlands area was once the site of a Communist Party designated 'liberated area', deep in the jungle, in the early days of the Emergency fifty years before; it was adjacent to the headquarters of the Communist North Pahang Regional Committee.

I was not at all prepared for what I saw when we arrived. The flattening of the hills around the airport was nothing at all compared with the levelling of mountains and the wholesale replacement of virgin jungle to create, what we were told, was the largest and most beautiful golf course in the world. No one seemed to be walking, motorised buggies were everywhere. We were taken round the golf course in two of these buggies and watched groups of young Japanese ladies dressed immaculately in smart baseball caps, dark glasses, Bermuda shorts, kneehigh socks and corespondent shoes playing some very good golf. After a gourmet Korean lunch, we went by cable-car four miles into the clouds, arriving with a bump in the bowels of a very large modern hotel. We discovered that there were three adjacent hotels which shared a stunningly beautiful swimming pool and a panoramic view of distant mountains on clear days. Immaculate lawns and well-kept gardens completed the picture and took our breath away in the refreshingly cool mountain air.

We were shown over the hotels which were run as casinos and interconnected at four levels. The highest level was the most resplendent, with high golden pillars shaped from single tree trunks, seemingly going on into infinity among the red and gilded dragons on the walls, and reflected clearly on the spotless marble floors. The rooms were lit by huge heavy Venetian glass chandeliers, said to cost £250,000 each, hanging from the ceiling to provide a sparkling light on the gilded tables and chairs below. At each table stood a young, slim, poker-faced Chinese lady croupier serving the punters who anxiously watched the turning of the cards. The next two floors were similar though not quite as spectacular and the stakes were lower. The first floor was devoted to rows and rows and rows of fruit machines, all being played with excitement by fat noisy children, supervised by professional uniformed minders, whilst their parents were busy up the stairs.

It was daytime outside and we were told that 12,000 people were playing at the tables: as evening approached, more people would arrive and the average daily total would rise to 25,000. Double that came at weekends; during Chinese New Year the gates would close at the foot of the hill when the figure reached 60,000. The Malaysian Government strictly prohibited the entry of Muslims, whose religion does not allow them to gamble. Entry was restricted almost entirely to Chinese, Thais and a few Japanese who came from Malaysia, Thailand, Japan and the countries round the Pacific rim.

The most successful of those who won at the tables were encouraged to stay in the hotels. We were shown the presidential suite, earmarked for the most successful gambler of all and his hastily gathered entourage, which contained the latest digital gimmicks: these included the largest domestic television screen in the world and a four-poster of which the bedhead was an enormous brightly-lit aquarium, full of large orange, grey and white carp. A comment from the managing director, which took our breath away again for an entirely different reason, was that the company's calculated investment in fruit machines was designed not as a convenient temporary nursery for the young, but to condition them for the day when they were old enough to be allowed to run upstairs . . . it struck us that this was indeed a pretty good depiction of Hell on Earth! The tock tock birds and the wah-wah monkeys started a never-ending evening chorus outside.

We left Malaysia by air and found Hanoi, the capital of North Vietnam, to be a striking contrast with mainland Malaysia. Although crowded, the pace was slow, much slower even than in China, and the people were slim, upright, bright and friendly. As we travelled by plane, taxi, bus and cyclo (a man-driven three wheeler tricycle for two people with hooded seats for the passengers) southward down the country we were amazed to see how the Vietnamese, with very little help from outside their country, had recovered from their wars. It was very much a series of flourishing agricultural and fishing communities and there was plenty of food for everyone. Fresh vegetables, a large selection of fruit and fish could be bought inexpensively along the roadsides and in all the country markets. Much to our surprise, the aroma of newly-baked French bread was everywhere we went.

It was only in Saigon (no one referred to it as Ho Chi Minh City – even the destination of buses travelling southwards was shown as Saigon) that we saw the effect of the wars: harsh modernisation and displaced people, many of them minus their limbs, crowded the suburbs. We were told there was much unemployment in Saigon. Travelling the last sixty miles to Saigon, we passed through the area where Catholic minorities from the north had been settled by the French colonial government after the Second World War. We saw pretty little churches every mile on both sides of the road. We discovered they had been built recently and each was of an entirely different design, brightly painted in the most attractive style.

On one Sunday, we attended Mass at 5 a.m. in a large Catholic church near Danang. It was very crowded and there were five hundred well-behaved school children in the congregation. The service was in Vietnamese. After his sermon, the priest went among the children for twenty minutes asking them, through his microphone, questions about the Gospel, chiding some gently and praising others. It was quite fascinating ... it struck us that this was a good example of Heaven on Earth!

There were little or no signs of the French connection, apart from the smell of French bread and the beautiful city boulevards. None of the enormous American bases, some of which I had visited in earlier days, were to be seen – all had been dismantled and absorbed into the countryside. However, it was crystal clear to us that the people still hated the Americans and the French; when they discovered that we were English, smiles appeared on their faces and they went out of their way to make us welcome. We discovered many cemeteries containing the graves of those killed in the French and American wars. Each could be seen from afar by its dazzling white concrete memorial, usually comprising well-sculpted concrete hands raised together in prayer 30 feet high on a small hill in the centre. Just outside Danang, we found part of a military museum had been dedicated to the mothers of North Vietnamese soldiers and guerrillas (i.e. the Viet Cong) killed in the two colonial wars. It took the form of 40,000 original identity cards pinned round the walls displaying the mothers' faces. It was a very moving place for us.

In 1999, a letter was published in the correspondence columns of *The Daily Telegraph* regretting the absence of any war memorial to women. This produced letters from a former serviceman who queried, 'Have you not seen the memorial in the Regent Palace Hotel, London, which reads "To all the girls who fell here during the war"?' And from me, drawing attention, firstly, to two memorial windows in Salisbury Cathedral, one dedicated to women in the armed forces and Women's Land Army, and one to prisoners of conscience of both sexes; and, secondly, to the forty thousand widows' memorial in far-away Vietnam.

To return to my last two years in Malaysia: where, for most of the time, I was the Acting Director of the Malaysian Special Branch.

In 1965 Joanna and I were asked to join a small group of senior political and government officials and their wives in learning to dance less well-known, but traditional, Malay *wronggeng* (dancing), and also to study and learn the latest crazes originating from Western Europe and America. Our instructors came from the National Culture Society and they were very strict with us. Joanna, who was much better than me, undertook most of these with enthusiasm. For the doubles, however, we decided to learn one main dance and try to perform it together as well as possible. We chose the Zappin, a modern Turkish dance then very much in fashion. Eventually, we danced as a group at various balls and parties, all great fun and it was nice to be the only Europeans in this group. Our first 'exhibition' together was at a ball in the Houses of Parliament given by the Sultans of Pahang and Selangor, both of whom we had come to know quite well. Joanna wore a long blue Malay dress of Kelantan silk with gold wiring inlay, a short coat of the same material, a small bag to match and lovely blue shoes. We were both asked to join the Sultans' parties for quite a long time and much enjoyed meeting old friends.

At about this time I was awarded the Kesatria Mangku Negara (Honorary KMN) by the Yang di-Agong (the King of Malaysia) for my services to Malaysia. The badge is a handsome one made of gold and enamel. A little later, I received Her Majesty the Queen's unrestricted permission to wear all the medals given to me by the Selangor State, Malayan and Malaysian Governments. Joanna and the boys thought I looked liked an American soldier with his good conduct medals all over his chest!

In early 1966, we attended a farewell dinner in honour of Dato Sir Claude and Lady Fenner given by the Combined Operations Council, of which I had been a member for some time, in the Malaysian Armed Forces officers' mess. We were placed above the Brigadiers and below the Major Generals. The highlight of the evening was a solo conjuring act performed by the Malay commander-in-chief, which ended up with his escape from being tied up with ropes in a large wooden box (the result of a terrorist coup, he said). We were very sad to see the Fenners go. Richard Buxton and I had gone through thick and thin with Claude, Huss, Rahman and Salleh and we had been a very happy team.

My meetings with visiting delegations seemed to become all too frequent; among the more interesting were the Australian Labour Party, the United States National War College and the Canadian Defence College delegations. *The Straits Times* said: 'the Australian Labour Party delegation led by its general secretary Mr C.S. Wyndham was given a full briefing and an insight into Indonesian Confrontation ... by Mr T.E. Hatton, the Acting Director of the Malaysian Special Branch, which lasted sixty-five minutes ... Mr Wyndham described it as very interesting.'

On 19 March 1966, John M. Cabot of the US National War College wrote to me: 'Your briefing and discussions on the Communist threat on your border with Thailand and your operations there were most beneficial and greatly appreciated ... the scope and clarity of your presentation provided insight into the problems and also your methods of coping with the situation ... a splendid presentation.'

Major General C.B. Wade of the Canadian National Defence College wrote later: 'the most interesting and comprehensive briefing which you gave us was one of the highlights of our visit ... we enjoyed our discussions and the illuminative insight given into your problems and methods of operation ... so much of value.'

These bread-and-butter letters were typical of many. They gave me great pleasure and I was especially glad to receive them as a British representative of the Malaysian Government – with government ministers present – some nine years after Merdeka.

A short while later, a dreadful incident occurred on the Thai border when Communist terrorists ambushed one of our patrols. Several of our people were killed and wounded and I went up to see if there were any lessons to be learnt; also to represent the Inspector General and the Commissioner of Police at the funerals. There was little I could do regarding the follow-up operations, although I used to know the area well in previous years. What distressed me was the condition of the wounded Malay policemen in hospital. Their wounds were dirty and they were starving. No one could tell me anything about their medical condition and their families had not been informed by the State Police Headquarters. I created Hell. I attended the funerals of those killed, all of whom were Chinese. They were buried in swampland, adjoining a cemetery; and, when the cheap, hastily-prepared coffins were lowered into the graves, they floated in the water. One fell apart and its occupant stared up at me with a cold reproachful look. I was the only mourner present and no one else appeared to have been informed of the funerals. I requested an interview with the Director of Medical Services and telephoned the Commissioner of Police. Immediate enquiries were held and those responsible were quickly identified and severely reprimanded. I continued to feel very strongly about this incident for a long time.

I decided to take Joanna, John (aged seven) and Richard (aged five) on a working tour up the east coast of mainland Malaysia, visiting Kuantan, Kemaman, Dungun, Besut, Kuala Trengganu and Kota Bahru, all places I had visited in 1946. In those early days, each of the many rivers flowing into the China Sea had to be crossed laboriously by an antique ferry using the current for traction. By 1966, bridges had been built over the smaller rivers, though the road was still hard going in places.

In Kuala Trengganu, a police launch took us out to the Perhentian Islands where we had a couple of days off and enjoyed the empty beaches, watching the dolphins at play and lazing around. On the way back, the local police insisted on taking us to the turtle beaches.

The Malaysian Government had just completed the renovation of their turtle farms, which were designed to protect the great sea turtle and to research into its life. Predators, pollution and tourists had become major hazards to the turtles' existence around the Pacific rim. Large areas of the Trengganu beaches had been wired off by the State Government and visitors were not allowed inside. The turtles would swim thousands of miles across the sea, lay their eggs high up on the sandy beaches and then return to the sea and swim away. The eggs would hatch, eventually, and the baby turtles would climb to the surface and make their perilous way down to the edge of the sea. A providence of some sort saved a very small number of these baby turtles, enabling them to obtain food and survive the many dangers at sea which beset them everywhere. Something inside the young turtles' heads seemed to guide them to join their parents, brothers and sisters, uncles and aunts then to return with them year after year, across thousands of miles of sea, to the same sites on the Trengganu beaches.

I wrote to my mother, 'We arrived just before darkness fell. There was a coldish wind blowing through the casuarina trees, it was half-tide and the waves were fairly strong and throwing spray into the air. The moon began to appear over the sea and disappeared into the clouds from time to time; one moment it was quite bright and we could see each other dressed in sweaters, caps and raincoats, the next moment it was dark; but the sea was luminous as the wind caught the crest of the waves. We had been told to make no noise in case the leading turtles took fright and swam away. It was quite a long wait and the boys were becoming cold and restless as Joanna and I peered anxiously out to sea through the spray. Suddenly, we spied a small dark shape coming very slowly through the mist some twenty yards away, floating towards us on the surface of the sea. We all saw it at the same time. "There it is!" we whispered to one another excitedly. And there it was, a black blob which got bigger and bigger until it drifted on to the beach a few feet from us.

'We began to discern its shape as it lost the buoyancy of the sea and started to drag itself ashore, its strong fins acted as arms and legs working in military unison as it laboriously humped its way up the beach. We followed it at a respectable distance, making sure the flashes from our torches did not distract its attention. After about ten minutes or so, it reached the softer sand at the top of the beach and paused. We approached to examine its leathery head and horny shell which was some four or five feet long and three or four feet wide. The boys gained courage and went right up to it, only to jump back in fright as it suddenly started to dig a hole with its hind legs flipping up clouds of sand. The turtle dug a neat hole, perhaps four feet deep, and then began laying its eggs. These were white and looked just like ping pong balls, about a hundred of them, perhaps more. The boys were distressed to see the turtle crying whilst laying its eggs; but our guide said the tears were nature's way of clearing its eyes, in case the wind blew the sand into them.

'The turtle made loud grunting noises too; then we became aware of many other noises and, looking about us in the night, we could see turtles emerging from the sea, struggling up the beach and throwing up miniature sandstorms before they laid their eggs. We had been mesmerised by our own turtle, and there must have been at least thirty others on our stretch of beach. We regarded ours as a special friend and watched it cover up its eggs and turn around somewhat exhausted, we thought, for a faster return down the beach to the sea, leaving tell-tale tracks across the sand. Thieves would come later in the night on unprotected turtle beaches and steal the eggs, which were much sought after as aphrodisiacs. As it swam away, we thought we saw it turn half-round and wave to us; but, perhaps, it was a trick of the moonlight on the spray.'

In April 1966, we flew to England on eight weeks' annual leave and stayed in Joanna's mother's bungalow in Chipperfield, visiting as many relations as we could fit in. We returned by air to Kuala Lumpur in June.

I resumed more or less where I had left off. I continued to visit the Borneo Territories, Thailand, Vietnam and Singapore regularly. I attended all the various national intelligence committees and kept an eye on the syllabus at the Special Branch school and revised my lectures. My help was requested on the setting up of anti-drug legislation (the old Colonial Acts were long out of date) and joint action with the Customs Department was long overdue. It took up a great deal of my time. Huss had ceased to be our director some time ago; he had been given the title Tan Sri and was at various times acting as Commissioner of Police Malaya or Inspector General of the Royal Malaysian Police Service, in Claude Fenner's absence. Rahman bin Hashim became the permanent Director of Special Branch but he, too, was a bit of a wanderer and stayed on as a key member of Malaysia's Special Delegation to the United Nations; he also accompanied ministers on various world tours. This meant I continued to hold the fort as acting director and had a great deal of extra work to do.

One day, my Indonesian general asked to see me at short notice at sea off Singapore. Doctor Ismail said I should go. I met the general in a very rough sea off an island to the south of Singapore. He was supposed to be inspecting an airfield in the Rhio Archipelago; but a fishing trip was his cover story. I had been given another fishing boat with a small escort armed to the teeth below decks. We had an amusing meeting and I nearly fell overboard when I misjudged a rising wave. He brought me up to date with current affairs in Jakarta. I reported back to Dr Ismail and the Minister for External Affairs, both of whom already knew most of what I had to pass on. However, I think it confirmed some important deductions already made on Indonesia's foreign policy. I agreed with my Indonesian friend that as Confrontation was faltering we could not go on meeting like this and, in future, he would deal openly and directly with the Malaysians.

I visited Hong Kong in September 1966 on my own and stayed three nights with Jim Patrick, the Security Liaison Officer, and his wife. Jim used to be the extremely friendly District Officer in Tampin when I was working with my cousin Colonel D'Arcy Mander and Major Nigel Bagnall. It turned out that his wife was a talented artist and, when she discovered that Joanna painted Chinese scrolls, she suggested that we should send them to her in Hong Kong and undertook to have them stretched and mounted

291

on our behalf. This proved to be of enormous help and we used her services on two or three occasions. On the work side, we discussed various projects which we wished to mount in Hong Kong against Communist couriers passing to and fro from China to the Borneo Territories, Indonesia and to Bangkok. Special Branch Hong Kong, and both MI6 and MI5, were horrified and declined to help in any way. Apart from that, we had a very pleasant social time. It was fun to be invited to a cocktail party on the aircraft carrier HMS *Victorious* and to be transported, pink gins in hand, up to the flight deck on an enormous aircraft lift. Whilst in Hong Kong, I was able privately to locate a well-situated safe house, for our possible secret use later, and to explore the airport and its facilities in some detail. On the way back, I stopped off in Bangkok for three days and found the Thai Special Branch very cooperative indeed. I visited the British Embassy, but was extremely circumspect about what I thought I might have to do. Rahman bin Hashim was delighted with the results of my meetings.

Later I was to return to Hong Kong with a false passport and a false medical certificate, both immaculately produced by Richard Buxton, together with a team of four incognito Malaysian Special Branch officers. I used the safe house I had earmarked on my previous visit and took a short holiday lease, setting up house with two of my colleagues acting as cook and gardener. I suspect the other two enjoyed themselves hugely among the low life in the Wan Chai district of Hong Kong Island. We met a plane coming in from Japan, introduced ourselves to a certain passenger, whose journey had started from Peking, confirmed that he was to catch another plane to Jakarta in two days' time and had a surprise talk with him. To our great relief, he proved as co-operative as we had hoped and he agreed to work for us; we arranged suitable contact methods for the future. All had gone smoothly and illegally.

Over the years, I got to know Richard Clutterbuck very well. He spent two long tours in Malaya and visited us from time to time thereafter. He eventually acquired a doctorate, became a major general (Her Majesty's Chief Engineer) and an acknowledged expert on terrorism around the world. Huss would not allow me to tell him anything about our successes or methods used in Pahang,

Selangor or our long-term projects in Federal HQ. But Richard had his own army friends in Johore and in Perak. His excellent books were based largely on his own experience whilst serving on the Director of Operations' staff and from his contacts in those States. However, I agreed to vet his work for historical accuracy, publishable intelligence matters and factual matters connected with the Emergency and the early days of Indonesian Confrontation. In return, he sent me presentation copies of his books. In one, entitled, *Riot and Revolution in Singapore and Malaya 1945–63*, he wrote, ' . . . this book . . . owes so much to you (though as you wish, I have expunged all references to your remarkably distinguished work) and the least I can do is to send you this copy though it is a very inadequate expression of thanks for all you did to help me . . .'

One of Malaysia's most talented artists of those days was Mohamed Hussein bin Enas who was born in Java in 1924. He came to Malaya and entered government service in 1952, and became an Assistant Protector of Aborigines, an FRSA and a trustee of the National Gallery of Malaya. His oil paintings of the indigenous people of Malaysia are, in my opinion, the best portraits of these people I have ever seen. He catches their liveliness, humour and character marvellously well.

Dick Noone was another friendly and approachable Protector and used to tell the story about his arrival in Malaya by parachute during the Japanese occupation. His headquarters in Ceylon sent a wireless message asking for confirmation that he had landed safely and the reply, 'No one here', had to be verified twice before it could be safely assumed that he had arrived and all was well.

I had a great friend in Howard Biles, another Assistant Protector, whom I got to know in Pahang. He lived twenty miles upriver from Kuala Lipis and had a lovely bungalow, with a large verandah around three sides, on a low hill in ten acres of grassland – an oasis in the jungle. He had a Malay cook, who produced the most delicious curries, and there were at least thirty *orang asli* (original people or aborigines) coming and going at any one time, half-naked, carrying long blowpipes, bulging quivers, smoking beedie cigarettes and bringing in their jungle produce for sale in Kuala Lipis market. Howard fought great battles against State Governments in Peninsular Malaya which administered the surrounding jungle. These administrations insisted on rehabilitating the orang asli; the result of this official interference with their lives was that they caught 'civilisation' diseases and whole families and groups had died. Howard used to tell surviving groups to run away from these rehabilitation areas and escape back into the jungle, where neither civil service official, nor security force patrol, nor Communist platoon could locate them if they decided to hide away. He spoke most of their several languages and had a great collection of out-of-print books by Sir Hugh Clifford, Sir Richard Winstedt and others, which I used to borrow.

I found Malay history intriguing and I read these books over and over again. Whilst at Kuala Selangor I had practised my Malay among the police constables and their families when I stayed in rural police stations, and in Pahang where I travelled extensively among the Malay kampongs preparing my papers on Bahaman and the Emergency, and I loved to explore the countryside with my Malay friends.

In the *Directory of the Malay Language*, Clifford and Swettenham say, 'Like French, Malay is essentially a diplomatic language and one admirably adapted for concealing the feelings and cloaking the real thoughts. Not even in French is it possible to be so polite, or so rude, or to say such rude things with every appearance of exaggerated courtesy, as it is the case in Malay.' C.C. Brown states in his book on Malay culture, 'The ability of Malays to use the right words at the right time shortens lengthy conversation and brings vague description sharply into focus.' He describes a Pahang Malay, whose answer to a charge of murderous assault on his wife was stated in two words '*mudah rioh*', a brevity which defies reproduction in English. He meant that his wife's voice would rise to an angry scream on no provocation, and he was overcome so much that he had to stop her at once.

Our government exams in Malay were usually based on ancient Malay literature such as the *Hikayat Abdullah*, *Pelayran Abdullah*, the *Hang Tuah*, *Hikayat Bayan Budiman* and sometimes on other *hikayats* (stories). We also had to have a knowledge of Malay sayings and *pantuns*. The latter were four-line verses of which the first couplet introduced the second couplet. My favourite, which I privately applied to myself quite often was:

Banyak orang bergelang tangan – Most people wear bangles on
                                their wrists
Sahaya sa-orang bergelang kaki – But I wear them on my ankles

Banyak orang larang jangan	– Many people tell me not to do something
Sahaya sa-orang terus hati	– But I do exactly as I please

The flouting of fashion in the first couplet introduces the flouting of advice in the second. I found pantuns great fun and very much part of the delightful Malay character. I discovered later that pantuns nearly always reflected the ups and downs of personal romance in the kampongs, but could be adapted to suit different situations.

Whilst in Pahang, and later on my visits to the east coast and elsewhere, I collected old Malay silver belt buckles (called *pendiung*), small silver plates, and inlaid betel boxes. I found most of these in pawnshops though some were given to me by Howard Biles. Much of the silver came from melted-down Maria Theresa dollars. These pieces were made in the the late nineteenth and early twentieth centuries by Malay silversmiths in South Thailand, Kelantan, Trengganu and Negri Sembilan. After a time, I was able to determine the States where they were made. I also had some Indonesian pendiangs, the designs of which were quite different and reflected more of the old Hindu culture.

Joanna decided to take the finals of her ikebana exminations, and I wrote home: 'Joanna sat or rather stood for her finals last week. She had four hours of practical work, having spent a fortune on collecting the required flowers and foliage to be used. She also had to survive a similar period of oral examination from a very nice American-speaking Japanese lady. It was the culmination of fifteen courses, each of six two-hour lessons, extending over several years. We already knew that the majority of candidates failed or simply gave up, or were given a low-standard pass. It was a great relief for all of us when it came to an end.'

The results were sent to Japan for judgement (a written report was prepared by the examiner and everything had to be recorded on coloured slides). It was nine months before Joanna received an oblong wooden plaque with nicely carved Japanese characters, together with two large certificates, to show that she had passed with 'Great Distinction' and had been elected a Professor of the Fourth Class in the Sogetsu School of Flower Arranging.

*

We decided that we would retire from Malaysia in April 1967 and we both had a very difficult time persuading people that we were serious. Our main concern was the education of John and Richard, who were eight and six years old respectively, and we did not wish to stay abroad flying the children out for their holidays. The Malaysian politicians offered me some very exciting prizes if I agreed to serve them for a further three years and I was sorely tempted. But family considerations prevailed.

In late February 1967 we were visited by the Head of MI5. He had the reputation of being a great bird watcher and members of his staff throughout the Far East got out their books on birds and studied them assiduously. My edition of Madoc's book on Malaysian birds was in great demand. He was entertained in Kuala Lumpur for two days and then we flew by Royal Malaysian Air Force Heron to Ipoh whence, at the request of the British Security Liaison Officer, I took him by helicopter to Fort Legap, deep in the jungle of Central Malaya. He thought this was a complete waste of time, even though I pointed out to him various jungle birds which he would not have seen elsewhere; he was in a frightful bate when we landed at Bel Retiro. the Governor of Penang's official residence. Rahman bin Hashim wished to get to know him on a personal basis over the next day or so, but the MI5 staff were most reluctant to leave them alone together. Hanif and I had the unenviable task of keeping his staff away so the two could meet privately, while the tock tock birds enjoyed their dangerous lives outside. We succeeded, but his colleagues were not at all pleased and blamed us for spoiling his visit.

I began to pay my farewell visits to the Borneo Territories and flew to all the familiar places. Many of the people I saw there were Malaysian families we had known in mainland Malaysia and I was berated for not bringing Joanna with me. They put me to shame by finding excuses to come to Kuala Lumpur instead, and joined the stream of visitors calling on us or staying with us.

I was accompanied on my final tour by Raja Adnan who had been designated my successor. When we visited Tawau in Sabah we were invited by Colonel 'Guinea' Graham to visit his Gurkha outposts deep inland along the border with Indonesian Kalimantan. We flew in by two helicopters provided by the aircraft carrier HMS *Bulwark*. Having been given a detailed security briefing and shown round the bases, we attended an excellent lunch to which the very young naval pilots were also invited. After several pink gins we took off for our return flight to Tawau. Unfortunately, it became quite misty down below and the pilots mistook Indonesian Tarakan, over the international border, for Malaysian Tawau and began to descend for landing. I signalled desperately to Raja Adnan's pilot and Raja Adnan waved his hands at my pilot. The urgency of our energetic gesticulations got through to the pilots when we were about 200 feet above the ground. A miscellaneous lot of Indonesian military, most of whom were wearing singlets and shorts, aimed their rifles at us. Our two helicopters banked and sped away. Raja Adnan and I both thought the Indonesians were actually taking pot-shots at us. The pilots, fearing for their careers, were greatly relieved to discover no bullet holes in their aircraft. We kept quiet.

To say farewell to as many friends and acquaintances as possible, we had a series of large parties at home helped by outside caterers. Whole roasted lamb on spits, satay parties, conversational dinners for eight at a time and drinks for all and sundry became the order of the day. Similarly, we were invited out by the highest and the lowest in the land, often being asked to select the guest lists ourselves. The Police Officers' mess in Venning Road not only gave a huge party for us both, but the wives asked that tradition should be broken and the party should be for both sexes. A record number of 180 people attended, to our great astonishment. My diary shows that on every day in the next ten weeks we were engaged with parties at home or out to meals.

Of our last big dinner I wrote home, 'We had another lamb roasted on a spit which operated outside under cover of our porch. The party was nearly ruined by a freak typhoon which blew a large heavy tree on top of us an hour before the guests were due to arrive – no electricity, no lights, no telephone and no oven! Fortunately the Prime Minister is on the same electricity line as us and it was repaired an hour later. The boys were thrilled, especially John, who imagined he was Robin Hood eating deer in Sherwood Forest. We had masses of roast potatoes, salad, curried vegetables, two varieties of rice, rolls and butter followed by fruit salad in four enormous pumpkins. The sort of party we shall never give again.'

We had a sale of our unwanted possessions and gave the cash and spare clothes to the Church Institute and to Flood Relief respectively. Joanna went to her own farewell dos given by the

Ikebana Society, the Japanese Embassy, the Police Depot Wives Association, the YWCA, the Paraplegics, her scroll-painting teachers and the wives of our Malay, Chinese and Indian friends. Many of the latter had been really close friends over the last ten years and they were particularly kind to Joanna and the boys prior to our departure. Puan Halimah, Rahman bin Hashim's wife, whose family home in Kedah we had visited, was every bit as friendly as Huss's wives, and so was Puan Sri Saodah, the Commissioner of Police's wife. Many others, including politicians and senior government servants seemed genuinely sorry that we were leaving. Former brother officers, inspectors and detectives as well as various friends of all ranks in the uniform branch found time to call in on us or invite us to their homes. We received shoals of letters in English, Malay, jawi script and in Chinese. Even the General Post Office examined its dead letterboxes and found several addressed to me by one of my Chinese names! I had a pleasant send-off given by the Selangor Philatelic Club of which I was still one of two vice-presidents, and a number of very nice letters from members all around the world. Tunku Abdul Rahman, Tun Razak and Dr Ismail gave me signed photographs of themselves in Selangor pewter frames. I gave Tan Sri Mohamed Salleh, the Commissioner of Police in mainland Malaya, a small antique desk which I had acquired some years ago from an antique shop in Malacca and was said to have been used by a junior clerk in the East India Company.

Richard had joined John at the Alice Smith School in Kuala Lumpur by then and both boys had flourished there making many friends. They went to their own farewells too. One day I judged that it was time for us to pay Mrs Duthie for the many extra-curricular Latin lessons she had given John. Her reply given with typical Scottish firmness was: 'I have enjoyed teaching him so much I couldnae possibly charge for it'.

Her Majesty the Queen directed that I should be appointed an Officer of the Most Excellent Order of the British Empire in the New Year 1967 Honours List in recognition of what was called my valuable services. There was a surprising follow-up to this. Just before we left Malaysia for the last time, Tan Sri Mohamed Salleh bin Ismael came round to our house and handed over a copy of the formal grounds for the recommendation, which he and Sir Claude Fenner had jointly submitted to the Secretary of State for Commonwealth Affairs some time before. He thought I would like to have it. In other words I was curious to see what they said and I was agreeably surprised. I quote from it, as it shows what people, whose opinion I greatly valued, thought of me:

During the early years of the Malayan Emergency when Communist terrorism was at its height Mr Hatton organised, directed and took part in a series of extremely effective operations against a particularly aggressive Communist terrorist organisation in his District. He displayed outstanding leadership and considerable personal courage on many occasions, sometimes in very great adversity. In 1952 Mr Hatton was transferred to the Special Branch and was posted to Pahang where he became responsible for the initiation, intelligence planning and detailed exploitation of several eminently successful national operations against the Malayan Communist Party headquarters and its supporting units. In conjunction with this aspect, Mr Hatton showed exceptional professional skill in conducting and co-ordinating highly delicate secret projects against selected important high level Communist leaders. That the Communist terrorist organisation in Central Malaya was virtually eliminated was in very great measure due to Mr Hatton's original detailed planning, ability to obtain the confidence and co-operation of senior military commanders and to his supreme professional competence.

In 1956 Mr Hatton was appointed a Divisional Head in the Federal Special Branch headquarters, where he immediately distinguished himself as a brilliant staff officer whose energy and initiative were of the highest order. He later served as Head of the Kedah Special Branch and in 1960 took charge of the strategically important Special Branch organisation in Selangor. His foresight and sound planning on the ground in Selangor laid the foundation for some of the country's most successful top secret operations. These projects have provided, and continue to provide, vital intelligence indispensable to the country's security.

Perhaps the real measure of Mr Hatton's valuable contribution to security intelligence in Malaysia has been over the last two years when he has held some of the highest appointments in the Malaysian Special Branch and has acted successfully as its Director on two occasions. He is a member of several important inter-professional and Government committees where his cool analytical approach to difficult problems on a national scale manifestly has won for him the admiration, friendship and respect not only of his brother officers but also of senior Malaysian Government officials and a host of others outside his service. It is true to say that the smooth running of the Malaysian Special Branch intelligence machine is in many ways due to Mr Hatton's abundant energy, unselfish approach to trying problems and outstanding moral courage . . .

Prime Minister Tunku Abdul Rahman asked Joanna and me to visit him informally one evening. Usually I went on my own, so it was quite an honour and a surprise to go together. Needless to say, Joanna was taken off by the ladies and her tummy felt gently for the last time. Tunku asked me to join him and watch the television news. Afterwards, he said he wished to thank me for my personal help to him over the last ten years. He said he was particularly grateful for the way Special Branch had been converted from a successful counter-terrorist organisation in Malaya, led almost entirely by British officers, into a Malaysianised organisation operating throughout Malaysia. He was very pleased with the way this had been accomplished and he looked forward to the future with complete confidence. We talked freely about the dangers of corruption (from outside sources into government, politics and finance, including banking); communalism (Lee Kuan Yew's 'interference'; the fundamentalist intentions of the Pan-Malayan Islamic Party and the imbalance of national education and wealth) and faltering commercial relationships with the British (i.e. the British High Commission in Kuala Lumpur) which, he said, gave him a series of headaches. He concluded by saying that he strongly supported Dato Nik Daud's wish that Joanna and I would come back to Malaysia one day (Nik Daud was our Permanent Secretary in the Ministry of Home Affairs). We were both very sad to leave as the Tunku and his household came outside to wave goodbye.

The time came for us to move into the Merlin Hotel for a night prior to going to the airport next morning. Even then, people came with small presents for the boys and Rahman bin Hashim presented me with a large wooden shield bearing two Malay kris (small daggers in wooden sheaths) and an inscription stating that it was a gift from the Director and Officers of the Malaysian Special Branch. We managed to find room for it in our baggage.

Next day, 6th April 1967, we were driven to Subang Airport and were seen off on the plane by a huge crowd of people including all my office staff and a host of friends wishing to say farewell to Joanna, John, Richard and me. Our forthcoming departure had been announced in the English, Malay and Chinese press and it was quite impossible to speak to everyone – anyway we were in tears. On looking around I noticed a vaguely familiar face next to the departure doors. Although our eyes met for just a moment, it was several hours later that I realised with quite a shock that it was the Chinese lady who accompanied Ah Kuk's two bodyguards and had surrendered to me for a second time in Mentakab fourteen years before. I wondered what was going through her mind.

Flying back home, with Joanna and the boys fast asleep in their seats, I became aware that the business of handing over aspects of my responsibilities to various people throughout Malaysia, and saying final farewells to people with many of whom I had served through every sort of experience, had come to an end. Now the final packing-up was over – everything was past history.

I had volunteered to join the army at the age of under eighteen. I had been commissioned into the 9th Gurkha Rifles. Most of my service had been in India, Malaya, Thailand, Indonesia and again in India during Partition. I had then joined the Colonial Service at the age of twenty-three, for what it was said would be no longer than five years. I was told that my main task would be concerned with handing over to local people so that they could run their own country. I joined the Malayan Police Service at a time when recruiting people was very much the order of the day, and my previous experience was no better than the majority of my colleagues. I was lucky to have served on the ground at the sharp end of the Emergency and also to have been an ADC: I had met and got to know many of the country's British leaders. Luckier still, I was able soon to develop my interest in languages and customs of the Malays and Chinese. I was one of the first to join the expanding Special Branch, ending up as its acting director on several lengthy occasions. We had made many friends in the Malay, Chinese and Indian communities. I had carried out my instructions to train local people to the best of my ability – though for a much longer period than first envisaged – and I had handed over a completely reorganised Special Branch which was an efficient, honest, loyal and going concern. I was forty-two years of age.

As far as a new job in England was concerned, I could offer good language skills and some knowledge of the Far East. I knew important people, many of them decision-makers or 'door-keepers' and I also knew the ropes. I hoped that MI6 or, perhaps, MI5 might find my experience useful. Unfortunately, I had already approached the Director of MI5 on his recent visit to Malaya; but I had caught him at a bad moment and I did not rate my chances highly. There were one or two large British companies which I knew I could help; the problems with these thoughts, however, was that I wished to be based in England, though I was prepared to travel abroad for short periods. Meanwhile I had to set up a home, find schools for the boys and make arrangements to keep an eye on my ageing mother, who was living alone in a large cottage surrounded by two acres of garden. No trouble with the short-term plans; but long-term employment seemed fraught with difficulties and it was clear that, to keep us alive, warm and happy, I would have to cast my bread upon the waters. Joanna had her own problems with starting a new life, feeding us and settling in as an English housewife. The boys had to get used to wearing shoes with laces, shirts with ties and living among strangers at a new school in summer and in winter.

We flew safely to Heathrow and were met by the same private taxi driver whom I had used to ferry us back and forth over the years.

We moved into my mother-in-law's bungalow and our first task was to get the boys off to a school. They had been put down for Ashdown House preparatory school near Forest Row in Sussex, where many of my family, on both sides, had been brought up. John went to Ashdown House straight away, as a boarder; Richard was too young, and for the next year or two went daily by bus to a preparatory school in Hertfordshire.

POSTSCRIPT TO THE COMMUNIST EMERGENCY
IN WEST MALAYSIA

When Chan Peng, Secretary General of the Communist Party of Malaya, left Pahang in 1953, he travelled north through deep jungle, crossed the Malaya/Thailand border and set up his headquarters in the Betong Salient northwest of Kroh in Upper Perak. This move enabled him to create a safe base free from the attention of Malayan security forces and to renew contact with the Communist Party of China and his own Party representatives in Peking. It is from this safe base that he took part in the inconclusive Baling talks of 1955; after which he began to run down the armed struggle and issued directives to the burgeoning subversive Communist organisations, operating secretly in mainland Malaya and in Singapore, aimed at building a united front of legal political parties to be led eventually by the Communist Party of Malaya.

In 1960 a senior party member, who had represented the CPM in Peking for several years, rejoined the CPM's armed units in South Thailand and took over as Acting Secretary General. Chan Peng thereupon left for Peking arriving there in mid-1961. He set up a new headquarters, established radio links with the Party in South Thailand and received financial support from the Communist Party of China. When the question of renewing the armed struggle in West Malaysia arose, the Party decided to resume its military activities across the border.

Several senior members of Chan Peng's group disagreed with the Party's decision to resume the armed struggle. The Acting Secretary General, at the sharp end on the Thai/West Malaysian border, was accused of lacking in enthusiasm and he was recalled to Peking. He was replaced by Siew Chong, a veteran Malayan Communist terrorist, who set about reorganising the remnants of his armed units still in South Thailand. Having already a nucleus of 300–500 armed men, he managed to recruit an additional 1,000 people who started training in the border camps. This major recruitment exercise enabled the Malaysian Special Branch to mount clandestine operations into these camps and to conduct psychological warfare on a most effective scale. Subsequent armed Communist forays into North and Central Western Malaysia along the mountain ranges achieved little success and received virtually no support from the Malaysian population.

Lack of success and further ideological disputes within the Party resulted in a number of murders and armed clashes among dissident Communist groups. By 1974 a state of war existed between them: but it was not until 1987 that the two main dissident groups surrendered to the Thai Government. This left the original Communist Party of Malaya, with a number of armed units totalling about 1,200 men, still based along the Thai/West Malaysian border.

Eventually the Malaysian and Thai Governments agreed to act jointly to end the state of 'Emergency' along the border. After protracted negotiations, Chan Peng, now firmly back in the driving seat as Secretary General of the Communist Party of Malaya, declared that, if the Party was recognised by the Malaysian Government as a legal political entity, he would agree to surrender and hand over all his arms. The Malaysian Government stood firm on any immediate recognition of the Communist Party; but agreed to let the Communists return to their homes without restraint. Chan Peng reluctantly agreed these terms and 1,200 Communist terrorists surrendered with their arms to the Malaysian and Thai authorities. A 'peace treaty' was signed on 2nd December 1989 – more than forty-one years after the declaration of the Emergency by the British High Commissioner to the Federation of Malaya in 1948.

A really dreadful disaster occurred in May 1969, two years after I had left Malaysia. Communal riots between Malays and Chinese raged around parts of Kuala Lumpur and a large number of people were killed or wounded. It brought back memories of the end of the Japanese occupation of Malaya in 1945. It also compelled the government to introduce urgent measures aimed at encouraging the population to consider themselves Malaysians rather than simply Malays, Chinese, Indians, Dyaks etc. I believe that this has been successfully achieved.

Little did I think that, in mid-1974, Tan Sri (as he became known) Abdul Rahman bin Hashim, the Director of the Malaysian Special Branch, would be murdered in the Lake Gardens near his home in Kuala Lumpur by a killer group of armed Communist terrorists, said to have come from one of the dissident Communist group based on the Thai/West Malaysian border. His wife and son, then a journalist in Ireland, had visited us in England a short time before. That this took place so far away from the terrorists' headquarters in the jungle still puzzles me – perhaps there is more to this story still to be told.

With Joanna, John and Richard outside Buckingham Palace

Tun Razak, deputy Prime Minister of Malaysia

Tim Hatton receiving an award from HM The King of Malaysia

Colonel W.N. Gray CMG., DSO.
Commissioner of Police Malaya 1948-53

Tunku Farid, self-portrait

Tunku Abdul Rahman Putra,
Prime Minister of Malaysia

Dato Dr Ismail, Minister Home Affairs
Malaysia

With HM King Constantine of the Hellenes and Roy McComish, June 1986

Tim and Sarah Hatton at the Doon School in India

12

Having settled into my mother-in-law's small bungalow in Chipperfield near Kings Langley in Hertfordshire, I read the job columns in *The Times*, *Daily Telegraph* and the Sunday newspapers. I replied to twenty advertisements. I also registered with the Overseas Services Resettlement Bureau (OSRB) and the Officers' Association, both of which interviewed me efficiently and at length before placing me on their books. I also spent much time in Watford library, where the librarian suggested material for me to read and bring myself up to date with current affairs. I opened a working file to record my progress on finding a job. Our daily financial requirements were met by 'end of service accumulated paid leave entitlement'.

Of the twenty newspaper advertisers, three acknowledged my application and sent me forms to complete. None was taken further. When I had no reaction from the OSRB, I asked politely if they were still in business. Its Chairman, Sir Edwin Arrowsmith, asked me to come and see him. Apparently the officer in charge of my case had to go to hospital with severe cancer of the throat, and had been unable to cope with his office work. Sir Edwin proved very helpful, however, and said he would take on my case himself. He undertook to post relevant offers to me. The Officers' Association came up trumps and sent me twelve interesting job specifications. The first one I opened contained an application form for the appointment of a Temporary Principal in the Administrative Grade of the Home Civil Service. This person would be responsible for the introduction of an entirely new government-funded Tourist Loan Scheme, to be run by the Development Commission in the rural areas of England and Wales. Something new, something different, an Adam-and-Eve situation which intrigued me. I decided to give it a try, though I was not particularly sanguine about my chances; my chief anxiety being competition from within the civil service and from people already in the tourist industry.

I completed the rather lengthy forms and, on Sir Edwin's advice, I enclosed references to cover my school career, army service and from the Chairman of the Public Services Commission in Malaysia. I delivered the envelope to 3 Dean's Yard, Westminster, crossed my fingers and admired the outside setting of the Commission's offices. Apart from an acknowledgment, I heard nothing more for a month; then came a letter from the Commission's Secretary inviting me to attend an interview. I duly presented myself at No 3 and was taken into a room furnished with a table, an ancient rickety chair and a small side table. Some sheets of plain white foolscap paper were lying on the table together with an inkpot, a pen with a steel nib and a large sealed envelope. A folded towel, a bar of Lux soap and a key lay neatly on the side table. The young lady who showed me in, said that all would be revealed when I opened the envelope and discovered my instructions. I was to read descriptions of five typical civil service problems, list all possible solutions and then outline my preferred plan. I had the rest of the day to produce the results of my deliberations. The soap and towel were to wash and dry my hands. The key was to open the door of a washroom located in a maze of corridors downstairs, and marked with a large X on an accompanying diagram. I found the problems simple and completed my work by lunchtime. I folded it up and placed it on the table. I decided to explore the loo, found it clean and bright and, on my return, I discovered another envelope on my table; inside was a formal acknowledgment of my work and a note that I would receive further information shortly.

In early September 1967, I was called for interview by the Development Commission's Chairman, Lady Albemarle, flanked by four Development Commissioners – a famous banker; a well-known trade union leader; a senior academic from the London School of Economics and the Chairman of a Rural Industries

Board. The banker wondered if I could speak any languages and asked me to outline the traffic problems in Singapore; the trade union leader asked me about the war in Vietnam and what I thought about the American intervention there; the academic asked me about the price of rubber, tin, fish and rice in Malaysia; the businessman asked me if I listened to *The Archers* on the wireless. Lady Albemarle asked me about my family life, children's education and what I thought of commuting to London. The Secretary informed us that my written answers to the five questions, compared with those submitted by other applicants, were by far the shortest; and he added, with a lugubrious smile, that he thought mine were the most amusing. I left them to their consider-ations. On 23rd September I received a letter from the Secretary; it said the interview board had recommended to HM Treasury that I should be appointed a Temporary Principal in the Development Commission. I would also act as Deputy to the Secretary and be responsible for introducing the Loan Scheme. This was later con-firmed in writing by the Treasury.

I was invited to join the Secretary of the Commission for lunch, so that he could brief me on what the Development Commission did and where I would fit in. He advised me to wear a bowler hat (I decided to borrow my father's ancient bowler), and to carry a rolled black umbrella in case it rained. I noticed afterwards that I was the only person to wear a bowler hat on the 7.30 a.m. train to London.

The Development Commission was a body of eight Com-missioners appointed by Royal Warrant, under the chairmanship of Lady Albemarle. Their statutory duty was to report to the Treasury on all applications for advances from the Development Fund, which had been established by Act of Parliament in 1909. Any scheme which benefited the rural economy in the Develop-ment Areas of England, Scotland and Wales would be eligible for assistance; providing there was no other statutory provision for helping it. The administrative staff consisted of the Secretary; the newly-appointed Principal (me); a Chief Executive Officer, who wore a Homburg hat and was responsible for the Factories Div-ision, and twenty members of staff.

My first task would be to introduce the Loan Scheme as soon as possible. The Secretary and I walked over to the Treasury offices, nearby in Whitehall, to discover exactly what was involved, how

307

much we could pay in loans and who would be responsible for running it after it had been set up. We went by appointment to meet a senior lady mandarin who kept us waiting outside her office for one hour. When we were ushered to our chairs in front of her desk, the Secretary, who did not smoke, put his hand in his pocket and was sharply admonished by our interviewer thus, 'I'll have none of that in here!' For once in his life, the Secretary, whom I soon came to know was rather sensitive, had nothing to say when he sheepishly produced his handkerchief and blew his nose with a triumphant trumpet. The Treasury lady enquired who was to be responsible and then addressed herself to me. We were to be given £750,000 to be replaced on a revolving basis as the loan and capital were paid off by the recipients. A part-time paid co-ordinator could be engaged; he should be a qualified accountant. The 'bank' would be the Rural Industries Loan Fund, which already came under the auspices of the Commission. My immediate task would be to carry out preliminary investigations, liaise closely with the co-ordinator in consultation with the Secretary and to produce a business plan of action for submission to the Treasury, through the Commissioners. That was it. I then had an infuriated Secretary to quieten down during lunch.

Of course, I knew next to nothing about tourism and there was no one around to whom I could turn for informed advice. I decided to go and see the secretaries of the Ramblers' Association, the Cyclists' Touring Club and the regional Tourist Boards. I also visited the National Trust offices and the Historic Houses Association. They were enormously helpful and full of ideas on how to attract more tourism into rural areas. All these visits enabled me increasingly to hold my own in conferences, financial planning and decision-making. I also received much wise advice from those running, or working for, the County Rural Industries Committees. It seemed that my market would be the couple who wished, on their own, to expand their accommodation up to a maximum of twelve bedrooms and the enlargement of their dining room and the provision of the necessary facilities. Unfortunately, my work was increased greatly when the co-ordinator fell ill with a serious heart attack and I had to share his workload with him. Eventually, the scheme got going, the capital was loaned and the revolving replacement of the fund began to work well. The Treasury lady, who was not at all a bad sort and very efficient, liked to be

308

informed of progress. She declared that she was pleased and in the following year the original loan capital was increased substantially.

There was more to my work than I realised at first. I would also be responsible to the Secretary for the policy and administrative side of financing forty five voluntary County Rural Industries Committees. They were extremely popular in the countryside and had been up and running for many years. This imposed no great problems for me, apart from the occasional troubleshooting aspect. However, the government wished to replace them with two entirely new centralised organisations one in England and Wales, and one in Scotland. It would be my responsibility to act as co-ordinator of this exercise, and work closely with those already running the Rural Industries headquarters organisation located on Wimbledon Common.

The first company was to be called 'The Council for Small Industries in Rural Areas (COSIRA)' of which Sir Paul Sinker (former Chairman of the British Council) was soon to be appointed its first chairman. We had to incorporate the Rural Industries Bureau, the Rural Industries Loan Fund and the forty-five largely independent County Rural Industries Committees into this new unified service. My task was to draw together existing policies in these organisations and to recommend necessary changes, and to prepare for the registration of the Council as a company, limited by guarantee. This involved consultations with the lawyers representing all sides; and with the Board of Trade regarding organisational and financial questions. Then, discussing the results with those involved on the ground, many of whom were volunteers and had their own very strong opinions. I accompanied Sir Paul on most of his consultations and meetings around the country, and I attempted to establish personal and friendly relations with their chairmen, and especially the hardworking Rural Industries Organisers who bore so well the brunt of the work in the countryside – not all of whom viewed the future changes with equanimity. All very exciting and worthwhile and I was able at first hand, over and over again, to observe the practised way Sir Paul Sinker dealt with tricky situations. Regarded as a bit of a cold fish by those who did not know him, he certainly warmed up in difficult situations and became an amusing, resourceful and successful negotiator. He proved a great friend to me though he did not hit it off with the Secretary.

The formation of a new company in Scotland, called 'The Small Industries Council for the Rural Areas of Scotland', involved me with the preparation of a memorandum and articles of association for the new council. I worked in conjunction with officers of the Scottish Department, the Board of Trade, the Scottish Country Industries Development Trust and their lawyers. Negotiations on policy were somewhat protracted as 'Scottish Nationalism' was not entirely absent from the proceedings! I found work with the Department and the Trust was extremely pleasant and rewarding. I really enjoyed this task.

Thus my day-to-day work outside the office was enjoyable and worthwhile. Inside 3 Dean's Yard, however, life was curious. Two rooms had been combined to form a large office for me; it had a circular glass dome in the middle of the ceiling and had been given a new carpet, new furniture and new curtains. I even had a new wooden pen, with a steel nib, an inkwell and a supply of lead pencils (I preferred my Parker 51). In my desk, I discovered several sheets of pink blotting paper in one drawer, and in another drawer were my old friends the clean white towel, the bar of soap and the key for the washroom; the latter was dedicated for use solely by the Secretary, the Principal and the Chief Executive Officer. My immediate staff consisted of two executive officers and two clerical officers. None of us could type. Typewriters were conspicuous by their absence. Incoming mail was opened by the Secretary and put on a file to be dealt with by way of notes on sheets of paper attached to the left-hand side of the file. The first notes started with the comments of a clerical officer, then the Executive Officers concerned had their say and, eventually, it landed in my in-tray for a decision, or a referral to the Secretary. Then, back went the file down the line again. When the time came for a reply to be sent to the originator, the clerical officer concerned drafted it out in longhand, according to the instructions outlined in the file, and took it over to the typing pool. Unfortunately, the pool was on the second storey of a rented house over a mile away across several busy roads. By the time the draft had been safely delivered by hand through all weathers, and explanations offered for illegible handwriting, plus a chit-chat with the four extremely bored unsupervised typists, to say nothing of the purchase of sandwiches for lunch and perhaps a visit to the betting shop, there was little left of the morning. I soon discovered that my typing problems could be short-circuited when the Secretary's secretary offered to type all my correspondence. I was amazed to discover more. The Secretary and his secretary were not on speaking terms; all communication between them for many years had been by written notes.

My efforts to improve the running of the office proved largely unsuccessful and when, with the Secretary's agreement, I put up costed proposals to HM Treasury for the redivision of my office back into its original halves, so that the typing pool could join us in No 3; it disappeared deep into HM Treasury, never to emerge despite polite reminders. Another unsolicited comment of mine, addressed to the Treasury, concerned the financial result of implementing Treasury instructions regarding who should authorise the issue of first and second class stamps to be placed on official mail. Recommendations had to be made right through the hierarchy of the Development Commission – from bottom to the top – and only the Secretary could make the final decision to enable a first-class stamp to be placed on an official letter. My submission costed each single decision at one shilling and sixpence (12½p) per stamped envelope. My recommendation on the postal class to be used was perfectly simple, it should be left to the decision of the writer. Once again no reply was forthcoming. A year later the Secretary agreed that the writer could exercise his or her discretion.

Another quaint decision was the Secretary's refusal to allow one of the Rural Industries officers to play a small, but highly relevant, part in *The Archers*, the popular BBC saga about everyday country folk. This decision caused considerable annoyance amongst his fellow officers. On the last working day before Christmas, the staff invited me to join them for a drink at the 'Albert' public house in Victoria Street. There was a tradition that everyone should pay for their own drinks and I accepted, thinking this would be a good way to get to know the staff socially; indeed, it was a very pleasant evening and I even discovered that a colleague's hobby was deep-sea diving. On the next working day after Christmas, I was summoned to the Secretary's office and told that Administrative Grade officers should not consort with their staff in pubs or canteens. Clearly, he felt very strongly about my 'misconduct' and was really quite pompous about it. I admit that I took some satisfaction in recalling that, a fortnight ago, he had been running around all the shops in Malvern trying to buy a wooden lavatory seat. It seemed that the Chairman of the Development Commission preferred to sit upon a wooden seat, but had found, to her dismay, that her en-suite hotel bedroom had a plastic one and the hotel did not run to wooden ones. The Secretary volunteered to remedy the situation. Unfortunately, it was late on a Saturday and it was some time before he came across a satisfactorily equipped bathroom in another hotel. We all moved into that hotel.

It took me about a year to come to terms with daily trips by car to the station, the train journey to London and then by underground to Westminster. Most days produced a headache in the afternoon, relieved by Veganin, and a sleep in the train on the return journey which, sometimes, resulted in unplanned visits to Leighton Buzzard at the end of the line. Here, the station staff came to know me well and would direct me to the correct platform for the return journey to Kings Langley, and a late supper at home.

At the end of two years or so, the Tourist Loan Scheme was in full swing and the two new companies in England and Scotland were settling down well. I considered that there was no likelihood of professional progress for me in the civil service, partly because I was older than my contemporaries; and partly because they had their careers carefully researched, and knew exactly where they planned to go. I did not wish to spend the rest of my working life in the Development Commission. I discussed my anxieties with Lady Albemarle and with Sir Paul Sinker who did their best to persuade me to stay on. Eventually, they gave me good references which I used to advantage. When I was about to leave, the Scottish Department and the Trust sent me moving letters of farewell; a typical one ended thus, 'I have been on many occasions grateful for your help and for decisions taken on behalf of the Trust. I'm afraid that the clock has now gone back a bit, in that your absence is bound to be noticed by a clogging of the works. If your steps ever take you this way be sure to invite yourself for a meal or a night...'

Having left the Development Commission, I started along the old familiar route writing to recruitment agencies and renewing my scanning of newspaper job advertisements. I sent off over one hundred replies and received eighty application forms. I was summoned to attend twelve interviews. I decided to try something entirely new and I joined Barbour Index two months later.

Barbour Index was a newcomer to the construction industry. Patrick Barbour, the managing director and 'owner', was a tireless entrepreneur who had discovered a lucrative niche for designing relevant information fact-sheets of manufacturers' products and distributing them into the libraries of architects and quantity surveyors throughout the industry. He not only helped individual manufacturers and suppliers to produce the information needed to describe and sell their products, but he also undertook to reorganise, on a continuing basis, the libraries of architects and others who wished to make their preferred selections from a wide variety of choices, set out in a universal language which they could readily understand. Both ends of this chain paid Patrick and he was seeking to consolidate the business and expand further.

Our headquarters were located on the top floor of Whiteley's departmental store in Bayswater, London. When Patrick acquired the original lease, the whole area was divided into a warren of corridors and little offices. As soon as the ink was dry on the lease, he removed all the partitions; thus more than doubling the office space and halving the original price per square foot. Thirty of us sat in open-plan fashion with a small boardroom on one side, washrooms at the far end and storage space off the other side. On the surface, everyone basked in an atmosphere of informality and we were all known by our first names. As some pointed out, it also gave Patrick a clear view of every desk and its occupants: he knew at once who was shirking, who was absent and how long people stayed chatting in the washroom. Office hours started at 8.30 a.m. sharp, an hour was allowed for lunch and work usually came to an end at 5.00 p.m. The often-stated company aim was to make money and the competitive spirit was strongly encouraged among the librarians and the sales people.

Patrick called me his 'intelligence officer' and, as a start, I was attached to each of the various sections of the company. The two main revenue-producing arms of the business were the twelve salesmen who visited the manufacturers, and the seventy young female librarians who drove around sorting out and maintaining the libraries. Their activities were supervised by more experienced ladies who also had responsibilities for recruiting architectural practices not already using our services. In addition to the sales department, there were supporting groups within the office such as the telephone sales, enquiries and information section; two product leaflet layout designers; a microfilm sales section and the administrators. The latter included a small typing pool, a store person, telephone operator and a company secretary. In-company training went on all the time, and extra people for research, or punch-card operations, were recruited on a temporary basis as required.

My first attachment was to shadow one of the salesmen. He was a large cheerful extrovert, whose own small building business did not produce enough money to support his family. He had joined Barbour Index because he liked selling services rather than playing around with glass, bricks and mortar. He had no difficulties in winning over the manufacturers' representatives and we were successful with our three calls in the Midlands.

I much enjoyed my time with the lady librarians. The majority were in the eighteen to twenty-four age group, unmarried, full of enthusiasm and determined to make a success of their first independent job, as well as to exploit, in the evenings, unsupervised use of their individual red-painted mini-cars readily identifiable by a large black letter 'B' on the doors. The girls were given a weekly programme of library visits. Here they were often offered lunch and were never short of personal invitations from their clients after-hours and at weekends. They soon learned their work and played an important professional part in the life of many practices. Turnover was frequent, partly because they left to marry and, partly, because Patrick caught them out when examining their weekly returns of work and petrol consumed. The few who failed to please were designated 'rogues' and disappeared without a trace.

Some people really like to use the telephone all day long (this was before the arrival of mobile telephones), and the telephone sales girls I sat beside in my first days at Barbour Index seemed to enjoy their work. I discovered they kept jolly and enthusiastic throughout a long day and sold our services to a high proportion of cold calls, producing a variety of useful leads for the salesmen and the librarians. Patrick had a friend who was an inventor and among his inventions was an easy-to-use, inexpensive-to-run micro-film machine: it was fascinating to see how this caught on throughout the industry.

Having completed my training, I took over my job at a desk next to Patrick. My routine day included visits to research groups working in companies throughout the industry, discussing their needs, their plans and their ideas for the future. Although some were reluctant to give trade secrets away, I received enormous help from the majority. The construction industry periodic journals, the

Building Research Station and the Building Centre in Bloomsbury proved mines of information. I made a great number of useful contacts and several valuable friends. Many of these people were interested in our work and I did my best to explain where we fitted into the scheme of things and how we might help them.

I attended the annual 'Book Festivals', 'Information Retrieval Seminars' and 'Construction Industry Fairs' in London, Munich and Paris. It was very interesting to meet the professionals involved and I took great pleasure in producing leads for our sales people to follow up. Unfortunately, our 'sales directors' seemed to change over rapidly as Patrick leaned on them to produce more business. I also visited the libraries of the larger architectural practices and the larger building contractors, and looked into their changing needs as new materials, processes and ideas came into the market place.

Then Patrick came up with two great ideas following a recent visit to the USA. The first was to emulate and improve upon McGraw Hill's information service on new building within the construction industry; and his second idea was to computerise the whole of our operation. There was no one with computer expertise within the company, so he persuaded a man from IBM to join us. In those early days of computerisation everything had to be done for the first time – another Adam and Eve situation, and an extremely tedious one.

I spent a great deal of time researching the construction industry's publications to discover the main supplier of new building reports. I found there was only one successful company. It had extremely good coverage in most of the important regions where building activities were taking place. It was run by two men in their sixties operating from a small office in London. After many telephone calls and letters, I managed to make an appointment to see them, having made all sorts of promises not to give away any commercial secrets. It seemed they had built up, over many years, a most productive network of informers throughout the industry. They were able to cover, in surprising detail, planning applications, planning approvals and the intentions and requirements of a huge variety of contractors, suppliers, builders merchants etc. Their sources were employed as part-time field workers, many of whom had retired from their careers in the building industry and had the necessary experience, and the time available, to do the ground research. I asked the two directors if they had any plans for eventual retirement and for the future of their company. They avoided giving a direct reply; but said that they knew of Barbour Index and approved the way our company had progressed over the years. They agreed that I could bring Patrick Barbour in to any future detailed discussions with them. I thought that computerisation of their information-collection and production would enable them to take on much more work: it seemed to me that they concentrated only on areas and detail with which they were personally familiar. I realised, too, that there was an insatiable demand throughout the construction industry for fast accurate and detailed advance information on which to plan and cost their tenders for new contracts. It seemed certain to me that a merger of the two companies would produce an exciting and profitable synergy.

Meanwhile, Patrick Barbour was pursuing grandiose ideas of his own for the future of the company. Although he was running a very successful business and his profits were increasing substantially every year, he still had great ambitions. A number of organisations were already expressing interest in taking us over or running joint projects to some of which we listened with interest. One of these, important in the international printing and publishing industry, was pressing for immediate negotiations. To my mind, the great minus point for us was that we were really a one-man-band. We had little or no capital for sustained expansion, the other directors and private shareholders either lacked enlightened interest in the business, or had insufficient practical experience. Everyone seemed to want Patrick on board; and I began to wonder whether these companies would be interested enough to run our little operations with enthusiasm. Suddenly, Patrick decided to move the company out of London to much larger premises in a rural location near Windsor. Moreover, he decided, quite rightly, to go public on the Stock Exchange. He thought, correctly as it turned out, there would be no difficulty in raising the money from his many contacts in the City. He decided to step down from being managing director so that he could mastermind the changes. The whole atmosphere of the business changed dramatically over night. The tock tock birds were already tocking away in my imagination but now they began drumming hard! I left in 1972.

So that was the end of my three and a half years in the construction industry. During the next week I received, out of the blue, a firm offer of a directorship in quite a large construction company; and my friends in the information collection business also offered me a provisional directorship. But I did not follow them up.

However, I followed up an advertisement for the appointment of clerk to the governors of the two Haberdashers' Aske's Schools. I attended interviews at the Haberdashers' Hall in the City of London, competing with several officers about to leave the armed services. The chairman of the interviewing board was a retired major general, so I did not rate my chances very high. Fortunately, I had visited both schools and had been given lunch by the heads. I thought this might give me a few Brownie points. To my surprise, I was offered the appointment and I accepted.

I reported to the Haberdashers' Company offices in Staining Lane on the following Monday and met the Chairman of the Haberdashers' Aske's Girls' School and the Company's Clerk. They informed me that my predecessor had died some months previously; there would be no handover and an office had been prepared for me in the headmistress's garage located beside the school in Acton.

My appointment would be on a gentleman's agreement for an initial period of two years. The other school in this section of the Aske Foundation was the boys' school in Elstree. Both schools had 'direct grant' status and were financed by the Department of Education. There was a senior domestic bursar in each school, neither of whom had applied for my job. Apart from my work for the governors of both schools, and my connections with the Haberdashers' Hall, my main task would be to organise the transfer of the 800-strong girls' school from Acton to a brand new site some twenty miles away, next door to the boys' school at Elstree in Hertfordshire. After the interview, I telephoned Miss Gillett, the headmistress in Acton, and arranged to visit her the next day.

Then started more unforeseen developments. Soon after I arrived home, the company Clerk telephoned to say that I had to report to his office at 9.00 a.m. the next day. On arrival, I was told that the company had decided that I should organise a full-scale appeal over the next two years to help pay for the construction of a swimming pool for the girls on the Elstree site. I was not permitted to employ an appeal organiser. I would have to do the job myself. My target would be £30,000 gross. Having no experience of organising an appeal, I began to have serious doubts about taking on the job. To play for time, I asked if my salary would be increased accordingly. I was told that, although the company would not increase my cash in hand, they would increase my salary by 10% and put it towards a company-funded pension. I agreed, with some misgivings, and the chairman and I shook hands. I never received a job description or written confirmation of our gentleman's agreement or any pension!

I was able to keep my appointment with the headmistress at Acton. I discovered that she too had been recently employed and was a very determined character who, previously, had survived several years as the head of a tough comprehensive school in Yorkshire. We took to each other immediately and talked together for several hours. Whilst driving home, I thought it was a good thing that we were both coming into a new situation and that it would be fun to work together.

Home was still my mother-in-law's new two-bedroomed retirement bungalow in Chipperfield, Hertfordshire. It was too small for our growing family and we had been taking weekends off looking for a slightly larger house within commuting distance of London. We soon realised that we could not afford a middle-size three- to four-bedroom house, so we were limited to a smaller house or a large rambling one. At that time no one seemed to want the larger older home so we aimed for something in that direction and, eventually, fell in love with the Old House, Mickleham, near Dorking, Surrey. A beautiful Carolean house (1636) and an acre or two of garden. The purchase proceeded, we liked the vendor and the deal went through without a hitch. We financed it by the sale of the bungalow, a loan from my mother's modest family trust and a topping-up mortgage from a building society.

Two things amazed me on my first full day at the girls' school in Acton. The first was the somewhat strange teacher-grouping in the common room. It seemed to me that there were three distinct groups who had been appointed by the three previous headmistresses; each had appropriated seating accommodation in their own particular corner of the room. These quite separate groups could be distinguished as much by their dress as by their conversation and mannerisms. But they seem to get on well enough together, anyway on the surface. It was stranger still to observe there was not a single male member of staff around! The second amazing experience came at lunchtime. The staff sat at a long top table. At first, I accepted an invitation to sit next to the headmistress; but I soon moved away in order to meet other members of staff. The only other male in the room was the peripatetic fencing master, a thin wiry man who was always darting around in a great hurry and stayed only to consume the main course. Also in the dining room were some 800 girls seated at long narrow tables chatting away vivaciously. Then, what a surprise! A most efficient waitress service was provided by a large number of matriarchal figures who not only served the food, but kept order in a firm no-nonsense fashion. I shall never forget the cacophony of 850 females and two males eating, laughing and talking at the same time. 'You've seen nothing yet,' said Miss Gillett, as she noisily threw a tough steel dish on the floor. There was an immediate drop in the sound index for a moment. But no one turned round or stood up to look. 'There, you see,' the headmistress said, 'You can always tell a Haberdashers' Aske's girl because she will never look round and enquire "Whatever was that?"'

Sombre matters soon began to appear as I thought about what I had seen. The boys' school had a modern self-service canteen. Any change to self-service for the girls would certainly be fraught with difficulty. I foresaw strong complaints from parents (no personal supervision at mealtimes, their daughters would learn bad manners, eat the wrong food, and probably develop anorexia); there would be terrible cries from the waitresses (many of whom had served in the school at lunchtime for more than thirty years; they relied heavily on their part-time occupations), and there would certainly be shocked interventions from the Old Girls' Association. As feared, all these situations arose and had to be dealt with sensitively – most fears disappeared by the end of the first term on the site.

To remedy my lack of experience as a fundraiser, I interviewed the managing directors of six leading fundraising organisations, and two independent appeals organisers. I soon discovered that the main problems for a girls' school appeal arose because most young ladies married and changed names and home addresses. Furthermore, the male partners of married couples tended to insist that any spare money should go to their old schools. There were also difficulties amongst public companies, charities and independent businesses – the relatively dull target of a swimming pool for girls was not a particularly attractive magnet for charitable money! I was told to set a gross target in the region of £20,000 to £30,000 achievable only by an experienced organisation and an appeals director. I was advised not to attempt the impossible on my own. A little chastened, but not put off, I decided to implement the constructive side of what I had been told. I divided the school constituency into twelve areas each with a volunteer leader, chosen by me, and I asked the Company 'to prime the pump' with a substantial donation. They gave me £10,000 and Haberdashers' liverymen covenanted a further £8,000 gross. The Old Girls' Association and the bursar revised and updated our records as best they could and I decided to drum up enthusiasm by persuading the Company, governors, common room, parents and students to take part in a garden fête. Apparently, nothing like this had been done by the school before and the staff thought that begging for money was not at all the done thing. Although, at first, many individuals were against the idea, others agreed to take part. I asked the Company to come up with a Very Important Person who might be asked to make a short speech and open the fête.

A number of distinguished Haberdashers were approached; but there was little enthusiasm; though honour was usually satisfied by a generous donation in lieu! I appealed to the staff; but, while they were not prepared to recommend a distinguished academic, they did suggest the names of a famous comedian, and a well-known racing driver, whose daughters attended the school. Neither was available. It so happened that the bursar had kindly arranged for a cup of coffee to be delivered to me in my garage every day by two sixth-form girls who volunteered on a rotation basis. One day, in desperation, I explained my predicament to them and they agreed to discuss the matter with their colleagues. Next day I was told that Lulu was their preferred candidate! This soon presented me with another dilemma. Neither the Clerk nor any member of the Haberdashers' Court of Wardens had heard of Lulu. They became quite restive until Lady Bowater, a pillar of strength on the school's governing body, told them that Lulu was an up-and-coming young Scottish pop singer who was a favourite with the young; moreover, she and Sir Ian Bowater thought Lulu was a splendid choice. I was given the Court's hesitant permission to approach Lulu. She agreed to come for two hours, on condition I gave her a small bottle of her favourite scent and that her boyfriend could be in attendance. The enthusiasm of the school grew daily; even some senior members of staff, who had spent most of their lives teaching in the school, overcame their disapproval of handling money. At 2.00 p.m. sharp, on a fine afternoon, Lulu swept into the school grounds in an open sports car driven by Maurice Gibb of the famous Bee Gees. A huge cheer went up from 800 girls, their parents, brothers, sisters and friends. Sir Ian and Lady Bowater joined in the fun and Lulu stayed till 6.00 p.m. We made £8,000 in cash, clear of expenses, and received appeal donations totalling a further £7,000.

At about this time, Dr Tom Taylor relinquished his appointment as head of the Haberdashers' Aske's Boys' School in Elstree. He wrote me a letter thanking me for my help and encouragement over the last year, and congratulated me on the initial successes of our appeal and on burgeoning plans for the girls' move to Elstree. His successor was Bruce McGowan. Bruce and his wife became great friends of mine for many years. Both worked hard and successfully to make sure the imminent arrival of Haberdashers Aske's Girls' School (commonly known as the HAGS!) on the Elstree campus would be warmly welcomed and supported by the boys' school.

A really sad series of events took place a few months after my arrival. Our energetic, strong-willed, admirable headmistress fell ill with a particularly painful form of cancer. She soon cut down her attendance at school and an air of depression came over the common room. I visited her at home and discussed the running of the school and our plan for the move to Elstree. I had to cut down the length of my visits as she weakened. The deputy head gradually took over all academic matters and made her own day-to-day decisions regarding the teaching staff. The domestic bursar became directly responsible for the routine administrative side of the school. I took on the rest in addition to my own responsibilities. The excellent Miss Gillett died at home having been looked after selflessly by a tireless faithful friend. I saw her the evening before she passed away. The only thing she said was 'God, it's awful.' I felt extremely sad and overcome, so I drove straight over to the McGowans who gave me an excellent supper and helped me recover and drive safely home.

I soon discovered that being a head of a large secondary girls' school was a major administrative task, and that the academic side would have to be delegated wholly to the deputy head. The latter had neither the time nor the inclination to deal with the mountain

321

of paperwork which, even in those days, dropped into the head's in-tray. The first port of call for all visitors, including parents, officers from the Department of Education, newspaper reporters, police, building contractors, etc. was me; so I had general responsibility for running the school until a new head could be selected and appointed. Meanwhile, I had to supply the energy and push to continue the appeal and, the biggest job of all, to co-ordinate plans for the detailed lay-out of the new school and the physical move to Elstree.

I enlisted the help of the boys' school's computer department in working out a timetable for buses and private cars to enter and leave the new school grounds in the morning and again in the evening. This would involve the daily transport of 800 girls from West London and adjacent suburbs. All our traffic had to be independent of the boys' school where an efficient system had been long established for the daily transport of their 1,200 boys. Entirely separate entrances, dropping-off points and picking-up areas had to be worked out, constructed and clearly signposted on the ground. Moreover, the arrival and departure of the teaching and administrative staff of both schools had also to be co-ordinated, together with the timing of trade deliveries to the site. Endless meetings with the traffic police, the bus companies and the staff of both schools took place. We had to ensure, somehow, that the narrow country roads round the site of the two schools were not blocked during 'commuting' times. No financial arrangements had been made for the extra parking space needed.

The original design of the new school at Elstree had been approved by the Worshipful Company of Haberdashers, before my arrival, in consultation with the headmistress, the headmaster of the boys' school and representatives of the Department of Education. The chosen building contractor had produced the detailed plans and had nominated the main sub-contractors. The company's architect was supposed to supervise the detail and an agent had been appointed who would live and work on site. However, a great deal of detail had been omitted, or postponed for later decision.

Strong-willed heads of departments demanded more room when they saw the plans of the new building; the scientists wanted fume-cupboards and the latest equipment for their laboratories; the language teachers wanted audio equipment; the computer department wanted to computerise everything in sight and to have what

322

later became a cyber café outside the classroom areas; the art department had their own original and often attractive ideas for design and decoration. The young and highly efficient school-keeper had excellent ideas regarding a security system throughout the site. The bursar abandoned, with regret, all hope of waitress service and wished to be involved fully with the selection of a caterer and with the management and layout of the canteen and kitchens. The sixth form wanted their own common room, which had not been included in the original design. The staff had their own ideas on the provision of lockers, chairs, desks and a separate quiet place to work. Games fields for the girls had to be agreed with the boys' school staff and entirely new ones for lacrosse had to be constructed and drainage provided where necessary. The gymnasium needed a sprung floor; not a wooden floor with a concrete base, as shown on the plan. Decisions had to be made on how much of the school should be carpeted and to what standard. The cost of these requirements had not been properly estimated and only provisional sums had been agreed without any real consideration of the detail. Fortunately, the boys' school staff took a constructive interest in all these problems and offered their help and advice. It took them a while to get over their amazement at seeing the old-fashioned well-worn classroom equipment currently in use at Acton (nearly all of it, they said, must have come out of the Ark!). Bruce McGowan supported me most effectively when I had to persuade the Company to provide extra cash for vital projects.

It was not just the equipment. The whole attitude to the education and welfare of girls throughout the school and, indeed, the Company was being shaken up and stirred as the move became a reality. No longer could the Haberdashers' Aske's Girls' School remain complacent and comfortable in its suburban backwater while the waves of change swept by. Gradually the atmosphere in the common room at Acton became lively, *The Times* crossword puzzle was left undone, people moved away from their institutional corners and I abandoned my thoughts of a common room in the round at Elstree to prevent any further bunching in the corners!

The boys' school, under its fresh, energetic and popular headmaster (he later became a most successful and innovative chairman of the Headmasters' Conference) presented all sorts of challenges to staff and students of the girls' school in almost every area of activity. Of course, we all realised that it would be impossible to achieve everything at once; but it provided wonderful opportunities to improve the quality of life throughout the school: and so it proved over the school's exciting first years at Elstree.

Unexpected developments began to impinge on my working day in Acton. A number of fourth-form girls began to arrive at school quite sick and had to be looked after in the sickroom. They had no appetite at lunch and slept soundly for most of the day: their parents were asked to come in and take them home. It soon appeared that the girls were not suffering from any disease, but were simply drunk and incapable. Investigations identified the real culprits to be three local publicans who had taken to selling under-aged girls bottles of vodka. These had been sampled in increasing quantities by these girls on their way to school. Interviews with parents, guardians, local police and certain members of the fourth form took a lot of time but there was no recidivism thereafter.

On another occasion, the editor of *The Jewish Chronicle* tele-phoned me to ask how many girls were attending a specified class on that particular day. Of course, I had no idea and, on visiting the classroom, I discovered the form teacher in front of only three girls. The remaining twenty-two had been withdrawn to join their families who were celebrating an important Jewish festival. The editor enquired later whether or not the school had a quota for the admission of Jewish girls. He went on to say, 'Did you not know that Jewish parents send their children to the Haberdashers' Aske's schools because they want them to be among a wide cross-section of students? If parents wanted an all-Jewish school they would send their children to the Jewish Free School.' The teacher in charge of admissions informed me that she always made her selections on ability and had not been given quotas based on race or religion. Ruffled feathers had to be smoothed very carefully.

Many members of the Jewish community in North West London sent their children to the Aske's schools and their parents took an active part in out-of-class activities, including the organisation of my appeal. However, the Yom Kippur War of 1973 affected greatly the members of the local Jewish community. I was told that they managed to collect more than £1 million cash over one weekend and transferred it to the government in Israel. Naturally, this produced an adverse effect on the flow of money into the appeal.

But the war was soon over and the generous donations recovered, to my selfish relief.

Halfway through the building of the new school, the economy of the country seemed to collapse. The Stock Exchange prices fell dramatically, there was a huge rise in inflation and a nationwide scarcity of building materials. All our orders for the delivery of reinforced steel joists (RSJs) were cancelled and there was despair among the building contractors. Fortunately, the site agent was an experienced reliable person with great *savoir faire*, a strong sense of humour and an extensive network of contacts in the construction industry. He installed a battery of telephones in his little office, and I bombarded my friends in Barbour Index for the telephone numbers of RSJ manufacturers and suppliers. He and I spent a whole week ordering the RSJs from all over the country and negotiating the best possible price. Eventually, we bought enough to ensure building could continue without further interruption. But we had to pay double the original estimated cost and this annoyed the Company's Clerk. However, he quietened down when he checked current prices which, by then, had risen to four times the original price. These costs never went back to the price we paid.

In order to achieve a reasonably uniform approach to colour, design and the supply of furniture throughout the school, we appointed the art mistress as the co-ordinator throughout the building. We also obtained from ICI the services, at no cost to us, of a lady adviser on the selection and quality of paint. They worked together and had a free hand – the results seemed to please everyone including a host of daily visitors from the Company. The only disagreement came from the person who first designed the building. He persuaded the Company to install reinforced glass doors throughout the school to prevent accidents occurring when doors were opened by girls approaching from different sides. He reasoned that, as they could see each other through the glass, one would politely give way. Eight doors were smashed on the first day and over twenty in the next week!

During the two years of my stewardship of the swimming pool appeal we managed to raise a total of £89,000 gross of which some £18,000 had been contributed directly by the Worshipful Company and its members. Our efforts had cost the Company nothing and had exceeded greatly our stated target. I am much indebted to our brilliant area leaders; particularly to the Polish community in Acton and to the many shipbroker families who seemed to have made Acton their home and, of course to the parents, staff and students who made collecting money such a pleasure. There was, in addition, a steady income from people who wished to donate cash or kind to pay for other projects in the school, e.g. pianos for the music department. These accounts became substantial and had to be kept separate from the appeal fund.

An important part of my job was to organise the appointment of a new headmistress to take over in September 1974, at the start of our first term in Elstree. Each candidate on the shortlist spent half a day at Elstree and I got to know them quite well: they all thought the school would not be ready on time. The governors' final selection was not quite unanimous and our chairman felt it necessary to resign. The new headmistress and the newly elected lady chairman worked well together and developed the vision and leadership which would ensure that the HAGS would go from strength to strength in their new home in Elstree – and so it proved.

The new headmistress, Mrs Wiltshire, took over on the first day of the autumn term and presided over the formal opening of the school by HRH Princess Margaret, Haberdasher, on 1st October 1974. As a postscript to this happy occasion, I nearly died of stress when, three days before the opening, the stone plaque was delivered on site inscribed with the wrong date! Back it had to go to the makers who pulled out all their stops and returned it (or another one, perhaps) just in time for the ceremony.

Meanwhile, I had discovered that the United Westminster Schools and the Royal Foundation of Greycoat Hospital were looking for a Clerk and Receiver to be based at their Westminster offices in Palace Street. As my time with the Worshipful Company of Haberdashers was coming to an end, and as Elstree was not within daily commuting distance from my home in Mickleham, I sent in my application for the appointment. I was interviewed, placed on a shortlist, interviewed again and was not chosen. Life went on as before in Acton and Elstree then, a month later, a short letter from Palace Street stated that their preferred candidate had failed his medical examination and, therefore, the appointment was mine – providing I passed my medical. My personal salary would be exactly twice the salary I was paid by the Worshipful Company;

furthermore, it would be revised annually after consultation with the Civil Service Pay Unit. I would also be eligible to join the combined schools final year's salary pensions scheme.

With the agreement of all concerned, I commuted between home, Acton, Elstree and London until 17th September 1974. Then my formal handover from the previous incumbent began. All went very well, apart from one irritating matter which made the tock tock birds sound urgent notes of warning in my imagination. My predecessor had said that one of the trust chairmen liked to arrive early in the Palace Street office and plant himself in the Clerk and Receiver's chair, sometimes for several hours on end. He would open the office mail before the arrival of the staff and then attend to his own private business affairs. Whilst this was going on, my predecessor was expected to make himself useful somewhere else; but he had managed to persuade the trustees to convert three basement rooms into a self-contained flat for his own use.

Bearing this in mind, I arrived at 7.00 a.m. on the first day after the handover. Despite my fears and the tock tock warnings, the chairman welcomed me so nicely on his arrival at 8.00 a.m. that I thought it safe to bring up the subject of accommodation in the office. We agreed that the flat should be made available for anyone who wished to use it on school business, and that the chairman should have his own desk in the sitting room, complete with a lockable drawer. Honour was satisfied all round.

The United Westminster Schools Foundation comprised a voluntary-aided day grammar school (Emanuel School for 850 boys in Wandsworth); a voluntary-aided non-diocesan Christian day grammar school (Westminster City School for 600 boys in Westminster) and an independent HMC boarding and day school (Sutton Valence School for 400 boys in Kent). The Royal Foundation of Greycoat Hospital comprised a voluntary-aided Church of England day grammar school (Greycoat Hospital for 600 girls in Westminster) and an independent boarding and day school (Queen Anne's School for 400 girls in Caversham, Berkshire).

During the sixteen years of my subsequent service with the foundations, Emanuel School was compelled by the Inner London Education Authority and the Department of Education to accept independent status; Westminster City became a comprehensive school and was enlarged to take 750 mixed-ability boys; and Sutton Valence opened its doors to girls throughout the school. Greycoat

327

Hospital amalgamated with St Michael's School, Pimlico and was enlarged to take 750 mixed ability girls. The sixth forms of both Westminster City School and Greycoat Hospital combined to form the South Westminster Consortium. In 1980 I stage-managed the purchase of the ailing Underhill Preparatory School in Kent, so that it might become an independent educational foundation, with its own governing body, and act as a feeder school for Sutton Valence. Numbers on the preparatory school role increased from 98 in 1980 to 335 boys and girls in 1990.

Some years after my appointment, *The Times* published the following letter from me:

Sir,
    I am a Clerk and Receiver and I have accepted letters addressed to me as

Sir Clarke Obe
The Clerk and Redeemer
The Old Horse, and
Mr Only the Clerk

Moreover, the Clerk occasionally protests at being linked with the Deceiver and the Receiver has been known to free himself from an association with the Shark.
    Yours faithfully,

This letter prompted Dr Briault, Chief Education Officer of the Inner London Education Authority, to suggest that, in his opinion, I should add a third leg to the stool of my authority and be called Foundations' Director. The Trustees took up this suggestion and we had to change our letterheads accordingly.

Whilst directing the Foundations in Palace Street, I was responsible generally to 100 trustees and governors and 9 chairmen, all at the same time. According to my daily diaries, the office serviced 700 meetings, each requiring an agenda and detailed minutes. I staged-managed the selection and appointment of 10 heads and 6 bursars and I redrafted 3 lengthy trust deeds, 6 general charitable trusts and set up a host of prize funds and articles of government. I also advised and took part in fundraising projects where I used my experience at the Haberdashers' Aske's Girls' School. I always insisted on the appointment of an appeal organiser who had a major interest in, and some knowledge of, the school concerned. Emanuel School appointed an Old Boy who had recently retired from his career in a national bank. He operated most successfully from my office for many years and gave his services free. I presented him with two new pairs of shoes, boxes of chocolates for potential donors' secretaries and a weekly programme of calls by appointment.

My secretary, Jean, and I made a hobby of helping indigent parents keep their children at school after money had run out. Jean kept an up-to-date annotated copy of the Directory of Grant-making Trusts to which she introduced the anxious mothers (fathers very seldom came); and encouraged them to compose carefully written letters to suitable potential donors. Determined mums were surprisingly successful. Over the years I collected, and zealously guarded, the private contact telephone numbers of individual donors who wished to support deserving families in financial need. I had an average of eight of these at any one time and between them they never let me down. Jean and I reckoned that we saved the Foundations annually rather more than the sum of our two combined salaries.

In 1978 I was admitted as a Freeman of the City of London which brought with it no exciting privileges, apart from a few boozy lunches in the City. At one of these I was introduced to an influential entrepreneur in the construction industry. He showed an interest in the world of education and I thought he might like to meet the Chairman of the Emanuel School Governors (a former Chairman of the Greater London Council) and the headmaster. I booked a table for lunch in the Festival Hall restaurant overlooking the Thames. They all arrived on time. Whilst enjoying a pre-prandial drink admiring the sunshine on the river and on St Paul's Cathedral in the background, our guest grabbed me by the elbow and, in a stage whisper, said, 'Tell those two to piss off.'

Unused as I was to carrying out such peremptory commands, I suggested that they might like to disappear into the Gents – and off they went like two small boys.

'It's a bloody con!' he exclaimed. 'How ever did you know?'

'Know what?' I asked.

He burst into tears, weeping copiously into a large white handkerchief. Eventually, he explained that while he was on fire duty during the Second World War, at a point exactly opposite where we were standing, a German aeroplane had dropped a bomb on a tug towing a barge along the river. He had jumped into the water to try and rescue two non-swimmers from the sinking barge. He managed to save one but not the other. 'I can still see her face clearly,' he said, as he regained his composure.

We enjoyed the lunch, my chairman was in good form and our guest said he would support the school financially. He wrote out a smallish cheque, sealed it in an envelope and handed it over to the headmaster. As he left, he said to me, 'You'll hear more from me later!' I thought I saw a wink of his eye; but the effect of the wine, and the lack of any tock tocks, may have affected my imagination. Two months later, I received a complicated legal letter transferring the equivalent of a very large donation to the school.

In early 1975, I was invited to become a committee member of the Inner London Council of the Association of Voluntary-Aided Secondary Schools (AVASS). Some thirty-two London schools were in membership, all of whom I visited several times. I learnt a great deal about their individual styles of management, their relationships with the Authority, the Department and their financial affairs. I consolidated my interests by transferring the venue of their regular meetings to our boardroom in Palace Street. Their National Chairman was Dr Lancelot Ware, a barrister with a degree in mathematics and a doctorate in biology. He was a founder-member of Mensa, which he set up in 1946 to be 'a club which had an objective qualification of intelligence as opposed to a subjective one of a shared interest'. Some sensitive people found him argumentative to the point of impatient rudeness. He did not suffer gladly those he considered less empowered than him with intelligence. Towards the end of his life Mensa awarded him the title 'Fons et Origo' and he was well pleased.

In July 1978, he summoned me to his office in the City. I was about to sit down on a chair with a broken seat in front of his desk, when he said, 'Bring up that one by the window; I use the other one to encourage the swift departure of unwelcome visitors.' He informed me that he had started on the quantitative assessment of his problems in AVASS and that it would give him great pleasure to put my name forward for the vacant vice-chairmanship of the National Association, did I have any objections? I did not; and so began a most productive and lively association, soon to be enhanced by his marriage to Francesca, a fellow barrister and

Charity Commissioner, who calmed him down and enabled him gracefully to achieve a ripe old age in music composer Vaughan Williams' former mansion deep in the Surrey countryside. At weekends, his snowy white hair and slim body, clothed only in an old pair of khaki shorts, might be observed emerging from a hole beneath his garden, down which he had vanished to repair the billy-engine which pumped water up the hill into his home. Their visitors would be welcomed with a bottle of House of Commons wine.

Unfortunately, our formal association was cut short by the actions of a large number of the AVASS National Committee who called an emergency meeting to discuss the chairmanship. A vote was past unanimously (I abstained) asking Lancelot to resign. He declined to do so and left the room in a huff. As vice-chairman, who had taken no part in calling the meeting, I was asked to act as intermediary and, after much consideration and reference to an array of law books, he agreed to go. I was offered the chairmanship, but I declined and a very efficient lady governor from a school in the Midlands was elected. I did not allow my name to go forward again as vice-chairman; but I continued to be a committee member of the National Association and, later, was elected Chairman of the Inner London Council of AVASS, until my retirement in 1990.

I was extremely fortunate to have some excellent people in the London office. John Plummer and Alan Faulkner, our two accountants, were there when I arrived and were there when I left; age had not wearied them. Rita Please, my secretary when I first arrived, left to look after her aged father at home and was replaced by Jean who saw me through my time. Alec Jackson, the Foundations' secretary, left to become the bursar of Emanuel School and was replaced by Mary Dobson, a Bachelor of Divinity, who became my PA and marked the occasion by accepting a proposal of marriage before the ink was dry on her contract with us. Jean, Mary and I helped each other out of all sorts of heavy seas and have remained friends ever since. Sue Coleman joined us as a junior and eventually became a most efficient assistant accountant when we took on Underhill Preparatory School.

We gained experience fast and took on extra work so that the annual cost of administration declined regularly as a percentage of the Foundations' total annual turnover. It also enabled me to accept in 1974 an invitation to join the governing body of Box Hill

School, opposite our home in Mickleham. The school was a co-educational independent secondary school for 260 pupils. I was immediately elected chairman of the Finance Committee and was mortified to discover the school had no endowment of its own and, though solvent, there was little left over for improvements.

I soon discovered that the safe of the school's consultant architect, our former chairman, contained important documents which would postpone my plans for a modest annual building programme, funded by annual surpluses on the school account. A completely new kitchen was long overdue; the Highway Authorities were insisting that the school should build a fresh main entrance away from the existing entry off the busy and dangerous A24. Headmaster, staff and pupils wanted better dormitories, modern laboratories, extended sixth-form accommodation, a reception area for 'swallows' (day girls), a much larger library and more on-site accommodation for staff. All this was needed to cope with local demand for boarding and day independent education. Fees had to be increased above inflation, fresh sources of finances had to be exploited, the market for students from abroad had to be researched and the possibility of introducing weekly boarders had to be examined. In lighter vein, I was filled with hope when I discovered the felicitous names of five members of the senior staff were Perfect, Topp, Masters, Read and Wright: moreover, the given first name of a bright West African student was Tenoutoften!

During the next ten years we gradually completed most of the above and were able to start implementing the long-delayed building plan, subject to many unhelpful restraining section notices issued by the local planning authority. Later, when I became chairman, I shamelessly replaced retiring governors with those whose expertise was much greater than mine and to whom I could delegate specific responsibilities. Sir Carl Aarvold a former High Court Judge (and English Rugby Fifteen Captain) rejoined; and in came a recently retired inspector of schools (also a designer of school buildings), a local lawyer (and popular TV scriptwriter), a civil engineer (and local politician), a chartered accountant, an architect, the chairman of a public company and two young and successful business ladies. They joined a Balkan prince, a German international company director, a well-known 'Bond' film actor, the extremely experienced Germany-based Director of the Round Square Group of International Schools and a nominee of the

Standing L-R   R McC   Kurt   Jean   Peter La S   Walter   John   HRH Prince   David   Martin   D.L.
     (Scout)   Wiecenhaupt   Teague   Draper   Gotell   Malvan   Tomislav   Gunter   De Laszlo   (Masseur)
     (Refd)   (Sub)   (Accounts)

Seated   Michael   Peter   Ros   Jocelin   T.E.   R. 'Barney'   Christine   Ben   Sir Carl
     Atkins   Ratcenbury   Dachtler   Winthrop Young   Hatton   Barnes   Clarke   Tatham   Aarvold
     L.S.M.   Captain   L.S.M.   A.C.E.M.

L.S.M. – Long Service Medal   A.C.E.M. – Also Captain of England Medal

333

Alumni Association. A very knowledgeable and happy team, two of whom were current parents [see cartoon on page 333].

Meanwhile, I started an education bulletin, published at two monthly intervals from the office in Palace Street, aimed at my thirty-plus voluntary-aided Inner London comprehensive secondary schools. The government and the ILEA were introducing so many major policy changes that governors, staff and parents needed simple explanations regarding the legal and financial implications and how to deal with, and extract advantage from, new situations as they arose. I hope that my literary efforts were of some help to them.

Every one of my one hundred trustees and governors were interesting people, genuinely united by a common wish to improve the education of the young. Inevitably, there was a fair cross-section of the community and some were more eccentric than others. For example, a certain, lean, ascetic theologian of a bishop would circulate recently composed doggerel to chosen recipients round the table during meetings. He liked to tell hair-raising stories of his travels in Africa with a lugubrious expression on his face. My favourite one described a visit to an African kraal, where he had been asked to pull the first flush of a newly-built school lavatory block. In he went through the open door, which had been lovingly decorated with streamers and balloons and disappeared inside. He pulled the chain and clouds of hot steam enveloped him as he rushed out with his mitre askew on the back of his head and his crook waving wildly in the air – the pipe had been connected to the hot-water tank – the children outside thought the Bishop had summoned up Satan from below; they fled into the bush. The Dean of Westminster, a Royal Peculiar to the core, wore his bicycle clips all day long and was wont to listen to test match commentaries on his earphones during meetings in our boardroom. Afterwards, he would cycle off to Buckingham Palace for his regular audiences with Her Majesty and would padlock his bicycle to the iron railings outside, much to the amusement of the Brigade of Guards and the undisguised petulance of the security police. Lady X would never vote for any candidate wearing a red dress. The Archdeacon of St Paul's travelled by train to Reading in his gaiters. He would keep the governing body of Queen Anne School waiting twenty minutes while he chatted with the engine driver, blessed the engine and thanked them both for a safe journey.

Meanwhile, Richard joined John at Ashdown House preparatory school and we hugely enjoyed visiting them, especially to see John playing the part of Alice in 'Alice in Wonderland' and speaking throughout in Latin. John went on to Charterhouse School, near Godalming in Surrey, and Richard joined him later, leaving Charterhouse at 16 and obtained his Diploma of Art (DA) at Epsom Art College. My mother continued to live in Chipperfield until her mid-eighties, suffering increasingly from rheumatism. She would not budge and when we persuaded her to sell the cottage, she insisted on showing people round. Although a pretty little cottage with a large garden and orchard, which the estate agent said would easily sell, no one made an offer. On investigation, we found that my mother went on and on to the prospective buyers about severe problems arising from heavy bomb damage during the war (it was never bombed!). She concluded her guided tour by announcing that an underground station was about to be built in the orchard. We had to retire her from her self-imposed task and the place quickly sold. She came down to live with us complaining bitterly that, now she had a little bit of money, there was nothing worthwhile to spend it on. Joanna looked after her in every way until my mother died two years later.

Four years on an even greater disaster overtook our little family. Joanna developed a melanoma and died of cancer six weeks later. John came up from Bristol University to be with her and to help me. It seemed the end of our world.

13

My knowledge of all things was won
Ere my life to lighten You came,
But the Land I knew, the Deeds saw done
Will never again be the same:
For You have come, like the rising Sun,
To golden my World with your flame.

SIR HUGH CLIFFORD

Life at home did not return to anything like normal for Richard, John or me. We were away during the day and the first one home in the evening cooked supper, the next one washed up and the last one laid the table for breakfast. The house was cleaned once a week by a most efficient motherly Spanish lady, who gave us friendly lectures on tidiness, cleanliness and how to cook paella.

I was helped greatly in my grief by Lynda Robinson, who had just completed with me a three-year History of Art course of evening classes run by the Inner London Education Authority, and had looked after our home in Mickleham when we were away. She was the Deputy Secretary of the Royal Watercolour Society, then located in very pleasant rooms in Conduit Street, London. Joanna and I had much enjoyed our evenings after the exhibitions in her gallery, where it was always good to see the self-portrait of Joshua Cristall, Joanna's ancestor and former President of the Old Water-colour Society, displayed over the entrance. I soon became a dab hand at stacking chairs.

One day, the telephone bell rang in the office and a female voice said that she had been given my address by a cousin of mine. Would I partner her to a Mencap Ball soon to be held at the Café Royal in London? I replied, 'Yes please,' and she gave me details of the date and time, adding that her name was Sarah. Unfortunately, she did not give me her telephone number or contact address; moreover, I was so surprised that I forgot to ask for identifying particulars and omitted to provide her with mine. Not withstanding this lack of vital information, I presented myself quite early at the Café Royal suitably clad and clutching an orchid for pinning upon my lady's breast. I reconnoitred the geography of the place, discovering the ballroom and the whereabouts of the loos; but I had no luck with nameplates on the dining tables. I concluded that the most advantageous place, from which to survey the multitude as they began to arrive, would be a perch located halfway up the wide carpeted staircase. I took up this position accordingly, and was soon joined by a very smart gentleman who sat down beside me and said,'Let's see whose girl arrives first!' After a while, he rose and, with a farewell smile and a wink to me, took his partner's arm and disappeared up the rest of the stairs. I was left on my own. Suddenly, my eyes alighted on a tall, willowy blonde wearing a striking all-black evening gown.

'Are you Sarah?' I enquired hopefully.

'Yes,' she said, 'are you Tim?'

Introductions successfully achieved, I shyly presented my orchid.

I proposed to Sarah a few months later during a private ball given in the Mansion House by Colonel Sir Ronald Gardner Thorpe, Lord Mayor of London. A neighbour sitting near us heard Sarah's reply to my proposal and it was reported to Sir Ronald, who thereupon conveyed the result to the enthusiastic diners!

Sarah was a convent-educated Catholic and regular attender at the Oratory in Brompton Road; she was twelve years younger than me. I was a typical Church of England widower. In order to be married to a Catholic, it seemed I had to be instructed in the theory and practice of the Catholic religion, even if I did not intend to change my faith. So it was, therefore, that I attended seven very interesting two-hour explanatory sessions. Although there were no examinations, I was deemed to have progressed satisfactorily enough and we were married on 22nd May 1981 in the Brompton Oratory, and the reception for our friends was held in the Challoner Club. My best man was Roy McComish, headmaster of Box Hill School; our honeymoon was spent in Venice. On our return, Sarah returned to her job as Deputy Appeals Director of Mencap and I resumed my work in Palace Street.

Sarah had been born in Harrow, where she lived throughout the Blitz. Their family house suffered many near misses from the bombs and the glass in their windows was blown out and had to be replaced several times. On one warm sunny evening they heard the unmistakable sound of a flying-bomb overhead. Suddenly, its engine cut out. The family dived for cover as the bomb exploded a few yards away, with a very loud bang, a shower of broken glass and a very nasty chemical smell. Utter silence followed. Then a group of neighbours made their way into the house. Sarah had received a deep cut on the back of her head between her plaits and her head was covered with blood. Friends took her home and offered her tea which her shaking hands spilled all over her dress – Sarah claims that the spilt tea, and the fear of possible reactions of her mother on seeing the stained dress, was far worse than the wound. She was soon classified as 'walking wounded' and became a heroine at her school ('Do let us look ... oooh!') until the bandages were finally removed. After the war, her family moved to Brighton where Sarah continued her convent education and attended all the shows at the Theatre Royal. She loved to watch the young new post-war group of brilliant actors, actresses and musicians as they began their careers in this theatre. Many were to become household names in the entertainment industry.

Ten years after my joining the governing body of Box Hill School, my fellow governors elected me their chairman and I began to take a greater interest in the day-to-day affairs of the Round Square Conference. This Conference was based on the original vision of Dr Kurt Hahn who was born into a rich, cultivated, German Jewish family on 5 June 1886. He was educated at Göttingen and at Christ Church, Oxford. At the end of the First World War he became secretary to Prince Max von Baden, the last Imperial Chancellor of Germany, whom he helped later to found a coeducational school (with Dr Hahn as headmaster), in the Prince's schloss (a castle and former Cistercian monastery) on the shores of Lake Constance. This school was named Salem (from the Jewish/ Islamic word 'shalom/salaam', meaning peace). Dr Hahn was arrested by the Nazis in February 1933 and imprisoned. His case was taken up by his Oxford friends who persuaded Prime Minister Ramsay MacDonald to intervene with Hitler. Hahn was released in July to go to Britain, a penniless, depressed refugee.

He soon recovered in the bracing Scottish air and, with the help of a friendly Scottish peer, he opened Gordonstoun School in 1934 and became a British subject in 1938. Following the school's temporary evacuation to Wales during the Second World War, and with the help of Sir Lawrence Holt, he started outward bound courses in Wales in 1941. In 1956 he helped the Duke of Edinburgh launch his Award Scheme and in 1962 he was a moving spirit behind the formation of the United World Colleges of the Atlantic.

In 1966 a group of six educationalists agreed, in the presence of Dr Hahn, to expand Hahn's ideas and methods of education further into British independent schools. It became known as the Round Square Conference and was the brainchild of Jocelin Winthrop-Young who became its Director for many years. Roy McComish, the headmaster of Box Hill School, was one of the founding members. The name came from the ancient round square located among the main buildings of Gordonstoun School. There were twelve schools when I became directly involved in 1974. Since then many more schools in Europe, North America, India, Africa, Australia and elsewhere have become members: the majority of these had no previous connection with Hahn; but had already independently adopted many of Dr Hahn's principles of educating 'the whole person'. The Conference is better known today as the Round Square Group of International Schools. Perhaps the most attractive of its international aspects is the implementation of student service projects which take place regularly in poverty-stricken areas of the world.

Kurt Hahn died in 1974 and *The Times* noted. 'No one else in our day has created more original ideas and, at the same time, possessed the gift of getting them into practice.'

The hands-on, influential and popular Chairman of the Round Square throughout my involvement was His Majesty King Constantine of the Hellenes. He was educated at Anavryta, then a Round Square school in Athens, and is an Olympian Gold Medallist. He is a large man in every sense of the word and has a strong very deep voice. His sense of humour is ever-present and often quite irreverent. He has a fund of amusing anecdotes about royalty and his wide circle of international friends. He is a past-master at answering awkward questions about his career, his exile and his relations with the Greek Government. He has the common touch, is very agreeable company, a most attentive generous host and is greatly admired by the many young people with whom he is in constant contact. He provides a natural leadership of the Round Square and, among many of his interesting innovations, he has invited HRH the Duke of York, Mrs Sonya Gandhi, Nelson Mandela and Dr R. Von Weizsacker, the former President of Germany, to join him as patrons of the Conference. All these patrons are highly popular with the students in their own particular ways, especially Nelson Mandela, who has an enormous following among the young, and the Duke of York who has a wonderful knack of relating to young people and treating them as equals. (Mention the word 'Falklands' and he will enthral a young audience for hours on end!)

My first difficult task within the organisation was to help my chairman change formal representation on the council from heads of schools in membership to the member schools themselves. Naturally this was not well received by some of the heads. But the aim was sure and worth pursuing. It would introduce continuity (headmasters were liable to change at short notice or disappear upon retirement) and reduce the feeling among some students that the Annual Conference was 'just another tea party for the headmasters and headmistresses'. It would increase the variety and quality of the governors' input (after all, they employ the heads); it would liberate the enthusiasm of the teaching staff; and it would produce a worthwhile forum for the students (sixth form or equivalent) who would feel free to bring forward original and constructive ideas. This change was achieved successfully during one of the Annual Conferences held at Salem where part of the *schloss* (castle) was used as a commercial brewery and a plentiful supply of beer was at hand.

My second task came just before Box Hill School hosted one of the Annual Conferences. His Majesty asked me to ensure that the plenary session of the conference would approve an application from the Doon School, which was situated in Northern India, for membership of the Round Square. Unfortunately, a straw-poll beforehand had revealed that there would be strong opposition from a few individuals who considered 'charity begins at home' and from those who wished to limit membership to schools in Europe and North America. Also there were many uncommitted members and others whose views were unknown. After much lobbying and some late-night meetings of certain delegates, the plenary session agreed to accept the Doon School's application to

340

great applause, especially from all the students present. But there were two disappointing adult resignations and one 'senior member' refused to allow his daughter to go on any future project to India. This successful application opened the door for subsequent membership of more Indian schools and new schools from Africa, Australia and the Middle East; and for a marked increase in the number of supervised student projects abroad run by the Round Square International Service.

My association with the Round Square as an occasional alternate chairman (at the request of His Majesty), as a member of the council and as an honorary member enabled me to put this experience to good use in Palace Street; also my experience of work in the British independent and state sectors was, I believe, of help to the Round Square. On the minus side, however, I was unable to introduce Round Square activities into the junior schools (preparatory schools), though this was developed most successfully after I left. Alas, too, I am ashamed to admit that I was unable to persuade the Round Square Council to consider the membership of qualified schools within the British state sector (especially comprehensive schools). I believed this to be short-sighted and divisive. State participation in the government of German schools has never been a reason for not allowing German schools to join.

I soon became acutely aware of how activities of the Round Square could have a beneficial effect on students. When Sarah and I were about to accompany our delegation to attend the Annual Conference in India, the parents of one of our student representatives withdrew their daughter. The teachers were reluctant to recommend a replacement. Then, at the last moment, one of the housemistresses said she would be delighted if we would relieve her of having to look after Sam, who was described as being distinctly slothful and naughty, but never deliberately wicked. Sam was far too campus-wise and suspicious to volunteer. But her mother gave her delighted approval and the headmaster, who was unable to attend the Conference, raised no serious objection. Sam was sullen, aloof and retired quietly into her shell on the outward flight to New Delhi; neither Sarah nor I could get beyond her politely reserved reaction to our attempts to interest her. On arrival in India, we travelled to Dehra Dun in a rickety country bus for fourteen hours, with stops to cool down the steaming radiator and to enjoy the culinary delights of curried lunch and supper at fly-blown wayside stalls. Most of us developed a tummy bug or suffered from withdrawal symptoms arising from unaccustomed thirst; but Sam came into her own and asked to take over our Red Cross box. She ministered to the medical requirements of the younger students and persuaded one or two members of staff to stop complaining of the heat and to get a grip on life and help her. On arrival at Dehra Dun, Sarah and I asked the headmaster, and a housemistress, to give Sam responsibilities during the Conference. On the last day's plenary session of the delegates, Sam was elected 'Girl Student Speaker' and spoke to a lively audience with flair, elegance and spirit. When the Conference was over, Sarah and I hired a bus and taxi to take our school delegation on a tour of North India for an additional unplanned fortnight. Sam turned out to be a really delightful companion throughout, revealing an unsuspected sense of humour and a passion to know and to understand more about the effects of poverty, so evident in the Indian countryside and cities through which we passed.

On our return to England, her housemistress commented on what she described as a sea-change in Sam's outlook on life. Sam was promoted to the equivalent of prefect and also deputy head of house. She surprised her experienced teachers by obtaining much better than forecast grades in her 'A' level examinations. I much enjoyed, and found it very useful, to talk about what I called 'the Sam factor' when explaining the Round Square ethos to parents and staff in my own school and in one or two nearby Round Square schools.

While we were staying in Dehra Dun, Sarah was taken seriously ill with diarrhoea, a temperature of 103 and severe sickness. She retired to her bed for a day or two until I asked the school's Indian doctor to look at her. We were roundly berated by him for not calling him in earlier. 'I could have cured Sarah at once; but now I will have to try something else'. He produced some foul-smelling medicine and left us. Next day, discovering her temperature was still very high, he gave her some enormous pills and produced a syringe and six phials. 'These pills may cause involuntary movements of your limbs. You may find your leg or arm will stick out at an angle and remain immobile. But not to worry. Use the syringe to inject yourself and your limbs will immediately return to normal,' he said. Sarah took some of the pills, suffered very bad nightmares and frequent spasms, but started to get better immediately when she looked at the syringe! On arrival at Delhi, after travelling fourteen hours again by country bus, she began to feel very much better. She decided that there was no need to fly home and, instead, much enjoyed our tour of Central India. On arrival in England our local doctor asked to examine the pills. He sent them for analysis and reported later that the substance had been banned in 1902 and even the Duke of Edinburgh had given up using them on his retired rheumatic horses!

In 1985, I was approached by two committee members of the British Atlantic Committee who asked if I would like to join their organisation. I already knew that the committee was a civilian group which supported the North Atlantic Treaty Organisation (NATO) and, on studying its aims and reading its literature, I thought it constructive and interesting; so I agreed to join. My twenty-four years' service in South-East Asia provided the rather limited basis of my military and political knowledge. So, of course, I was out of date and I knew little about NATO activities, apart from what I had read in the newspapers and magazines. I was unlikely to provide any informed contribution to the deliberations of its members; who seemed mostly to comprise members of parliament, retired ambassadors, trade union leaders, university professors, school teachers and former Foreign Office officials.

The British Atlantic Committee was serviced by a Director, who was a retired and extremely efficient major general of the Royal Engineers, a young lady graduate was the secretary and there were two or three helpers in the office; all of whom formed a happy team and looked after us very well.

Soon after I was relieved of my annual subscription, I was approached by the Director who said he would like to put my name forward for election to honorary treasurer; I ascertained that, if elected, I would be required to attend regular meetings in the UK and to join the BAC's delegation to international conferences abroad. I agreed, knowing that my election would be in competition with other much more qualified people. Suddenly, Sarah and I began to receive at home several strongly worded telephone calls expressed in a guttural male voice, insisting, 'You must withdraw at once,' 'You are splitting the committee,' 'We do not want you,' and similar uncomplimentary remarks. I thanked him politely for his advice, reported our one-way conversation to the Director and then held my peace. Much to my surprise, I was elected. The

343

Director and I had no problem identifying the owner of the guttural voice from his persistent, aggressive and frequently irrelevant questioning of the chairman at the annual general meetings.

My chairman was Sir John Killick, a former ambassador to Soviet Russia, who never stopped talking and was greatly feared by young Treasury officials who tried to restrict our expenditure. He was extremely energetic and I found his fund of amusing stories, garnered from his career in the Foreign Office, lit up many a dull meeting. I cannot recall that he ever lost an argument. He was a virtuoso at circumnavigating difficult questions. An even stronger character was Sir Frank Roberts, who had a long and distinguished diplomatic career and served as HM Ambassador to Bonn, Moscow and to NATO. He had a deep understanding of the Slav character and seemed to know intimately almost all the main players behind the Iron Curtain. In the words of the Director, 'Frank was diminutive and dashingly urbane'. He was always in the forefront of our meetings, our activities and our travels abroad, on which he was accompanied by his charming wife, the daughter of Sir Said Shincair Pasha, financial adviser to the Sudan Government. They were both very kind to me and I learnt a great deal from them. His acerbic wit and ability as a superb raconteur made history come alive for young and old. He always listened intently. I knew at once when he was in a good mood because his eyes would sparkle and he would smile urbanely. He was interested in everything, liked the company of young people and was at home in their company. He often acceded to my requests for him to lecture on 'The Russian Bear' to sixth-form would-be politicians.

The British Atlantic Committee's practical work was supervised by an experienced education adviser and carried out by education committees responsible for promotional work in secondary schools, youth organisations, colleges and universities. NATO games among competing sixth forms in secondary schools were very popular. The secretariat was responsible for organising guided visits to NATO offices around Europe by students, politicians and a host of other interested groups. I much enjoyed my participation in all these areas and made it my business to attend conferences, seminars, visits abroad and to help Sarah entertain foreign visitors.

None of my colleagues were particularly interested in fund-raising and my chairman regarded it with huge disdain. The only occasion I used him was for an approach to a rich city gentleman who I was sure would be sympathetic. I had already contacted the rich man's consultant lawyer and I believed that, if we were lucky, we might well obtain a substantial sum of money. After much grumbling, my chairman agreed to have a go on his own. During my detailed briefing beforehand, I suggested that the rich man would probably interrupt him by asking, 'Well, how much do you want?'and I went on to say that he should reply, '£50,000 would be most welcome.' Apparently, all went according to plan at the meeting until he clean forgot the figure I had given him. Eventually he stuttered, '£15,000'. It was quite unlike my chairman to forget his lines or to be at a loss for words. When the cheque arrived he admitted his lapse of memory to me, but the Committee thought he had done extremely well!

Having completed my three years as honorary treasurer, I was talked into serving another two years, and then someone else took over in 1991. I became a member of the committee and continued to attend meetings in the UK. In 1993 the BAC amalgamated with an organisation named 'Peace through NATO' and changed its name to 'The Atlantic Council of the United Kingdom' under a new chairman, the Rt. Hon. Sir Richard Luce. My good friend Alan Lee Williams became the new Director. I continued as a member of the President's Advisory Council.

In 1986, I was asked by their Majesties King Constantine and Queen Anne-Marie of the Hellenes to join Roy McComish as one of the two British governors of the Hellenic College of London. The remaining governors were either Greek or Greek Cypriot. Our extremely practical president/patroness was Her Majesty. My first tasks were to help with the appointment of a new headmaster and then a new bursar. We were extremely fortunate in both and the college experienced a dramatic revival in examination results and in the number of successful university entrance examinations. The main educational difference from British schools was the need to teach Greek as a compulsory subject to all students until they became not only bilingual in English and Greek, but also had acquired a full understanding and appreciation of their own national culture.

Soon after my appointment as a governor, I was coming down the main staircase in the college when I saw a small Greek girl crying, halfway down the stairs. I realised, to my horror, that I was unable to say in Greek, 'What is the matter?', 'Can I help?' or even, 'Come with me, I will take you to the matron'. I had to pass by and alert the telephone operator/receptionist down below. Thereupon, I enrolled myself for a Greek language course lasting two years, run by a Greek lady in Dorking Adult Education Centre; then I attended classes in Hellenic College under the auspices of a delightful Greek nursery school teacher over the next five years. Their combined efforts enabled me to speak simple modern Greek; to improve my oral fluency, I made a point of talking to all and sundry within the college. Fortunately, my gubernatorial colleagues conducted their meetings in English; though, when there was a need to raise money for a particular project, they would adopt a serious mien and chat away very fast in low conspiratorial voices which left me far behind. The only remark I understood was 'I have no cash, my ships are rusting in the Piraeus!' Despite this, my Greek colleagues spent a great deal of their own money behind the scenes supporting indigent parents and improving various aspects of school life. They were generous, took a great deal of interest in the day-to-day running of the college and were always extremely friendly to me.

During one of our regular meetings in 1995, the chairman noted that there was only one Governor present who had not given an Address to the College on Speech Day. His Majesty raised his bushy eyebrows, Her Majesty smiled at me encouragingly and the Chairman said to me, 'It's your turn'. Unfortunately, a few weeks before, Roy McComish had died suddenly from a heart attack, which had left me as the only British governor present. The moment of truth had arrived and I felt unable to refuse. 'Yes, whatever you wish,' I said airily and with the correct shake of my head. I memorised my speech in Greek and ended up with a short appreciation of Roy's contribution to the college, also given in Greek, but repeated in English to make sure it came across accurately. As I was about to leave the stage, His Eminence Archbishop Gregorios of the Greek Orthodox Church climbed laboriously on to the stage and proceeded to fling his arms around me, pat me on my back and kiss me several times on both cheeks. I felt myself going as red as a beetroot, more so when Her Majesty then asked me to sit beside her.

My next task, which was given to me by King Constantine, was to help the headmaster introduce additions to the curriculum so that conditions could be met for becoming a member of the Round

Square Group of Schools. I think that we were the first urban school to apply and we had to substitute a much wider range of required social activities in the deprived areas of London; in place of the countryside activities so favoured by all the other Round Square schools. Our application had the strong support of governors, parents, students and from the Alumni Association. The college was inspected by the Director of the Round Square and our application was approved. We rapidly gained valuable experience of working with other international schools and taking part with them in the various projects run by the Round Square International Service. I retired in 1997 having completed six years as a governor of the Hellenic College of London.

In 1994 I retired, after twenty years as a governor of Box Hill School and was succeeded by Vice-Admiral Sir James Weatherall KCVO, KBE (an Old Boy of Gordonstoun School) as chairman of the governors. I handed over to him my version of what I believed the school governors' aims should be. (See page 355, What is a Round Square School?) I remained a trustee of the school. Meanwhile Box Hill School continued to flourish and grow steadily under the leadership of Dr Rodney Atwood and his supportive wife Harriet.

In 1992, Sarah and I agreed that The Old House, Mickleham, was much too big for us; so we put it on the market. Eventually, in 1994, we received an offer and began looking for a smaller house within reach of London. Selling the property was an unpleasant task, the buyers were argumentative and had endless financial problems; final payment came months after completion. Buying our new home was quite a different matter. Sarah drew my attention to an article in *The Daily Mail* describing the delights of a smaller house in Salisbury. We visited Salisbury the next day and liked the vendor and her house so much that we put in an immediate offer. Unfortunately, other people also liked the house and other offers were made. Eventually, it went out to sealed tender and our revised offer was accepted. During negotiations I discovered that our cheerful and delightful vendor was the widow of Brigadier Desmond Shean with whom I had flown around Central Malaya more than forty years ago. Sybil was his second wife and had never been to Malaya. She was very interested to hear of my life there. We have remained good friends since then.

Sarah attends St Osmund's Catholic church, and I go to the

Cathedral some five hundred paces away. Sarah obtained her diploma in teaching illiterates to read and write whilst we were living in Surrey, and continued to do this in Salisbury. Her main interest at present is managing a help-line for needy members of her local medical practice. Over the last few years she has mastered the computer, use of the internet and e-mail. Meanwhile I enjoy being in charge of no one! I enjoy my work as a guide in Salisbury Cathedral, as a steward in the Chapter House and as an occasional guide round the Old Bishops' Palace. I like to research and write about obscure people and places connected with the history of Wiltshire. We are both active in the English-Speaking Union, of which I have been a member for nearly fifty years.

My eldest son John runs a successful business in Sydney, Australia. I visit him and his family every other year. Richard is a talented freelance artist and lives in West Sussex.

I occasionally meet Hokkiens (often Taiwanese) in the Cathedral and enjoy talking to them in the dialect which I was taught, but which has since become extremely old-fashioned. It makes the very young ones laugh, and the very old ones' faces crinkle with delight.

What of the tock tock birds? I occasionally hear them, but too far away to enable me to play dab cricket with the tocks. Actually, they are being replaced by the ticonderoga (R.L. Stevenson's 'utterances of the dead') as I walk across the green green grass of the Cathedral Close which covers up so many people buried down below – but that is another story!

APPENDICES

ACRONYMS EXPLAINED

AVASS, Association of Voluntary Aided Secondary Schools

BO, British Officer in the Indian Army
BAC, British Atlantic Committee

CCO, the Clandestine Communist Organisation in Sarawak
CEP, Captured Enemy Personnel
CO, Commanding Officer
COSIRA, Council for Small Industries in the Rural Areas
CP, Commissioner of Police
CPC, Communist Party of China
CPM, Communist Party of Malaya
CPO, Chief Police Officer of a State in Malaya
CSC, Civil Service Commissioners (UK Examination Body)
CT, Communist Terrorist
CTO, Communist Terrorist Organisation

DID, Drainage and Irrigation Department
DO, District Officer
D OF OPS, Director of (military) Operations
DSO, Distinguished Service Order
DWEC, District War Executive Committee, during Malayan
    Emergency

ECO, Emergency Commissioned Officer in the Indian Army, i.e.
    not a 'Regular'
ENSA, Entertainments National Service Association
E/Sgt, European (Police) Sergeant, later renamed Police
    Lieutenant

351

FMS, Federated Malay States

GM, George Medal
GO, Gurkha Officer, the equivalent of Viceroy's Commissioned
    Officer, in the Gurkha Brigade
GOC, General Officer Commanding a military formation
GR, Gurkha Rifles
3/9th GR, 3rd Battalion 9th Gurkha Rifles

HABS, Haberdashers' Aske's Boys' School
HAGS, Haberdashers' Aske's Girls' School
HMC, Head Masters' Conference

IGP, Inspector General of Police

KL, Kuala Lumpur
KMT, Kuo Min Tang, the Chinese Nationalist Party led by Chiang
    Kai Shek
KOYLI The King's Own Yorkshire Light Infantry

LMG, Light Machine Gun

MB, Mentri Besar, the Prime Minister of a Malay State
MCA, Malayan Chinese Association
MCP, Malayan Communist Party
MCS, Malayan Civil Service
MIC, Malayan Indian Congress
MIO, Military Intelligence Officer
MMG, Medium Machine Gun
MPABA, Malayan People's Anti-British Army
MPAJA, Malayan People's Anti- Japanese Army
MRLA, Malayan Races Liberation Army
MRLL, Malayan Races Liberation League

NATO, North Atlantic Treaty Organisation
NCO, Non-Commissioned Officer
NCP, Nautical College Pangbourne, now called Pangbourne
    College

OC, Officer Commanding

OCPD, Officer in Charge of a Police District
OSPC, Officer Superintending a Police Circle, senior to an OCPD
OSRB, Overseas Services Resettlement Bureau
OTS, Officers Training School in India

PKI, Communist Party of Indonesia
PWD, Public Works Department

RSC, Round Square Conference
RSIS, Round Square International Service
RSJ, reinforced steel joist

SB, Special Branch
SC, Special Constable
SEP, Surrendered Enemy Personnel
SMIS, Special Military Intelligence Staff
SNIL, Selangor National Independence League
SS, Straits Settlements
SWEC, State War Executive Committee in the Malayan
   Emergency

TNI, Tentera National Indonesia – the Indonesian Armed Forces

UMNO, United Malays National Organisation

VCO, Viceroy's Commissioned Officer in the Indian Army

WOSB, War Office Selection Board

GLOSSARY OF EASTERN
TERMINOLOGY

Amah – childen's nanny in the Far East
Attap – nipah palm fronds used for thatching a small house
Babu – an Indian clerk
Bandobast – administrative arrangements
Bandook – Gurkhali word for shotgun (see top of page 37)
Bania – a Hindu money-lender
Batcha – a young boy
Belukar – long grass growing wild
Bilalo – Gurkhali word for cat
Bin or **Binte** – son of or daughter of a Malay person, part of a full
name
Bn – a battalion, an infantry unit of 600–900 soldiers commanded
by a Lt Colonel
Bumiputra – sons of the soil (the Malays)
Burong Malas – the lazy bird, one of many Malay nicknames for
the long-tailed nightjar or Tock Tock bird
Cafilla – a caravan or travelling group of people in India, also
cafilla party
Caste – Hindu hereditary class of socially equal people united in
religion and similar occupations
Char wallah – a tea person, a popular camp follower
Cheetal – a deer
Cheng-beng – annual grave-cleaning task undertaken by Chinese
in Malaya
Chips – rupees in India
Chukka – a term used in polo. A journey round a place
Cyclo – a pedal-driven two seater vehicle used in Vietnam
Dak Bungalow – formerly a mail staging post in India, latterly a
Government Rest House

Dancing Team – code name for a surveillance team on suspects
Dashera – an important Hindu religious fetival
Dato – formerly a distinguished elderly person: now an Order of Knighthood in Malay chivalry
Devanagari – the Nepali script
Gudwara – a Sikh temple
Gurang da guroong – onomatopoeic Gurkhali word for thunder
Haj – the Holy Pilgrimage to Mecca: Haji, one who completes the Holy Pilgrimage
Hueh Hsih – study and practice, the Chinese Communist method of indoctrination
Imam – a senior mosque official in Malaysia
Jawi – the Malay language script, similar to Arabic
Jemadar – a Viceroy's junior Commissioned Officer or a junior Gurkha Officer, often platoon commander
Jheel – a countryside lake often attracting game-birds
Kampong – a Malaysian village
Kebun – a gardener
Kempei-tai – the much-feared Japanese secret police in the Far East during the Second World War
Ketua – a Malay leader or headman of a village
Khan Sahib – of Mogul origin: a respected person in the community
Konfrontasi – confrontation in the context of Indonesia's war with Malaysia
Kongsi – a long shed usually inhabited by several Chinese families
Kow Thau San – Dog's Head Mountain, outlined in the sky like the head of a dog
Kukri – a Gurkha knife used as a weapon or for chopping wood
Lambedar – a village leader in India
Lathi – a wooden pole used by police to control an unruly mob in India
Mahoot – person in charge of an elephant
Maidan – the town square
Mentri Besar – the Prime Minister of a Malay State
Meo – the name given to the descendants of Hindus converted to Islam by the Moguls in the Punjab
Merdeka – freedom or independence from colonial rule
Mewat – the region in India where Meos lived (or used to live, prior to 1947)

Mui-tsai – Chinese concubine (often the partner of an overseas Chinese male in SE Asia)

Munshi – a language teacher in the Far East

Naik – an Indian Army Corporal

Nautch – a dance

Orang Asli – the preferred description of an aboriginal in Malaysia

Padang – an open space, usually in a town or city in Malaysia

Pancasilas – the five principles much quoted in Indonesian politics

Panchayat – a semi-legal council especially in rural India

Panjies – sharpened bamboo spikes at the bottom of a pig or man trap

Pengawa – a senior village official in Northern Malaya eg. Kelantan State

Penghulu – a senior village official in Malaya

Pirudli-pirudli – Gurkhali onomatopoeic word for lightning

Pondok – a small hut

Purdah – the wearing of a veil to protect women from men or strangers

Putra – a Prince, a **Putri** is a Princess

Sarthi – a Gurkhali word for a friend

Sikh – a member of a monotheistic religion in the Punjab founded in early 16th century

Shikari – a wild-animal hunt

Songkok – a Malay hat

Subedar – a Viceroy's senior Commissioned Officer or a senior Gurkha Officer

Subedar Major – the Viceroy's most senior Commissioned Officer or the most senior Gurkha Officer in a Gurkha battalion

Sutton Boy – a National Service recruit in the Malayan police during the Emergency

Tai-pan – the director of a trading house in the Far East

Taxi-girls – professional dancing partners for short-term hire in Malayan dance halls

Tan Sri – the equivalent of a Baron in Malaysian chivalry

Tehsildar – a Muslim police officer in India

Tonga – a pony trap in India

Trishaw – a pedal driven three-wheeler carrying one or two passengers

Tuanku – honorific title applied when speaking directly to a Malay Sultan

Tun – the equivalent of a Lord in Malaysian chivalry

Tunku or **Tengku**– Prince of a Royal House in Malaysia

Urzi – a plea, often in a legal sense

Viceroy's Commissioned Officer or **Gurkha Officer** – roughly the equivalent of a Warrant Officer

Wayang kulit – a puppet show using homemade leather puppets

Wronggeng – Malay dancing where the participants do not touch one another

WHAT IS A ROUND SQUARE SCHOOL?

There is more in you (than you think)

The name Round Square was the brainchild of Jocelin Winthrop-Young and was adopted during the first conference held in Gordonstoun School attended by Kurt Hahn in 1967. Its principles were agreed at the second conference held in Box Hill School in 1968 also in the presence of Kurt Hahn: all schools present accepted these as the basis of their membership of the Round Square. With this in mind, the Box Hill School Governors' own statement is as follows:

1. As Governors of one of the founder schools of the Round Square, we believe that education should be concerned with the development of the whole man or woman in the pursuit of truth. Whilst examination success is vital for entry into the professions and the universities, and to obtain stimulating employment, we also believe that our task is to encourage pupils to develop moral integrity, self-confidence, individual responsibility, an interest in the arts, service to the community and an understanding of the value of personal fitness and positive health.
2. We attach great importance to the provision of a wide range of physical activity alongside a challenging academic programme for every child.
3. Whilst we encourage the young to develop self-confidence and their particular gifts to the full, they should also be prepared to sacrifice a measure of freedom and self-interest to help other people. Emphasis is placed on training pupils to accept personal responsibility for their own self discipline and to take part in graded, supervised, outdoor challenges aimed at developing

stamina, endurance under stress, an ability to face hardship and to accept failure with dignity and success with humility. In the words of Roy McComish, our founder Head Master, it is not only what is done; but the way in which it is done.

4. We give young people special responsibility of a demanding nature in recognition of the fact that school is a partnership between adults and young people in which mutual trust and understanding play an important part, and in which participation and involvement is encouraged. Responsibilities are graded according to maturity.

5. We believe that service to the less fortunate is an obligation. We aim to provide opportunities for the young to serve with compassion and competence others both inside and outside the school at home and abroad. Experience of the spiritual dimension and Christian teaching is basic to our aims and we strongly support our Rector and Parish Church. We shall continue to play positive roles in our community.

6. Our pupils should reflect the composition of society at large as far as financially possible. We wish our boys and girls to become international citizens through experiencing the enrichment of sharing their lives in school, and on Round Square International Service projects with others from a dissimilar background. Familiarity with a wide range of human circumstance, during the years when attitudes are flexible but hardening is a cornerstone of our policy.

7. We shall continue to demonstrate an active concern for the natural environment, appreciating proven environmental problems and playing our part in tackling these.

Mickleham
1984

Edited by Tim Hatton
Chairman

INDEX OF NAMES

362

366